9

D0070490

Traditionally the province of chemists, the problem of environmental pollution is being tackled increasingly using methodologies which have a biological basis. This volume provides a range of examples of how biotechnology can offer sensitive and ecologically relevant new ways of monitoring the presence of biohazards in our environment and, once detected, how these biohazards can be removed in an ecologically safe way through bioremediation. Additional chapters on economic, legislative and policy aspects set the topic in its social context, resulting in a broad-ranging volume of value to all those concerned with the science of ecologically effective environmental protection and management.

Series Editor

James Lynch, School of Biological Sciences, University of Surrey, UK

Advisory Editors

Donald Crawford, Department of Microbiology, Molecular Biology and Biochemistry, University of Idaho, USA
Michael Daniels, Sainsbury Laboratory, John Innes Centre, Norwich, UK
Jonathan Knowles, Glaxo Wellcome Research and Development S.A., Geneva, Switzerland

Biotechnology Research

This series of contributed volumes provides authoritative reviews of selected topics in biotechnology aimed at advanced undergraduates, graduate students, university researchers and teachers, as well as those in industry and government research. The scope of the series is as broad-ranging as the applications of the research itself, encompassing those topics in applied science and engineering, ranging from agriculture to the design of pharmaceuticals, which are not well served by the existing literature. Each volume therefore represents a significant and unique contribution to the literature, comprising chapters by the leading workers in the field who review the current status of the specialisms and point the way to future research and potential applications.

Titles in the series

(Volumes 1–5 were originally published under the title Plant and Microbial Biotechnology Research Series.)

Biotechnology Research Series: 7
Series Editor: James Lynch

**Environmental Biomonitoring:
The Biotechnology Ecotoxicology
Interface**

UK Government Chief Scientific Adviser, Professor Sir Robert May, FRS deploys a potential bioremediation product (compost) in planting a rare 'recycled' tree (Variegated London Plane *Platanus* × *hispanica* 'Suttneri'). He is watched by the Chief Executive of the Natural Environment Research Council (Professor John Krebs, FRS).

The editors would like to acknowledge the help of Mr Gordon Hartman (Lecturer in Biochemistry, School of Biological Sciences, University of Surrey) who obtained the tree described above, for replanting at the University of Surrey, Guildford, UK in 1996.

Environmental Biomonitoring: The Biotechnology Ecotoxicology Interface

James M. Lynch and Alan Wiseman

School of Biological Sciences, University of Surrey, Guildford, UK

OECD
OCDE
PARIS

CAMBRIDGE
UNIVERSITY PRESS

98·302

PUBLISHED BY THE PRESS SYNDICATE OF THE UNIVERSITY OF CAMBRIDGE
The Pitt Building, Trumpington Street, Cambridge CB2 1RP, United Kingdom

CAMBRIDGE UNIVERSITY PRESS
The Edinburgh Building, Cambridge CB2 2RU, United Kingdom
40 West 20th Street, New York, NY 10011-4211, USA
10 Stamford Road, Oakleigh, Melbourne 3166, Australia

First published 1998

Printed in the United Kingdom at the University Press, Cambridge

Typeset in Garamond 10/12pt [VN]

A catalogue record for this book is available from the British Library

Library of Congress Cataloguing in Publication data

Lynch, J. M. (James Michael)
    Environmental biomonitoring: the biotechnology ecotoxicology
interface / James M. Lynch and Alan Wiseman.
      p. cm. – (Biotechnology research series; 7
    Includes index.
    ISBN 0 521 62141 0 (hardbound)
    1. Environmental monitoring. 2. Bioremediation. I. Wiseman, Alan.
II. Title. III. Series.
QH541.15.M64L95 1998
571.9'5–dc21   97–14837 CIP

Contents

Contents

Contributors

R. M. Atlas Department of Biology, Life Sciences Building/Room 139, University of Louisville, Louisville 1, KY 40292, USA

M. J. Bailey Natural Environment Research Council, Institute of Virology and Environmental Microbiology, Mansfield Road, Oxford OX1 3SR, UK

S. Battersby Consultant Adviser, 120 Wilton Road, London SW1V 1JZ, UK

M. J. Bazin Division of Life Sciences, King's College London, Campden Hill Road, London W8 7AH, UK

H. Bogaert Laboratory for Microbial Ecology, University of Ghent, Coupure Links 653, B-9000 Ghent, Belgium

P. A. Bramwell Natural Environment Research Council, Institute of Virology and Environmental Microbiology, Mansfield Road, Oxford OX1 3SR, UK

R. R. Colwell University of Maryland Biotechnology Institute, 1123 Microbiology Building, College Park, MD 20742, USA

F. A. A. M. De Leij School of Biological Sciences, University of Surrey, Guildford, Surrey GU2 5XH, UK

B. R. Evans Chemical Technology Division, Oak Ridge National Laboratory, PO Box 2008, Oak Ridge, TN 37831-6194, USA

Z. Fuzesi Facts Foundation, Pecs, Hungary

K. Gernaey Laboratory for Microbial Ecology, University of Ghent, Coupure Links 653, B-9000 Ghent, Belgium

P. S. Goldfarb School of Biological Sciences, University of Surrey, Guildford, Surrey GU2 5XH, UK

Contributors

V. V. S. R. Gupta Cooperative Research Centre for Soil and Land Management, Private Bag No. 2, Glen Osmond, South Australia 5064, Australia *and* Department of Soil Science, Waite Institute, University of Adelaide, SA, 5064, Australia

H. Kawashima National Institute of Agro-Environmental Sciences, 3-1-1 Kannondai, Tsukuba 305, Ibaraki 305, Japan

J. H. Koeman Department of Toxicology, Agricultural University, Wageningen, The Netherlands

J. R. Krebs Natural Environment Research Council, Polaris House, North Star Avenue, Swindon SN2 1EU, UK

D. R. Livingstone Natural Environment Research Council, Plymouth Marine Laboratory, Citadel Hill, Plymouth, Devon PL1 2PB, UK

J. M. Lynch School of Biological Sciences, University of Surrey, Guildford, Surrey GU2 5XH, UK

Sir Robert May UK Goverment Chief Scientific Adviser, Office of Science and Technology, Albany House, 84–86 Petty France, London SW1H 9ST, UK

B. J. Nordenstam Faculty of Environmental Studies, College of Environmental Science and Forestry, State University of New York, Syracuse, NY 13210, USA

K. Okamoto National Institute of Agro-Environmental Sciences, 3-1-1 Kannondai Tsukuba 305, Ibaraki 305, Japan

C. E. Pankhurst CSIRO Division of Soils, Private Bag No. 2, Glen Osmond, SA, 5064, Australia

S. L. Rogers Cooperative Research Centre for Soil and Land Management, Private Bag No. 2, Glen Osmond, South Australia 5064, Australia *and* Department of Soil Science, Waite Institute, University of Adelaide, SA, 5064, Australia

S. Shohet Segal, Quince, Wicksteed Ltd, The Grange, Market Street, Swavesey, Cambridge CB4 5QG, UK

I. P. Thompson Natural Environment Research Council, Institute of Virology and Environmental Microbiology, Mansfield Road, Oxford OX1 3SR, UK

L. Tistyan Fact Foundation, Pecs, Hungary

L. Van Vooren Department of Applied Mathematics, Biometrics and Process Control (BIOMATH), University of Ghent, Coupure Links 653, B-9000 Ghent, Belgium

P. Vanrolleghem Department of Applied Mathematics, Biometrics and Process Control (BIOMATH), University of Ghent, Coupure Links 653, B-9000 Ghent, Belgium

A. Vari   Hungarian Academy of Sciences, Institute for Social Conflict Research, Benczur U.33, Budapest 1068, Hungary

W. Verstraete   Department of Applied Mathematics, Biometrics and Process Control (BIOMATH), University of Ghent, Coupure Links 653, B-9000 Ghent, Belgium

A. Wetzel   Philipps-Universität Marburg, Fachbereich Biologie, Karl-von-Frisch-Strasse, D-35032 Marburg, Germany

J. M. Whipps   Horticulture Research International, Wellesbourne, Warwickshire, UK

A. Wiseman   School of Biological Sciences, University of Surrey, Guildford, Surrey GU2 5XH, UK

J. Woodward   Chemical Technology Division, Oak Ridge National Laboratory, PO Box 2008, Oak Ridge, TN 37831-6194, USA

Foreword

by Sir Robert May FRS
UK Government Chief Scientific Adviser

This book, which originated from an Organization for Economic Co-operation and Development (OECD) Workshop and the creation of Centres for Toxicology and Environmental Biotechnology at the University of Surrey, emphasizes the inter-disciplinary approach which is needed to solve environmental problems. I welcome its publication. I would like to think that, to some extent at least, the creation of the Centres was stimulated by our activities in the Office of Science and Technology (OST). Certainly, many of the themes explored in this book reflect recent developments in UK science and technology policy, notably the Foresight Programme which is the central plank of that policy.

The primary aim of the Foresight Programme is to identify market opportunities for UK industry and to foster the creation of networks between industry and the science base which will enable the UK to exploit those opportunities. One of the priorities identified is:

Securing a cleaner world through the development and application of environmental sciences and technologies for pollution control, clean processing and clean energy, and product life cycle analysis.

In line with this, environmental considerations and the biological sciences feature prominently in the reports produced by the sectoral Panels which are the spearhead of the Programme.

Foresight is fundamentally about promoting closer collaboration between the users and providers of science. A number of mechanisms are now available for encouraging university/industry research partnerships, notably the LINK scheme run by OST which is increasingly geared to Foresight priorities. There are now nearly 800 individual LINK projects, involving 1100-plus companies and 170 science and engineering base institutes. Biotechnology, toxicology and environmental Science are well represented in the 15 LINK programmes announced since the scheme was relaunched to focus on Foresight priorities in March 1995 and in the research programmes run by the various UK Research Councils funded by OST. For example, the Natural Environment Research Council is launching a major new programme on 'Ecological Dynamics and Genes' bringing together population and molecular biology to address previously intractable issues of the spatial and temporal dynamics of ecological processes related to microbial diversity and function and to the hazards associated with the release of genetically modified organisms.

The environment is a global responsibility and dealing with the effects of pollution a global problem. This is reflected in the book with chapter contributions from Europe, where current negotiations on the EU Fifth Framework Programme offer the opportunity to establish sustainable development as a key cross-cutting theme, the United States, Australia and Japan. Risk assessment, which is fundamental to the process of determining both safety criteria and priorities in toxicology research, is also featured.

Nobody should be in any doubt that the importance of environment, biotechnology, biomonitoring and ecotoxicology has been recognized where it counts. The contents of this book reflect that importance. I hope that it will be of interest to all those working in the field.

Acknowledgement

The editors would like to acknowledge the contribution made by Dr Peter Goldfarb (Reader in Molecular Biology, School of Biological Sciences, University of Surrey) for his suggestion, *inter alia*, of the title adopted for this book, and for helpful discussions on molecular toxicology.

Introduction: the value of biomonitors in bioremediation strategies against ecotoxicants

James M. Lynch and Alan Wiseman

Introduction

Since 1979, the Organization for Economic Co-operation and Development (OECD) has funded a co-operative research programme on Biological Resource Management for Sustainable Agricultural Systems. There are four themes, the first of which concerns safe exploitation of micro-organisms in plant/soil systems (Coordinator: Professor Jim Lynch). In the theme since 1995, the six topics which all have a biotechnological dimension are:

- methods for molecular ecology;
- identification of physiochemical aspects of the soil environment which regulate microbial function;
- risk analysis and toxicology of the use of micro-organisms;
- production and delivery of microbial inoculae;
- reduction of the load of chemical pesticides, fertilizers and organic wastes on the soil ecosystem;
- assessment of biodiversity in plant/soil systems.

Two of the major beneficial effects of micro-organisms which have been covered in previous books in this series are biocontrol (Hokkanen & Lynch, 1995) and bioremediation (Crawford & Crawford, 1996). In achieving progress in the latter field, it is necessary to be able to monitor ecotoxicants. The primary function of the present volume is to provide the linkage in environmental biotechnology and solution of ecotoxicological problems by monitoring processes biologically.

Some new approaches are required to supplement, or substitute for, present-day abilities to assess environmental hazards: precise and meaningful 'accurate-for-purpose' (AFP) biomonitoring is essential in the prediction of risk hazard indices (RHI) in air, soil and aqueous environments. Favoured techniques may require resort to approaches through molecular genetics, biophysical specific electrode development, molecular-electronic devices: in addition to the use of living organisms. A variety

Table 1. *Selection criteria in environmental biomonitoring*

General
* Be scientifically valid, robust, representative and understandable
* Allow intersite comparisons and linkages between ecosystem components
* Diagnose 'health' at the individual, population, community and ecosystem level
* Be responsive to environmental stress and changes
* Preferably be simple and cheap to use

Biomarkers
* Be cellular *or* subcellular including metabolic products, enzymes, antibodies and nucleic acids
* Respond sensitively to environmentally relevant contaminants
* Be dose and time responsive
* Be tested in the laboratory, validated in the field

Social and regulatory considerations
* Must be understood by policy makers and enforceable by regulators
* Document genuine reduction and prevent further risk to human health and environment, not just to legislation or public concern
* Be acceptable in public perception

of scientific, environmental and social aspects are necessary for the development of a biomonitor and some of these are outlined in Table 1, developed in discussion with Dr Sarah Cowell, Centre for Environmental Strategy, University of Surrey.

Following this introductory chapter, the first main chapter of the book provides a perceptive account of the directions for much-needed research on ways of dealing with present and future environmental hazards.

Ecotoxicology and biomonitoring

Detection of environmental hazards

The opening chapter of Part I of this book provides the essential 'historical' background and invaluable insights into pollution through long personal experience in the field. Then the role of polynuclear aromatic hydrocarbons in soil (Chapter 3) provides invaluable information on this recurrent problem: as does the following chapter (Chapter 4) on the application of micro-organisms and enzyme assays to assess 'risk of utilization' of polluted soil.

Gene-release and biomonitoring strategies

In Chapter 5 the wide scope of application of recombinant DNA gene release into the environment is indicated. It provides an important and novel technique for following the subsequent distribution and fate, especially in soils, of such genetically manipulated organisms (GMOs), which can be readily identified by the biomonitoring of their recombinant DNA directly, or indirectly through their particular phenotypic characteristics thereby introduced. Several ingenious new applications are manifest in published accounts of gene-release strategies and tactics as utilized for fundamental research. In addition, success is evident in the solving of industrial problems relating to spillage and leakage of effluents and other chemicals, including feedstocks and saleable products.

The advent of 'gene-release', in a variety of genetically engineered recombinant forms of micro-organisms and plants (and possibly in some animal species), has led to the development of biomonitoring of the particular DNA base sequence(s) that characterize the gene(s) released into the environment. In this context, Chapter 6 details studies on gene probing with tissues of the common mussel *(Mytilus edulis* L) gathered from polluted littoral sea-tidal beach environments (also studied in several species of fish). Particular pollutants in the water environment led to the induction of characteristic isoenzyme forms of the ubiquitous iron–protohaem enzyme generically named as cytochrome P-450 (cyt P-450). In particular, the cytochrome P-450 1A1 isoenzyme form is induced by benzo(a)pyrene-binding to the Ah receptor for aromatic hydrocarbons: this leads to gene expression and the consequent biosynthesis of the corresponding messenger RNA occurs. The particular messenger RNA form can be identified readily, even in the complex mixtures arising from tissue extraction. This is achieved by the popular technique of 'Northern-blotting' identification of gel electrophoresis patterns using *in situ* hybridization (specific bonding) with radiolabelled gene probe DNA: this DNA is constructed to recognize that particular messenger RNA through specific tight bonding because of pre-arranged complementary structure hydrogen bonding opportunities. This observed structure is found also in the DNA–DNA naturally occurring double helix, and is used to detect particular DNA base sequences in the analogous 'Southern-blotting' hybridization technique with agarose gel electropherograms.

Ecotoxicology and bioremediation

In Part II of this book, Chapter 7 defines the advantages and problems of bioremediation using added micro-organisms: case studies are provided in the following chapter. Chapter 9 deals with the employment of biocatalysts, including natural enzymes, in cellulose waste minimization. The opportunities for nitrogen biosensors to be used in assessing the removal of nitrogen from aqueous waste are covered in the next chapter. In Chapter 11, the public are made aware of the problems of nitrate leaching to groundwater as a hazard to both human and environmental health. An analysis is presented of future problems world-wide associated with excessive use of nitrogen-containing fertilizers in agricultural production of foods for people, and for domestic animal feeding purposes. Reduction of fertilizer usage would result in less groundwater leakage of nitrate and gaseous emissions which damage the ozone layer.

Biosafety, regulations, and economics

Part III of this book opens with an account of risk perception in the public, associated with environmental lead contamination in Hungary. This is followed by Chapter 13 on risk assessment and then Chapter 14 with an analysis of legal problems associated with the environment. In Chapter 15, the economic consequences of bioremediation strategies world-wide are considered. Exploitation of the opportunities of environmental biotechnology will only be realized if economic and regulatory conditions are satisfied, and if there is public acceptance.

Directional pointers to future environmental problems

In the final section of the book, a concluding chapter (Chapter 16) attempts to identify 'fail-safe strategies' (FSS) in some cases based on the partial coupling of biomonitoring techniques with automatic responses to deal with the set-point prediction of looming crisis. In this way, bioremediation strategies that can be detected as failing could, through early warning systems, be supplemented (or diverted) to avoid real-time build-up of risky scenarios of significant environmental damage ahead, as pre-defined by the adopted strategy programme.

Much further research and prototype testing will be essential to perfect such FSS abilities.

References

Crawford, R. L. & Crawford, D. L. (eds.). (1996). *Bioremediation: Principles and Applications.* Cambridge: Cambridge University Press.

Hokkanen, H. M. T. & Lynch, J. M. (eds.). (1995). *Biological Control: Benefits and Risks.* Cambridge: Cambridge University Press.

The editors, August 1997

Part I
Ecotoxicology and biomonitoring

I

Our environmental future: the role of science

John R. Krebs

1.1 Introduction

During the past 30 years, the environmental agenda has included, in succession, depletion of the Earth's resources (1960s), regional pollution (e.g. acid rain) (1970s), global change (e.g. stratospheric ozone 'hole') (1980s) and sustainability (1990s). The concept of sustainability serves as a description label for the environmental agenda, but requires careful analysis before it can be used prescriptively.

In the next 10 years the six major issues on the UK's environmental agenda will be: global change; pollution; waste; biodiversity; natural and man-made risks and hazards; sustainable management of resources including earth and marine resources, freshwater supplies; land and the coastal zone. Local and global environmental pressures will increase because of global population growth and the increasing impact of UK and EU environmental legislation on all sectors of the economy, including: manufacturing industry, transport and leisure. The environment also offers a commercial opportunity for providing goods and services.

Science has a key role to play in underpinning sound legislation and regulation, sustainable management of the environment and development of new solutions. An important challenge for environmental scientists in the future is not only to develop better knowledge, understanding and prediction of the environment, but also to link this knowledge to economics, perceptions of risk and societal values.

Many areas of public policy formation benefit from access to a strong science and engineering base. Indeed, the OECD's Committee on Scientific Policy recommended, in 1963, the integration of science with general policy (Skoie, 1993). This chapter explores the role of science in underpinning sound legislation, sustainable management of the environment, and development of new solutions.

Table 1.1. *UK's rank performance in environmental and geo-sciences (combined)*

World ranking	% share of world papers (1981–94)	% share of world papers (1981–94)	Relative citations per paper (1981–94)
1	USA	USA	USA
2	Canada	UK	Australia
3	UK	Canada	Switzerland
4	Germany	Australia	UK
5	France	France	Norway
6	Australia	Germany	Sweden

Source: Bureau of Industry Economics (1996). Australian Science: Performance from published papers.

1.2 The role of science

Most countries have formal scientific advisory systems. Scientists provide advice on technical issues beyond the competence of government officials and ministers. They also bring objectivity and rationality to decision-making.

Unless the causal chains leading to changes in our environment and its resources are properly understood, effective policies cannot be devised. For science to be of use, it must be of the highest quality, impartial, internationally respected and authoritative. UK environmental science is respected internationally. During the period 1981 to 1994, the UK ranked ahead of all other European Union countries in terms of the percentage share of world papers and world citations, and in terms of relative citations rate per paper in the environmental and geo-sciences (Table 1.1).

Science, which underpins policy, may arise in unexpected ways. It is not easy to predict precisely which pieces of information will be needed. Therefore, customers of research, like NERC, must be able to support a range of quality science that will lead to fundamental understanding of the environment. Environmental science must have regard for other disciplines. It must be linked effectively and closely with an understanding of economics, and sociological psychological issues such as the perception of risk and the aspirations of individuals and society as a whole.

1.3 Environmental policy formation

The UK reasserted its policy of basing 'decisions . . . on the best possible scientific information and analysis of risk' in 1994 with the publications of '*Sustainable Development: The UK Strategy*' (HMSO, 1994). Increasingly, environmental policy development is informed by multi-disciplinary scientific advisory committees.

8

These may include environmental scientists, but may also draw on experience from the medical, transport and other sectors. Examples of such bodies within the UK include: the Expert Panel on Air Quality Standards (EPAQS), the Group of Experts on Scientific Aspects of Marine Pollution (GESAMP), and the Advisory Committee on Releases to the Environment (ACRE).

Science may also influence policy formulation through other bodies such as the UK's Advisory Committee on Business and the Environment (ACBE), the Royal Commission on Environmental Pollution (RCEP) and the Technology Foresight Programme (OST, 1995). ACBE's most recent report, published in April 1996 (DTI/DoE, 1996), acknowledges the scientific input provided by NERC in the area of urban air quality, and emphasizes the importance of integrated multidisciplinary research programmes to inform policy-making.

The Government's 1996 White Paper, *This Common Inheritance* (HMSO, 1996) outlined progress on 642 environmental policy commitments. Many of these require science to underpin policy development and monitor progress. Working with other bodies, DoE funds science (£114 million in 1996/7) activities to support its Departmental Policy, statutory, operational, regulatory and industrial sponsorship responsibilities. NERC's investment in environmental science is directed towards long-term strategic and basic science.

1.4 The Natural Environment Research Council's (NERC) contribution

NERC is the lead UK environmental science organization. Its role is complementary to that of policy-making bodies or regulatory authorities (for example, DoE, MAFF, Environment Agency). Its mission is to develop knowledge, understanding and prediction of all aspects of the environment and natural resources. It does this by fostering research, survey and monitoring, education and training, technology development and the provision of environmental data. NERC is also required to provide advice and enhance public understanding of the environment. Environmental issues are almost invariably transnational. Much of NERC's science is therefore linked into international programmes both within Europe and throughout the world. NERC contributes to the development of the UK policy on the EC's Framework Programmes for Research and Technological Development.

The total budget of the NERC from the Office of Science and Technology is in the region of £160 million. In addition, NERC receives about £38 million from external sources, including Government bodies and the EC. These monies are used to carry out research into issues high on the UK's environmental agenda, embracing: biodiversity; environmental risks and hazards; global change; natural resources; pollution; and waste. Figure 1.1 illustrates the percentage breakdown of funding (science budget and external) for these six environmental and natural resource issues.

J. R. Krebs

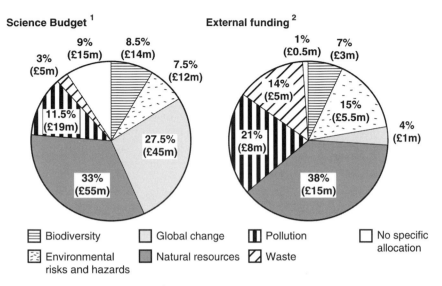

Fig. 1.1. NERC expenditure (1996/97) against six environmental and natural resource issues.
[1]Percentages calculated on the basis of science budget allocation (SB) of £165m at 1996–97
planning figures. [2]Percentages calculated on the basis of forecasts of external funding for
research (EF) of £38m in 1996–97.

1.5 Science and policy development

Rachel Carson's (1962) book *Silent Spring* provided a turning point in our attitude
towards human impacts on the environment. Rachel Carson 'blew the whistle' by
amassing circumstantial evidence to show that organochlorines such as DDT
persist in the food chain and damage animals other than the target species. In
particular, she suggested that these chemicals damage the predators of the target
insects and the predators of the predators. Their persistence in the food chain not
only indicated damage to environmental health but also raised the possibility that
they could damage human health. These disbenefits, if substantiated, had to be
weighed against the undoubted benefits of pesticides in agriculture and in controlling
vectors of human disease. At the time of *Silent Spring*, the evidence was by no means
watertight. Now it is, and most organochlorines are banned in the UK and other
countries of the European Union.

1.6 Agrochemicals and the environment

The key paper establishing the link between raptors and DDT was published by a
NERC scientist, Derek Ratcliffe, in 1967, and this, together with much subsequent
work, eventually led to legislation in most industrialized countries. Since phasing
out of organochlorines, raptors have recovered substantially in the UK. There has

been a three-fold increase in sparrowhawk population since 1972 and a five-fold increase in peregrine falcons since 1960. The possible impacts on human health are still a matter of debate. Interestingly, although UK scientists did much of the critical research, the UK in 1986 was the last developed nation to ban DDT, aldrin and dieldrin. The key science came from an unexpected quarter: observations on the deaths of birds in and around fields treated with organochlorines, and the discovery of broken egg shells in raptor's nests which were not accountable to predation. It may now seem obvious that birds' nests may act as an environmental marker for DDT, but it was by no means so at the time. A complete analysis of the causal chain was necessary to underpin the development of policy.

1.7 Global atmosphere and climate change

Another defining moment in the role of science in underpinning policy development was the discovery in 1985 by NERC scientist Joe Farman at the British Antarctic Survey of the 'ozone hole' in the stratosphere over Antarctica. This was the first time that concrete evidence of human action influencing the global environment was reported. Within 2 years, the Montreal Protocol had been adopted, and now more than 150 countries have signed the Protocol, with its subsequent Copenhagen amendment.

The principal concern about ozone in the stratosphere is that it screens out UV-B, and thus protects humans from skin cancer and cataracts as well as protecting crops and natural ecosystems from the damaging effects of UV-B. The measurements which led to the discovery of the 'ozone hole' have been made on a regular basis since 1957. Although NASA had been measuring stratospheric ozone over Antarctica, it had programmed its computers to reject outlying data points and, therefore, had not seen the evidence of depletion. The reason why the 'ozone hole' is over Antarctica (and now increasingly over the Arctic) is because, at very low temperatures, the chemical interactions between chlorofluorocarbons (CFCs) and stratospheric ozone (9–30 miles up in the air) lead to the breakdown of ozone. They act as catalysts and are not destroyed in the chemical reaction that breaks down ozone. Paradoxically, when CFCs were first introduced, it was the *New Scientist* which stated 'no other chemicals are as harmless in the home as CFCs'. New technologies are always likely to carry with them potential environmental risks. The effect of new technology on our health and the environment is the subject of a new book by Edward Tenner (1996), in which he assesses how and why new technologies and processes often help us to do things better, but make us and the environment feel worse.

1.8 Acid deposition

The acidifying effect of airborne sulphur was recognized by chance in the 1960s by Swedish agricultural scientists studying geochemistry. Sulphur deposition resulted in damage to acid-sensitive freshwater and soils in Europe. The problem had to be addressed at an international level because the pollution travelled long distances and crossed political boundaries. The first step was to understand the processes operating and then to develop a policy for reducing the pollution to a level at which environmental damage did not occur.

NERC-sponsored scientists provided the scientific underpinning for UK policy relating to the European transport and deposition of acidic pollution. Through greater understanding of the processes, the UK has developed a policy which relies on the application of a critical loads approach, in which the sensitivity of the landscape to acidic inputs and current deposition is assessed and mapped. Different landscapes reveal different tolerance levels. This approach identifies areas of exceedence and estimates the reduction necessary to protect them. The current UK policy for sulphur is designed to close the gap between deposition and the threshold for effects, by 60% by the year 2010, and is on course to do so. Since 1970, sulphur dioxide emissions within the UK have been reduced from about 6.5 million tonnes to under 4 million tonnes.

1.9 Air pollution

Science has informed, and continues to inform, policy developments in this area. A major route to the development of the Department of the Environment's technical policy on air quality comes via its scientific research programme (Williams, 1996). Together with medical evidence synthesized through such bodies as the Department of Health's Advisory Group on the Medical Aspects of Air Pollution Episodes and the Committee on Medical Effects of Air Pollutants, advice on recommending standards for air quality is provided by the Expert Panel on Air Quality Standards. The Government published for consultation in August 1996 a National Air Quality Strategy (DOE, 1996). The Strategy is the first of its kind in Europe. It includes standards for all the main air pollutants: nitrogen dioxide, particles, ozone, sulphur dioxide, carbon monoxide, lead, benzene and 1-3 butadiene, based on the recommendations of independent experts.

1.10 Sewage and the environment

An example of how NERC scientists have influenced policy development at the regional level is the work of NERC's Institute of Freshwater Ecology (Elliott & Reynolds, 1996). Since 1945, nutrient concentrations and algal populations have been measured weekly in Lake Windermere. From about 1965, winter concentrations of phosphorous have increased. This enrichment promoted larger populations of algae, especially in summer, and had a negative impact on the size of the fish population in the lake. The increase in phosphorous was related to the switch, in 1965, from the disposal of sewage in septic tanks (which discharge mainly to soils) to mains sewerage and the discharge of mineral-rich, treated, effluent directly into the lake. This discharge reached a maximum in 1991 by which time it provided 13.6 of the 19.5 tonnes of the phosphorous reaching the lake each year. The rest of the phosphorous entered the lake in run-off from the land.

North West Water have accepted advice on the diagnosis and control of the enrichment by introducing a tertiary treatment, designed to precipitate ('strip') phosphorous from the final effluent from the sewage works. Efficiency is less than 100% because in wet weather the greater volume of fast-running water means contact times are shortened. Nevertheless, since 'stripping' began in April 1992 there has been an average 70% reduction in the sewage-derived phosphorous supplied to the lake. The dramatic response in the winter phosphorous concentrations since then, as well as the reduction in algal biomass to levels not seen since the early 1970s, have resulted in the density of the local fish population increasing.

1.11 Radioecology

Radioecological research at NERC's Institute of Terrestrial Ecology (ITE) has had a number of impacts at policy level. Shortly after the Chernobyl accident in 1986, ITE produced the first and most comprehensive contamination map in the UK (Allen, 1986). The map was used extensively by DoE and the Ministry of Agriculture, Fisheries and Food (MAFF) to direct their response and impose appropriate restrictions. The stratified sampling used to compile the map enabled contaminated upland areas to be identified. Restrictions were subsequently placed on the movement and slaughter of sheep in some upland areas, some of which still remain in place today.

Subsequently, ITE carried out an experiment to show that contaminated lambs removed from the upland to lowland farms lost their radiocaesium burden rapidly (Howard *et al.*, 1987). In a further experiment it was revealed that the contaminated faeces and urine deposited on these lowland pastures would not give rise to elevated levels in lowland vegetation, because of the binding of the radiocaesium ions by clay minerals in these soils (Crout, Beresford & Howard, 1991). This enabled MAFF to sanction the sale and movement of hill lambs for fattening and subsequent slaughter.

1.12 Beyond environmental science

Environmental and natural resource issues will continue to increase in importance. Population and economic growth will inexorably increase pressure on the environment. Each month, the equivalent of a New York city is added to the world's population, and economic growth inevitably means a greater impact on the environment. At the moment, one-fifth of the world's population live in the industrialized nations: they use two-thirds of the resources and create four-fifths of the pollution. New environmental problems are likely to become acute, including problems of water supply and of urban pollution.

J. R. Krebs

Legislation and regulations are having an ever-increasing impact on industry. This is both a threat and an opportunity for UK business. New technologies will have new impacts on the environment. Introduction of the so-called 'harmless' CFCs is known to have a damaging effect on the environment. One of the important new technologies that will develop over the next few years is biotechnology. When genetically modified organisms are released into the environment, their effects will have to be studied carefully and predicted.

There is a key challenge for environmental scientists to understand and ensure that their knowledge meshes with the perceptions and values of individuals and of society as a whole. Nowhere is this difficult area more obvious than in discussions and analysis of risk. Science has never shirked from facing up to uncertainty. As O'Riordan and Cameron (1994) state, uncertainty comes in three fundamental forms: lack of data where uncertainty arises through ignorance; variability of process where uncertainty arises through changing conditions and how organisms and the environment respond to these changes; and uncertainty through indeterminacy where the systems being studied operate processes that cannot be encapsulated in traditional scientific terms.

1.12.1 Public and political perception of the environment

Public and political perception of the environment is a further important factor. In the 1960s and 1970s environmental policy treated the marine environment as a resource, whose exploitation was limited only by considerations of the effect of one group of people upon another (MacGarvin, 1994). During the 1980s there was a significant shift in north-west European marine environmental policy when it became apparent that substances released into the North East Atlantic were by no means rapidly diluted and dispersed from inshore water and coastal seas such as the North Sea and the Baltic. The NERC North Sea research programmes made a major input to the Quality Status Reports on the North Sea during this period (and subsequently). The most significant development, the precautionary principle, was given explicit form at the 1987 Ministerial North Sea Conference.

For natural scientists, risk estimation is largely a matter of statistical analysis and scientific understanding of causal chains such as those in the examples provided in this chapter. The estimation of risk is then combined with some estimate of trade-offs to complete the risk analysis. For social scientists, individual perceptions, beliefs and aspirations, may be as important or more important than technical scientific analysis. In particular, individuals perceive as high risk things that are unusual, over which they have no control, which act with a long time delay, and about which there is some uncertainty of the consequences. In the environmental sphere, an example is the decommissioning of the Brent Spar. The scientists say (and this was confirmed in the Report of the independent expert group set up by NERC in response to a request from the Minister for Energy) 'the impact on the environment will be negligible'. Media responses to the publication of this Report illustrate how difficult it is to draw unambiguous conclusions about an issue in which there are no simple answers. The *Daily Express's* 'oil rig can be dumped at sea' seems to be at odds with Lloyds List's 'dumping at sea fails to win support'. The *Glasgow Herald, Nature* and *Wall Street Journal* steered a middle course with, respectively: 'Report gives both sides some comfort', 'Report stays neutral on deep-sea disposal' and 'UK Report on rig disposal stirs differing praise'. Other papers headlined specific points, such as 'Brent Spar dumping site "not ideal"' (*Daily Telegraph*) and 'Shell "ignored" sea experts' (*Times Higher Education Supplement*). As the Report acknowledges, the scientific evidence on potential environment impacts of disposal at sea is not the whole story: 'social, economic, ethical and aesthetic considerations' must also come into play and there must be open and public debate on such issues.

In the terminology used by DOE, risk estimation (which is what the scientific and engineering skills help to achieve) must be combined with risk evaluation (including the other factors referred to by the Report) to form a complete risk assessment. The issue of marrying scientific evidence with the somewhat less tangible elements of risk evaluation is a major challenge and one which will continue to require scientific knowledge, understanding and prediction to underpin environmental policy and legislation.

References

Allen, S. E. (1986). Radiation: a guide to a contaminated countryside. *The Guardian*, 25 July, 17.

Bureau of Industry Economics (1996). *Australian Science: Performance from Published Papers*, Australian Government Publishing Service, Report 96/3, pp. 1–88.

Carson, R. (1963). *Silent Spring*, pp. 1–293. London: Hamish Hamilton.

Crout, N. M. J., Beresford, N. A. & Howard, B. J. (1991). The radioecological consequences for low land pastures used to fatten upland sheep contaminated with radiocaesium. *Science of the Total Environment*, **103**, 73–87.

DoE (1996). New air quality strategy promises end to smog episodes (UK takes lead on air quality management). *Department of the Environment Press Release* (356), 21 August 1996.

DTI/DoE (1996). *Sixth Progress Report and Response from the President of the Board of Trade and the Secretary of State for the Environment*, April 1996, pp. 1–118. Advisory Committee on Business and the Environment.

Elliott, M. & Reynolds, C. (1996). Lake enrichment and Windermere Charr. *Biological Sciences Review*, May 1996, 17–20.

HMSO (1994). *Sustainable Development: The UK Strategy*, Cm. 2426, pp. 1–268.

HMSO (1996). *This Common Inheritance: UK Annual Report*, Cm. 3188, pp. 1–163.

Howard, B. J., Beresford, N. A., Burrow, L., Shaw, P. V. & Curtis, E. J. C. (1987). A comparison of caesium 137 and 134 activity in sheep remaining on upland areas contaminated by Chernobyl fallout with those removed to less active lowland pasture. *Journal of the Society of Radiological Protection*, **7**, 71–3.

MacGarvin, M. (1994). Precaution, science and the sin of Hubris. *Interpreting the Precautionary Principle*, ed. T. O'Riordan & J. Cameron, pp. 69–101. London: Earthscan Publications Ltd.

O'Riordan, T. & Cameron, J. (1994). (eds.). *Interpreting the Precautionary Principle*, pp. 62–8. London: Earthscan Publications Ltd.

OST (1995). *Progress Through Partnership*. Report from the Strategy Group of the Technology Foresight Programme 1995, pp. 1–126.

Ratcliffe, D. A. (1967). Decrease in eggshell weight in certain birds of prey. *Nature*, **215**, 108–210.

Skoie, H. (1993). Science and technology advice to governments – a Norwegian perspective. *Science and Public Policy*, **20** (2), 79–86.

Tenner, E. (1996). *Why Things Bite Back: New Technology and the Revenge Effect*. Fourth Estate, pp. 1–346.

Williams, M. L. (1996). Urban air quality: policy issues. *Proceedings of a Conference held at the Environmental Change Research Centre, University College London*, Friday 23 September 1994, pp. 59–64.

2

Pollution and its ecotoxicological consequences

J. H. Koeman

Ecotoxicology is an interdisciplinary field of science that was established 'stepwise' over the last 50 years, although the history of ecotoxicological testing, like the development of fish toxicity tests, dates back even to the last century. The first test methods were already developed in 1863 (see Hunn, 1989). Generally, the main objective is to assess the possible impact of pollutants on animals, plants and ecosystems. However, there is an increasing tendency to include man within the scope, because one starts to realize that the protection of ecosystems is not just a luxury problem, aimed to please the environmentalists in our society, but is an essential condition for the survival of the human species. Part of the field is covered by the term 'fish and wildlife' toxicology or just 'wildlife' toxicology. Here, the emphasis is put on the effects on populations of vertebrates, especially fish, birds, mammals and occasionally amphibians and reptiles. In the United States, 'wildlife toxicology' mainly stands for effects of chemicals on species hunted for 'sport' or food. Elsewhere in the world, 'wildlife toxicology' generally comprises 'non-game animals' as well.

2.1 Historical overview

In the history of the discipline, one can broadly distinguish five periods as outlined in Fig. 2.1. First, the period of discovery. This phase was triggered by calamities, such as mass mortalities in fish and birds caused by large-scale applications of pesticides the use of which had increased markedly since the mid-1940s. From 1946/47 until the mid-1950s, a lot of spectacular cases came to light, especially in the United States. The main compounds involved were DDT and the related pesticide DDD (e.g. Hotchkiss & Pough, 1946; George & Mitchell, 1948; for an overview, see Rudd, 1964). The studies made in this period were largely empirical and case orientated. Most of the early observers were wildlife biologists or amateur naturalists. It became clear that the use of pesticides may pose a serious risk for a variety of non-target species. One also learned that pollutants can accumulate in

HISTORY OF ECOTOXICOLOGY

- 1945 - 1960 Discovery

- 1960 - 1969 Alarm

- 1969 - 1980 Recognition

- 1980 - 1990 Maturation

- 1990 -   'Eco' concern

Fig. 2.1. History of ecotoxicology.

the tissues of fish and wildlife and be bio-accumulated in food chains (Hunt & Bischoff, 1960). Virtually all the early studies were carried out in North America and the UK, probably because at that time there were already more scientists involved in fish and wildlife research in these countries than in other places. Moreover, in North America a lot more types of habitats were treated with pesticides than in Europe, including forests, lakes and marshlands, which made it more likely that effects on non-target species would come to light.

The period from the mid-1950s until about the end of the 1960s could be referred to as the period of alarm. Special working parties and research study groups were created, not only in the US but also in Europe. Reports appeared, to alert and/or advise governments (e.g. the Zuckerman & Sanders reports produced in the UK in 1955 and 1961, respectively, were probably the first formal documents in this sort in Europe). These actions also led to the first restrictions in the use of pesticides. For instance, in the UK the dressing of seeds with pesticide mixtures containing aldrin, dieldrin and heptachlor for spring sowings was withdrawn in 1961, one year before the most influential publication ever written on the subject, *Silent Spring*, was published in the US (Carson, 1962). It is noteworthy that pesticides were the first chemicals that attracted the attention of those concerned about the environment. Problems with pesticides preceded those by other chemicals, and in many countries Pesticide Acts were the first legislative measures aimed at the protection of man and environment against possible undesirable effects of chemical contaminants. An important event in the 1960s was the international workshop convened by Dr Norman Moore at Monks Wood Experimental Station in the UK in 1965 (Moore, 1966). The first specialized journal, the *Bulletin of*

Environmental Contamination and Toxicology, appeared in 1966. Considerable progress was also made in analytical chemistry in that period, which led to the discovery of many more environmental pollutants, e.g. the PCBs (Jensen, 1966). The invention of the electron-capture GLC detector by Lovelock and Lipsky (1960) was especially a major breakthrough in this context.

The period from 1969 to about 1980 could be called the period of recognition. Governments and industry could no longer ignore the fact that industrial, agricultural and infrastructural developments had a considerable impact on environmental quality. Chemical pollution was recognized as a phenomenon of major concern. The consequences were spectacular. In many countries steps were taken to expand the legislative framework in order to control pollution, research was stimulated, special institutes and departments were created and in quite a few countries the Minister for Environment made his or her appearance. Environmental research was stimulated and the number of scientists involved increased exponentially. Consequently the major publishers noticed that there was a new gap in the market and many of the specialized pollution- and ecotoxicology-orientated international periodicals were introduced (about 15 new journals appeared between 1970 and 1977). In 1969, the French toxicologist Dr R. Truhaut introduced the term ecotoxicology. In 1972 during the Man and Biosphere Conference at Stockholm, UNEP (the United Nations Environment Programme) was established. At the beginning of the 1970s the first international agreements and treaties were made on pollution issues, such as the Copenhagen Agreement (1971) and the Oslo Convention (1972) on marine pollution. The OECD started to play a leading role in the international coordination of environmental monitoring activities and the drafting of guidelines for testing of chemicals (e.g. OECD, 1981). In 1967 the EEC made the first steps for the control of dangerous chemicals by launching Directive 67/548/EEC. From that moment on, ecotoxicologists were asked to contribute to the generation of ecotoxicity tests and procedures for risk assessment within the registration and notification processes. The latter development had a boom-effect on the field. Since the early 1970s, ecotoxicology developed along two lines, first as an applied field within the regulatory framework and secondly as a more purely scientific field dedicated to the mechanisms underlying the fate in the environment and effects on organisms (Fig. 2.2). In that period, relatively little attention was paid to the ecological consequences of chemical pollution (Koeman, 1982).

In the 1980s it became obvious that an appropriate characterization and assessment of risks of chemicals would require in-depth analyses of the complex fate of chemicals in the environment and of their effects on organisms and ecosystems. For this reason, a more professional input was needed from the main supporting disciplines: toxicology, (environmental) chemistry and ecology. Some of the main targets studied in these 'sub-disciplines' are shown in Fig. 2.3.

Environmental chemistry attempts to describe, quantify and understand the movement and transformations of chemicals released in the environment (Mill,

J. H. Koeman

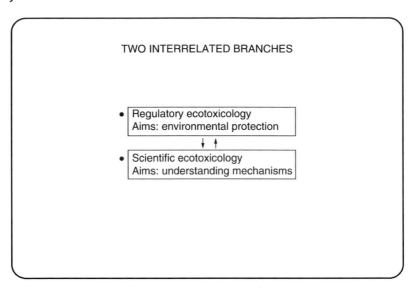

Fig. 2.2. Two interrelated branches.

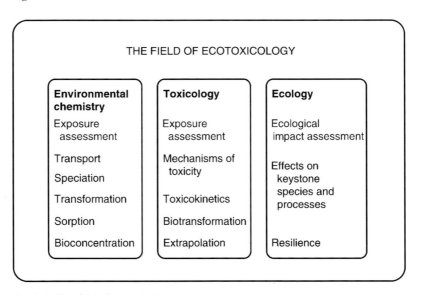

Fig. 2.3. The field of ecotoxicology.

1993). This requires an input not only by chemists but also, for instance, by soil scientists, specialists in air quality research and microbiologists. Of special practical importance within the context of ecotoxicological risk evaluations is the determination of the quantity of a chemical or chemical mixture, which is potentially available for uptake by organisms within their natural range (exposure assessment). A well-known parameter in this context is the predicted environmental concentration (PEC). Environmental chemists have also made considerable contributions towards the prediction of the fate and effects of chemicals on the basis of their chemical properties through the development of QSAR modelling (quantitative structure activity relationships). Using simple parameters, such as the octanol–water partition coefficient (P_{oct}/water, indicators for the lipophilicity of compounds) and the LC50 quantitative models for the prediction of toxicity have been established (e.g. Hermens & Opperhuizen, 1991). Some progress has also been made in linking other structural features of molecules (e.g. molecular connectivity) to particular effect parameters.

The main objective of toxicology is to assess the toxic effects chemicals may cause. Traditionally, toxicology was mainly concerned with effects on a limited number of mammalian species, mostly rodents, because the protection of man used to be the main target. Within the framework of ecotoxicology, many more target species are being considered, including almost all animal taxa and a number of plants. Toxicology deals with the interactions between chemicals and organisms. The toxic effects are studied both in a qualitative and quantitative sense: qualitatively, in order to identify (i) the fate of the chemicals in the organisms (e.g. kinetics, biotransformation), (ii) the organs and physiological functions that are affected, and (iii) the molecular mechanisms involved. In general, comparative studies are required in order to learn whether experimental studies with a limited range of laboratory models also apply to species living in the natural environment. To date, in toxicological research, more emphasis has been put on similarities among species than on differences. Research in comparative physiology forms an essential condition for the identification of species, populations and physiological processes, which are particularly vulnerable to the toxic effects of pollutants (Koeman, 1991). Insight into the mechanisms may also lead to the identification of appropriate biomarkers of effect (see later section). Most important in a quantitative sense within the framework of effect(s) assessment in regulatory ecotoxicology is the assessment of dose–response relationships. These show at which dose levels toxic effects may occur and how the response increases in proportion to the dose. Threshold levels of effect are derived from the dose–response curves. The better the insight into the mechanisms underlying critical toxic effects of chemicals, the more accurate and sensitive threshold levels such as NELs (no effect levels), NOELs (no observed effect levels), NOECs (no observed effect concentrations) or NAELs (no adverse effect levels) can be measured. The basic fields of science supporting toxicology are physiology, pathology, biochemistry and other more specialized derivatives of these sciences such as neurophysiology, immunology and molecular biology.

The professional input by ecologists has only become meaningful rather recently. Most of the earlier studies did not go far beyond the population level. Moreover, generally little attention was paid to species that play key roles in food webs and ecological processes. Ecologists study the distribution, abundance and population dynamics of species; the structure of food webs; interactions among species; the influence of physical factors on the performance of individuals and populations; community structures, the diversity of communities and systems and the functional properties of ecosystems, such as the fluxing of energy and matter; and the decomposition of organic matter. Ecologists and related specialists such as wildlife biologists play a predominant role in studies concerning the analysis of suspected causes of ecotoxicological effects (environmental epidemiology). Ecologists also contribute to the identification of biological responses, which can be used as indicators for laboratory and field studies aimed at the assessment of ecotoxicological properties of chemicals. Finally, they contribute to monitoring activities within the framework of the implementation of risk management policies.

Of the three major components of ecotoxicology mentioned, ecology is one that is still lagging behind. A large number of individual species have been studied but not sufficiently within the context of their possible role in the structure and functioning of ecosystems. This implies that it is highly uncertain at present whether the risk management strategies, devised on the basis of the prevailing risk assessment procedures, will provide sufficient protection to the world's ecosystems.

2.2 Future prospects

First of all, it must be recalled that the increased awareness of the problem, the better insight into the hazardous properties of chemicals and the determination of governments to abate and prevent the occurrence of undesirable effects have led to remarkable improvements. A number of dangerous pesticides and other chemicals have either been banned completely or substantially restricted in their use. For instance, most of the chlorinated hydrocarbon pesticides have been banned, almost on a world-wide scale, the use of metals and compounds like PCBs has been restricted or stopped and in many countries considerable efforts have been made to reduce emissions from factories. It is also notable that these measures have been successful. Many species of organisms, like birds of prey and fish-eating birds, which were seriously threatened in their existence in former periods, have shown a remarkable recovery. It is noteworthy that a relatively large number of species have been saved through measures against a relatively small number of chemicals. The explanation is that these chemicals, such as some of the chlorinated hydrocarbon pesticides, were dominant pollutants in many habitats in many countries.

However, one can not yet state that all the problems have been solved. It is true that drastic effects like mass mortalities in populations and severe effects on the reproduction of species have become uncommon, but there are indications that the remaining chemical pollutants still contribute to the deterioration of ecosystems in many places of the world. Presently, there is a tendency in ecotoxicological field studies to focus on the possible impact of the total chemical stress resulting from multiple diffuse sources on species and processes that play a key role in the structure and function of food webs and in ecological processes in general.

However, due to the fact that many ecosystems are subjected simultaneously to other stress factors such as acid rain, fertilizers, withdrawal of groundwater, landscape fragmentation and recreational pressure, it is scientifically difficult to prove that pollutants are involved and to quantify their role.

A development that may possibly meet the present needs to a considerable extent concerns the research on biomarkers. There is some variation in the definitions given, but the basis of most of them is that biomarkers are cellular, biochemical or molecular alterations that can be measured in organisms and other substrates either to obtain information about the physical condition or functional status of organisms and ecosystems or to provide qualitative and quantitative information about the presence and biological availability of pollutants in the environmental compartments concerned (e.g. Fossi & Leonzio, 1994; Koeman et al., 1993; Peakall, 1992; Walker, 1995). Considerable achievements have been made in this field as a spin-off of developments in molecular biology, particularly in molecular genetics, and in comparative mechanistic studies in toxicology.

Generally, biomarkers are classified into three categories: biomarkers of exposure, biomarkers of effect, and biomarkers of susceptibility (indicating differences in susceptibility among species in ecosystems or individuals in populations). Biomarkers can also be classified according to the degree of specificity of their indicator potency. For instance, acetylcholine-esterase inhibition in blood is a rather specific biomarker of exposure for defined chemical groups (organophosphorous compounds and carbamates), whereas induction of mixed function oxidases, such as cytochrome P450 1A, are much less specific biomarkers, in view of the range of organic pollutants to which this biotransformation enzyme may respond.

Many biomolecular biomarker systems have been developed in recent years. For the assessment of exposure and effects of mutagenic compounds, techniques are applied in animals and plants that were developed primarily to assess exposure and effects in human populations, such the measurement of DNA adducts, PCR (polymerase chain reaction) and gene expression (e.g. Minear et al., 1995; Vincent et al., 1995). Polyclonal and monoclonal antibody techniques are also applied to measure enzymes and proteins that are, to some extent, indicative of the presence and toxic effects of certain classes of chemicals (e.g. Husoy et al., 1996). A very promising development concerns the construction of recombinant receptor/reporter gene assays. These are recombinant cell-based bioassay systems that respond to chemicals that elicit their toxic response through the mediation of intracellular receptors and a subsequent reaction with specific DNA motifs, referred to as REs (responsive elements). Reporter genes are induced through this pathway, yielding gene products that can be measured to quantify the response. Receptors that have been incorporated successfully in such systems include the AhR (arylhydrocarbon receptor) and oestrogen receptors (e.g. Aarts et al., 1995; El-Fouly et al., 1994; Garrison et al., 1996; Zacharewski et al., 1995). Most systems developed make use of the luciferase reporter gene. A schematic outline of this approach is presented in Fig. 2.4.

J. H. Koeman

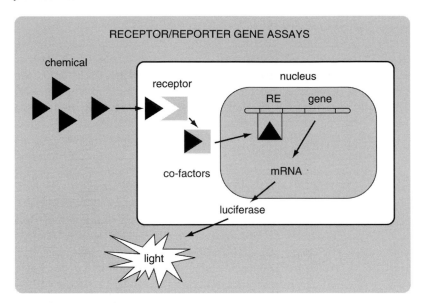

Fig. 2.4. Receptor/reporter gene assays.

These recombinant cell lines are now used for the detection and relative quantitation of complex mixtures of dioxin-like compounds and pollutants with oestrogenic potential. A major advantage over traditional instrumental methods is that the receptor/reporter gene bioassays provide information on the total biological potency, because they also integrate antagonistic, synergistic and/or additive interactions that may occur in response to complex pollutant mixtures that occur in the environment. Comparable reporter systems or biosensors have been developed, using bioluminescent reporter bacteria. They are used to investigate dynamic environmental changes on catabolic gene expression and bacterial physiology under *in situ* conditions (e.g. Heitzer *et al.*, 1995). Such systems may be developed further into ecological biomarker systems, through which basic ecological functions could be assessed as measures for 'ecosystem health'.

Insight into molecular mechanisms involved at the onset of toxicity, and in the subsequent toxicological response, has also resulted in the development of sensitive and specific biomarkers that can be used in biomonitoring programmes (e.g. Aldridge, 1996). Insight into the mechanisms of action of pollutants generally forms a prerequisite for the analysis of possible causal relationships between exposure and effect. For instance, the analysis of the role of PCBs in population changes in wild mammals and birds only became possible after it could be demonstrated that molecular mechanisms characteristic for the toxicity, that were identified in the laboratory, also occurred in wild species. These mechanisms include the role of AhR and the disruptive effects on endocrine functions, especially

24

the interference with thyroid hormone and retinol metabolism (Brouwer *et al.*, 1988, 1989; Murk *et al.*, 1994).

In spite of the progress made, there are still obvious gaps in our understanding of the structures and keystone functions of ecosystems that are, for instance, critical for their resilience to stress or, reversely, critical for their vulnerability. A meaningful future for ecotoxicology will, therefore, largely depend on breakthroughs in the field of ecology.

References

Aarts, J. M. M. J. G., Denison, M. S., Cox, M. A., Schalk, M. A. C., Tulis, K., de Haan, L. H. J. & Brouwer, A. (1995). Species specific antagonism of Ah receptor action by 2,2',5,5'-tetrachloro- and 2,2',3,3',4,4'-hexachlorobiphenyl. *European Journal of Pharmacology, Environmental and Toxicological Pharmacology Section*, **293**, 463–74.

Aldridge, W. N. (1996). *Mechanisms and Concepts in Toxicology*. London, Bristol (US): Taylor & Francis.

Brouwer, A., Blaner, W. S., Kukler, A. & Van den Berg, K. J. (1988). Study on the mechanism of interference of 3,4,3',4'-tetrachlorobiphenyl with the plasma retinol-binding proteins in rodents. *Chemico Biological Interactions*, **68**, 303–17.

Brouwer, A., Reijnders, P. J. H. & Koeman, J. H. (1989). Polychlorinated biphenyl (PCB)-contaminated fish induces vitamin A and thyroid hormone deficiency in the Common seal (*Phoca vitulina*). *Aquatic Toxicology*, **15**, 99–105.

Carson, R. (1962). *Silent Spring*. Boston: Houghton Mifflin.

El-Fouly, M. H., Richter, C., Giesy, J. P. & Denison, M. S. (1994). Production of a novel recombinant cell line for use as a bioassay system for detection of 2,3,7,8-tetra-chlorodibenzo-*p*-dioxin-like chemicals. *Environmental and Toxicological Chemistry*, **13**, 1581–8.

Fossi, M. C. & Leonzio, C. (eds.). (1994). Nondestructive biomarkers in vertebrates. Boca Raton, Ann Arbor, London, Tokyo: Lewis Publishers.

Garrison, P. M., Tullis, J. M. M., Aarts, J. G., Brouwer, A., Giesy, J. P. & Denison, M. S. (1996). Species-specific recombinant cells as bioassay systems for the detection of 2,3,7,8-tetrachlorodibenzo-*p*-dioxin-like chemicals. *Fundamental Applied Toxicology*, **30**, 194–203.

George, J. L. & Mitchell, R. T. (1948). The effects of feeding DDT-treated insects to nestling birds. *Journal of Economics of Entomology*, **40**, 782–9.

Heitzer, A., Webb, O. F., Digrazia, P. M. & Sayler, G. S. (1995). A versatile bioluminescent reporter system for organic pollutant bioavailability and biodegradation. In *Applications of Molecular Biology in Environmental Chemistry*, Chap. 13. Boca Raton, New York, London, Tokyo: Lewis Publishers.

Hermens, J. L. M. & Opperhuizen, A. (eds.). (1991). *QSAR in Environmental Toxicology-IV*, Procedures of the 4th International Workshop, The Netherlands, 16–20 Sept. 1990, Elsevier, Amsterdam.

Hotchkiss, N. & Pough, R. H. (1946). Effects on forest birds of DDT used for Gypsy Moth control in Pennsylvania. *Journal of Wildlife Management*, **10**, 202–7.

98-302

J. H. Koeman

Hunn, J. B. (1989). *History of Acute Toxicity Tests with Fish, 1863–1987*. Investigations in fish control no. 98. UK Fish and Wildlife Service, PO Box 818, LaCrosse, Wisconsin 54602, 10 pp.

Hunt, E. G. & Bischoff, A. I. (1960). Inimical effects on wildlife in periodic DDD applications to Clear Lake. *California Fish Game*, 46, 91–106.

Husoy, A.-M., Straetkvern, K. O., Maaseide, N. P., Olsen, S. O. & Goksoyr, A. (1996). Polyclonal and monoclonal antibodies against immunoaffinity purified Atlantic cod (*Gadus morhua*) CYP1A. *Molecular Marine Biology and Biotechnology*, 5, 84–92.

Jensen, S. (1966). Report of a new chemical hazard. *New Scientist*, 32, 612.

Koeman, J. H. (1982). Ecotoxicological evaluation: the eco-side of the problem. *Ecotoxicological and Environmental Safety*, 6, 358–62.

Koeman, J. H. (1991). From comparative physiology to toxicological risk assessment. *Comparative Biochemistry and Physiology*, 100C, (1/2), 7–10.

Koeman, J. H., Köhler-Bünther, A., Kurelec, B., Rivière, J. L. & Walker, C. H. (1993). Applications of biomarker research. In *Biomarkers*, ed. D. B. Peakall & L. R. Shugart. NATO ASI Series, vol. H 68, Berlin, Heidelberg: Springer-Verlag.

Lovelock, J. E. & Lipsky, S. R. (1960). Electron affinity spectroscopy. A new method for the identification of functional groups in chemical compounds by gas chromatography. *Journal of the American Chemical Society*, 82, 431–3.

Mill, T. (1993). Exposure assessment for predictive risk assessments. In *Ecological Risk Assessment*, ed. G. W. Suter II *et al.* Boca Raton, Ann Arbor, London, Tokyo: Lewis Publishers.

Minear, R. A., Ford, A. M., Needham, L. L. & Karch, N. J. (eds.). (1995). *Applications of Molecular Biology in Environmental Chemistry*. Boca Raton, New York, London, Tokyo: Lewis Publishers.

Moore, N. W. (ed.). (1966). Pesticides in the environment and their effects on wildlife. *Journal of Applied Ecology*, 3, (Suppl.), 311 pp.

Murk, A. J., Van den Berg, J. H. H., Fellinger, M., Rozemeijer, M. J. C., Swennen, C., Duiven, P., Boon, J. P., Brouwer, A. & Koeman, J. H. (1994). Toxic and biochemical effects of 3,3',4,4'-tetrachlorobiphenyl and Clophen A50 on Eider ducklings (*Somateria mollissima*), *Environmental Pollution*, 86, 21–30.

OECD (1981). *Guidelines for Testing of Chemicals*. Paris: OECD.

Peakall, D. (1992). *Animal Biomarkers as Pollution Indicators*. London, New York, Tokyo, Melbourne, Madras: Chapman and Hall.

Rudd, R. L. (1964). *Pesticides and the Living Landscape*. Madison.

Vincent, F., Jaunet, S., Galgani, F., Besselink, H. & Koeman, J. H. (1995). Expression of *ras* gene in Flounder (*Platichtys flesus*) and red Mullet (*Mullus barbatus*). *Biochemical and Biophysical Research Communications*, 215, 659–65.

Walker, C. H. (1995). Biochemical markers in ecotoxicology – some recent developments. *Science of the Total Environment*, 171, 189–95.

Zacharewski, T. R., Berhane, K., Gillesby, B. E. & Burnison, B. K. (1995). Detection of oestrogen- and dioxin-like activity in pulp and paper mill black liquor and effluent using *in vitro* recombinant receptor/reporter gene assays. *Environmental Science and Technology*, 29, 2140–6.

3

Advances in biomonitoring: sensitivity and reliability in PAH-contaminated soil

Astrid Wetzel

3.1 Introduction to exposures and modes of action of PAHs (also see Chapter 4)

Polyaromatic hydrocarbons (PAHs) constitute a group of priority-rated pollutants, which are present at high concentrations in the soils of many industrially contaminated sites (Wilson & Jones, 1993). They are found in sewage sludge in the range of 1 to 10 mg kg^{-1}, which is significantly higher than found in normal agricultural soil (Table 3.1). Normal levels of PAHs in soil range between 0.1 and 1 mg kg^{-1} (Edwards, 1983). Prominent sources of PAH contamination in soils include oil spills and leakages from petrol stations, and former gasworks. They are also associated with gas-production and wood-preserving industries (Table 3.2).

PAHs consist of two or more fused benzene rings in linear, angular or cluster arrangements. They are formed whenever organic materials are burned (Fig. 3.1), with temperature influencing the particular mixture produced. Although PAHs behave in a particular way in the environment, each PAH component has a unique set of physical and chemical properties (Jacob *et al.*, 1984/1986). The stability of the PAHs is indicated by the ring arrangement, linear being the most unstable and angular rings (rings in steps) being the more stable forms (Table 3.3). Volatility decreases with increasing number of fused rings. They are relatively insoluble in water and are therefore associated primarily with the particulate phase, or with lipid-containing locations. The soil processes that determine the fate of PAHs are volatilization, abiotic losses (leaching, hydrolysis, photodecomposition) and biodegradation (of at least two- and three-ring PAHs). Loss of PAHs with four and more rings is considerably less significant. Most four- and five-ring PAHs are strongly adsorbed to the organic fraction of the soil and generally exhibit half-lives of >100 days.

A number of PAHs, such as benzo(a)pyrene, are proven or suspected to be carcinogenic in animals and man and/or mutagenic, in a variety of systems: at least after MFO(mixed function oxygenase)-mediated cation radical formation (Sullivan,

Table 3.1. *Summary of PAH concentration found in sewage sludge along with some of their physico-chemical properties*

Organic compound	Range (mg kg^{-1})	Median (mg kg^{-1})	log K_{ow}	Hc	Water solubility (mg l^{-1})
Naphthalene	0–5.8	1.0	3.59	4.79 E-2	31.7
Phenanthrene	2.1–8.3	4.3	5.61	1.625 E-3	1.08
Fluoranthene	2.2–28.5	9.1	5.33	2.69 E-4	0.26
Pyrene	1.2–36.8	4.9	5.32	2.1 E-4	0.132
Benzo(b)fluoranthene	2.1–14.8	7.5	6.57	4.96 E-4	0.001
Benzo(a)pyrene	0.1–7.5	2.6	6.30	6.46 E-5	0.0016
Benzo(ghi)perylene	nd.–0.3	0.2	7.23	2.23 E-6	0.245 E-4

K_{ow}: Concentration in octanol phase/concentration in aqueous phase.
Hc (Henry's constant): Concentration in the gas phase/concentration in the liquid phase.
Hc = Pa m^3 mol^{-1} = vapour pressure/aqueous saturation concentration in mol m^{-3} (vapour pressure can be expressed as atm or Pa. 1 Pa is equal to 9.872 E-6 atm).
Adapted from Wild & Jones, 1992.

Table 3.2. *Concentrations of PAHs (mg kg^{-1}) at contaminated sites*

Contaminant	Wood-preserving		Creosote production	Coking plant	Gas works
	Surface	Subsoil			
Fluoranthene	35	1629	21–1464	34	614–3664
Benzo(a)pyrene	28	82		14	45–159

Adapted from Wilson & Jones, 1993).

1985). The principal mechanisms that mediate PAH toxicity to organisms are:

- binding of the unaltered molecule to hydrophobic sites, thereby causing disturbances in normal function of membranes and cells;
- induction of biotransformation enzymes by binding to the Ah(aromatic hydrocarbon)-receptor;
- binding of PAH metabolites to macromolecules such as proteins and nucleic acids (resulting in molecular and cellular damage).

(For details see Ayrton *et al.*, 1990; Molven & Goksøyr, 1993.)

3.2 Bioaccumulation of PAHs in the terrestrial environment

The study of PAHs in the terrestrial environment is related mainly to concern over food-chain contamination and potential human exposure (Lo & Sandi, 1978; Speer

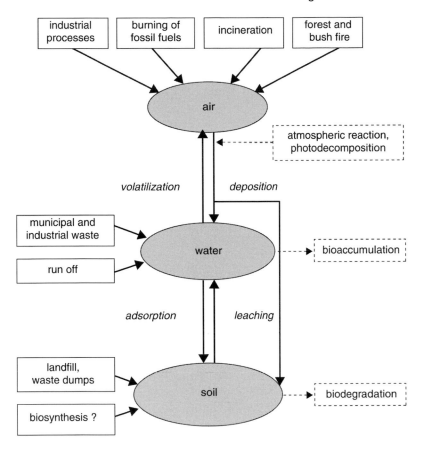

Fig. 3.1. Sources, sinks and transfer processes of PAHs in the environment (adapted from Bahadir *et al.*, 1995).

& Montag, 1989; Tuominen, Pyysalo & Sauri, 1988). Concentrations of PAHs in the range of 0 to 100 μg kg^{-1} have been detected in plant tissues, suggesting that some PAHs, particularly the lower molecular weight compounds, have been taken up from soil (Larsson, 1985; Coates, Elzerman & Garrison, 1986; Haas, Schreiber & Koss, 1990; Münch, 1992). In recent studies, however, on PAHs in crops from long-term field experiments amended with sewage sludge, there were only a few indications of PAH uptake via roots (Wild & Jones 1992; Niederer, Maschka-Selig & Hohl, 1995). On the other hand, atmospheric deposition seems to provide an important input of PAHs onto plant leaves (Debus *et al.*, 1989) and is considerably greater than inputs via root uptake and translocation, especially if these plants possess a huge leaf surface area and large amounts of cuticular waxes.

Hydrophobicity is the driving force for uptake of hydrophobic compounds by

Table 3.3. *Summary of half-lives of certain PAHs*

Organic compound	$T_{1/2}$
Naphthalene	<125 d
Phenanthrene	25 d–5.7 a
Fluoranthene	44–322 d
Pyrene	229 d
Benzo(b)fluoranthene	67–252 d
Benzo(a)pyrene	269–420 d
Benzo(ghi)perylene	9.5 a

Adapted from Wild & Jones, 1992.

organisms. For aquatic organisms, a relationship is often found between the partition coefficient in an octanol/water system (K_{ow}) and the bioconcentration factor (BCF), which is the coefficient for the equilibrium partitioning process between water and lipid (in the organism). The linear relationship between K_{ow} and BCF is broken only for compounds with log $K_{ow} > 6$ or for those that are easily metabolized (Axelmann *et al.*, 1995).

The relationship of K_{ow} and BCF is also found to be valid in partitioning processes in soil as they relate to the concentration of the PAHs in the soil-pore water. Since PAHs are adsorbed strongly to the soil organic matter and consequently the concentration of PAHs in soil-pore water is generally low, the uptake by soil organisms is considerably less than in the aquatic environment (Belfroid *et al.*, 1995). From our own investigations on the influence of sorption on bioavailability and toxicity of PAHs, we know that the amount of PAHs taken up from the soil into roots and shoots is not only reduced by an increasing content of soil organic matter but also by increasing the time-period of contamination. Comparative tests with freshly contaminated soil and soil that has been contaminated several years ago (but had the same methylene chloride-extractable amount of PAHs) suggested that the older-contaminated soil exhibited far less toxicity to plant growth (see Fig. 3.3) than the freshly contaminated soil. The uptake was quantified by the extraction of fluoranthene from root and shoot tissues. Hardly any PAHs were found in alfalfa plants grown on soil contaminated long ago, but transfer rates increased in soil with freshly applied PAHs (Wetzel & Werner, 1995). Additional investigations of fluoranthene uptake with *Lepidium sativum*, *Lolium multiflorum* and *Medicago sativa* showed significant species-dependent differences of fluoranthene uptake. It was not clear whether or not this was due to different accumulation (or metabolism) rates of PAH, but it is obvious that, for predictions of PAH bioconcentration factors for plants on the basis of K_{ow} values, the species-specific physiology has to be considered.

3.3 Biotransformation and biodegradation of PAHs in soil

Despite the high accumulation potential of high molecular weight PAHs, they are also subject to metabolism: usually activation. In fungi (Bumpus, 1989) and mammals (Zander, 1980), the initial activation (oxidation) in PAH-transformation processes is catalysed by monooxygenases (MFO) that are part of the cytochromes P-450 enzyme super-family. Intermediate metabolites of PAH degradation include dihydrodiols, phenols and arene oxides, many of which have been identified as mutagenic (and therefore likely to be carcinogenic): and some may be teratogenic. Arene oxides, especially, tend to bind to nucleophilic sites in DNA, thus forming DNA-adducts that may increase the mutation rate in a particular organism.

Bacteria characteristically produce dioxygenases, which incorporate two oxygen atoms into aromatic compounds (Cerniglia & Heitkamp, 1989). Metabolic degradation proceeds in one of two ways: either as the sole source of carbon and energy for the bacterium or by co-metabolism, e.g. co-oxidation. Co-oxidation has been observed to enhance the degradation of high molecular weight PAHs (Sims & Overcash, 1983; Smith, 1990). Biodegradation becomes difficult when the PAHs are adsorbed within the very fine pores within soil aggregates and are no longer reached by micro-organisms. The higher the content of organic matter in soil, the slower the microbial degradation (Weissenfels, Klewer & Langhoff, 1992). It is a subject of on-going discussion whether PAHs or PAH-metabolites are immobilized chemically by integration into the humus fraction of soil, and whether they are regained unchanged after eventual humus degradation (Qui & McFarland, 1991). If they could be fixed irreversibly in this way, appropriate investigations might prove this to be an acceptable remediation procedure (Rippen, Held & Ripper, 1994).

In studying the potential ecotoxicological effects of pollutants on plants, we must be aware that plants often modify these pollutants by biotransformation but do not mineralize them. Negeshi et al. (1987) demonstrated that soybeans grown in benzo(a)pyrene (BaP) polluted soil produce BaP alcohols and quinones, in addition to glucuronides and sulphate conjugates that correspond to metabolites and detoxification products of higher organisms.

3.4 Biomonitoring methods: prospective and retrospective strategies

Methods of biomonitoring can generally be divided into two categories: prospective and retrospective strategies (Fig. 3.2). To anticipate how PAHs are likely to impact on ecological systems (prospective strategy), biotests are carried out with suitable organisms (or suborganismic units) in the laboratory or as enclosure-type experiments with appropriate design (positive and negative references can assist in the evaluation of the data). The investigated biomarkers can be defined generally as xenobiotically induced variations in cellular or biochemical components, processes, structures or function. Biomarkers are divided into those that indicate exposure

A. Wetzel

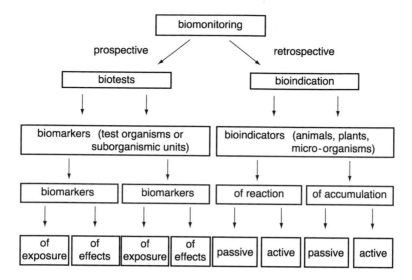

Fig. 3.2. Biomonitoring strategies.

to chemicals and those that demonstrate specific effects resulting from that exposure.

In retrospective biomonitoring an attempt is made to assess what changes have already taken place in ecological systems under the influence of released substances. These are the type of tests that are applied with so-called 'existing chemicals' for which actual effects in the field may still be unknown. The retrospective strategy involves the use of bioindicators: plants, animals or micro-organisms, with specific accumulation or reaction patterns for particular chemicals. Studies are related to particular circumstances and hence are usually carried out in effluent/emission streams, and also in receiving ecosystems. They enable *in situ* monitoring, with integration over the spatial and temporal heterogeneity of the system. Bioindication may be 'active' by introducing the bioindicators into the receiving ecosystem or may be 'passive' by analysing the natural inhabitants.

Various techniques have been derived to measure dose-response relationships and to investigate the mode of action at each step from the introduction of a xenobiotic to the experimental system to the final series of effects. This continuum of monitoring points can be outlined as follows.

- Molecular parameters of genotoxic effects: DNA-adducts, sister-chromatid exchange, micronucleus formation. They are predictive for exposure but not necessarily predictive for effects on a population.
- Physiological parameters of chemical stress: heat shock proteins, lowered chemical energy reserves, specific enzyme activities, MFO-activity, enhancement or inhibition of macrophages.

Table 3.4. *Evaluation of chemicals according to the soil function: the retention capacity of soil and endangering of groundwater*

Method	Reference	Parameter
Luminescence test with *Photobacterium phospheum*	DIN 38412 section 34	Light emission
Algae test	DIN 38412 section 9 OECD 201 (1984)	Growth
Daphnia immobilization test	DIN 38412 section 11 OECD 202 (1984)	Immobilization
Nematode mortality test	Debus & Niemann (1994)	Mortality
Fish mortality test	OECD 203 (1984)	Mortality
Ames-Test	DIN UA 12 (1994)	Mutagenicity
SOS-Chromotest	Xu (1989)	Activation of SOS-system
Umu-test	DIN UA 12, T3 (1994)	Mutagenicity

- Histological and behavioural parameters: cellular injury, lipid peroxidation, deformation of cell structures, changes in biomass, chlorosis, lesions, parasitism, tumours, abnormal levels of various salts or cytogenetic damage. Detailed knowledge of the normal cycles and natural history of the organisms and their environment is necessary to interpret the data correctly.
- Population parameters: mortality, reproductive indices, density, and alterations in genetic structure, i.e. the frequency of certain marker alleles. Indicators of reproductive effects include biochemical and physiological changes. The appropriate sampling strategy is important in relation to the reliability of the predictions made from the collected data.
- Community parameters: species diversity, species richness and composition, trophic composition, species abundance and condition.

As soon as generally valid response mechanisms are established and the impact range of a toxicant is known, all above-mentioned parameters may also be used as biomarkers in receiving ecosystems.

Several of the above-mentioned parameters have already been used for the evaluation of effects of PAHs in marine ecosystems (for references, see Molven & Goksøyr, 1993). Far fewer studies deal with terrestrial ecosystems, although the contamination levels in soils caused by decades of uncontrolled emission of PAHs are within an order of magnitude where destabilizing effects on the ecosystem have to be taken into consideration. Despite the low accumulation of PAHs in plants, they might nevertheless disturb plant growth due to hormone-like effects (Graf & Nowak 1966; Beteigne *et al.*, 1989), and further monitoring is therefore advisable. Another need for biomonitoring is to measure the effectiveness of soil detoxification in soil remediation processes of point contaminations.

Tables 3.4, 3.5 and 3.6 give an overview about appropriate biotests for the

Table 3.5. *Evaluation of chemicals according to the soil function: living-space for plant production*

Method	Reference	Parameter
Bacillus cereus contact test	Liu & Strachan (1981)	Dehydrogenase activity
Root growth	ISO 11269-1 Part 1	Root growth
Root-symbiosis test	Wetzel & Werner (1995)	Nodulation
Terrestrial plant test	OECD 208 (1984)	Plant shoot growth
Summer barley yield test	Kehres *et al.* (1994)	Yield
Terrestrial plant life cycle test	Sheppard *et al.* (1993)	Complete generation

Table 3.6. *Evaluation of chemicals according to the soil function: living-space for soil communities*

Method	Reference	Parameter
Soil microflora enzyme activity	Alef (1991)	Enzyme activities
Microflora dehydrogenase activity	BBA, VI 1-1 (1990)	Dehydrogenase activity
Microbial actual respiration rate	Hund & Schenk (1994)	Respiration rate
Substrate-induced respiration	ISO/DIS 14240-1 (1994)	Induced respiration rate
Nitrification test	ISO/DIS 14228 (1994)	Nitrification
Enchytraeus test	Römbke (1991)	Biomass, mortality and reproduction
Nematode abundance test	Hund & Traunspurger (1994)	Reproduction
Collembola reproduction test	ISO/TC 190 SC4 WG2	Reproduction
Earthworm mortality test	OECD 207 (1984)	Mortality
Earthworm reproduction test	ISO/DIS 11268-2 (1994)	Reproduction
Aleochara life cycle test	BBA VI 23-2.1.10 (1994)	Mortality and hatching rate

investigation of PAH-contaminated soil. As soil has various functions in the terrestrial ecosystems (water retention, substance retention, plant production and living space for micro-organisms) the test methods are grouped according to the various objectives of protection of soil. The Tables include tests that have been standardized by the OECD, the International Organization for Standardization (ISO) and other regulatory agencies as well as those that are not yet fully established. They are described in more detail by the Dechema publication – *Ad hoc* Arbeitsgruppe (1995): *Fachgespräch: Biologische Testmethoden für Böden*.

The strategy of ecotoxicological tests using aqueous extracts is based on the assumption that the particular chemicals affect the soil organisms via the aqueous phase, and that a potential hazard for the groundwater by water-soluble toxic substances can be identified. However, for the preparation of the aqueous extract, no standardized guideline exists at present. One common procedure is to shake soil with water (1 : 10) for 24 h (DIN 38414 Teil 4). However, several authors are doubtful about the environmental relevance of these extracts because the extraction is performed with a high content of water and therefore the ionic strength, which influences the solubility of contaminants, is lower than in the pore water of the soil (Friege, 1990). Consequently, in some investigations, lower soil/water ratios are used. Alternatively, solvents, such as DMSO, may be added to increase the solubility, but some of these solvents exhibit toxic effects themselves. Another problem is that media used for the tests may interact with the components of the test samples, rendering them more or less toxic than will in fact occur on the land. For example, dense suspensions and coloured solutions may not allow sufficient light for algal growth.

Aquatic and terrestrial plants are essential components of the ecosystem: they are primary producers of oxygen and primary food sources for all heterotrophic organisms whether they are animals, fungi or bacteria. Assessment of the likelihood of risks to humans, livestock and wildlife from potentially toxic constituents in water and soil requires knowledge of their toxic effects on plants. Plant studies at present deal mostly with germination, survival, growth rate and seed formation of individual species. A characteristic of this area of research is the emphasis on physiognomic plasticity of plants: parameters are change of leaf size, leaf position or total leaf area index.

Because the root zones of plants (rhizosphere) especially influence with soil processes, root parameters should be included in the assessment strategies. The root elongation test is the most widely used method in this respect. However, inhibited roots tend to develop a mass of laterals, which may weigh as much as normal roots; or they may not show any reduced growth, although the shoot is already damaged. In both cases, the sensitivity of the test has to be questioned.

One of the most challenging problems of ecotoxicological research, not just in soil, is the design of a proper control situation. An unchanging reference soil is essential to ensure that the interpretations do not vary with time and can be attributed to the contaminant and not to unfavourable pH, water or temperature conditions. In most cases, no consistent reference soil can be guaranteed, because non-affected areas will always differ from the influenced area. Most authors, therefore, use a synthetic soil, created from the reliable components peat, sand and expanded rock that matches the contaminated soil as closely as possible. By using dilutions of the soil sample with the synthetic soil or standard test soil, various EC (effective concentration) estimates can be obtained.

3.5 Biomonitoring of PAHs in soil bioremediation

Toxicity studies are essential in soil remediation, not only because intimate association of PAHs with the soil matrix may render the PAHs unavailable but also because metabolites have the potential to be more toxic than the parent compound. Hund and Traunspurger (1994) have recently developed an ecotox-evaluation strategy for soil bioremediation and have validated it for a PAH-contaminated site with a concentration of 4.5 g PAHs kg^{-1} soil. The investigations included biotests with the aqueous extract of the soil and with the soil itself. The tests took the different trophic levels of destruents, primary consumers, producers and secondary consumers into account.

3.5.1 Tests with soil eluate (prepared by shaking with deionized water (soil: water = 1 : 2.5) for 24 h)

- Luminescence test (*Photobacterium phosphoreum*)
- Bacteria respiration test (*Pseudomonas putida*)
- Daphnia acute immobilization test (*Daphnia magna*)
- Algae growth test (*Scenedesmus subspicatus*)
- Fish mortality test (*Brachydanio rerio*)

The high sensitivity of the luminescence test (Microtox® assay), compared to all other test systems, has been described for many pure organic substances and also for the assessment of contaminated soils with a mixture of contaminants. Hund and colleagues found that, even 21 months after the bioremediation procedure, the Microtox® assay still indicated the toxicity of the soil extracts. An uncertainty remains whether the toxicity determined with the Microtox® test is due to the contamination or whether the organisms also react on natural soil components in the eluate. In this case, an assessment of a bioremediation success solely based on the Microtox test could lead to false-positive results. For daphnids, a significantly increased short-term toxicity was observed. The temporary increased toxicity for daphnids indicates the formation of intermediate products for which the daphnids seem to possess specific reaction sites, whereas the potential for *Brachydanio rerio* and *Scenedesmus subspicatus* seems to be unspecific.

3.5.2 Tests with soil and introduced organisms

- Plant growth test (*Avena sativa/Brassica rapa*)
- Earthworm mortality test (*Eisenia fetida*)

The results of the tests with *Brassica rapa*, *Avena sativa* and *Eisenia fetida* were in accordance with the aquatic tests. They indicate that, in contact assays, a significant reduction of the toxicity also occurred during bioremediation. One problem in interpreting the results is that reduced growth of single plants need not be due necessarily to adverse effects by chemicals but may be a result of nutrient parameters and parameters of soil structure.

Eisenia fetida is exposed to soil contaminants in direct contact with the soil-pore water and through dietary uptake of soil. There is a correlation between increasing survival rate in this test and decreasing toxicity with the aquatic test. The measurement of weight was included in the test design but showed no significant correlation to other toxicity parameters.

3.5.3 Tests in soil with natural soil organisms

- Nematode abundance
- Microbial actual respiration rate
- Microbial substrate-induced respiration rate
- Nitrification

Nematodes present the group of metazoan organisms with the greatest number of individuals and species. Compared to other soil species, their abundance is 10 to 100 times higher (Scheffer & Schachtschabel, 1989). Furthermore, nematodes play a significant role in the nutrient cycle. Grazing, bioturbation and excretion products led to stimulation of the micro-organism population. Many authors have therefore suggested their use as test organisms, but because they are very heterogeneous in their ecological demands, only test protocols with water, agar or soil eluate have been developed. However, as part of a test battery, the recovery of a nematode population during a soil remediation process can be a useful indicator for (the decrease of) chemical stress. The monitoring of the nematode population showed that, after a survival rate of 100% had been achieved in this test, the natural recolonization of the soil started.

The actual microbial respiration rate is a measure of the momentary heterotrophic microflora under the present chemical and physical conditions. When the content of easily degradable carbon sources falls below the maintenance-carbon requirements, the biomass necessarily decreases leading to reduced respiration rates (Anderson & Domsch, 1985/1990). The suitability of this parameter, in combination with the potential respiration rate determined after addition of an easily biodegradable carbon source, as indicator of easily bioavailable carbon sources and contaminants, has already been shown by Hund and Schenk (1994).

The high sensitivity of the nitrifiers compared to heterotrophic micro-organisms was proved by Blum and Speece (1991), who tested about 70 organic chemicals in aqueous medium. The method was adopted for soil samples and used for monitoring the bioremediation process. All investigated parameters, with the exception of the actual microbial respiration rate, indicated a toxicity at the beginning of the bioremediation. During the time course of the remediation process, the authors found (except for the *Daphnia* test) a more or less continuously decreasing toxicity for the test organisms. After 7 months, when nearly all easily biodegradable PAHs (two- and three-ring PAHs) were degraded and the biodegradation had nearly stopped, a significant reduction of toxicity was observed.

3.5.4 Test sensitivity at low contamination levels

Most of the standardized biotests, except those with micro-organisms, operate on the individual or population level and use mortality, growth or reproduction as effect parameters. They have a clear predictive value, in that the level of organization is understood clearly but they are not very sensitive with respect to low contamination levels.

In order to find early warning biomarkers for chronic exposure, there is growing interest in analysing molecular and biochemical biomarkers. One example of a specific mode of action of a chemical toxicant and the target molecule is the binding of PAHs to the DNA (see below).

3.6 Early warning biomarkers: DNA adducts

Many organic xenobiotics interact with the DNA and form adducts, which may cause mutations. In the case of benzo(a)pyrene exposure, the formation of DNA adducts has been demonstrated in several fish species and human beings and correlated with carcinogenic events (Varanasi, Stein & Nishimoto, 1989; Newman et al., 1990). They have also been detected in plant tissue (Rether et al., 1990). Recently, the ^{32}P-postlabelling determination of DNA-adducts in the earthworm Lumbricus terrestris exposed to PAH-contaminated soil has been published by Walsh et al. (1995). It was shown that earthworms exposed to PAH-contaminated soils exhibited a 3.5- to 15-fold increase in DNA adducts over non-exposed (control) animals. They found this to be a powerful technique for determining the effective PAH concentration in endogenous animal populations, and suggested its use as an early warning biomarker. The advantage of this biotest is that the target concentration of the contaminant, and thus uptake and metabolism properties of the organisms are included instead of relating (or mis-relating) the contaminant concentration in the medium to effects in the test organisms. Unfortunately, the ^{32}P-postlabelling procedure is quite time-consuming and requires appropriate laboratory equipment (and expertise in radioactive labelling). Another disadvantage in these investigations is that PAH–DNA adducts may go unnoticed in the organism: consequently these are biomarkers of exposure but not necessarily of observed effects.

3.7 The root nodule symbiosis test

With the intention of finding sensitive effect-parameters with a significant ecological relevance, many authors prefer the use of microcosm systems, with an experimental design as close as possible to natural conditions. The soil core microcosm (SCM), which was developed initially for the evaluation of pesticides on an agroecosystem, consists of plants, soil invertebrates and microbial processes. The soil cores are derived from the outdoor environment and brought into a laboratory setting with control of the environmental variables. Although an ASTM standard exists (ASTM, 1987), only a few samples of SCM experiments for PAHs exist in the published literature. This may be due to the specialized facilities required and to the high costs for the performance of multi-species toxicity tests. The section below introduces an alternative multispecies toxicity test, without high expense for laboratory or personal equipment.

The test is based on the sensitivity of nodulation in the *Rhizobium*–legume symbiosis. The legume root nodules are the site of biological nitrogen fixation in this symbiosis. They are an organ unique to this symbiosis, and are morphologically as well as physiologically distinct from other plant organs. Evidence has been presented that the formation of nodules may serve principally for ecotoxicological evaluation of contaminated soil samples (Wetzel, Klante & Werner, 1991; Wetzel & Werner, 1995). The test uses the decrease of the nodulation rate as the effect parameter. Because specific microbe–plant root interactions such as the *Rhizobium*–legume symbiosis (or mycorrhiza) play a dominant role in nutrient interactions, a decrease of nodulation in this interaction, caused by toxic substances, is of clear predictive value for the ecotoxicological effects of these substances.

The test is performed in Petri dishes on a solid agar, Gelrite® matrix, respectively, with three plants per dish. Preferred leguminous plants are *Medicago* and *Trifolium* because they are small enough to be kept in Petri dishes for the 14-day experimental period. Before planting, the matrix is inoculated with Rhizobia (*Rhizobium meliloti, Rhizobium trifolii*). Several cultivars of *Medicago* and different *Rhizobium meliloti* strains were tested to find the most sensitive combinations, but all tested cultivars and strains showed comparable sensitivity against the test substances. However, to ensure reliability of the test, the seeds should germinate evenly with fewer than 5% showing aberrations after 7 days' growth. All batches of seeds have to be tested routinely against standard toxicants to prove and ensure their sensitivity.

This test can be used for the evaluation of pure chemicals, mixtures of substances, soil eluates or soil samples. Soil samples or water-soluble substances are mixed with Gelrite®, before pouring into the dishes. Water-insoluble substances are sprayed as ethereal solutions on to the agar surface. When applying pure chemicals, mineral nutrients have to be added to the matrix: when applying soil samples, the pH and eventually the ammonium ion concentration have to be adjusted. The pH value and ammonium ion concentrations are factors that influence the nodulation process also in the natural habitats and should therefore be kept within specified limits. The samples under test are compared either to uncontaminated mineral medium or to a control soil where the contaminants have been eliminated by solvent extraction (Fig. 3.3). Particular parameters and factors may influence the sensitivity and reproducibility of the root-symbiosis-test and have to be carefully documented (see Table 3.7).

Within specified limits, the nodulation test is found to be very robust and highly reproducible. In most cases, nodulation decrease is a more sensitive parameter towards PAHs toxicity than are root and shoot growth depression. The only element of uncertainty is the genomic heterogeneity of the plant material, leading to high standard deviations in the nodule number per plant (Table 3.8).

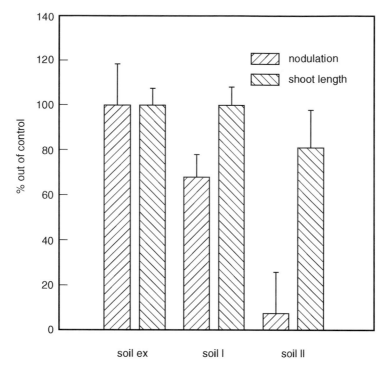

Fig. 3.3. Influence of time-elapse since contamination, on nodulation and shoot length of *Medicago sativa* in symbiosis with *Rhizobium meliloti*. Soil ex = methylene chloride extracted soil; soil I = old contamination; soil II = recent contamination.

3.7.1 Mode of action of PAHs: flavonoid synthesis

The mode of action of PAHs in plant toxicity is not understood fully. Experiments with fluoranthene, phenanthrene and fluorene also revealed a decrease of anthocyanins in shoots. We therefore suggest that PAHs interfere with the phenyl-propane pathway, which would not only affect the anthocyanin production but would also affect the synthesis of flavonoids. The release of flavonoids from the plant roots is one important precondition for a successful nodulation. A lack of flavonoids restricts the microbe–plant communication: the infection process fails. A supplementation of fluoranthene-treated plants with the flavone, luteolin, cancelled the toxic effects of fluoranthene (Wetzel, Parniske & Werner, 1995).

3.8 Future studies

Future studies should concentrate on community-orientated approaches (species diversity, species richness and composition, trophic composition, species abundance

Table 3.7. *Controlled and standardized parameters of the root symbiosis test*

Procedure	Parameters
Contamination of substrate	Nutrients, pH, water, composition of control soil, contamination procedure
Inoculation with rhizobia	Preculture condition, growth phase, strain specificity
Planting of legume seedlings	Surface sterilization technique, germination rate, cultivar specificity
14 days growth cabinet	Light, humidity, temperature
Accumulation of substances	Volatilization rate, plant transpiration rate
Nodulation	Normal distribution, statistical significance, coefficient of variation

Table 3.8. *Toxicity data for selected PAHs in the root symbiosis test*

	Fluoranthene		Fluorene		Phenanthrene	
	EC10	EC50	EC10	EC50	EC10	EC50
Root dry	50	3000	60	600	60	1000
weight	(7–100)	(50–n.d.)	20–90	400–700	20–70	400–1300
Shoot dry	No effect up to		70	300	130	800
weight	1000 μg		(15–90)	(200–800)	(100–150)	(500–1300)
Nodulation	1.1	10	8	130	50	200
	(0.3–2)	(3.5–70)	(0.3–25)	(30–400)	(20–65)	(100–250)

Personal communication: Neumann (1995).
Data are derived from box and whiskers-plot analysis and give the arithmetic mean as well as the 25- to 75-percentile (in brackets). The EC concentrations are given in μg per dish because the test substances are applied on to the surface of the matrix (all values should be multiplied by the factor 40 to obtain the corresponding litre data).

and condition). This approach is already in use in plant-sociological studies, but deals mainly with eutrophication. Implementation and potential of this plant-sociological approach for ecotoxicological purposes in PAH-monitoring are not recognized fully at present.

Acknowledgements

Many thanks to the organizing committee of the EB96 conference and to Professor Werner for the opportunity to publish this chapter, to T. Batinić for the constructive comments on the manuscript and to S. Pueppke for English corrections.

A. Wetzel

References

Alef, K. (1991). *Methodenhandbuch Bodenmikrobiologie*. Landsberg am Lech: Ecomed.

Anderson, T. H. & Domsch, K. H. (1985). Determination of ecophysiological maintenance carbon requirements of soil microorganisms in a dormant state. *Biology and Fertility of Soils*, 1, 81–9.

Anderson T. H. & Domsch, K. H. (1990). Metabolic processes and soil microbial biomass. *Soil Biology and Biochemistry*, 22, 251–255.

ASTM E 1197-87 (1987). Standard guide for conducting a terrestrial soil-core microcosm test. In: *Annual Book of ASTM Standards*. American Society for Testing and Materials.

Axelmann, J., Broman, D., Näf C. & Pettersen, H. (1995). Compound dependence of the relationship log K_{ow} and log BCF_L. *Environmental Science and Pollution Research*, 2, 33–6.

Ayrton, A. D., McFarlane, M., Walker, R., Neville, S., Coombs, M. M. & Ioannides, C. (1990). Induction of the P-450 I family of proteins by polycyclic aromatic hydrocarbons: possible relationship to their carcinogenicity. *Toxicology*, 60, 173–186.

Bahadir, M., Parlar, H. & Spiteller, M. (eds.). (1995). *Springer Umwelt Lexikon*, pp. 760. Berlin: Springer.

BBA VI 1-1 (1990). Auswirkungen auf die Aktivität der Bodenmikroflora. Richtlinien für die amtliche Prüfung von Pflanzenschutzmitteln. *Biologische Bundesanstalt für Land und Forstwirtschaft*, Braunschweig.

BBA VI 23-2.1.10 (1994). Vorschlag für eine Prüfung von Pflanzenschutzmitteln. *Biologische Bundesanstalt für Land und Forstwirtschaft*, Braunschweig.

Belfroid, A. C., Seinen, W., van Gestel, K. C. A. M., Hermens, J. L. M. & van Leeuwen, K. J. (1995). Modelling the accumulation of hydrophobic organic chemicals in earthworms. *Environmental Science and Pollution Research*, 2, 5–15.

Beteigne, M., Rose, C., Gérard, J. & Dizengremel, O. (1989). Effects of polyaromatic hydrocarbons on the forest ecosystem and woody plants. *Annals Science Forest*, 46, 561–5.

Blum, D. J. W. & Speece, R. E. (1991). A database for chemical toxicity to environmental bacteria and its use in interspecies comparisons and correlations. *Research Journal WPCF*, 63, 198–207.

Bumpus, J. A. (1989). Biodegradation of polycyclic aromatic hydrocarbons by *Phanerochaete chrysosporium*. *Applied Environmental Microbiology*, 55, 154–8.

Cerniglia, C. E. & Heitkamp, M. A. (1989). Microbial degradation of polycyclic aromatic hydrocarbons in the aquatic environment. In *Metabolism of Polycyclic Aromatic Hydrocarbons in the Aquatic Environment*, ed. U. Varanasi, pp. 41–68. Boca Raton, Florida: CRC Press.

Coates, J. T., Elzerman, A. W. & Garrison, A. W. (1986). Extraction and determination of selected polycyclic aromatic hydrocarbons in plant tissues. *Journal of the Official Association of Analytical Chemists*, 69, 110–14.

Debus, R., Dittrich, B., Schröder, P. & Volmer, J. (1989). Biomonitoring organischer Luftschadstoffe: polyzyklische aromatische Kohlenwasserstoffe. In *Angewandter Umweltschutz*, ed. J. Vogl, A. Heigl & K. Schäfer, pp. 17–21. Landsberg am Lech, Germany: Ecomed.

Dechema – *ad hoc* Arbeitsgruppe (1995). Methoden zur toxikologischen/ökotoxikologischen Bewertung von Böden. *Biologische Testmethoden für Böden*, ed. G. Kreysa & J. Wiesener. Frankfurt: Deutsche Gesellschaft für Apparatewesen, Chemische Technik und Biotechnologie.

DIN 38 412 Teil 11 (1985). Bestimmung der Wirkung von Wasserinhaltsstoffen auf Kleinkrebse. Testverfahren mit Wasserorganismen (Gruppe L). Deutsches Institut für Normung, Arbeitsgruppe Biotests, Beuth-Verlag, Berlin.

DIN 38 412 Teil 9 (1985). Bestimmung der Wirkung von Wasserinhaltsstoffen auf die Zellvermehrung von *Scenedesmus supspicatus*. Testverfahren mit Wasserorganismen (Gruppe L). Deutsches Institut für Normung, Arbeitsgruppe Biotests, Beuth, Berlin.

DIN 38 412 Teil 34 (1991). Bestimmung der Hemmwirkung von Abwasser auf die Lichtemission von *Photobacterium phosphoreum (Vibrio fischeri)* – Leuchtbakterien-Abwassertest mit konservierten Bakterien (L34). Deutsche Einheitsverfahren zur Wasser, Abwasser- und Schlammuntersuchung (Gruppe L).

DIN 38 414 Teil 4 (1984). Bestimmung der Eluierbarkeit mit Wasser (S4). Deutsche Einheitsverfahren zur Wasser-, Abwasser- und Schlammuntersuchung; Schlamm und Sediment (Gruppe S).

DIN UA 12 (1994). Entwurf: Bestimmung des erbverändernden Potentials von wässrigen Bodeneluaten mit dem *Salmonella*-Test (Ames-Test), Deutsches Institut für Normung, Arbeitsgruppe Biotests.

DIN UA 12, T3 (1994). Entwurf: Bestimmung des erbgutverändernden Potentials von wärigen Eluaten und Extrakten mit dem umu-Test, Deutsches Institut für Normung e.V., Arbeitsgruppe Biotests.

Edwards, N. T. (1983). Polycyclic aromatic hydrocarbons (PAHs) in the terrestrial environment – a review. *Journal of Environmental Quality*, 12, 427–41.

Friege, H. (1990). Bewertungsmaßstäbe für Abfallstoffe aus wasserwirtschaftlicher Sicht. *Müll und Abfall*, 7, 413–26.

Graf, W. & Nowak, W. (1966). Growth stimulation in lower and higher plants by carcinogenic polycyclic aromatic compounds. *Archive Hygiene Bakt.*, 150, 513.

Haas, R., Schreiber, I. & Koss, G. (1990). PAK- und Schwermetall-Aufnahme in Getreide. *Z. Umweltchem. Ökotox.*, 2, 66–70.

Hund, K. & Schenk, B. (1994). Microbial respiration quotient as indicator of bioremediation processes. *Chemosphere*, 28, 477–90.

Hund, K. and Traunspurger, W. (1994). Ecotox: evaluation strategy for soil bioremediaton exemplified for a PAH-contaminated site. *Chemosphere*, 29, 371–90.

ISO 11269-1-Part 1: Method for the measurement of root growth. In: *Soil Quality: Determination of the Effects of Pollutants on Soil Flora*. International Organization for Standardization.

ISO/DIS 11268-2 (1994). Effects of pollutants on earthworms (*Eisenia fetida*) – Part 2: Method for the determination of effects on reproduction. In *Soil Quality*. International Organization for Standardization.

ISO/DIS 14228 (1994). Soil quality: determination of nitrogen mineralization and nitrification in soils and the influence of chemicals on these processes, International Organization for Standardization.

ISO/DIS 14240-1 (1994). Soil Quality: Determination of soil microbial biomass, Part 1: Respiration method. International Organization for Standardization.

ISO/TC 190 SC4 WG 2 (1994). Effects of soil pollutants on collembola: Determination of the inhibition of reproduction. International Organization for Standardization.

Jacob, J., Karcher, W., Belliardo, J. J. & Wagstaffe, P. J. (1984/1986). Polycyclic aromatic

A. Wetzel

compounds of environmental and occupational importance. Part I and II. Fresenius Z. *Anal. Chem.* 317/323, 101–14/1–10.

Kehres, B, Gottschall, R. & Vogtmann, H. (1994). Bestimmung und Bewertung der Pflanzenverträglichkeit von Kompost mit Sommergerste. *Müll und Abfall*, 4, 238–43.

Larsson, B. K. (1985). Polycyclic aromatic hydrocarbons and lead in roadside lettuce and rye grain. *Journal of Science of Food in Agriculture*, 36, 463–70.

Liu, D. & Strachan, W. D. J. (1981). A rapid biochemical test for measuring chemical toxicity. *Bulletin of Environmental Contamination and Toxicology*, 26, 145–9.

Lo, M.-T. & Sandi, E. (1978). *Polycyclic Aromatic Hydrocarbons (Polynuclears) in Foods*, pp. 35–85. New York: Springer-Verlag.

Molven, A. & Goksøyr, A. (1993). Biological effects and biomonitoring of organochlorines and polycyclic aromatic hydrocarbons in the marine environment. In *Ecotoxicology Monitoring*, ed. M. Richardson, pp. 137–62. Germany: VCH, Weinheim.

Münch, D. (1992). Soil contamination beneath asphalt roads by polynuclear aromatic hydrocarbons, zinc, lead and cadmium. *Science of the Total Environment*, 126, 49–60.

Negeshi, T., Nakano, M., Kobayashi, S. & Ho Kim, C. (1987). Isolation and determination of benzo(a)pyrene glucuronide and sulfate conjugates in soybean leaves. *Bulletin of Environmental Contamination Toxicology*, 39, 294–8.

Newman, M. J., Weston, A., Carver, D.C., Mann, D.L. & Harris, C.C. (1990). Serological characterization of polycyclic aromatic hydrocarbon diolepoxide: DNA adducts using monoclonal antibodies. *Carcinogenesis*, 11, 1903–7.

Niederer, M., Maschka-Selig, A. & Hohl, C. (1995). Monitoring polycyclic aromatic hydrocarbons (PAHs) and heavy metals in urban soil, compost and vegetation. *Environmental Science and Pollution Research*, 2, 83–9.

OECD Guideline for Testing of Chemicals 201 (1984). *Alga, Growth Inhibition Test*, updated, Paris: OECD.

OECD Guideline for Testing of Chemicals 202 (1984). *Daphnia sp., Acute Immobilization Test and Reproduction Test, Part II*, updated, Paris: OECD.

OECD Guideline for Testing of Chemicals 203 (1984). *Fish, Acute Toxicity Test*, updated, Paris: OECD.

OECD Guideline for Testing of Chemicals 207 (1984). *Earthworm, Acute Toxicity Test*, updated, Paris: OECD.

OECD Guideline for Testing of Chemicals 208 (1984). *Terrestrial Plants, Growth Test*, updated, Paris: OECD.

Qui, X. & McFarland, M. J. (1991). Bound residue formation in PAH contaminated soil composting using *Phanerochaete chrysosporium*. *Hazardous Waste and Hazardous Materials*, 8, 115–26.

Rether, B., Pfohl-Leskowicz, A., Guillemaut, P. & Keith, G. (1990). Benzo(a)pyrene induces nuclear DNA-adducts in plant cell suspension culture. *Federation European Biochemical Societies*, 263, 172–4.

Rippen, G., Held, T. & Ripper, P. (1994). Microbiological remediation of waste-oil polluted soils: ecotoxicological and toxicological considerations. *Environmental Science and Pollution Research*, 1, 185–9.

Römbke, J. (1991). Entwicklung eines Reproduktionstests an Bodenorganismen - Enchytraeen. UBA – Bericht, FUE-Vorhaben Nr. 106 03 051/01, Batelle Institut, Frankfurt.

Scheffer, F. & Schachtschabel, P. (1989). *Lehrbuch der Bodenkunde.* Stuttgart: Ferdinand Enke Verlag.

Sheppard, S. C., Evenden, W. G., Abboud, S. A., Stephenson, M. (1993). A plant life-cycle bioassay for contaminated soil, with comparison to other bioassays: mercury and zinc. *Archives of Environmental Contamination and Toxicology*, 25, 27–35.

Sims, R. C. & Overcash, M. R. (1983). Fate of polynuclear aromatic compounds (PNAs) in soil plant systems. *Residue Reviews*, ed. F. A. Gunther & J. D. Gunther, 1–67.

Smith, M. R. (1990). The biodegradation of aromatic hydocarbons by bacteria. *Biodegradation*, 1, 191–206.

Speer, K. & Montag, A. (1989). PAHs in nativen pflanzlichen Ölen. *GIT Supplement*, 2, 16–21.

Sullivan, P. D. (1985). Free radicals of benzo(a)pyrene and derivatives. *Environmental Health Perspectives*, 64, 283–95.

Tuominen, J. P., Pyysalo, H. S. & Sauri, M. (1988). Cereal products as a source of polycyclic aromatic hydrocarbons. *Journal of Agricultural Food Chemistry*, 36, 118–120.

Varanasi, U., Stein, J. E. & Nishimoto, M. (1989). Biotransformation and disposition of polycyclic aromatic hydrocarbons (PAHs) in fish. In *Metabolism of Polycyclic Aromatic Hydrocarbons in the Aquatic Environment*, ed. U. Varanasi, pp. 93–149. Boca Raton, Florida: CRC Press.

Walsh, P., Aldlouni, C. El., Mukhopadhyay, M. J., Viel, G., Nadeau, D. & Poirier, G. G. (1995). ^{32}P-postlabeling determination of DNA adducts in the earthworm *Lumbricus terrestris* exposed to PAH-contaminated soils. *Bulletin of Environmental Contamination and Toxicology*, 54, 654–61.

Weissenfels, W. D., Klewer, H. J. & Langhoff, J. (1992). Adsorption of polycyclic aromatic hydrocarbons (PAHs) by soil particles: influence on biodegradability and biotoxicity. *Applied Microbiology and Biotechnology*, 36, 689–96.

Wetzel, A. & Werner, D. (1995). Ecotoxicological evaluation of contaminated soil using the legume root nodule symbiosis as effect parameter. *Environmental Toxicology and Water Quality*, 10, 127–33.

Wetzel, A., Klante, G. & Werner, D. (1991). Biotoxizitätstests mit PAK: Die Nodulation in der Leguminosen-Rhizobien-Symbiose als sensibler Wirkungsparameter. UWSF. *Zeitschrift Umweltchemie Ökotoxicologie*, 3, 66–271.

Wetzel, A. Parniske, M. & Werner, D. (1995). The pleiotropic effects of fluoranthene on anthocyanin synthesis and nodulation of *Medicago sativa* is reversed by the plant flavone luteolin. *Bulletin of Environmental Contamination Toxicology*, 54, 633–9.

Wild, S. R. & Jones, K. C. (1992). Organic chemicals entering agricultural soils in sewage sludges: screening for their potential to transfer to crop plants and livestock. *The Science of the Total Environment*, 119, 85–119.

Wilson, S. C. & Jones, K. C. (1993). Bioremediation of soil contaminated with polynuclear aromatic hydrocarbons (PAHs): a review. *Environmental Pollution*, 81, 229–49.

Xu, H. (1989). Microtitation SOS-Chromotest. A new approach in genotoxicity testing. *Toxicology Association*, 4, 105–14.

Zander, M. (1980). Polycyclic aromatic and heterocyclic hydrocarbons. In *Environmental Chemistry. Vol. 3, Part A: Anthropogenic compounds*, ed. O. Hutzinger. Heidelberg: Springer.

4

Microbial parameters for monitoring soil pollution

Clive E. Pankhurst, Stephen L. Rogers and Vadakattu V. S. R. Gupta

4.1 Introduction

As a result of increasing industrialization and the spread of intensive agricultural practices, the soils of the world have become increasingly contaminated with a range of potentially toxic organic and inorganic chemicals. These chemicals include those deliberately introduced into the soil to maintain and increase plant production, such as pesticides, chemical fertilizers and other agrochemicals. Disposal of industrial wastes to land, atmospheric deposition of industrial contaminants and the land application of biosolids and sewage effluent all have the potential to contaminate soil with a range of organic and inorganic chemicals. Classes of industries and land-uses associated with soil contamination are detailed by ANZECC/NHMRC (1992). The area of both urban and rural land affected by soil contamination is significant. Burns, Rogers & McGee (1996) noted that there are an estimated 4000 contaminated hazardous waste disposal sites in the US, whilst the estimate of the number of potentially contaminated rural and industrial sites in Australia has been put at 60 000 (Forrest, 1993). Numerous studies have demonstrated that soils in urban areas (whether in parks or domestic gardens, cities or small towns) have become so contaminated with a wide variety of inorganic compounds (mainly heavy metals) that any baseline differences originating from the local geology are difficult to trace (Purves, 1985; Adriano, 1986). Tiller (1992) in a survey of contaminated urban soils in Australia noted that the 'background' levels of Pb in urban soils ranged from $16-185 \, mg \, kg^{-1}$, whilst Pb concentrations at 'contaminated' sites ranged from $2000 \, mg \, kg^{-1}$ to $100 \, 000 \, mg \, kg^{-1}$. Typical Pb concentrations in rural soils ranged from $2-160 \, mg \, kg^{-1}$. Purves (1985) also noted that concentrations of many heavy metals in both urban and rural soils are now two to more than ten times higher than the levels in uncontaminated soils. Moreover, the potentially 'bioavailable' levels of these pollutants, defined as the fraction extractable using mild reagents such as $0.1 \, M \, CaCl_2$ or $0.1 \, M \, Ca(NO_3)_2$ (Beckett, 1989), have also increased markedly in urban soils (Purves, 1985).

Whilst analytical techniques for the detection, quantification and monitoring of contaminants in soils are well defined, and guidelines are available that determine 'safe' concentrations of contaminants in soils with respect to human health criteria and contaminated site management (Langley and El Saadi, 1991; ANZECC/ NHMRC 1992; Langley & Van Alphen, 1993; Edwards, Van Alphen & Langley, 1994), there are few, if any, guidelines or accepted criteria for assessing the impact of contaminants on the biological health of soils. As a consequence there is an urgent need to (a) characterize suitable techniques and (b) assess the impact that contaminants are having on soil health.

4.2 Soil micro-organisms and soil microbial activity as biomonitors

Soil micro-organisms (bacteria, actinomycetes, fungi, microalgae, protozoa) contribute significantly to the maintenance of soil health by controlling the decomposition of plant and animal residues, biogeochemical cycling (including N_2 fixation), the formation and maintenance of soil structure, and the fate of agrochemicals and organic pollutants entering the soil. Soil micro-organisms also make up the bulk (~85%) of the biomass in the soil and contribute ~90% of the CO_2 efflux (Reichle, 1977). These properties plus their sensitivity to low concentrations of pollutants (Witter, 1992) and their rapid response to soil perturbation have led to soil microbial properties being considered as good candidates for monitoring soil pollution (Elliott, 1994; Pankhurst, 1994; Brookes, 1995; Mhatre & Pankhurst, 1997). Not unexpectedly, however, there are also many problems with using populations of micro-organisms or microbial activity as soil biomonitors. These include the generally large natural variation in population size and activity of all micro-organisms in the soil and the major influence that soil chemical factors (e.g. pH) and soil physical factors (e.g. clay content, soil moisture) can have on their activity and interaction with pollutants. But, despite these inherent difficulties, the use of microbial parameters as biomonitors of soil pollution has attracted considerable interest and investigation.

4.3 Criteria for selection of microbial parameters for biomonitoring

To be useful as a biomonitor, a microbial parameter would be required to meet a number of criteria. These criteria have been discussed by Brookes (1995) and include: (i) general scientific validity and relevance to soil health; (ii) is easily measured; (iii) can be measured accurately across a wide range of soil types and soil conditions; (iv) has sufficient sensitivity to indicate pollution but is sufficiently robust not to give false alarms; (vi) is of a nature that background (control) measurements can be made so that effects of pollution can be precisely determined. In view of the high spatial heterogeneity that is generally encountered in the field, a suitable sampling strategy is also required if any measurements are to be meaningful.

4.4 Microbial parameters with potential as biomonitors of soil pollution

Microbial parameters, which may be useful as biomonitors, can be subdivided into several groups. The first and probably the most widely used group of measurements includes the measure of soil microbial biomass, soil respiration and various derived parameters. A second group includes other measures of microbial activity such as N mineralization and enzyme activity. A third group includes measures of functional groups of micro-organisms (e.g. mycorrhizal fungi, protozoa) and a fourth and more recent group includes measures of the composition and functional diversity of the microbial community. These measurements and examples of their application in polluted soils are discussed below.

4.5 Soil microbial biomass and soil respiration

Microbial biomass is defined as the living component of soil organic matter and normally constitutes between 1 and 5% (w/w) of the total soil organic C (Jenkinson & Ladd, 1981). Typical methods for determination of microbial biomass include fumigation-incubation, fumigation-extraction, or substrate-induced respiration (Sparling & Ross, 1993). It has been suggested that the microbial biomass could be a sensitive indicator of changes in soil processes because it has a much faster rate of turnover than the total soil organic matter (Jenkinson & Ladd, 1981; Paul, 1984), and several authors have suggested that trends in the microbial biomass content of soils will predict longer-term trends in total organic matter contents (Powlson, Brookes & Christensen, 1987; Sparling, 1992).

Soil microbial biomass measures have been used to assess the impact of fungicides (Heilmann, Lebuhn & Beese, 1995), herbicides (Wardle & Parkinson, 1990) and heavy metal contaminants (Brookes et al., 1986b; Fliessbach et al., 1994; Brookes, 1995; Leita et al., 1995) on soil health. In general, microbial biomass has not been a sensitive indicator of the effects of herbicides except when added at more than the recommended dosage, when microbial biomass and soil respiration was decreased. Usually, when used at the recommended dosages, only small effects of pesticides on the soil microbial biomass have been reported. In contrast, heavy metals at high concentrations (e.g. >0.1%) can have marked effects on the microbial biomass. Brookes and McGrath (1984) reported that the microbial biomass of soils at the Woburn experimental site that had been amended with heavy metal contaminated sewage biosolid over 30 years previously was still lower than uncontaminated soil. In the contaminated soil there was no relationship between microbial biomass and total organic C, unlike the uncontaminated soils from the same experiment. Similar results were obtained for other experiments at Ludington, Lee Valley and Gleadthorpe (Chander & Brookes, 1991b, 1993). In each case the biomass C as a percentage of total soil organic C was two to three times higher (1.5–2.0%) in the untreated soils or soil treated with non-contaminated sewage biosolid than in soils treated with biosolids that were principally contaminated with Cu or Zn (0.4–1.0%). As a consequence of these effects of the heavy metals on the soil microbial biomass, the biosolid-treated soils in these experiments showed an accumulation of organic matter (10–30%) compared with the control soils (Brookes, 1995). A decrease in the biomass C as a percentage of total organic C was also noted by Rogers (1996) at a long-term biosolids trial in New South Wales, Australia. The percentage biomass C was three times higher in the controls (1.5%), compared to soils receiving heavy metal contaminated biosolid applications (0.5%). The contaminated soils had over double the organic carbon content of the control soils, yet there was no significant difference in biomass C. Fractionation of carbon in the soils receiving biosolids has indicated a large pool of recalcitrant, biologically inactive material compared to controls (S. L. Rogers, unpublished data). It is hypothesized that the decline in the biomass C / organic C ratio is a result of the recalcitrance of this organic carbon to microbial mineralization, and not an effect of heavy metals reducing the efficiency of microbial carbon substrate utilization, as has been demonstrated in other biosolid studies (Chander & Brookes, 1991a, b). Therefore, when using this measurement of biomass C/organic C percentages, care must be taken in interpreting a decline in the percentage as a sign of contaminant impacts, as other factors can cause a decline in this ratio as shown by Rogers (1996).

Soil respiration is a well-established parameter for monitoring organic matter decomposition (Anderson, 1982), but it is also highly variable and can show wide natural fluctuation depending on substrate availability, moisture and temperature (Orchard & Cook, 1983; Alvarez, Santanatoglia & Garcia, 1995). This high variability means that this measure taken alone is very difficult to interpret in terms of soil health (Brookes, 1995). For valid comparison between soils, respiration measurements must normally be made under controlled laboratory conditions (Anderson, 1982). Under these conditions, Brookes (1995) noted that soil respiration appears to be little affected by contamination of soils with biosolid heavy metals at levels currently permissible in Europe (CEC, 1986). However, studies of biosolid heavy metal impacts on soil respiration in Australian soils, at concentrations equivalent to current European regulations (Rogers & Tiller, 1996), have recorded negative impacts of metals on soil respiration. The lack of agreement between these studies highlights the potential problems of using microbial biosensors of soil contamination to compare across different soil types. Contaminant impacts are likely to be a function of soil type, soil chemistry, contaminant bioavailability, the composition of the soil microbial population, and the sensitivity of individual components of the microbial population to the contaminant. If this is the case, the development of contaminant guidelines, i.e. concentrations of contaminants that are considered not to impact on soil biological health, and are universally applicable across a number of soils and contaminated sites, may be difficult.

Combining measures of soil microbial biomass and soil respiration to give the amount of CO_2 evolved per unit of biomass (biomass specific respiration or the respiratory quotient) has, in contrast, been found to be a subtle indicator of

49

C. E. Pankhurst, S. L. Rogers and V. V. S. R. Gupta

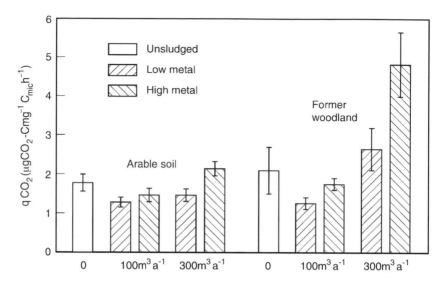

Fig. 4.1. qCO2 in soil samples of the Ap horizon of experimental soils. From Fliessbach *et al.* (1994).

environmental stress. The use of qCO_2 as a measurement of microbial stress in soils is based on the community respiration theories of Odum (1985). He states that an increase in community respiration should be the first sign of stress, since repairing damage caused by a disturbance requires diversion of energy from growth and reproduction to cell maintenance. Therefore, if the soil microbial biomass is under stress, it will direct more energy into maintenance, rather than growth, so that an increased proportion of C taken up by the biomass will be respired as CO_2. An example showing the potential usefulness of the respiratory quotient (qCO2) is given by Fliessbach *et al.* (1994) who examined the effects of two levels of sewage biosolid (with low and high metal contents) applied to two different soils on microbial biomass C, soil respiration and qCO_2. They found that the ratio of biomass C to total organic C decreased with increasing metal load to the soil, although soil respiration generally showed an increase. The qCO_2 values showed an increase with increasing metal concentration suggesting that, at the higher metal levels, the biomass was under stress (Fig. 4.1). However, the use of qCO_2 to indicate microbial community stress is not without its critics. Wardle & Ghani (1995) published a critique of the use of qCO_2 as a bioindicator of microbial disturbance, and noted that this measurement fails to distinguish between the effects of ecosystem disturbance (such as ploughing or liming) and stress. Despite this criticism, qCO_2 continues to be used successfully in studies of heavy metal contaminant impacts on soil microbial ecosystems.

An example that illustrates the potential value of combining measures of microbial biomass, respiration and qCO_2 to elucidate the impact of heavy metal contamination on soils is given by Rogers & Tiller (1996), who investigated the ecotoxicological impact of contaminated biosolid application to agricultural soils in South Australia. Biosolids from a rural and urban waste water treatment works were applied to the soil, a red-brown earth (pH $4.6_{(0.01\underline{M}CaCl2)}$ organic C 0.93%), at the rate of 500 t ha^{-1} in order to simulate long-term agricultural application rates (10–20 t ha^{-1} yr^{-1}). Biosolids were applied to give three heavy metal loading rates equivalent to current Australian regulations (NSW EPA, 1995), an intermediate metal loading, and metal concentrations equivalent to USEPA Rule 503 biosolid regulations (USEPA, 1993). In order to achieve USEPA maximum permissible metal loadings, the urban biosolid was spiked with metal salts. Biosolid loading rates and soil organic matter, C and N, were identical in each of the three treatments. The final metal concentrations present in the biosolid treated soil and the effect that these treatments had on microbial biomass, soil respiration, and the respiratory quotient of the soil are given in Table 4.1. Of particular interest was the finding that the soil receiving the rural biosolid with the lowest total heavy metal concentration displayed the greatest impact on all of these microbial parameters (e.g. relative decline in microbial biomass and soil respiration; and largest increase in qCO$_2$ compared with the urban biosolid treatment), despite the fact that the rural biosolid contained similar levels of Cu and significantly less Cd and Zn than the urban biosolid. The authors investigated metal bioavailability in these soils using solid phase sequential extraction techniques (Beckett, 1989) and showed that the bioavailability of metals in the rural biosolids was significantly higher. For all three metals, but most noticeably for Zn, the concentration of metals present in the exchangeable or organic forms (potentially bioavailable pool) in the soil receiving the rural biosolid was 15 to 20 times higher than the urban biosolid. Of Zn in the urban biosolid, 96% was bound to oxide surfaces; heavy metals in this form are generally considered to have low bioavailability (Harter & Naidu, 1995). The results of this study are in conflict with previous investigations on the impact of metal-contaminated biosolid application to soils on microbial biomass and respiration. Studies by Chander & Brookes (1991a, b) and Fliessbach et al. (1994) both indicated that biomass decline and microbial stress increased with increasing total concentrations of heavy metals in soils, whereas the study by Rogers and Tiller (1996) demonstrates that it is the bioavailable forms of heavy metals and not their total concentration that should be considered when assessing the impact of a contaminant on soil health. This example illustrates (i) that each of the microbial parameters measured was able to detect differences in the bioavailability of metals in these two biosolids, and that chemical and biological measurements of metal bioavailability were closely correlated, and (ii) that bioavailability of metals is independent of the total metal concentration in biosolids and soils receiving biosolid applications.

The ability of micro-organisms to utilize added substrate is another parameter that has been used as a bioindicator of heavy metal contamination (Bardgett & Saggar, 1994). Micro-organisms living in metal-contaminated soils exhibit reduced

Table 4.1. *Impact of three different biosolid heavy metal loading rates on soil microbial biomass, respiration and metabolic quotient*

	Soil Cd (mg kg^{-1})	Soil Cu (mg kg^{-1})	Soil Zn (mg kg^{-1})	Biomass C Fumigation-Extraction (g g^{-1})	Soil Respiration 28-day incubation (g CO$_2$-C g^{-1} d^{-1})	Metabolic Quotient qCO$_2$ (g CO$_2$-C mg biomass C^{-1} d^{-1})
Rural biosolid (Current Australian biosolid regulations)	1.2	306	280	442[a]	25.6[a]	5.7[a]
Urban biosolid	5.7	260	528	1342[b]	40.6[b]	2.9[b]
Urban biosolid + metal addition (Current US biosolid regulations)	19.0	760	1451	1068[c]	35.4[c]	3.2[b]

Values within columns followed by a different letter are significantly different LSD P = 0.001. Modified from Rogers and Tiller (1996).

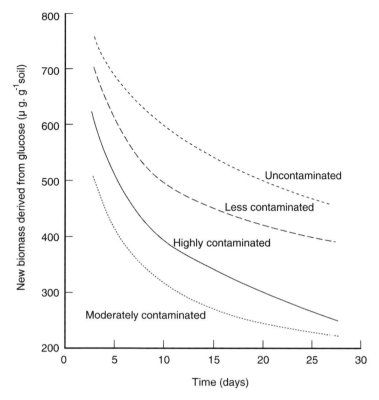

Fig. 4.2. Effect of increasing heavy metal concentration on new biomass derived from added ^{14}C-glucose (Bardgett & Saggar, 1994, as presented by Elliott, 1997).

efficiency of added substrate incorporation into new microbial biomass because they tend to expend more energy to survive compared with those under less stressful conditions (Chander & Brookes, 1991a). Gupta et al. (1996) observed similar results in herbicide-treated soils. Bardgett and Sagger (1994) monitored the effects of increasing heavy metal contamination on the status of soil micro-organisms in a contaminated pasture in New Zealand by measuring the efficiency of conversion of added ^{14}C-glucose into new microbial biomass (Fig. 4.2). They found that microbial biomass in contaminated soils was less efficient at incorporating added ^{14}C into new biomass and suggested that the amount of new biomass was a sensitive indicator of the level of metal contamination in the soil.

4.6 Nitrogen transformations

Nitrogen transformations in the soil include the release of ammonium N from organic N, a process (ammonification) carried out by the majority of soil micro-organisms; the oxidation of ammonium to nitrite and nitrate (nitrification) and the reduction of nitrite and nitrate to N_2 gas (denitrification), processes carried out by more specialist groups of chemotrophic bacteria; and nitrogen fixation, a process carried out by a range of autotrophic, heterotrophic and symbiotic organisms (Alexander, 1977; Sprent, 1979; Lynch, 1983). Ammonification does not generally appear to be affected by organic xenobiotic compounds or heavy metals, possibly because of the wide range of organisms capable of carrying out this process (Hicks, Stotzky & Van Voris, 1990). In contrast, soil pollutants, especially heavy metals, have been found to decrease nitrification and denitrification, although effects are often conflicting (Duxbury, 1985; Hicks et al., 1990). Nitrification may be a much more robust process in its resistance to the ecotoxicological impacts of contaminants than other microbial bioindicators. For instance, Rogers & Tiller (1996) in the biosolid study previously discussed, also measured nitrification rates. Whilst biomass, respiration and qCO_2 all indicated a toxicological impact of soil metals on microbial populations, no negative effect was noted on nitrification rates.

Considerable attention has been focused on the process of N_2 fixation, especially autotrophic N_2 fixation carried out by cyanobacteria and symbiotic N_2 fixation carried out by Rhizobium/Bradyrhizobium spp. as indicators of soil pollution. Using a laboratory assay, Brookes et al. (1986a) demonstrated a decline in N_2 fixation by cyanobacteria in response to a gradient of heavy metal pollution. However, this could not be repeated in other soils, possibly due to the low amounts of cyanobacteria present (Lorenz, McGrath & Giller, 1992). Similarly, N_2 fixation by Rhizobium leguminosarum biovar trifolii in symbiotic association with Trifolium repens (white clover) was found to be highly sensitive to soils containing high levels of Zn, Cu, Ni, and Cd (McGrath, Brookes & Giller, 1988). This was found to be due to the survival of metal-tolerant rhizobia that were ineffective in N_2 fixation in the metal-contaminated soils (Giller, McGrath & Hirsch, 1989). These observations have led to a lot of interest in using the Rhizobium–legume symbiosis as an indicator of soil pollution by heavy metals. However, results from other work have been conflicting (Kinkle, Angle & Keyser, 1987) suggesting the need for more research.

4.7 Soil enzyme activity

The activity of approximately 50 enzymes has been identified in soils (Ladd, 1985). Undoubtedly, the number in soils is far greater, but techniques for determining the presence or activity of other enzymes have not been developed for soils. The enzymes studied most often are oxidoreductases (e.g. catalase, dehydrogenase), hydrolases (e.g. cellulase, phosphatase, sulphatase and urease), and transferases. Enzymes are present in two general locations in soils: those associated with living cells (intracellular) and those that are extracellular or abiontic (Burns, 1982). Because it is difficult to extract enzymes from soil, their activity is generally

Table 4.2. *Soil enzyme activity in pasture soils (0–5 cm) contaminated with heavy metals*

	Degree of contamination		
	Control	Medium	High
Cu (mg kg^{-1})	38	140	900
Cr (mg kg^{-1})	50	132	842
As (mg kg^{-1})	8	148	1124
Dehydrogenase	12.4	12.2	2.2*
Urease	1.32	0.89*	0.41*
Phosphatase	4.19	3.12*	2.95*
Sulphatase	0.56	0.57	0.14*

From Yeates *et al.* (1994); *Significantly different from control (P < 0.05).

measured in laboratory assays under defined and optimal conditions. A major problem with assaying soil enzyme activity is that abiontic activity cannot readily be separated from that of the intracellular enzymes of living cells.

Soil enzyme activity has been used as a sensitive indicator of the effect of heavy metals on soils (Baath, 1989; Hicks *et al.*, 1990; Dick, 1994; Yeates *et al.*, 1994; Serra-Wittling, Houot & Barriuso, 1995). In general, most soil enzymes are inhibited by high concentrations of heavy metals in the soil (Baath, 1989; Hicks *et al.*, 1990; Dick, 1994). An example of this is given in Table 4.2 where heavy metal contamination of a pasture soil in New Zealand was shown to inhibit the activity of four enzymes significantly (Yeates *et al.*, 1994). In most cases, enzyme reactions are inhibited by metals through complexation of the substrate, by combining with the reactive functional groups of the enzymes, or by reacting with the enzyme–substrate complex. The degree of inhibition may also be affected by soil type. Enzymes are more likely to be inhibited by metals in soils with low cation exchange capacity and low organic matter content as these soils have reduced potential to inactivate metals via complexation or sorption reactions (Speir *et al.*, 1995).

Measurement of soil enzyme activity also has potential for assessing the impact of accidental spills of hydrocarbons on to soils and in following the effectiveness of remediation (Song & Bartha, 1990). An example of this is shown in Fig. 4.3. In the absence of bioremediation (addition of fertilizer, tillage and liming), jet fuel at 50 and 135 mg g^{-1} soil inhibited fluorescein diacetate (FDA) hydrolysis over an 18-week incubation. However, with bioremediation, during the first 2 weeks, FDA hydrolysis was initially inhibited but then stimulated, reaching a peak after most of the jet fuel had been mineralized. Such results support the potential for enzyme assays to monitor biological activity in soil after an environmental impact.

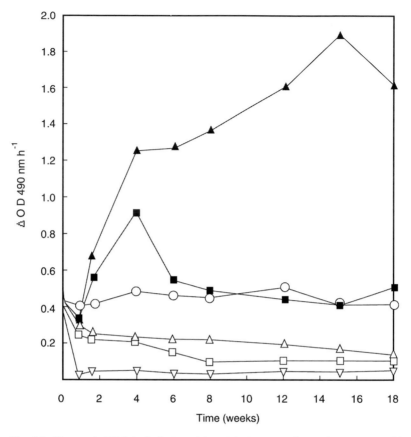

Fig. 4.3. Changes in FDA hydrolysis activity with time in surface soil contaminated by jet fuel. Symbols: ○, no jet fuel, no bioremediation; □, 50 mg of jet fuel g of soil^{-1}; △, 135 mg jet fuel g of soil^{-1}; ■, 50 mg of jet fuel g soil^{-1} plus bioremediation; ▲, 135 mg of jet fuel g soil^{-1} plus bioremediation; ▽, poisoned control (1% HgCl$_2$). (From Song & Bartha, 1990.)

4.8 Mycorrhizal fungi and plant growth

Mycorrhizae are ubiquitous symbioses which can mediate uptake of some plant nutrients, especially phosphorus (Mosse, Stribley & Le Tacon, 1981). They are also known to enhance uptake of heavy metals such as copper and zinc when these essential metals are deficient. High concentrations of Zn, Cu, Ni and Cd can, however, severely reduce plant root infection by arbuscular mycorrhizal (AM) fungi (Graham, Timmer & Fardelman, 1986; Koomen, McGrath & Giller, 1990; Leyval, Singh & Joner, 1995).

For example, in a glasshouse experiment, Koomen *et al.* (1990) noted a significant reduction in the amount of mycorrhizal root infection of white clover grown in soil

Table 4.3. *Shoot and root dry weights and mycorrhizal infection levels of clover sown in soil previously treated with farmyard manure (FYM) or sewage sludge: (a) results for naturally occurring mycorrhizal fungi (plants harvested at 8 weeks); (b) results for both naturally occurring mycorrhizal fungi (−inoc) and* G. mosseae *(+inoc) (plants harvested at 6 weeks)*

	FYM			Sludge		
	Shoot	Root		Shoot	Root	
	dry wt (g)		% infection	dry wt (g)		% infection
(a)						
Experiment 1	4.66	11.22	60	4.52	5.67	1
(b)						
Experiment 2						
− inoculum	2.46	4.99	21	3.11	5.97	0
+ inoculum	2.03	4.44	46	3.66	7.41	0

Modified from Koomen *et al.* (1990).

that had been treated with sewage biosolids contaminated with heavy metals (Table 4.3). When the soil was inoculated with spores of a standard AM species (*Glomus mosseae*), there was substantial infection of clover roots in the uncontaminated soil but no infections in the contaminated soil after 6 weeks. However, in a field experiment, infection was observed on plants in the contaminated soil but not until the autumn, 8 weeks after sowing. It was concluded that these infections arose from the growth of metal-tolerant strains which took time to develop. Similarly, Leyval *et al.* (1995) found that spore numbers, mycorrhizal infectivity and spore germination of indigenous mycorrhizal fungi were lower in soils contaminated with heavy metals and that AM fungi isolated from the contaminated soils were more tolerant to metals than those isolated from non-polluted soils.

4.9 Protozoa

Because of their delicate external membranes and rapid growth rates, protozoa, in particular the ciliate protozoa and testate amoebae, have been found to be sensitive bioindicators of heavy metals and pesticides in soil (Foissner, 1994; Gupta & Yeates, 1997). Active forms of protozoa show measurable sensitivity in their growth and behaviour (motility and cellular abnormalities) to the presence of undesirable compounds in their environment. In short-term (~24 h) laboratory assays, the growth and behaviour of protozoan species such as the ciliate *Colpoda steinii*, flagellates *Oikomonas* sp. and *Bodo* sp. and naked amoebae *Acanthamoeba* sp. were found to be related strongly to the concentration of heavy metal in its 'active' (bioavailable) form rather than the total concentration, suggesting that protozoan

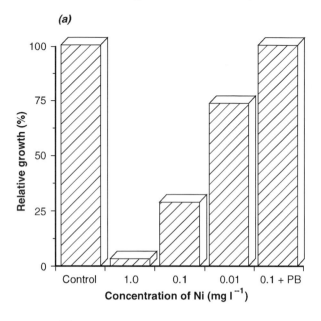

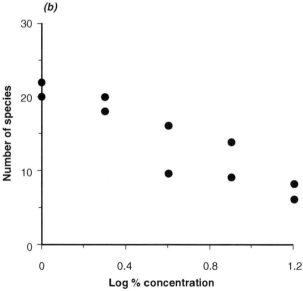

Fig. 4.4. Results from laboratory bioassays showing (*a*) relative growth of the soil ciliate *Colpoda* sp. at different concentrations of Ni and the effect of phosphate buffer (PB) in test solution (Gupta, VVSR, unpublished observations) and (*b*) survival of protozoan species in microcosms developed with leachates from a soil (VAFL 1) contaminated with heavy metals (e.g. Cu, Cd, Ni, Pb and Zn) (Pratt *et al.*, 1988).

bioassays could be used to assess the bioavailability of heavy metals (Pratt *et al.*, 1988; Schreiber & Brink, 1989; Forge *et al.*, 1993; Gupta, VVSR unpublished data). For example, Gupta VVSR (unpublished data) observed that the concentration of Ni that reduced the growth rates of the ciliate *Colpoda* sp. (Fig. 4.4(*a*)) and the naked amoebae *Acanthamoeba* sp. was between 0.1 and 0.01 mg l^{-1}. The growth rate of *Colpoda* sp. was improved significantly in the presence of phosphate buffer in the media which reduces the level of Ni in its 'active' form thereby reducing its bioavailability (Fig. 4.4(*a*)). He also observed that an increase in concentration of Ni from 0.01 to 0.1 mg l^{-1} increased the percentage of deformed cells (27.5 % to 57.5% at 0.01 and 0.1 mg l^{-1}, respectively). In their work using aquatic protozoan as species test organisms, Pratt *et al.* (1988) found that leachates from an uncontaminated agricultural soil showed no toxicity in laboratory tests, whereas leachates from soils contaminated with toxic wastes (e.g. heavy metals, coal, organic pesticides) showed different degrees of toxicity. They found a significant negative relationship between the survival of protozoan species and the concentration of leachates from a soil contaminated with heavy metals such as Cu, Cd, Ni, Pb and Zn (Fig. 4.4(*b*)).

4.10 Microbial populations

Measuring the effects of soil contaminants on total populations of micro-organisms in the soil has been used in many studies (Hicks *et al.*, 1990). However, there are many problems associated with these measurements, including high variability and insufficient knowledge of the effects of ecological and physiological factors on the growth of micro-organisms in the soil. In general, algae and photosynthetic bacteria appear to be more susceptible to xenobiotics than other groups, probably because many of the compounds that have been tested inhibit photosynthesis. Actinomycetes and saprophytic fungi appear to be more resistant to the action of xenobiotics, and for many of the compounds tested, an increase in their numbers was detected (Simon-Sylvestre & Fournier, 1979). This trend, which also occurs with heterotrophic bacteria, may be due to the compound being used as a carbon source by the micro-organisms or due to its suppression of predatory micro-organisms such as protozoa (Schreiber & Brink, 1989).

4.11 Analysis of microbial communities

During the last decade a number of methodologies have been developed that provide new approaches to the analysis of the structure and biodiversity of soil microbial communities (Pankhurst *et al.*, 1996). Several of these methodologies including analysis of the fatty acid composition of phospholipids extracted directly from soil (Frostegård, Tunlid & Bååth, 1993), and reassociation kinetics of DNA molecules extracted from soil (Torsvik *et al.*, 1990) do not rely on the culturing of micro-organisms. Other methods, including the pattern of utilization of carbon substrates (BIOLOG) and aromatic substrates (Reber, 1992) rely on the growth of organisms in the community but provide valuable insight into the functional capability (functional diversity) of the community. All of these methods provide new approaches to using the structure and functioning of the microbial community as an indicator of the effect of pollutants on soils. Some examples of this are discussed below.

4.12 Fatty acid analysis

The structure of soil microbial communities can be examined by measurement of ester-linked fatty acids derived from hydrolysed lipids extracted from soil. The fatty acid methyl esters (FAMEs) are measured using gas chromatography and analysed using the MIDI system (Microbial ID, Inc., Newark, DE, USA). The soil FAME profiles tend to be complex because many fatty acids are common to different micro-organisms and interpretation may be difficult. However, with application of principal component analysis to the FAME profiles, it has been possible to define similarities and differences between microbial communities in soil subjected to different agricultural managements (Pankhurst, 1997).

Restricting the analysis of soil fatty acids only to those derived from phospholipids (PLFA) and/or lipopolysaccharides in the soil markedly increases the capacity to detect differences in soil microbial community structure in soils subjected to different agricultural practices (Zelles et al., 1992) and soil exposed to various pollutants (Frostegard et al., 1993). In their study, Frostegård et al. (1993) followed the effects of five heavy metals on microbial biomass, activity and community structure in two soil types over a 6-month period. Gradual changes in community structure revealed by PLFA analysis were found in response to increasing amounts of metal contamination, suggesting the development of a metal-tolerant community. These changes were, in general, detected at similar or even lower metal concentrations than those, at which effects on ATP and respiration occurred, indicating that community analyses could be a sensitive way of detecting environmental perturbations. In another example, Pennanen et al. (1996) showed a shift in the PLFA profiles of soil sampled at increasing distance from the Harjavalta smelter in S.W. Finland (Fig. 4.5). These changes were associated with Cu levels in the soil, which decreased with increasing distance from the smelter. Calculating the fungal/bacterial biomass ratio (from known fungal and bacterial fatty acids in the PLFA profiles), they showed that the fungal component of the microflora was the most sensitive to the Cu in the soil. Such analysis of individual fatty acids ('signature fatty acids') from the PLFA profile not only permits quantification of specific functional groups of micro-organisms (bacteria, fungi, actinomycetes) in the soil, but the presence of specific fatty acids, e.g. cyclopropane PLFA, may also provide information about the nutritional status (degree of stress) of the microbial community (Tunlid & White, 1991; Frostegård, Tunlid & Bååth, 1996; Pennanen et al., 1996).

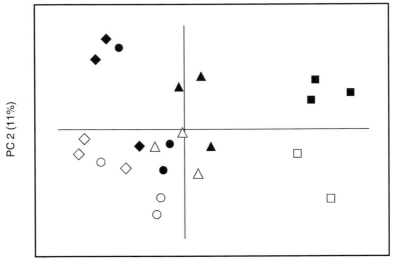

PC 1 (63%)

Fig. 4.5. Score plot of principal component analysis of PLFA profiles of soils at different distances from the Harjavalta smelter, Finland. Black and unshaded symbols indicate two different sampling occasions. Distances from the smelter are indicated as follows: squares, 0.5 km; triangles, 2 km; circles, 4 km; and diamonds, 8 km. (From Pennanen *et al.*, 1996.)

4.13 DNA approaches

Several approaches based on DNA technology have been used successfully for measuring the composition of soil microbial communities (Saylor *et al.*, 1992). These include (i) use of DNA probes to identify community members, (ii) estimations of total genetic diversity via DNA reassociation kinetics, (iii) estimations of genetic diversity within groups of organisms via the construction and analysis of ribosomal DNA libraries and (iv) a wide range of DNA hybridization techniques. All techniques have been made possible by advances in the quantitative extraction of DNA from soil (Holben, 1994). However, to date, very few of these methods have been used to investigate the effect of pollutants on soil microbial communities. One example is the use of DNA reassociation kinetics to follow the impact of application of the herbicide 2,4,5-T on soil (Atlas *et al.*, 1991) (Fig. 4.6). DNA extracted from the herbicide-treated soil showed a decreased rate of reassociation indicative of the development of a genetically less diverse microbial population in response to the perturbation. This paralleled a significant decrease in taxonomic diversity, based on characterization of randomly selected isolates by phenotypic tests and cluster analysis. The populations that became dominant in the herbicide-treated soil demonstrated enhanced nutritional versatility for carboxylic acids (Atlas *et al.*, 1991). The decrease in genetic diversity could have resulted from the

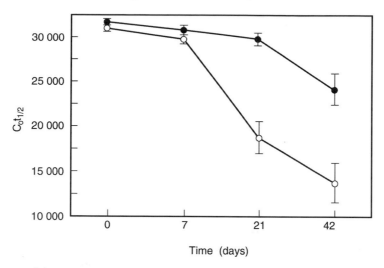

Fig. 4.6. Graph showing changes in genetic diversity (C_0t values for 50% reannealing of DNA) following 2,4,5-T treatment (○) and in untreated control (●) soil microbial communities. $C_0t_{\frac{1}{2}}$ values = moles × litre^{-1} × seconds. (From Atlas *et al.*, 1991.)

increased prevalence of similar genes, e.g. a proliferation of plasmids could cause such a decrease in genetic diversity while at the same time result in enhanced nutritional versatility.

4.14 Utilization of carbon substrates

A simple approach to examining the functional diversity of microbial communities in a given soil is examination of the number of different substrates that are utilized by the community. Using the BIOLOG microplate identification system (BIOLOG, Inc., Haywood, CA, USA) which tests the capacity of bacteria to utilize 95 different substrates, Garland and Mills (1991), Grayston, Campbell and Vaughan (1994) and Zak *et al.* (1994) were able to obtain an assessment of functional differences between soil bacterial communities from a variety of soils. Knight, McGrath & Chaudri (1996) have used the BIOLOG system to examine the effects of heavy metal contamination of soils on soil bacterial communities. Principal component analysis of substrate utilization patterns demonstrated positive effects of the metals (Cu, Cd and Zn) on the extracted bacterial community. As the microbial biomass of the tested soils was very similar, the change in substrate use was attributed to a combination of a shift in microbial community structure and/or a change in the activity/vitality of the same community. They suggest that this technique has potential to detect stressed populations which would not be possible from measurement of total biomass size. Whilst the technique has thus far only been used for analysis of bacterial communities, it may also be adaptable to other micro-organisms (e.g. actinomycetes, fungi and protozoa).

A similar approach based on the ability of isolated soil bacteria to use 20 different aromatic substances was used successfully by Reber (1992) to show that the diversity and degradative capacity of bacterial communities is soils contaminated with heavy metals was reduced compared with communities in uncontaminated soils. In a similar study, Doelman *et al.* (1994) developed a sensitivity–resistance ratio for bacteria isolated from soils contaminated with Cd or Zn. This ratio was consistently lower for bacteria isolated from contaminated soils. They also showed that the metal-resistant bacteria had reduced capacity to utilize a range of aromatic substances.

4.15 Concluding remarks

It seems clear that, whilst several microbial parameters fulfil the criteria desired of a biomonitor of soil pollution, there is no single parameter that is superior to all others for this purpose. Major difficulties remain in interpreting the response of microbial parameters to soil perturbations, particularly because of natural fluctuations in microbial populations and microbial activity. These fluctuations are often larger than the effects due to pollution (Brookes, 1995). There is also the problem of not having suitable reference values against which to gauge the magnitude of the microbial response to a perturbation and hence determine its significance. This can be achieved in controlled field experiments where direct comparisons between treated and non-treated soils can be made, but alternative strategies based on the use of some form of internal control, e.g. the ratio of biomass C or enzyme activity to total organic C will be required in situations where such control soils are unavailable. More research is needed to develop and evaluate these measurement strategies.

Some of the microbial parameters more recently investigated, e.g. incorporation of ^{14}C into new microbial biomass, protozoan growth rates (*in vitro* bioassays) and microbial community analysis (using a variety of approaches), warrant further research and have the potential to complement or even replace currently more well-established biomonitors such as measures of total microbial biomass, soil respiration and soil enzyme activity. These newer parameters offer similar advantages to the well-established parameters in that they are sensitive to low levels of pollutants, respond rapidly to pollutant perturbations, and have the capacity to provide information about the bioavailability of the pollutant in the soil matrix. However, they may be less subject to the inherent variability encountered by the use of other microbial parameters.

References

Adriano, D. C. (1986). *Trace Elements in the Terrestrial Environment.* New York: Springer-Verlag.
Alexander, M. (1977). *Introduction to Soil Microbiology.* New York: John Wiley.

Alvarez, R., Santanatoglia, O. J. & Garcia, R. (1995). Effect of temperature on soil microbial biomass and its metabolic quotient *in situ* under different tillage systems. *Biology and Fertility of Soils*, 19, 227–30.

Anderson, J. P. E. (1982). Soil Respiration. In *Methods of Soil Analysis, Part 2, Chemical and Microbiological Properties*. pp. 831–71. Madison WI: American Society of Agronomy.

ANZECC/NHMRC (1992). Australian and New Zealand Guidelines for the Assessment and Management of Contaminated Sites. Australian and New Zealand Environment and Conservation Council, National Health and Medical Research Council, Canberra ACT.

Atlas, R. M., Horowitz, A., Krichevsky, M. & Bej, A. K. (1991). Response of microbial populations to environmental disturbance. *Microbial Ecology*, 22, 249–56.

Bååth, E. (1989). Effects of heavy metals in soil on microbial processes and populations (a review). *Water, Air and Soil Pollution,* 47, 335–79.

Bardgett, R. D. & Saggar, S. (1994). Effects of heavy metal contamination on the short-term decomposition of labelled [^{14}C]glucose in a pasture soil. *Soil Biology and Biochemistry*, 26, 727–33.

Beckett, P. H. T. (1989). The use of extractants in studies on trace metals in soils, sewage sludges, and sludge treated soils. In *Advances in Soil Science*, ed. B. A. Stewart, Vol. 9, pp. 143–76. New York: Springer-Verlag.

Brookes, P. C. (1995). The use of microbial parameters in monitoring soil pollution by heavy metals. *Biology and Fertility of Soils,* 19, 269–79.

Brookes, P. C. & McGrath, S. P. (1984). Effects of metal toxicity on the size of the soil microbial biomass. *Journal of Soil Science*, 35, 341–6.

Brookes, P. C., McGrath, S. P. & Heijnen, C. (1986a). Metal residues in soils previously treated with sewage-sludge and their effects on growth and nitrogen fixation by blue-green algae. *Soil Biology and Biochemistry,* 18, 345–53.

Brookes, P. C., Heijen, C. E., McGrath, S. P. & Vance, E. D. (1986b). Soil microbial biomass estimates in soil contaminated with metals. *Soil Biology and Biochemistry*, 18, 383–8.

Burns, R.G. (1982). Enzyme activity in soil: location and a possible role in microbial activity. *Soil Biology and Biochemistry,* 14, 423–7.

Burns, R. G., Rogers, S. L. & McGee, I. (1996). Remediation of contaminated urban and industrial soils. In *Contaminants and the Soil Environment in the Australasia–Pacific Region*, ed. R. Naidu, M. McLaughlin, R. Kookana, S. Rogers & D. Oliver, pp. 411–50. Dordrecht: Kluwer Academic Publishers.

CEC (1986). Commission of the European Communities. Council Directive of 12 June 1986 on the protection of the environment, and in particular of the soil, when sewage sludge is used in agriculture. *Official Journal of the European Communities*, L181 (86/278/EEC), 6-12.

Chander, K. & Brookes, P. C. (1991a). Microbial biomass dynamics during the decomposition of glucose and maize in metal-contaminated and non-contaminated soils. *Soil Biology and Biochemistry*, 23, 917–25.

Chander, K. & Brookes, P. C. (1991b). Effects of heavy metals from past applications of sewage sludge on microbial biomass and organic matter accumulation in a sandy loam and a silty loam UK soil. *Soil Biology and Biochemistry,* 23, 927–32.

Chander, K. & Brookes, P. C. (1993). Effects of Zn, Cu, and Ni in sewage sludge on microbial biomass in a sandy loam soil. *Soil Biology and Biochemistry,* 25, 1231–9.

Dick, R. P. (1994). Soil enzyme activities as indicators of soil quality. In *Defining Soil Quality for a Sustainable Environment*, ed. J. W. Doran, D. C. Coleman, D. F. Bezdicek & B. A. Stewart, pp. 107–24. Madison WI: Soil Science Society of America Special Publication No. 35.

Doelman, P., Jansen, E., Michels, M. & van Til, M. (1994). Effects of heavy metals in soil on microbial diversity and activity as shown by the sensitivity-resistance index, an ecologically relevant parameter. *Biology and Fertility of Soils*, 17, 177–84.

Duxbury, T. (1985). Ecological aspects of heavy metal responses in microorganisms. *Advances in Microbial Ecology*, 8, 185–235.

Edwards, J. W., van Alpen, M. & Langley, A. (1994). Identification and Assessment of Contaminated Land. Contaminated Sites Monograph Series No. 3. South Australian Health Commission, Adelaide SA.

Elliott, E. T. (1994). The potential use of soil biotic activity as an indicator of productivity, sustainability and pollution. In *Soil Biota: Management in Sustainable Farming Systems*, ed. C. E. Pankhurst, B. M. Doube, V. V. S. R. Gupta & P. R. Grace, pp. 250–6. Melbourne: CSIRO Press.

Elliott, E. T. (1997). Rationale for developing bioindicators of soil health. In *Biological Indicators of Soil Health*, ed. C. E. Pankhurst, B. M. Doube & V. V. S. R. Gupta, pp. 49–78. Wallingford, Oxford: CAB International.

Fliessbach, A., Martens, R. & Reber, H. H. (1994). Soil microbial biomass and microbial activity in soils treated with heavy metal contaminated sewage sludge. *Soil Biology and Biochemistry*, 26, 1201–5.

Foissner, W. (1994). Soil protozoa as bioindicators in ecosystems under human influence. In *Soil Protozoa*, ed. J. F. Darbyshire, pp. 147–94. Wallingford, Oxford: CAB International.

Forge, T. A., Berrow, M. L., Darbyshire, J. F. & Warren, A. (1993). Protozoan bioassays of soil amended with sewage sludge and heavy metals using the common soil ciliate *Coploda steinii*. *Biology and Fertility of Soils*, 16, 282–6.

Forrest, W. (1993). Harmonising health and environmental criteria: environment based criteria. In *The Health Risk Assessment and Management of Contaminated Sites*, ed. A. Langley & M. van Alpen, pp. 5–7. Proceedings of the Second National Workshop on the Health Risk Assessment and Management of Contaminated Sites. Adelaide: South Australia.

Frostegård, A., Tunlid, A. & Bååth, E. (1993). Phospholipid fatty acid composition, biomass and activity of microbial communities from two soil types experimentally exposed to different heavy metals. *Applied and Environmental Microbiology*, 59, 3605–17.

Frostegård, A., Tunlid, A. & Bååth, E. (1996). Changes in microbial community structure during long-term incubation in two soils experimentally contaminated with metals. *Soil Biology and Biochemistry*, 28, 55–63.

Garland, J. L. & Mills, A. L. (1991). Classification and characterization of heterotrophic microbial communities on the basis of patterns of community-level sole-carbon-source utilization. *Applied and Environmental Microbiology*, 57, 2351–9.

Giller, K. E., McGrath, S. P. & Hirsch, P. R. (1989). Absence of nitrogen fixation in clover grown in soil subject to long-term contamination with heavy metals is due to survival of only ineffective *Rhizobium*. *Soil Biology and Biochemistry*, 21, 841–8.

Graham, J. H., Timmer, L. W. & Fardelman, D. (1986). Toxicity of fungicidal copper in soil to citrus seedlings and vesicular–arbuscular mycorrhizal fungi. *Phytopathology*, 76, 66–77.

Grayston, S. J., Campbell, C. D. & Vaughan, D. (1994). Microbial diversity in the rhizospheres of different tree species. In *Soil Biota: Management in Sustainable Farming Systems, Poster Papers*, ed. C. E. Pankhurst, pp. 155–7. Melbourne: CSIRO Press.

Gupta, V. V. S. R. & Yeates, G. W. (1997). Soil microfauna as indicators of soil health. In *Biological Indicators of Soil Health*, ed. C. E. Pankhurst, B. M. Doube & V. V. S. R. Gupta, pp. 201–33. Wallingford, Oxford: CAB International.

Gupta, V. V. S. R., Fettell, N., Eberbach, P., Neate, S. & Wilhelm, N. (1996). Impact of herbicides on the populations and activities of soil biota. *Australian Microbiology*, 17, A51.

Harter, R. D. & Naidu, R. (1995). Role of metal organic complexation in metal sorption by soils. In *Advances in Agronomy*, Vol. 55, ed. D. L. Sparks, pp. 219–64. San Diego: Academic Press.

Heilmann, B., Lebuhn, M. & Beese, F. (1995). Methods for the investigation of metabolic activities and shifts in the microbial community in a soil treated with a fungicide. *Biology and Fertility of Soils*, 19, 186–92.

Hicks, R. J., Stotzky, G. & Van Voris, P. (1990). Review and evaluation of the effects of xenobiotic chemicals on microorganisms in soil. *Advances in Applied Microbiology*, 35, 195–253.

Holben, W. E. (1994). Isolation and purification of bacterial DNA from soil. In *Methods in Soil Analysis. Part 2. Microbiological and Biochemical Properties*, ed. R. W. Weaver, S. Angle, P. Bottomley, D. Bezdicek, S. Smith, A. Tabatabai & A. Wollum, pp. 727–51. Madison WI: Soil Science Society of America.

Jenkinson, D. S. & Ladd, J. N. (1981). Microbial biomass in soil: measurement and turnover. In *Soil Biochemistry*, ed. E. A. Paul & J. N. Ladd, Vol. 5, pp. 415–71. New York and Basel: Marcel Dekker, Inc.

Kinkle, B. K., Angle, J. S. & Keyser, H. H. (1987). Long-term effects of metal-rich sewage sludge application on soil populations of *Bradyrhizobium japonicum*. *Applied and Environmental Microbiology*, 53, 315–19.

Knight, B., McGrath, S. P. & Chaudri, A. M. (1996). Biomass carbon measurements and substrate utilization patterns of microbial populations from soils amended with Cd, Cu or Zn. In *1st International Conference – Contaminants and the Soil Environment – Extended Abstratcts*, pp. 75–6. Adelaide, Australia: Glenelg Press.

Koomen, I., McGrath, S. P. & Giller, K. G. (1990). Mycorrhizal infection of clover is delayed in soils contaminated with heavy metals from past sewage sludge applications. *Soil Biology and Biochemistry*, 22, 871–3.

Ladd, J. N. (1985). Soil enzymes. In *Soil Organic Matter and Biological Activity*, ed. D. Vaughan & R. E. Malcolm, pp. 175–221. Boston: Martinus Nijhoff.

Langley, A. & El Saadi, O. (1991). Protocol for the Health Risk Assessment and Management of Contaminated Sites. Summary of a National Workshop on the Health Risk Assessment and Management of Contaminated Sites. Adelaide: South Australian Health Commission.

Langley, A. & van Alpen, M. (1993). The Health Risk Assessment and Management of Contaminated Sites. Proceedings of the Second National Workshop on the Health Risk Assessment and Management of Contaminated Sites, Adelaide: South Australian Health Commission.

Leita, L., Nobili, M. De, Muhlbachova, G., Mondini, C., Marchiol, N. & Zerbi, G. (1995). Bioavailability and effects of heavy metals on soil microbial biomass survival during laboratory incubation. *Biology and Fertilty of Soils*, **19**, 103–8.

Leyval, C., Singh, B. R. & Joner, E. L. (1995). Occurrence and infectivity of arbuscular mycorrhizal fungi in some Norwegian soils influenced by heavy metals and soil properties. *Water, Air and Soil Pollution*, **84**, 203–16.

Lorenz, S. E., McGrath, S. P. & Giller, K. E. (1992). Assessment of free-living nitrogen fixation activity as a biological indicator of heavy metal toxicity in soil. *Soil Biology and Biochemistry*, **24**, 601–6.

Lynch, J. M. (1983). *Soil Biotechnology: Microbiological Factors in Crop Productivity*, Oxford: Blackwell Scientific.

McGrath, S. P., Brooks, P. C. & Giller, K. E. (1988). Effects of potentially toxic metals in soil derived from past applications of sewage sludge on nitrogen fixation by *Trifolium repens* L. *Soil Biology and Biochemistry*, **20**, 415–24.

Mhatre, G. N. & Pankhurst, C. E. (1997). Bioindicators to detect contamination of soils with special reference to heavy metals. In *Biological Indicators of Soil Health*, ed. C. E. Pankhurst, B. M. Doube & V. V. S. R. Gupta, pp. 349–69. Wallingford, Oxford: CAB International.

Mosse, B., Stribley, D. P. & Le Tacon, F. (1981). Ecology of mycorrhizae and mycorrhizal fungi. In *Advances in Microbial Ecology*, ed. M. Alexander, Vol. 5, pp. 137–210. New York and London: Plenum Press.

NSW EPA (1995). *Environmental Management Guidelines for the Use and Disposal of Biosolid Products*. Environmental Protection Authority, New South Wales.

Odum, E. P. (1985). Trends expected in stressed ecosystems. *BioScience*, **35**, 419–22.

Orchard, V. A. & Cook, F. J. (1983). Relationship between soil respiration and soil moisture. *Soil Biology and Biochemistry*, **15**, 447–53.

Pankhurst, C. E. (1994). Biological indicators of soil health and sustainable productivity. In *Soil Resilience and Sustainable Land Use*, ed. D. J. Greenland & I. Szabolcs, pp. 331–51. Wallingford, Oxford: CAB International.

Pankhurst, C. E. (1997). Biodiversity of soil organisms as a bioindicator of soil health. In *Biological Indicators of Soil Health*, ed. C. E. Pankhurst, B. M. Doube & V. V. S. R. Gupta, pp. 297–324. Wallingford, Oxford: CAB International.

Pankhurst, C. E., Ophel-Keller, K., Doube, B. M. & Gupta, V. V. S. R. (1996). Biodiversity of soil microbial communities in agricultural systems. *Biodiversity and Conservation*, **5**, 197–209.

Paul, E. A. (1984). Dynamics of organic matter in soils. *Plant and Soil*, **76**, 275–85.

Pennanen, T., Frostegård, A, Fritze, H. & Bååth, E. (1996). Phospholipid fatty acid composition and heavy metal tolerance of soil microbial communities along two heavy metal-polluted gradients in coniferous forests. *Applied and Environmental Microbiology*, **62**, 420–8.

Powlson, D. S., Brookes, P. C. & Christensen, B. T. (1987). Measurement of soil microbial biomass provides an early indication of changes in total soil organic matter due to straw incorporation. *Soil Biology and Biochemistry*, **19**, 159–64.

Pratt, J. R., McCormick, P. V., Pontasch, K. W. & Cairns, J. (1988). Evaluating soluble toxicants in contaminated soils. *Water, Air, and Soil Pollution*, **37**, 293–307.

Purves, D. (1985). *Trace-Element Contamination of the Environment*. Amsterdam: Elsevier.

Reber, H. H. (1992). Simultaneous estimates of the diversity and the degradative capability of heavy-metal-affected soil bacterial communities. *Biology and Fertility of Soils*, 13, 181–6.

Reichle, D. E. (1977). The role of soil invertebrates in nutrient cycling. In *Soil Organisms as Components of Ecosystems*, ed. U. Lohm & T. Persson, vol. 25, pp. 145–56. Ecological Bulletin (Stockholm).

Rogers, S. L. (1996). Effects of biosolids on nutrient cycling, microbial activity and population diversity in soils from the Glenfield long term biosolids application trial. In *Biosolids Research in NSW. Proceedings of Biosolids Summit, BCRI Rydalmere June 1995*, ed. G. J. Osbourne, R. L. Parkin, D. L. Michalk & A. M. Grieve, pp. 181–6. NSW Agriculture.

Rogers, S. & Tiller, K. (1996). Influence of metal contaminated sewage biosolid application to soils on C and N mineralisation and microbial biomass. *Water Techology*, pp. 99–105. Sydney: Australian Water and Waste Water Association Inc.

Saylor, G. S., Nikbakht, K., Fleming, J. T. & Packard, J. (1992). Applications of molecular techniques to soil biochemistry. In *Soil Biochemistry*, ed. G. Stotzky & J. M. Bollag, Vol. 7, pp. 131–72. New York: Marcel Dekker.

Schreiber, B. & Brink, N. (1989). Pesticide toxicity using protozoa as test organisms. *Biology and Fertility of Soils*, 7, 289–96.

Serra-Wittling, C., Houot, S. & Barriuso, E. (1995). Soil enzymatic response to addition of municipal solid-waste compost. *Biology and Fertility of Soils*, 20, 226–36.

Simon-Sylvestre, G. & Fournier, J. C. (1979). Effects of pesticides on the soil microflora. *Advances in Agronomy*, 31, 1–92.

Song, H. G. & Bartha, R. (1990). Effects of jet fuel spills on the microbial community of soil. *Applied and Environmental Microbiology*, 56, 646–51.

Sparling, G. P. (1992). Ratio of microbial biomass carbon to soil organic carbon as a sensitive indicator of changes in soil organic matter. *Australian Journal of Soil Research*, 30, 195–207.

Sparling, G. P. & Ross, D. J. (1993). Biochemical methods to estimate soil microbial biomass: Current developments and applications. In *Soil Organic Matter Dynamics and Sustainability of Tropical Agriculture*, ed. K. Mulangoy & R. Merckx, pp. 21–37. Chichester: Wiley.

Speir, T. W., Kettles, H. A., Parshotam, A., Searle, P. L. & Vlaar, L. N. C. (1995). A simple kinetic approach to derive the ecological dose value, ED_{50}, for the assessment of Cr(VI) toxicity to soil biological properties. *Soil Biology and Biochemistry*, 27, 801–10.

Sprent, J. I. (1979). *The Biology of Nitrogen-fixing Organisms*. London: McGraw-Hill Book Company (UK) Limited.

Tiller, K. G. (1992). Urban soil contamination in Australia. *Australian Journal of Soil Research*, 30, 937–57.

Torsvik, V., Goksoyr, J. & Daae, F. L. (1990). High diversity in DNA of soil bacteria. *Applied and Environmental Microbiology*, 56, 782–7.

Tunlid, A. & White, D. C. (1991). Biochemical analysis of biomass, community structure, nutritional status, and metabolic activity of the microbial communities in soil. In *Soil Biochemistry*, ed. J. M. Bollag & G. Stotzky, vol. 7, pp. 229–62.

USEPA (1993). United States Environmental Protection Agency. Standards for the Disposal and Utilization of Sewage Sludge. *US Federal Regulations, Title 40, Parts 257 and 503.*

Wardle, D. A. & Ghani, A. (1995). A critique of the microbial metabolic quotient (qCO_2) as a bioindicator of disturbance and ecosystem development. *Soil Biology and Biochemistry*, 27, 1601–10.

Wardle, D. A. & Parkinson, D. (1990). Effects of three herbicides on soil microbial biomass and activity. *Plant and Soil*, 122, 21–8.

Witter, E. (1992). Heavy metal concentrations in agricultural soils critical to microorganisms. National Swedish Environmental Protection Board (SVN), Solna. Naturvardsverket Rapport No. 4079.

Yeates, G. W., Orchard, V. A., Speir, T. W., Hunt, J. L. & Hermans, M. C. C. (1994). Reduction in soil biological activity following pasture contamination by copper, chromium, arsenic timber preservative. *Biology and Fertility of Soils*, 18, 200–8.

Zak, J. C., Willig, M. R., Moorhead, D. L. & Wildman, H. G. (1994). Functional diversity of microbial communities: a quantitative approach. *Soil Biology and Biochemistry*, 26, 1101–8.

Zelles, L., Bai, Q. Y., Beck, T. & Breese, F. (1992). Signature fatty acids in phospholipids and lipopolysaccharides as indicators of microbial biomass and community structure in agricultural soils. *Soil Biology and Biochemistry*, 24, 317–23.

5

Release of genetically modified micro-organisms and biomonitoring

F. A. A. M. De Leij, M. J. Bailey, J. M. Whipps, I. P. Thompson,
P. A. Bramwell and J. M. Lynch

5.1 Introduction

This chapter describes and evaluates the first risk assessment study with a free-living (non-symbiotic) genetically modified micro-organism (GMM) in terrestrial systems in the UK. The aim of the study was to increase the understanding of the behaviour of free-living GMMs in the environment by inserting genes that enable the detection, selection and quantification of the GMM on simple culture media. The novel genes and insertion procedures were designed to minimise alterations of the behaviour, fitness and function of the GMM in the environment when compared with the non-modified wild-type strain. These markers also allowed gene transfer to indigenous micro-organisms to be assessed.

5.1.1 *Potential of recombinant technology*

Recombinant technology enables the transfer of genes between different organisms and, consequently, allows organisms to be modified in a variety of ways to express novel traits. For example, micro-organisms could exhibit enhanced ability to degrade toxic compounds and be of benefit by decontaminating polluted environments. Others could be used for mineral leaching, changing soil nutrient status or for biological control of pests and diseases.

Although the potential benefits of GMMs are numerous, the large-scale use of GMMs requires a knowledge of the wider ecological impacts that such organisms might have once they are released into the environment. Micro-organisms, once released, may not only multiply, but may also be subjected to evolutionary selection pressures in the environment which might enhance their ecological fitness (Tiedje *et al.*, 1989). Also the ability of micro-organisms to exchange genetic information with related or non-related micro-organisms increases the uncertainty of the fate and effects that novel genetic elements might have on the environment. Therefore, there is a need to differentiate perceived from real risks associated with the release of GMMs.

To provide appropriate information for the risk assessment of a large-scale GMM release, a better understanding of the behaviour and impact of GMMs in the environment is needed. Such information is normally acquired by a stepwise approach divided into three phases comprising pre-release studies in contained environments, the release itself and subsequent post-release monitoring. First, information on the survival, establishment and dissemination of GMMs in the environment is acquired. This may consider localized, microhabitat studies of spread and persistence on plants and in soil, in addition to larger-scale dispersal studies to identify how fast, and how far, GMMs can spread in a range of different habitats. Secondly, information is needed on the likelihood of the transfer of introduced genetic material to indigenous micro-organisms, because there is ample evidence that bacteria can exchange DNA in natural environments, both within and between different species and genera. Transfer of genetic information between micro-organisms may be mediated by a great variety of mobile genetic elements such as conjugative plasmids, transposons and transducing phages, and therefore the stability of any genetic transfer using these mobile elements should be monitored carefully. Thirdly, information is needed on the possible interactions of GMMs with other species and/or biological processes in the environment where releases will take place, including effects of the products produced by the inserted genes. However, few quantitative data are available that provide a measure for the magnitude of consequences caused by GMM releases in general.

5.1.2 Risk assessment

In the process of evaluating the risks associated with the release of GMMs, a stepwise assessment takes place that is divided into hazard identification, likelihood of realizing identified hazards, consequence of hazard being realized and estimation of risk. The hazard identification takes into account the properties of the GMM and factors such as genetic stability of the inserted genetic elements, the genetic stability of the host, pathogenicity, potential of dissemination and establishment in the environment, and impact on other micro-organisms and ecological processes. The consequence of hazards being realized estimates what effect potential hazards might have on the release environment. Finally, estimation of risk is defined as the product of the likelihood of a hazardous event and the consequence of such an event on the environment. Therefore, a properly conducted risk assessment should identify:

(a) if there are any potential hazards posed by the GMM to the environment;
(b) the likelihood of the potential hazards being realised in the environment;
(c) the consequence of hazards being realized;
(d) estimation of risk as the product of likelihood and consequence;
(e) whether any management procedures are required to control the risks and prevent or minimize damage to the environment;
(f) whether monitoring is required to confirm the risk assessment and to establish that any risk control measures are effective.

F. A. A. M. De Leij *et al.*

However, there may be occasions where even a thorough risk assessment is not able to give definitive answers to all the questions considered, i.e. there is a degree of uncertainty of the extent of environmental risk as identified in the risk assessment. This may arise, for example, due to a lack of data relevant to the risk assessment.

Before a field release of a GMM can be undertaken, a risk assessment involving a series of pre-release studies under contained conditions should be done. A brief overview of these studies is given below to aid comparison between results obtained in the field following release of this GMM with those obtained under containment.

The pre-release work had two main phases. Initially, the microbial populations in soil and the phytosphere of both sugar beet and spring wheat were quantified in the field and in glasshouse microcosm experiments using a variety of techniques (De Leij *et al.*, 1993*a*, 1994*a*; Ellis, Thompson & Bailey, 1995; Thompson, Ellis & Bailey, 1995*a*). This provided data on naturally occurring microbial populations and helped to assess whether microcosm experiments could be used to examine accurately the behaviour of microbial populations in the field. By comparing the fatty acid methyl ester (FAME) profiles of some of the isolated bacteria with an existing library of FAME profiles of described bacterial species, isolated bacteria were identified to the species level (Bailey & Thompson, 1992; Thompson *et al.*, 1993*a,b*). Also, using this technique, a common, non-pathogenic isolate was selected and identified for genetic modification purposes. The bacterial strain selected for marking was a *Pseudomonas fluorescens* isolated from the phylloplane of sugar beet.

The novel genes and insertion procedures were designed to minimize alterations of the behaviour, fitness and function of the GMM in the environment when compared with the non-modified wild-type strain (Bailey *et al.*, 1995). It was marked on the chromosome in two well-separated, presumed non-essential sites, with *lacZY* marker genes that provide the ability to utilize lactose (Drahos *et al.*, 1992), a kanamycin resistance gene (*aph*1) giving resistance to the antibiotic kanamycin and the *xylE* gene that confers the ability to degrade catechol to the organism (Bailey *et al.*, 1995, 1994; Williams & Murray, 1974). The insertion of two marker gene cassettes into the chromosome of the selected bacterium, not only enabled extremely sensitive detection of this organism in environmental samples (De Leij *et al.*, 1993*a*) but also generated the possibility of detecting gene transfer of the inserted genes to related organisms.

Subsequently, after construction of the GMM, a range of experiments were carried out in contained glasshouse facilities with plants grown to maturity to investigate survival, establishment and dissemination. Wheat plants were grown in large, undisturbed cores of silty loam soil taken from the field and sugar beet plants were grown in pots filled with heavy clay soil. The GMM was introduced on to the seed of either spring wheat or sugar beet, and also sprayed on to the phylloplane of wheat. Subsequently, survival, establishment and dissemination of the GMM in soil, the rhizosphere and the phylloplane was determined. In

72

addition, the ability of the GMM to survive, establish and disseminate in the target habitats and the ability of the GMM to colonize some common commercial crops and common weed species was examined. Also, survival of the GMM in the two soil types at different temperatures and the ability of the GMM to survive desiccation on wheat roots was studied.

To evaluate the effect of the GMM on the population dynamics of indigenous microbial populations, seed inoculations with the GMMs were compared with inoculation with the non-modified *P. fluorescens* strain and non-inoculated systems. Impact on total culturable bacteria, filamentous fungi, yeasts and *Pseudomonas* were determined during the growing season. These data were complemented with measurements on the microbial community structure over time in the different treatments.

The pre-release studies that were carried out indicated that the release of the genetically modified *P. fluorescens* into the field was likely to be of low environmental risk. The results from these experiments were used to draft a model release proposal which formed the basis of an application to the Secretary of State for the Environment and the Minister of Agriculture, Fisheries and Food for consent to release the GMM into the UK environment. The main aim of this release was to assess the ability of the marked bacterium to survive in the target habitats and surrounding natural environments in order to provide information and to evaluate the risk of releasing GMMs into the environment. The goals of this project are summarized as follows:

(a) to provide data on the survival, establishment and dissemination of deliberately released bacteria;

(b) to investigate the colonization of plants by a phytosphere bacterium that has been marked genetically for rapid identification;

(c) to evaluate the potential for natural chromosomal gene transfer *in situ*;

(d) to assess the environmental impact of introducing large inocula on closely related species groups and other microbial phytosphere organisms;

(e) to monitor the persistence of introduced bacterial inocula in soil and ability to colonize crops planted the following year;

(f) to provide data relevant to the regulatory authorities for evaluating future field releases;

(g) to develop protocols which can be used to assess the risks of future field releases of functionally modified micro-organisms.

5.2 Experimental approach

Two widely grown, economically important crops, wheat and sugar beet, were used for this study. The wheat was grown in a silty loam soil (Hamble series), while sugar beet was grown in a heavy clay soil (Evesham series). By using such morphologically different plants and different soils, the amount of information that could be obtained for testing the risk assessment process was maximized.

5.2.1 Selection of bacteria for genetic modification

The organism that was chosen for genetic modification was isolated from the phylloplane of sugar beet and initially identified by fatty acid methyl ester (FAME) analyses as *Pseudomonas aureofaciens*. Subsequently the bacterium was identified as *P. fluorescens* using 16S ribosomal restriction analyses. This bacterium formed part of a group of fluorescent pseudomonads, and was one of the most commonly found bacterial species on the phylloplane and in the rhizosphere of both wheat and sugar beet. This bacterial species was considered to be non-pathogenic to humans, animals and plants and was not found to be antagonistic to other microbial inhabitants of the phytosphere. The *P. fluorescens* isolate that was used for the purpose of genetic modification was named *P. fluorescens* SBW25 and it contained no plasmid DNA (Bailey *et al.*,1995).

5.2.2 Genetic modification of Pseudomonas fluorescens SBW25

The marker genes were chosen to facilitate identification and detection of the GMM by simple plate and culture methods and positioned in the chromosome at separate sites to ensure genotypic and phenotypic stability. They also allowed assessment of gene transfer between microbial populations on the two crops. The first marker gene cassette contained the *lacZY* genes which confer ability to utilize lactose (*lacY*). Expression of these genes also allows detection in media containing the chromogenic substrate 5-chloro-4-bromo-3-indolyl-β-D-galactopyranoside (X-gal), because this compound is cleaved by the action of β-galactosidase (*lacZ*) to yield a blue product (Barry, 1988; Drahos, Hemming & McPherson, 1986). The second marker gene cassette, *aph*1-*xylE*, encoded for resistance to the antibiotic kanamycin (*aph*1) and for the enzyme catechol 2,3 dioxygenase (*xylE*), which converts catechol to an identifiable yellow compound: 2-hydroxymuconic semi-aldehyde (Williams & Murray, 1974).

The two different sets of marker genes were introduced into two well-separated, presumed non-essential sites of the chromosome of strain SBW25 by site-directed homologous recombination, to create the GMM (SBW25EeZY-6KX). These two sites, in chromosome fragments Ee and 6, were approximately 1 megabase pair (Mbp) (15% of the genome) apart on the chromosome, as determined from a physical map of the SBW25 chromosome (Rainey & Bailey, 1996). The method developed for the chromosomal marking of SBW25 avoided the retention of vector sequences, plasmid replicons and other mobile genetic elements including transposon or insertion sequences. The use of selectable phenotypes for the chromosomal marking of the recipient bacterium enabled the construction of a GMM free of unwanted extraneous genetic material.

The *lacZY* marker genes (lactose utilization and β-galactosidase activity), as used in the Clemson/Monsanto investigations (Drahos *et al.*, 1992) were isolated from pMON7117 on a *XbaI* fragment which was inserted into the unique *BglII* site in the chromosomal fragment Ee isolated from SBW25. The marked chromosomal fragment (EeZY) was introduced into recipient SBW25, on a mobilizable suicide integration vector (pBGS19M, kanamycin resistant). The recombinant SBW25EeZY was selected on lactose minimal media and the absence of the vector (kanamycin resistant) was confirmed by replica plating and Southern blot hybridization.

The kanamycin gene (*aph*1) derived from *Tn*903 was isolated from pUC4K (Pharmacia) and inserted, in the opposite orientation to the *xyl*E gene (derived from the TOL (pWW0) plasmid) isolated from MOB-TNP5XYLE (H. Joos, Plant Genetic Systems), in the vector pUC18N, to generate pUC18NKX. The *aph*1-*xyl*E cassette was isolated and inserted into the middle of SBW25 chromosomal fragment 6 in plasmid pUC119-6. Fragment 6KX was purified by agarose gel electrophoresis and used to transform SBW25EeZY. Recombinant SBW25EeZY-6KX (GMM) was selected on lactose minimal media supplemented with kanamycin. GMM identity was confirmed phenotypically by a colour change of the colonies when exposed to catechol and X-gal and genotypically by Southern blot hybridization.

The marked sites were genetically stable, and no loss of genotype or phenotype was observed after continuous subculture of the GMM in antibiotic-free L-broth at 28 °C for more than 200 generations. Correct orientation and single site insertion into the recipient chromosome was confirmed by appropriate Southern blot analyses.

Both *lacZY* and kanamycin-resistant phenotypes were commonly expressed in the indigenous microbial populations that inhabited the soil (0.03% and 3.5% of the culturable bacterial cells, respectively; De Leij, Whipps & Lynch, 1995c). No evidence of catechol 2,3 dioxygenase activity was detected in the microbial communities that were extracted from the wheat or sugar beet field sites. However, the *xyl*E gene or its product are unlikely to give a fitness advantage to the recipient organism, because the *xyl*E gene forms part of a large operon involved in aromatic ring degradation. Therefore, the *xyl*E gene on its own was not considered to provide a phenotypic advantage. Apart from the phenotypic differences expressed by the GMM, no difference between the GMM and the non-modified recipient organism could be detected. In competition and growth rate experiments in nutrient broth, both behaved similarly. Also, survival of the wild-type and the GMM in water was identical. Therefore, on the basis of these studies, there appeared to be no difference between the GMM and wild-type in terms of ecological fitness.

5.2.3 Sites and experimental design

The GMM release experiment was carried out during 1993/1994 on both spring wheat (*cv* Axona) and sugar beet. The wheat site was at Littlehampton, West Sussex, on a silt loam soil (Hamble series; 17% sand, 68% silt, 15% clay, 1.4% C, pH 6.0) with a cropping history of wheat for the previous 4 years. The experimental area was situated in the middle of a 3 ha spring wheat field. The experiment itself consisted of 15 plots; five were treated with GMM, five were treated with the non-modified wild-type organism and the remaining five plots were not treated with bacteria (controls) (Fig. 5.1). The treatments were randomized completely.

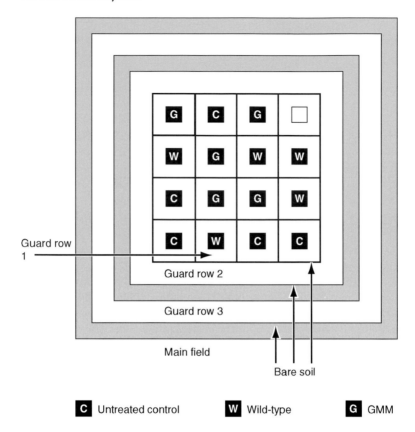

Fig. 5.1. Field site design for spring wheat at Littlehampton. C = uninoculated control; G = GMM; W = wild-type.

Each treated plot was 1.5 m wide and 1.5 m long and was hand sown with 13 rows of wheat. The treated plots were surrounded by three guard rows of wheat and three fallow areas to minimize recombinant spread to the surrounding environment (Fig. 5.1). The first guard row was 2 m wide and separated from the second, 3 m wide guard row, by a 50 cm wide fallow zone. The third 3 m wide guard row was separated from both the second guard row and the main field by 3 m wide fallow zones.

The sugar beet site was at Wytham (Oxford) adjacent to agricultural fields and woodland and had been undisturbed pasture land for over 100 years prior to ploughing and planting with sugar beet. The soil was a heavy clay soil (Evesham Series; 24.9% sand, 21.6% silt, 53.5% clay, 8.5% C, pH 7.7). A 40 m × 25 m enclosure of 2 m high deer and hare fencing designed to exclude large animals was erected near to the centre of the field.

Within the fenced area, nine open plots were established in a Latin square randomized arrangement, three for each treatment of GMM and wild-type and

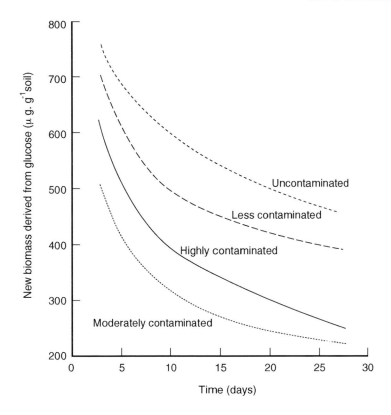

Fig. 5.2. Field site design for sugar beet at Wytham, Oxford. C = uninoculated control;
G = GMM; W = wild-type.

three were untreated controls. The plots were surrounded by three guard rows of untreated plants to minimize edge effects and provide material for the assessment of recombinant dissemination (Fig. 5.2). Walk boards 30 cm wide were placed on the centre of the 1.0 m wide margins of bare soil surrounding the first guard rows, in order to reduce the possibility of GMM transfer on the footwear of personnel. A double boundary, each of three rows of untreated plants, separated by 1.0 m of bare soil, was sown around each treatment block. Bare soil was maintained throughout the study between the third boundary row and the fence by regular weeding and application of herbicides.

5.2.4 Application of bacterial inocula

Wheat

Wheat seeds were inoculated with bacteria by vacuum infiltration. After inoculation, excess inoculum was removed and each batch of inoculated seeds was suspended in

1.25% guar gel. Subsequently, the seeds were fluid drilled into 2 cm deep furrows at a rate of one seed/cm. The distance between the furrows was 12.5 cm, which meant that each plot (1.5 × 1.5 m) received approx. 2000 seeds, each of which contained between 10^7 and 10^8 colony-forming units (cfu). After drilling, the seeds were covered with soil. In total, between 10^{11} and 10^{12} cfu of both the GMM and the wild-type *P. fluorescens* were released initially into the field by seed inoculation.

Sugar beet

Commercially pelleted sugar beet seeds were soaked in suspensions of bacteria in quarter strength Ringer's solution for 10 minutes and dried on filter paper (control treatments were soaked in sterile quarter strength Ringer's solution). Subsequently, each experimental plot of 5 m^2 was planted to a depth of 3 cm with 100 treated sugar beet seeds at 23 cm intervals. The number of GMMs introduced per seed was estimated to be 7.0×10^6 cfu g^{-1} seed, and in total 2.1×10^9 GMM cfu were released into the field.

Spray application

The GMM and the non-modified *P. fluorescens* were also applied to the phylloplane of wheat by spraying. Inoculum (100 ml/plot) containing 3.2×10^{10} cfu/ml of 0.25 strength Ringer's solution was sprayed on to the plants of each plot as a fine mist with a pressurized sprayer. The control plots were sprayed without bacteria. In total, approximately 1.6×10^{13} cfu of both the GMM and the wild-type *P. fluorescens* were released by spray application.

To minimize drift of GMMs by wind, the inoculum was applied during an almost still evening and the plots were surrounded by a 1 m high polyethylene sheet, supported by a wooden frame. These screens were left for one week after the spray application. To monitor inoculum drift, settle plates containing a GMM selective agar medium were positioned at various sites around the GMM-treated plots. The settle plates were left open during the spray application and removed immediately after all the plots were sprayed. They were then incubated, and GMM colonies were enumerated.

5.2.5 Monitoring

The following variables were monitored for this risk assessment study using a variety of techniques.

- Survival, establishment and dissemination of the GMM was monitored in soil and the phytosphere of volunteer wheat seedlings, sugar beet regrowth, resown wheat and sugar beet plants, weeds and the surrounding environment.
- Distant loci and selectable marker genes were chosen specifically to enable gene transfer of the marker genes from the GMM to indigenous microbial populations to be evaluated.
- Mercury heavy metal resistance was used to evaluate gene transfer from indigenous microbial populations to the GM *P. fluorescens*.

- Total culturable microbial populations, specific culturable populations, community structure analyses (r- and K-strategists), fatty acid methyl ester analyses (FAME) and enzyme profile analyses (BIOLOG) were used to evaluate impact of the GMM and the wild-type on indigenous microbial populations.

5.3 Survival, establishment and dissemination

The survival and establishment of GMM populations in soil and the phytosphere of wheat and sugar beet was monitored for a year after release into the field. Also, the dissemination of the GMM into the surrounding environment was investigated, as was the ability of the GMM to re-establish on volunteer wheat plants, regrowth of sugar beet, resown wheat and sugar beet and weeds that established in the GMM-treated plots. The constitutive expression of the marker genes (*lacZY* and *aph*1-*xylE*) enabled extremely sensitive recovery of the GMM from the environment (De Leij *et al.*, 1993*a*).

5.3.1 Survival and establishment of the GM P. fluorescens on inoculated plants

Wheat

The GMM established and survived on roots at levels $> 10^6$ cfu/g root during the whole of the growing season and up to 7 months after harvest on the decaying wheat roots. The only sharp decline (> 1 log unit) occurred between the seedling stage and tillering. This decline was unlikely to be the result of a real decline of the GMM population in the rhizosphere but is most likely related to the fact that, at the seedling stage, the root system consisted mainly of roots originating directly from the seed, while at subsequent sampling occasions, the roots consisted mainly of those originating from the stem base. Because roots originating from the seed were in direct contact with the GMM inoculum, their GMM load was likely to be high, while roots originating some distance away from the point of inoculum would have less chance to become colonized by the GMM than those that originated from the seed.

From the results obtained with the microcosm experiments, it was expected that the GMM would persist on the roots until wheat maturity and then a sharp decline would occur when roots decayed after harvest (De Leij *et al.*, 1994*a*). The GMM did not decline until 7 months after harvest, when the roots had virtually fully decayed. Therefore, the GMM decline found on recovered decaying roots that were kept at 100% relative humidity (RH) at a temperature of 25 °C (De Leij *et al.*, 1994*a*) did not resemble the GMM decline on decaying roots in soil. It is possible that the decay rate of the GMM at 25 °C on extracted roots was much more rapid than the decay rate in soil at between 5 and 10 °C because of greater microbial antagonism or competition on the recovered roots at the higher temperature.

As expected, colonization of the phylloplane by GMMs from a seed inoculation was restricted to the first emerging leaves (De Leij *et al.*, 1994*a*), but survival after spray application with GMMs was much greater in the field than in the glasshouse

(10^5 cfu/g leaf tissue at ripening in the field, compared to < 1 cfu/g leaf tissue at ripening in the glasshouse). After spray application, GMM cfu/g tissue on the phylloplane increased from 10^5 to 10^7 cfu/g leaf tissue during the first month and declined subsequently to a level of approx. 10^5 cfu/g tissue at harvest.

This pattern was very different from the GMM survival found in the glasshouse after spray application where GMM cfu/g tissue declined within 70 days from $> 10^7$ cfu/g tissue to almost non-detectable levels at harvest (De Leij *et al.*, 1994*b*). The reasons for these differences between field and glasshouse grown plants could be manifold. Even though the wheat plants in the glasshouse were sprayed regularly with water, the relative humidity within the field-grown crop was likely to be higher and more constant than the relative humidity encountered by isolated plants grown in the glasshouse. Also, temperatures in the field were lower (between 5 and 25 °C) than in the glasshouse (between 15 and 40 °C). Furthermore, the level of nutrients available for microbial growth was likely to be greater in the field than in the glasshouse as a result of availability of dust, pollen and honeydew depositions, all of which were less available in the contained glasshouse. Such nutrient-rich depositions would also explain the sharp increase of GMM numbers after spray application in the field, in addition to the fact that total bacterial numbers on the phylloplane of field grown plants were up to 4 log units higher than those in the glasshouse.

No GMMs were ever recovered from the ears of wheat plants during the field release. This was in agreement with the distribution of the GMM found in the glasshouse after spray application (De Leij *et al.*, 1994*a*). It suggests that the GMM cannot actively colonize the phylloplane, but that dissemination on to later emerging leaves occurs through the expansion of leaves that are already colonized by the GMM, the ear being enclosed at the time of spraying. Subsequent establishment then takes place through GMM multiplication (for example, GMM numbers on the flag leaf increased from approx. 100 cfu/g leaf at booting to approx. 10^5 cfu/g leaf at ripening).

Sugar beet

The GMM was detected in all of the habitats examined on all sampling occasions throughout the 270-day growing season. The largest number of GMMs detected at any one time in the study was approx. 5×10^6 cfu/g on senescent leaves, 88 days after the release. Considerable fluctuations in GMM numbers were found between habitats and replicates. Greatest fluctuations in numbers were found in rhizosphere soil, with GMM numbers varying up to six orders of magnitude over the season. In most cases, however, GMM numbers in the leaf and root habitats varied by less than two orders of magnitude on consecutive sampling times.

In all the sampled habitats, the GMM represented only a small fraction of the culturable bacteria. On average, over the whole season, the GMM represented less than 0.07% of total bacteria and 0.37% of the total *Pseudomonas* populations. Only on one sampling occasion, in one habitat (immature leaf on day 28), did the GMM represent more than 1.0% of the total isolated bacterial community (32.8% of the total *Pseudomonas* population). From the total culturable bacterial community, the GMM represented the greatest proportion on the immature leaves and the smallest proportion in the root cortex.

These results are very different from the results that were obtained in the glasshouse investigations where the GMM established a relatively large population, representing >85% of all isolates that were isolated from the immature leaves. In comparison, absolute numbers of GMMs/g of leaf tissue, GMM populations in glasshouse and field studies were similar, indicating a possible carrying capacity in the sugar beet phyllosphere for the GMM. However, because numbers of GMM/g tissue were similar on field and the glasshouse-grown plants, this difference in relative numbers was a reflection of the fact that field-grown plants supported up to 1000 times as many culturable bacteria as glasshouse-grown plants.

The fluctuations in the numbers of GMMs/g tissue, particularly on the mature leaf, correlated positively with total *Pseudomonas* numbers. This indicated that the GMM behaved as a normal member of the indigenous *Pseudomonas* community and was an active colonizer of sugar beet.

5.3.2 Vertical dissemination through soil

Silty loam; wheat

The GMM disseminated vertically through the silty loam soil, and 2 months after the initial release, GMMs could be found up to a depth of 45 cm at levels of around 3.5×10^3 cfu/g soil. It is likely that the GMM dissemination was actually more extensive, as numbers of GMMs found at 45 cm depth were not significantly different from the numbers found in the top 10 cm of the soil profile. However, 45 cm was the maximum depth that the soil sampler could reach. Although extensive vertical dissemination did occur, the number of GMMs/g soil declined steadily over time and reached non-detectable levels (< 1 cfu/g soil) 319 days after the release.

These findings differed from the ones obtained by Drahos *et al.* (1992) and Ryder *et al.* (1994) who both found limited spread down the soil profile of *lacZY*-modified *Pseudomonas* species. Also, the results from the experiments on dissemination of the GMM that were carried out in the glasshouse in undisturbed soil cores suggested that dissemination of this bacterium was restricted to the rhizosphere when introduced as a seed inoculum, and dissemination to the soil was limited (De Leij *et al.*, 1994a). The reason for these differences is most likely to be the very wet conditions immediately after sowing and during the field release, resulting in movement of the GMM in the soil water.

Heavy clay; sugar beet

Dissemination of the GMM through clay was limited. No GMMs were found in the top 10 cm of the soil profile using standard dilution plating on to GMM-selective medium. Using enrichment methods, GMMs could be detected (< 1 cfu/g soil) on two sampling occasions in a small proportion (2%) of the samples taken from the top 10 cm of the soil profile.

It is possible that dissemination of GMMs is limited in clay soil because it contains only small pores; the negatively charged clay particles would further limit dissemination of the GMMs. However, it is also possible that a large proportion of the inoculum was trapped in the clay seed coating surrounding the seeds, so that only a few GMM cells were free to disseminate into the soil. This would have resulted in limited GMM dissemination, irrespective of the soil type to which the inoculum was applied.

5.3.3 Lateral dissemination in soil

Silty loam; wheat

GMMs were recovered from soil up to a distance of 2 m away from the release plots at levels of around 1 cfu/g soil. GMM levels were around 100 cfu/g root tissue in the rhizosphere of wheat plants growing at the same place.

This was in contrast to the findings of Drahos *et al.* (1992) who never found GMMs further than 36 cm away from the point of inoculum. This difference cannot be explained solely by the fact that the recovery system of the GMM (De Leij *et al.* 1993*a*) was more sensitive than the one used by Drahos *et al.* (1992). Possibly, as the GMMs were applied to the seed in our experiment rather than as a drench (Kluepfel *et al.*, 1991), initial survival of the GMM inoculum was enhanced, and hence a larger viable population of GMMs in the soil was established. Also, differences in soil moisture and soil type might have been contributing factors to the differences found between the two studies. It is also feasible that GMMs were found in the guard row soil as a result of the GMM dissemination that occurred after the spray application with GMMs.

Although dissemination of GMMs in the soil was found, survival of the GMM in soil was limited. From a density of 10^4 GMM cells/g soil, 58 days after inoculation, levels dropped steadily to a level of approx 200 cfu/g soil, 132 days after inoculation. These results were similar to the ones found on survival of the GMM in pot experiments (De Leij *et al.*, 1994*a*). Because the GMM does not decline in sterile water and does not enter a non-culturable state (Colwell *et al.*, 1985), the most likely reason for the observed GMM decline in soil must be sought in factors such as competition by other micro-organisms and predation by protozoa and nematodes (Scott *et al.*, 1994).

Heavy clay; sugar beet

No GMMs could be isolated from non-rhizosphere soil sampled at distances of 10, 40 or 100 cm away from the GMM-treated plots.

5.3.4 Dissemination of GMMs into the guard rows

Wheat

Even though an evening with very light winds was chosen for the spray application and each plot was surrounded by a polyethylene enclosure, densities in excess of 1–2 GMM cfu/cm^2 were recorded immediately after the spray application on settle plates that were placed 2 m away from the plots. However, subsequent sampling of the wheat surrounding the treated plots failed to yield GMMs, suggesting that, even though spread by wind had occurred, the subsequent establishment of these GMM cells on the phylloplane was poor. However, 50 days after spray application, GMMs could be recovered from the phylloplane of wheat plants that grew in the first guard rows that surrounded the treated areas. Either dissemination from the sprayed plots to the first guard row occurred, or the few GMM cells that established in the first guard row after the spray application were able to multiply subsequently, to levels of > 100 cfu/g leaf. As with the initial increase on the sprayed plants, GMM numbers declined thereafter to non-detectable levels.

Sugar beet

GMMs (< 100 cfu/g tissue) were isolated from sugar beet leaves from the guard rows, in eight out of 144 leaf samples taken on four sampling occasions. Only leaves that were in direct contact with treated plants yielded GMMs. No GMM dissemination to the outer guard rows (1 m from treated plots) was found.

5.3.5 Establishment of GMMs on to volunteer wheat seedlings and regrowth of sugar beet

After harvest, the GMM re-established on the phylloplane and rhizosphere of volunteer wheat seedlings that grew in the treated plots. Six months after harvest, the GMM occurred at a level of around 1000 cfu/g root of these volunteer seedlings, while on the leaves the GMM level was around 1 cfu/g leaf. Because the level of GMMs in soil was around 100 cfu/g soil, the wheat roots must have had an enriching effect on the GMM. However, the GMM levels never reached the levels observed on the inoculated plants.

Phylloplane samples of the sugar beet plants which had overwintered and had not yet produced new growth were collected in mid March 1994 (11 months after sowing). No GMMs were detected on these samples. However, when new leaf tissue and the rhizosphere were sampled in May 1994 (over 12 months after sowing), GMMs could be detected on the phylloplane but not in the rhizosphere.

This indicates that GMMs could persist over the winter at levels below the level of detection. The young plant tissues that subsequently formed seemed to provide suitable growth conditions for the GMM to multiply and recolonize the sugar beet plant.

F. A. A. M. De Leij *et al.*

5.3.6 Establishment of GMMs on resown plants
Wheat

Replanting with wheat, 1 year after the GMM release, resulted in re-establishment of the GMM on the wheat seedlings in three out of the five plots (in one plot GMMs were recovered from the roots and in two other plots from the phylloplane), even though GMMs could only be detected in the soil of one of the five plots at the time of replanting.

When residual root tissue from the previous season's growth was sampled, GMMs were found to persist at levels of approx. 10^5 cfu/g root material. This indicates the importance of plant material as a means for GMM survival in the soil and suggests that young wheat roots had an enriching effect on the GMM.

Sugar beet

GMMs were detected (<50 cfu/g tissue) on the phylloplane on three out of nine plants that were sampled following resowing, but no GMMs were detected in the soil or rhizosphere, again demonstrating the enriching effect of young tissue on the GMM.

5.3.7 Establishment of GMMs on weeds
Wheat

Dissemination and establishment of the GMM on weeds that grew during the winter on the plots was highly variable. Only on the roots of scarlet pimpernel (*Anagallis arvensis* L.) were large numbers of GMMs found ($>10^3$ cfu/g root), while the roots of the other common weed species (annual meadow grass, common field speedwell, corn spurry and groundsel) were almost free of GMMs.

Sugar beet

From 68 weed samples taken on three separate sampling occasions, GMMs were isolated from two leaf samples only, both buttercup ($< 10^4$ cfu/g leaf tissue). No establishment of GMMs on the roots of any of the weed species was found.

Even though the GMM was able to multiply on weed species such as thistle, nettle, dandelion and chickweed in the glasshouse, the GMM appeared restricted in its ability to colonize most of the common weed species that grew at the release sites. This suggests that either the GMM was not as ubiquitous as originally thought, or the temperature and inoculum level in the soil limited GMM establishment on most weed species.

5.3.8 Implications

Large differences in dissemination of the GMM were found between the two sites. Extensive dissemination occurred in silty loam, but dissemination was virtually absent in clay soil. The reasons for these differences might be related to the fact that dissemination of GMMs is indeed restricted in clay soils, but might also be governed by the way the GMMs were applied. The aerial spray application, coupled to the seed inoculation, may have enhanced dissemination in the wheat crop, but the clay pellet used for the sugar beet inoculum may have restricted dissemination in comparison with the fluid drilling system that was used for wheat. If dissemination of GMMs can be prevented by applying such bacteria to a clay seed coat, this might have important implications for future releases of GMMs. If extensive dissemination of GMMs to non-target environments is regarded as an environmental risk, such risks might be minimized by choosing formulation and application methods that restrict microbial movement through soil, but allow the GMM to colonize the phytosphere of the inoculated plants.

The results on survival and establishment showed that the GM *P. fluorescens* used in this release study was more persistent, and its dissemination on the inoculated plant was greater, than could be predicted from the pre-release experiments that were conducted under contained conditions in microcosms and pot experiments. The survival and establishment was also greater than that found by other independent release studies with GMMs.

Consequently, even though pre-release experiments in contained environments are thought to be necessary before any GMM is released into the environment, the value of such experiments is somewhat limited, because they cannot fully reflect conditions in the field. As a consequence they might under- or over-estimate the environmental risks associated with GMM survival and establishment. Nevertheless, in our study, because this work was carried out with a non-pathogenic bacterial strain that was modified purely for monitoring purposes, the under-estimation of GMM survival and establishment which was found did not result in any hazard or risk to the environment.

Even though survival of the GMM in non-rhizosphere soil was limited, the GMM was able to survive, disseminate and re-establish on new plant growth, including weeds, volunteer wheat seedlings and replanted crops. If survival of GMMs in the environment is regarded as an environmental risk, candidate GMMs must be evaluated with great care. Ubiquitous organisms, such as the strain of *P. fluorescens* used in this study, should be avoided as potential carriers of functional genes. Once released, such organisms are likely to establish permanently in the environment, making predictions of their long-term effects on the environment difficult to make.

If it is accepted that the survival, establishment and dissemination of free-living, ubiquitous GMMs in the environment at large is difficult to predict, care should be taken that genetic modifications of such organisms and the resulting characteristics of the GMMs are neutral or of benefit to the environment. If modifications are carried out that might pose a possible hazard to the environment, recipients will have to be chosen with a clearly defined niche, in which case dissemination through the environment is restricted and, therefore, of no real significance.

5.4 Gene transfer

Concerns have been raised about the use and widespread release of GMMs in respect of the impact that they may have on the target and wider environment by perturbing established populations or by exchanging genetic material. Although the most probable mediators of gene transfer in the phytosphere are considered to be conjugative plasmids (Bailey *et al.*, 1994; Bailey, Lilley & Diaper, 1996), little or no evidence exists to describe the frequency of such gene transfer events. Knowledge of the frequency and probability of natural transfer is essential for making predictions of the fate and impact of released GMMs and their genes, particularly if new functional genes are introduced. However, for this risk assessment study, only marker genes were introduced, and transfer of these genes was minimized by inserting them into the chromosome.

Gene transfer was assessed in two ways. First, the transfer of the introduced marker genes to the indigenous *Pseudomonas* community was estimated by isolation on selective, indicator media. Secondly, the ability of the GMM to acquire DNA from indigenous microbial populations and express a novel phenotype was assessed. Mercury resistance was chosen as this phenotype because it was known to be associated with mobile genetic elements (transposons and conjugative plasmids) present in the phytosphere bacteria of sugar beet.

5.4.1 Transfer of the marker genes (lacZY and aph1-xylE) to indigenous microbial populations

From *in vitro* studies involving continuous co-culture with the wild-type in broth or as patches of colonies on agar, the rate of chromosomal gene transfer, in the absence of promiscuous mobilizing factors, was predicted to be lower than the limit of detection of 1 in 10^{10}. Thus, co-cultivation of the wild-type and the GM *P. fluorescens* in non-selective, antibiotic-free L-broth at 28 °C and diluted 1000-fold daily for 20 days (> 200 generations) did not result in greater growth of any one form, the loss of either genotype or phenotype or any discernible gene transfer. Gene transfer was assessed by plating the bacterial culture mixture on to agar medium containing the antibiotic kanamycin and the chromogenic substrate X-gal. Any white colonies would have been sub-cultured and evaluated by hybridization to determine whether the *lacZ* had been lost or whether the *aph*1-*xylE* cassette had been transferred. However, no kanamycin-resistant, white colonies were found, which suggests that no gene transfer occurred under these conditions (Bailey *et al.*, 1995).

With the methods developed, based on simple plating procedures, the limits of detection for transconjugants depended on the number of GMMs per g of soil or root. At its most sensitive, the limit of detection using this method is in the region of 1 transconjugant per 10^5 *Pseudomonas* cfu present in a soil or phyllosphere sample.

Not only does the detection of gene transfer of novel genetic elements depend on the frequency with which such an event is likely to occur, but it also depends on the selective advantage that the acquisition of those elements gives to a recipient organism. If acquisition of the novel genetic elements resulted in rapid multiplication of the recipient, even infrequent gene transfer would be detected. However, the selective advantage of acquiring *lacZY* or *aph*1-*xylE* in the phytosphere was thought to be nil because three of the phenotypes were already present in the environment (lactose utilization, β-galactosidase activity and kanamycin resistance). The *xylE* gene is present in micro-organisms capable of degrading toluene, but is only one gene in a large operon involved in aromatic ring degradation. Catechol -2,3-dioxgenase activity was not detected in the environment, because it is not constutively expressed in environmental isolates, but needs to be induced by chemicals such as *m*-toluate. The *xylE* gene, on its own, is of no advantage to a recipient organism when the other genes that make up the operon involved in aromatic ring degradation are missing. Taking into account the fact that transfer of genes between donor and recipient microbial populations is also dependent on the frequency with which such populations make contact in the soil and the rhizosphere (estimated to be in the order of 10^{-8}), transfer of the marker genes to other microbial populations in the environment was a highly unlikely event.

Not surprisingly, no transfer of the *lacZY* or *aph*1-*xylE* genes to indigenous *Pseudomonas* spp. present in the phytosphere was detected in the field either on spring wheat or sugar beet.

5.4.2 Gene transfer from indigenous micro-organisms to the GM P. fluorescens

To investigate whether transfer of mercury resistance plasmids into the released GMM occurred in the natural environment at detectable frequencies, GMM colonies that were isolated from the phytosphere of mature sugar beets were screened for mercury resistance and the presence of plasmid DNA. Mercury resistance plasmids were known to be widely distributed at the field site in Wytham and could be isolated throughout the growing season (Lilley *et al.*, 1996). These types of plasmids are also readily transferred (one transconjugant per 10^3 to 10^7 possible recipients) to alternative hosts *in vitro* (Lilley *et al.*, 1994).

On the first sampling occasion (88 days after seed inoculation), three mercury-resistant GMM colonies were isolated from the leaves of plants collected from two of the three study plots. Each isolate contained a unique plasmid. On the following sampling occasion, 123 days after planting, mercury-resistant GMMs were again isolated from the rhizosphere and phylloplane of sugar beet but from one plot only. Restriction endonuclease (REN) profiling and cross-hybridization showed that these plasmids were closely related to two of the previously isolated plasmids but different from the other previously isolated plasmid. GMM isolates with resistance to mercury represented a significant proportion of the isolates in some habitats. It was estimated that plasmid transfer frequencies in the environment were greater than one transconjugant per 3×10^7 recipients (Lilley & Bailey, 1997).

The ability of the plant habitat to enhance or stimulate the transfer of mercury resistance plasmids has been demonstrated following the introduction of both donor and recipient cells of *Pseudomonas* spp. to the rhizosphere 24 h before sampling (Lilley *et al.*, 1994). The transfer of mercury resistance plasmids to GMMs colonizing the plants resulted from an active interaction between the inoculum and the indigenous microflora that maintained these mercury resistance plasmids. This implies that the GMM must remain metabolically active after inoculation, because conjugation and plasmid maintenance are considered to be active processes. Furthermore, the presence of the mercury-resistant GMM bacteria in the phytosphere reflects true colonization and not carryover of surviving, contaminating inocula from the seed. The sensitivity of detection for the recipient bacteria (GMM) provided by the introduced genes was central to this investigation and allowed the important observation that natural transfer is a measurable event in the field.

It should be emphasized that only one transferable phenotype, mercury resistance, was assessed in this study. It is probable that other cryptic functions exist in the natural environment which are also carried on conjugative replicons. Until detection methods are improved, an assessment of the actual transfer frequency of these and other transfer elements will not be possible. It is nevertheless apparent that conjugative transfer occurs in the natural terrestrial environment at detectable frequencies. The exchange of genetic material between populations is most probably an effective strategy for survival in extreme and fluctuating environments such as those experienced in the phylloplane and rhizosphere.

In theory, the diversity in the isolated plasmids could be explained by reassortment, or point mutation, within the plasmid. However, no evidence for reassortment or mutation was found *in vitro* or on the plant. Therefore, it is most likely that each plasmid lineage that was isolated from the GMM populations on the phytosphere represented an individual transfer event.

5.4.3 Implications

These findings provide strong evidence that conjugative gene transfer occurs in, and may be stimulated by, the phytosphere under natural non-selective (undefined) conditions. Furthermore, the occurrence of this phenomenon suggests that better methodologies should be developed to investigate the frequency and consequence of gene transfer, not only for risk assessment purposes but also in developing our understanding of bacterial population genetics in the natural environment.

5.5 Impact studies

Investigations into the effects of the GMM on the microbiology of the soil and the phytospheres of wheat and sugar beet were undertaken. The microbial populations on non-treated plants were compared with those on plants treated with GMMs and plants treated with the non-modified wild-type *P. fluorescens* over an entire growing season. The magnitude and effects of such perturbations is an important part in the risk assessment of GMMs. Selected microbial populations, total culturable bacteria, *Pseudomonas* spp., filamentous fungi and yeasts were quantified and microbial communities were analysed using a range of techniques. These measurements were used to determine whether or not the released microbial inocula had any direct measurable impact on the ecology and natural succession of microbial populations in soil and the phytosphere.

5.5.1 Impact on total microbial populations in the rhizosphere

In general, there were no significant overall effects on microbial populations as a result of the release of either the wild-type or the GM *P. fluorescens*. However, there were a few exceptions. Applications of bacteria to wheat seeds resulted in a significant reduction of the *P. putida* and yeast populations on the seed and the hypocotyl at the seedling stage, while the numbers of filamentous fungi were in general higher on the roots treated with bacteria compared with the control treatment.

Yeasts, as well as indigenous *Pseudomonas*, were also affected negatively by introductions of either wild-type or GM *P. fluorescens* in the contained environment studies at the early stages of the wheat development (De Leij *et al.*, 1994*a*). The large load of introduced bacteria on the seed and the hypocotyl presumably competed with indigenous *Pseudomonas* populations as well as with yeasts, preventing the initial build-up of these populations. As filamentous fungal counts are derived from both conidia and hyphae, any effects on filamentous fungi are likely to be obscured by large numbers of conidia which are relatively unaffected by bacterial competition. Despite the fact that some microbial populations were affected by the seed application, no significant differences were found between the wild-type and the GM *P. fluorescens* treatments.

If biologically significant, these effects might be explained either in terms of competition in the case of negative effects or by the release of extra nutrients from the added biomass in the case of positive effects. However, since such effects were transient, and differences between the wild-type and the GMM were small or non-existent, no environmental significance should be attached to them.

5.5.2 Impact on total microbial populations in the phylloplane

Spray applications with wild-type and GM *P. fluorescens* on the phylloplane of wheat at tillering resulted in effects on the microbial populations on the third and fifth leaves. The increase of total bacteria, *Pseudomonas* as well as *P. putida* populations at the end of the growing season on plants that were sprayed with bacteria, might be the result of nutrients being released from the extra microbial biomass that was added. Smaller populations of *P. putida* and yeasts, shortly after spray application, might be the result of competition of these populations with the quickly establishing *P. fluorescens* inocula. The establishment pattern of the GM *P. fluorescens*, which increased rapidly on leaves 3 and 5 up to the time that the ears emerged but declined thereafter, supports these explanations.

The total number of culturable bacteria, *Pseudomonas*, *Erwinia*, filamentous fungi, pink and white yeasts were monitored throughout the growing season on immature, mature and senescent sugar beet leaves, rhizosphere, rhizoplane and root cortex. Large variations in the size of these populations between replicates meant that no significant differences could be detected between the three treatments.

5.5.3 Microbial community analyses

Analyses of the total bacterial community structures in the rhizosphere of wheat following seed inoculations with wild-type and GM *P. fluorescens* showed that no lasting effects occurred. Significant time-inconsistent differences were found between the total bacterial population structures of inoculated and non-inoculated plants at the early growth stages.

Some of the microbial community structures derived from the total bacterial population on the phylloplane of wheat were affected by the spray application with bacteria. At flowering, leaves 3 and 5 that were sprayed with wild-type and GM *P. fluorescens* had more fast-growing isolates whilst at wheat ripening, they had less, or differences were not significant. Again, effects were inconsistent with time and therefore a buffering effect of initial microbial perturbations occurred.

Pseudomonas community structures on the phylloplane of wheat were extremely variable and no clear trend could be observed. The phylloplane is an environment that is far less buffered compared with the soil, and it is possible that the observed fluctuations were a result of phenotypic changes in the *Pseudomonas* populations on the phylloplane (Rainey, Bailey & Thompson, 1994). For example, a spell of hot, dry weather before wheat flowering resulted in a slow-growing *Pseudomonas* population, whilst samples taken after wet weather resulted in a fast-growing *Pseudomonas* population.

Results derived from FAME analyses of bacterial communities on the rhizoplane of sugar beet suggested that an inoculation effect occurred, which resulted in some replacement of bacterial genera. However, no significant differences in the genera composition and the bacterial diversity could be found between rhizosphere microbial communities of plants treated with the wild-type compared with those treated with the GM *P. fluorescens*.

The diversity of the bacterial community on the phylloplane of sugar beet was, in general, significantly lower than that on the rhizoplane. This might be related to the fact that the phylloplane is a harsher and less stable environment compared with the rhizosphere. As a result, the more specialized bacterial communities fluctuate dramatically in space and time. Such large fluctuations are likely to obscure any effect caused by the wild-type and the GM *P. fluorescens*.

5.5.4 Implications

The release of wild-type and GM *P. fluorescens* resulted in significant but transient perturbations of some components of the indigenous microbial community that inhabited the phytosphere. In terms of hazard and risk assessment of GMM releases, the observed perturbations seemed to be of minor importance. First, the wild-type *P. fluorescens*-induced effects that were not significantly different from those induced by the GMM, as was predicted from the contained glasshouse studies. Secondly, the effects were, in general, small and transient. Thirdly, effects did not affect plant growth or plant health. As long as perturbations of the microbial community are not transmitted to more stable components in the environment, such as the soil, hazards as well as risks to the environment are bound to be minimal. If microbial changes were to be transmitted to the soil or other stable environments, an evaluation of the consequences in terms of soil processes, soil productivity and effects on plant health should be made.

5.6 Final remarks

5.6.1 Use of genetic marker systems to obtain ecological information

Genetic modification of micro-organisms to provide novel traits can be used as a powerful tool for the identification and quantification of these cells in the environment. The incorporation of the *lacZY*, kanamycin resistance and *xylE* genes enabled the detection of fewer than one GMM cfu/g soil using simple microbial techniques such as dilution plating and Most Probable Number estimates. These kinds of sensitive recovery techniques enabled GMM survival, establishment and dissemination in the environment to be monitored in great detail during these release studies.

Furthermore, because of the simplicity of the methodologies used, large numbers of samples could be processed, increasing the amount of information that could be obtained on the behaviour of the GM *P. fluorescens* in the environment.

The marker strategy with two sets of selectable marker genes inserted into different positions on the chromosome of *P. fluorescens* was not only designed to allow sensitive monitoring of the GMM in the environment, but should also allow the detection of transfer of the inserted genes to indigenous microbial populations. This approach is valid if the marker genes are both selectable, and are absent in the indigenous microbial community. However, to minimize the risk of the genetic modifications, the novel phenotypic characteristics (lactose utilization and resistance to the antibiotic kanamycin) were both commonly expressed in the indigenous microbial communities of the release sites. Therefore, the transfer of these genes could only be monitored in populations which could be selectively recovered from the environment, and could either not utilize lactose or exhibit kanamycin resistance. Of these, *Pseudomonas* spp. were considered likely candidates, being of the same genus. Obviously, this approach is limited. Failure to detect gene transfer in such a small proportion of the microbial community was by no means a guarantee that transfer of the marker genes did not occur. Furthermore, the marker genes were supposed to give no fitness advantage to a potential recipient, making detection of transconjugants in the environment even more unlikely.

In order to establish if chromosomal gene transfer does actually occur in the environment, the inserted genes should be unique to the environment, selectable and preferably give a fitness advantage to a potential recipient.

Therefore, the release of a selectable, well-characterized microbial population (the GM *P. fluorescens*) into the field, gave the opportunity to screen GMM cells that were subsequently recovered from the field, for characteristics which were absent from the released population. By screening the recovered GMM population for mercury resistance, it could be shown that gene flow from indigenous micro-organisms to GMMs via plasmids was a measurable event in the natural environment (> 1 transconjugant/10^7 potential recipients). This means that, despite careful characterizations, released GMM populations are not genetically stable, increasing the difficulty of predicting their behaviour in the environment. However, exchange and alteration of genetic information is a normal evolutionary process which enables organisms to exploit their environment more efficiently. The release of a GMM would add (or distract) little to this evolutionary process, especially when inserted genes encode for characteristics which are already present in the environment where release takes place.

The argument that the uncertainty of the fate of novel genetic elements following the release of a GMM is itself a risk (National Academy of Sciences, National Research Council, 1989) seems to be somewhat over-cautious. The stability of the inserted genes, as well as the stability of a GMM, cannot be guaranteed in the environment over long periods. Even chromosomal DNA can be mobilized through phages and other mobile genetic elements, whilst GMMs can take up plasmids from indigenous microbes or can mutate into different forms. Such events are likely to change the ecological characteristics and fitness of GMMs and, therefore, the fate of the novel genetic elements. Consequently, it seems logical to determine if the inserted genes themselves can pose a risk to the environment. If the expression of certain genes poses a significant risk, it could be argued that such genes should not be used, even in recipients that occupy a defined ecological niche.

When used to examine microbial behaviour in general, GMMs are only of value if survival and ecological fitness are equivalent to that of the parental, non-modified organism. Because the non-modified bacterium cannot be monitored in non-sterile environments, information on GMM fitness has to be obtained from comparisons of the growth curve and survival characteristics of the GMM with those of the non-modified organism in sterile environments. In non-sterile environments, an indication of GMM fitness can be obtained by quantifying the impact of introductions of non-modified and modified organisms on the plant/soil ecosystem. Such comparisons might give a good indication of the ecological fitness of the GMM, but they can never be completely conclusive. Consequently, if the only reason for genetically modifying the parental organism is to provide a marked strain for ecological studies of the organism itself, a better strategy may still be to utilize non-modified strains in combination with specially developed selective media or antibiotic-resistant mutants of natural strains.

However, if the aim of the genetic modification is to provide organisms that can be used for novel functional roles such as biological control, bioremediation and mineral leaching purposes, other criteria come into play. Although ecological fitness is important for the successful use of such organisms, the ecological behaviour of the GMM does not have to be identical when compared with its non-modified parent; its ecological fitness should be equal or diminished outside the target environment in order to minimize the occurrence of ecological risks. Nevertheless, marker genes for sensitive detection, if introduced at the same time as functional genes, would be of great value to determine the behaviour of such GMMs in the environment.

Although the use of selective media proved to be a sensitive method to monitor dissemination and survival of GMMs in non-sterile environments, there might be some concern about the general applicability of these methods, since they are entirely based on the ability of a GMM cell to grow on, or in, laboratory media. It is thought that a large proportion of the bacteria in environmental samples are present in a viable, but non-culturable, state (Colwell *et al.*, 1985). If GMM cells entered a non-culturable state once released into the environment, dilution plating alone would underestimate the size of the GMM population. As yet, no evidence has been found that *Pseudomonas* spp. can enter a non-culturable state; but other bacteria may do this. If genetic modifications were to be carried out with such bacteria, alternative detection systems such as direct microscopic counts would have to be used. Modification with other marker genes could be of benefit here. For example, use of the *lux* genes would enable selective GMM counts after activation with aldehyde substrate and charge-coupled device (CCD) imaging. Alternatively, polymerase chain reaction (PCR) procedures might provide a solution to this problem.

5.6.2 Relevance of glasshouse studies for GMM risk assessment

There were significant differences in microbial population dynamics of indigenous bacteria and the GMM between microcosm and field studies. Consequently, it could be argued that microcosm experiments might give unreliable results in terms of GMM behaviour and ecological impact. This may well be true, but such studies on GMMs should still be performed in contained environments to ensure that any potential harmful environmental impacts are detected. However, during such studies, attention should be paid to the design of the microcosm as well as the glasshouse or controlled environment used, so that the field situation can be simulated. Thus, well-designed microcosm studies can give valuable information on GMM behaviour, but they can never be equated fully with the field situation.

Although the soil/rhizosphere environment can be mimicked to some extent in the glasshouse, the phylloplane environment is more difficult. In the glasshouse, microbial populations on the phylloplane are protected from harmful UV radiation and seasonal as well as diurnal temperature fluctuations, while humidity and wind speeds are different from the field situation. Also, nutrient depositions on the leaf surface as well as rain are, in general, absent in the glasshouse. Furthermore, microbial populations are monitored on individual plants, ignoring the effects of a crop situation where many plants create a distinct crop micro-climate. Therefore, it is not surprising that, for example, microbial numbers/g leaf were often 3 to 4 log units larger in the field than in the glasshouse. If the situation is sub-optimal for the GMM as well as other microbial populations, lack of environmental harm in the glasshouse is no guarantee of the safety of a GMM in the field.

If it is accepted that the conditions in the field (especially on the phylloplane) cannot be mimicked in the glasshouse, contained experiments should be designed to create conditions that are optimal for GMM survival and multiplication ('worst case scenario' conditions). If, in such a situation, no undesirable effects are found, the risks associated with the release of such an organism into the environment are also likely to be minimal.

Therefore, the value of microcosm experiments should not necessary lay solely in the accurate simulation of a specific field situation, but more as a range of tests that will evaluate possible harmful effects under optimal conditions. What these optimal conditions entail will be dependent on the GMM, and should, therefore, be evaluated case by case.

If, in a worst case scenario situation the negative effects of a GMM outweigh potential benefits, then the release of such a GMM into the environment should be prohibited. However, if no, or limited, environmental harm results from application of the GMM under optimal conditions, it is likely that the undesirable effects that might result from a release into the environment will be even smaller.

5.6.3 Significance of the two releases

Application method, test crop, soil type and meteorological conditions differed between the two sites. Therefore, it is perhaps not surprising that the two releases resulted in very different GMM survival, establishment, dissemination and subsequent ecological impact. It is difficult to suggest which of these different features had the greatest influence on the behaviour of the released GMM and, consequently, implies that it is very difficult to predict the behaviour of a GMM in all the habitats that exist within the environment as a whole.

Other studies on wheat with similar GMMs on different continents under different conditions (Drahos et al., 1992; Ryder et al., 1994), showed different degrees of dissemination of GMMs from those found here. This indicates again, that no matter how realistic pre-release contained studies or related field experimentation are, it is not possible to test and predict conclusively the risks to the environment that might result from a GMM release. Consequently, because it is not feasible to test GMM behaviour and impact conclusively using realistic systems, the design of contained environment experiments that mimic a worst case scenario might be of more value in a risk assessment procedure.

5.6.4 Relevance of methodologies used and other approaches

The chromosomal double marking strategy used in these studies was designed to ensure that the methods for monitoring survival, establishment and dissemination of the GMM and for assessing gene transfer were simple, reliable and sensitive.

Consequently such methods should be used in any future similar studies involving *Pseudomonas*. Molecular methods such as PCR can also be used for the detection of GMMs. However, such methods were never as sensitive as the assays using selective media.

Dilution plating on non-selective and selective media will give information about the presence of viable culturable cells in a microbial community. Because these methods are quick and simple to use, a range of habitats can be frequently targeted during the growing season, giving data that can be analysed statistically. The use of selective media will extend this type of information for specific populations that are present in the phytosphere. Such media include selective culture techniques that are designed to quantify certain bacterial or fungal genera or species that are present in the soil. Alternatively, selective media can be used to quantify functional groups of organisms such as cellulose utilizers, chitin utilizers, denitrifying organisms, nitrifying organisms or physiological groups of organisms that are present in the phytosphere. The use of differential counting over time (De Leij *et al.*, 1993*b*), which was developed during this project, is another example of a method that provides information about ecological groups of bacteria present in time and space in the phytosphere.

All these methods have two distinct drawbacks. First, only information about organisms that are culturable is acquired (95% of the microbial population is viable but non-culturable (Colwell *et al.*, 1985); in the phytosphere this percentage might be lower). To overcome the problems associated with culturability of micro-organisms, direct detection techniques have been developed. Direct microscopic counts of bacterial cells normally yield one to two orders of magnitude larger counts but fail to distinguish between dead and viable cells. Addition of nalidixic acid encourages cell elongation of viable cells (but not division) and, in theory, this should enable the separation of dead and viable cells by direct counting. This works well with single populations, but is almost impossible for natural soil microbial communities that represent many bacteria with different cell sizes. In addition, the single concentration of nalidixic acid employed may not be suitable for each species present.

Other methods that are aimed at estimating the viable cell count in a bacterial community include the slide culture method (enables quantification of cells with limited cell divisions) and methods based on the ability of viable cells to respire (for example, by measuring the uptake of membrane-potential dyes such as tetrazolium). All these methods that aim to quantify viable cells yield estimates that fall between the under-estimated values of plate counts and the over-estimated values of the direct microscope counts and, therefore, are a useful addition to dilution plate counts. Nevertheless, all these methods are extremely time-consuming and tedious in comparison with dilution plating, and the quality of data required must be assessed at the beginning of any such study.

The second drawback of dilution plating is the inability of this method to distinguish between active and non-active cells which give rise to colony-forming units. Spores (Gram-positive bacteria), conidia (fungi) and Gram-negative cells that are in an inactive state can produce a colony on a dilution plate. It is obvious that inactive microbial cells are of less importance for the functioning of an ecosystem than active ones. To measure microbial activity, a number of techniques are available such as CO_2 evolution, O_2 consumption, enzyme measurements (urease, acid and alkaline phosphatases, arylsulphatases and dehydrogenases), and molecular techniques are available such as quantification of the amount of mRNA present in a microbial community. Besides the fact that all these measurements are rather non-specific, the overriding problem with using these methods is that microbial activity is influenced by the sampling and incubation procedures. Consequently, the measured activity does not necessarily reflect microbial activity *in situ*.

Although there is no direct comparative evidence from these studies, dilution plate methods are probably as good as or better than alternative methods such as biomass estimations and measurements of microbial activity, in that they seem to be sensitive enough to detect microbial perturbations as a result of GMM introductions. A spectrum of comparative studies should be carried out to verify this.

The detection of microbial community differences on the basis of species/genera composition (FAME), growth rate characteristics (r- and K-strategists) and ability of a microbial community to utilize specific combinations of carbon sources (BIOLOG) seems to be governed by the complexity of the microbial community and the sensitivity of the methodology to detect discriminating characteristics. The more overlap there is between communities, the more difficult it is to find discriminating characteristics.

When the microbial community as a whole is analysed, the discriminating factors become rarer in relation to the complexity of the microbial community. This problem can be solved by increasing the sensitivity of the method. In the case of the BIOLOG system, a diverse microbial community will result in most carbon sources being utilized at roughly the same level, making it difficult to detect differences using a coarse scale. It is possible that by using an image analyser to analyse more sensitively the optical density in each well of the microtitre plate used for substrate utilization, a better resolution can be obtained and, hence, increase discrimination between communities.

Alternatively, the community has to be split into simpler groups. To some extent, this is always done, even in attempts to analyse the whole microbial community, since only dilutions of the original sample are used for analyses. This approach requires that the number of samples taken from a community increases proportionally to the dilution, so that the community as a whole is still represented in the samples that are analysed. FAME and r- and K-analyses both aim to characterize individual isolates (which represents an extreme simplification of the microbial community) for the purpose of describing a microbial community.

During the test period, 120 isolates were identified from a library of 40 000 potential profiles (or classes) using the FAME procedure and 1000 isolates were divided into seven potential classes using the r- and K-strategists procedure. It could be argued that the latter system was relatively insensitive because of the limited number of classes; nevertheless it still yielded statistically significant results. Sensitivity could perhaps be improved by increasing the number of classes and this option is worth pursuing. FAME analyses, however, suffered from the opposite problem; the ratio of isolates to classes was too small. This meant that the microbial community as a whole was not represented adequately in the different classes. So, although the potential sensitivity of the system was great, the results were not statistically meaningful. To overcome this problem, the number of classes would have to be reduced dramatically, or the number of characterized isolates increased. Because the method is labour intensive, only the first option could be attempted. Instead of identification up to species or subspecies level, isolates were grouped into genera. In this way, more meaningful results could be obtained. However, in view of the lengthy procedures involved in FAME analyses, simpler techniques, such as selective media, could be a more cost-effective approach.

5.6.5 Impact studies

The release of wild-type and GM *P. fluorescens* resulted in significant but transient perturbations of some components of the indigenous microbial community that inhabited the phytosphere. In terms of hazard and risk assessment of GMM releases, the observed perturbations seemed to be of minor importance. First, the wild-type *P. fluorescens* induced effects that were not significantly different from those induced by the GMM; as was predicted from the contained glasshouse studies. Secondly, the effects were in general small and transient. Thirdly, effects did not affect plant growth or plant health. As long as perturbations of the microbial community are not transmitted to more stable components in the environment, such as the soil, hazards as well as risks to the environment are bound to be minimal. If microbial changes were to be transmitted to the soil or other stable environments, an evaluation of the consequences in terms of soil processes, soil productivity and effects on plant health should be made.

What the measured microbial perturbations mean in terms of soil productivity and plant growth is difficult to quantify using microbial population studies. This makes assessments of effects on ecosystem functioning, let alone hazards and risks to the environment, almost impossible. Examining effects on plant and soil productivity could also be useful; in addition to studying functional aspects of microbial ecology, using a variety of methods could be of value for impact assessment. Plant growth, plant health and soil structure can be measured in systems with and without GMMs. Physiological disorders, occurrence of plant diseases, shoot/root ratios and plant growth can all be used to detect imbalances or disruptions in soil ecosystem functioning. If such imbalances were to be detected as a result of a GMM introduction, further targeted investigations could be undertaken to determine the causes of these effects using combinations of the techniques described above.

It is generally assumed, that because GMMs are alive and able to multiply and disseminate in the environment, if environmentally hazardous GMMs are released into the environment they may cause permanent adverse effects if they become established. In contrast, environmentally hazardous chemicals are inanimate and adverse effects are likely to be temporary. This premise, however, is worthy of further consideration and critical assessment. Even though environmentally harmful chemicals themselves might not persist, they can, in some instances, induce environmentally harmful genetic mutations in organisms that inhabit the environment; induction of pesticide resistance in insects and antibiotic resistance in bacteria in hospitals are only two examples. Organisms that are genetically altered through exposure to chemicals are capable of multiplication, dissemination and are likely to persist in the environment. Therefore, the only difference between chemically induced mutants and GMMs is that chemicals induce unpredictable mutations whereas, with GMMs, there is some control over the genetic elements that are incorporated. Furthermore, chemically induced mutants may also undergo environmental selection on a large scale, resulting in organisms that are environmentally fit and adapted. Therefore, it is a misconception that the effects of chemicals are transient because they are inanimate.

Consequently, it seems logical to continue to restrict the use of mutagenic chemicals but to simplify legislation on GMMs without compromising human and environmental safety. Ultimately, the use of chemicals as well as GMMs should be evaluated for their benefits as well as possible harm to man and the environment.

Acknowledgements

The work presented in this chapter was funded by the Department of the Environment and has been published previously in a more extensive form by the Department (Anon., 1996) and elsewhere (De Leij *et al.*, 1995*a*, *b*; Thompson *et al.*, 1995*b*). Evaluations and opinions expressed are those of the authors and not necessarily those of the Department of the Environment.

References

Anon. (1996). Risk assessment and genetically modified microorganisms: final release report. *DoE Research Report no. 7*, 66 pp. Department of the Environment, London.

Bailey, M. J. & Thompson, I. P. (1992). Detection systems for phylloplane pseudomonads. In *Genetic Interactions between Microorganisms in the Microenvironment*, ed. E. M. Wellington & J. D. van Elsas, pp. 126–41. New York: Pergamon Press.

Bailey, M. J., Kobayashi, N., Lilley, A. K., Powell, B. J. & Thompson, I. P. (1994). Potential for gene transfer in the phytosphere: isolation and characterisation of naturally occurring plasmids. In *Environmental Gene Release*, ed. M. J. Bazin & J. M. Lynch, pp. 77–98. London: Chapman & Hall.

Bailey, M. J., Lilley, A. K., Thompson, I. P., Rainey, P. B. & Ellis, R. J. (1995). Site directed chromosomal marking of a fluorescent pseudomonad isolated from the phytosphere of sugar beet; stability and potential for marker gene transfer. *Molecular Ecology*, 4, 755–64.

Bailey, M. J., Lilley, A. K. & Diaper, J. D. (1996). Gene transfer in the phyllosphere. In *Microbiology of Aerial Plant Surfaces*, ed. C. E. Morris, P. Nicot & C. de Nguyen, pp. 103–23. New York: Plenum Publishing.

Barry, G. F. (1988). A broad-host range Shuttle system for gene insertion into chromosomes of Gram-negative bacteria. *Gene*, 71, 75–84.

Colwell, R. R., Brayton, P. R., Grimes, D. J., Rossak, D. B., Huq, S. A. & Palmer, L. M. (1985). Viable but non-culturable *Vibrio cholerae* and related pathogens in the environment: implications for release of genetically engineered microorganisms. *Biotechnology*, 3, 817–20.

De Leij, F. A. A. M., Bailey, J. M., Whipps, J. M. & Lynch, J. M. (1993*a*). A simple most probable number technique for the sensitive recovery of a genetically modified *Pseudomonas aureofaciens* from soil. *Letters in Applied Microbiology*, 16, 307–10.

De Leij, F. A. A. M., Whipps, J. M. & Lynch, J. M. (1993*b*). The use of bacterial colony development for the characterisation of bacterial populations in soil and on roots. *Microbial Ecology*, 27, 81-97.

De Leij, F. A. A. M., Whipps, J. M., Sutton, E. J. & Lynch, J. M. (1994*a*). Spread and survival of a genetically modified *Pseudomonas aureofaciens* on the phytosphere of wheat and in soil. *Applied Soil Ecology*, 1, 207–18.

De Leij, F. A. A. M., Whipps, J. M., Sutton, E. J. & Lynch, J. M. (1994*b*). Effect of a genetically modified *Pseudomonas aureofaciens* on indigenous microbial populations of wheat. *FEMS Microbiology – Ecology*, 13, 249–58.

De Leij, F. A. A. M., Sutton, E. J., Whipps, J. M., Fenlon, J. S. & Lynch, J. M. (1995*a*). Field release of a genetically modified *Pseudomonas fluorescens* on wheat: establishment, survival and dissemination. *Bio/Technology*, 13, 1488–92.

De Leij, F. A. A. M., Sutton, E. J., Whipps, J. M., Fenlon, J. S. & Lynch, J. M. (1995*b*). Impact of field release of genetically modified *Pseudomonas fluorescens* on indigenous microbial populations of wheat. *Applied and Environmental Microbiology*, 61, 3443–53.

De Leij, F. A. A. M., Whipps J. M. & Lynch, J. M. (1995*c*). Traditional methods of detecting and selecting functionally important microorganisms from the soil and the rhizosphere. In *Microbial Diversity and Ecosystem Function,* ed. D. Allsopp, R. R. Colwell & D. L. Hawksworth, pp. 321–37. Wallingford, Oxford: CAB International.

Drahos, D. J., Hemming, B. C. & McPherson, S. (1986). Tracking recombinant organisms in the environment: β-galactosidase as a selectable non-antibiotic marker for fluorescent pseudomonads. *Bio/Technology*, 4, 439–44.

Drahos, D. J., Barry, G. F., Hemming, B. C., Brandt, E. J., Kline, E. L., Skipper, H. D. & Kluepfel, D. A. (1992). Use of *lacZY* chromosomal marker system to study spread and survival of genetically engineered bacteria in soil. In *Environmental Release of Genetically Engineered Microorganisms,* ed. M. J. Day & J. C. Fry, pp. 147–59. London: Academic Press.

Ellis, R. J., Thompson, I. P. & Bailey, M. J. (1995). Metabolic profiling as a means of characterising plant-associated microbial communities. *FEMS Microbiology – Ecology*, 16, 9–18.

Kluepfel, D. A., Kline, E. L., Skipper, H. D., Hughes, T. A., Gooden, D. T., Barry, G. F.,

Hemmings, B. C. & Brandt, E. J. (1991). The release and tracking of genetically engineered bacteria in the environment. *Phytopathology*, **81**, 348–52.

Lilley, A. K. & Bailey, M. J. (1997). The acquisition of indigenous plasmids by a genetically marked pseudomonad population colonising the phytosphere of sugar beet is related to local environmental conditions. *Applied and Evironmental Microbiology*, **63**, 1577–83.

Lilley, A. K., Fry, J. C., Day, M. J. & Bailey, M. J. (1994). *In situ* transfer of an exogenous isolated plasmid between indigenous donor and recipient pseudomonad spp. in sugar beet rhizosphere. *Microbiology*, **140**, 27–33.

Lilley, A. K., Bailey, M. J., Day, M. J. & Fry, J. C. (1996). Diversity of mercury resistance plasmids obtained by exogenous isolation from the bacteria of sugar beet in three successive seasons. *FEMS Microbiology – Ecology*, **20**, 211–28.

National Academy of Sciences (NAS), National Research Council (1989). *Field Testing Genetically Modified Organisms: Framework for Decisions.* Washington, DC: National Academy Press.

Rainey, P. B. & Bailey, M. J. (1996). Physical and genetic map of the *Pseudomonas fluorescens* SBW25 chromosome. *Molecular Microbiology*, **19**, 521–33.

Rainey, P. B., Bailey, M. J. & Thompson, I. P. (1994). Phenotypic and genotypic diversity of fluorescent pseudomonads isolated from field grown sugar beet. *Microbiology*, **140**, 2315–31.

Ryder, M. H., Ophel-Keller, K., Dhindsa, H. & Veal, D. (1994). Detection and characterisation of a genetically modified biocontrol bacterium in field soil. In *Improving Plant Productivity with Rhizosphere Bacteria*, ed. M. H. Ryder, P. M. Stephenson & G. D. Bowen, pp. 261-263. Adelaide: CSIRO.

Scott, E. M., Rattray, E. A. S., Prosser, J. I., Killham, K., Glover, L. A., Lynch, J. M. & Bazin, M. J. (1994). A mathematical model for dispersal of bacterial inoculants colonising the wheat rhizosphere. *Soil Biology and Biochemistry*, **27**, 1307–18.

Thompson, I. P., Bailey, M. J., Ellis, R. J. & Purdey, K. J. (1993*a*). Sub-grouping of bacterial populations by cellular fatty acid composition. *FEMS Microbiology – Ecology*, **12**, 75–84.

Thompson, I. P., Bailey, M. J., Fenlon, J. S., Fermor, T. R., Lilley, A. K., Lynch, J. M., McCormack, P. J., McQuilken, M., Purdy, K. J., Rainey, P. B. & Whipps, J. M. (1993*b*). Quantitative and qualitative seasonal changes in the microbial community from the phyllosphere of sugar beet (*Beta vulgaris*). *Plant and Soil*, **150**, 177–91.

Thompson, I. P., Ellis, R. J. & Bailey, M. J. (1995*a*). Autecology of a genetically modified fluorescent pseudomonad on sugar beet. *FEMS Microbiology – Ecology*, **17**, 1–14.

Thompson, I. P., Lilley, A. K, Ellis, R. J., Bramwell, P. A. & Bailey, M. J. (1995*b*). Survival, colonisation and dispersal of genetically modified *Pseudomonas fluorescens* SBW25 in the phytosphere of field grown sugar beet. *Bio/Technology*, **13**, 1493–7.

Tiedje, J. M. Colwell, R. K., Grossman, Y. L., Hodson, R. E., Lenski, R. E., Mack, R. N. & Regal, P. J. (1989). The planned introduction of genetically engineered organisms: ecological considerations and recommendations. *Ecology*, **70**, 298–15.

Williams, P. A. & Murray, K. (1974). Metabolism of benzoate and the methyl benzoates by *Pseudomonas putida* (Arvilla) mt-2: evidence for the existence of a TOL plasmid. *Journal of Bacteriology*, **125**, 416–23.

6

Biomonitoring in the aquatic environment: use of cytochrome P4501A and other molecular biomarkers in fish and mussels

David R. Livingstone and Peter S. Goldfarb

6.1 Introduction

The amount, variety and number of industrial, agricultural and other chemicals produced by man is continually increasing (Walker & Livingstone, 1992; Lemaire & Livingstone, 1993; Rand, 1995). A part of this potentially toxic material enters aquatic and other environments, where it is readily taken up into the tissues of resident organisms, including pelagic fish (Varanasi *et al.*, 1992; Porte & Albaigés, 1993; Khan, Al-Ghais & Al-Marri, 1995; Van der Oost *et al.*, 1996) and sessile mussels (Livingstone & Pipe, 1992; Widdows & Donkin, 1992; Livingstone *et al.*, 1995). The contaminants comprise a diverse range of chemicals of both long-standing and more recent concern. The former include polynuclear aromatic hydrocarbons (PAHs) (Neff, 1979; Rainio, Linko & Ruotsila, 1986; Varanasi, 1989; Speer *et al.*, 1990), organochlorine pesticides (1,1,1,-trichloro-2,2-bis(*p*-chlorophenyl)ethane (DDT), dieldrin), organochlorine industrial products (chlorophenols, poly-chlorobiphenyls (PCBs), hexachlorohexanes, hexachlorobenzenes) (Livingstone, 1992; Varanasi *et al.*, 1992), and various metals (Cd, Hg, Ag, Pb, Zn, Cu, Fe) (Livingstone & Pipe, 1992; Rodriguez-Ariza *et al.*, 1992). Contaminants of more recent concern include polychlorinated dibenzo-*p*-dioxins (PCDDs) and dibenzofurans (PCDFs) (Cooper, 1989), nitroaromatic and other heterocyclic compounds (Fu, 1990; Balch, Metcalfe & Huestis, 1995; Hetherington, Livingstone & Walker, 1996), organotin antifouling agents such as tributyltin (TBT) (Fent, 1996), organophosphate fertilisers (Van der Oost *et al.*, 1996), oestrogenic compounds such as alkylphenol ethoxylate surfactants and a range of other xenobiotics (Granmo *et al.*, 1989; Lech, Lewis & Ren, 1996; Nimrod & Benson, 1996; Routledge & Sumpter, 1996): and pro-oxidant chemicals such as particular transition metals (for example Cr, Ni, Va, Mn) (Stohs & Bagchi, 1995), and hydrogen peroxide production related to levels of organic matter in water (Price, Worsfold & Mantoura, 1992; Fujiwara *et al.*, 1993).

Uptake of foreign chemicals (xenobiotics) such as contaminants in water environments by fish and mussels can take place from bottom sediments, suspended particulate material, the water column and food sources (Livingstone, 1991a, 1992, 1993; Varanasi et al., 1992). The major routes of input of contaminants will depend on the dietary and ecological lifestyle of the particular organism (Van Veld, 1990; Livingstone, 1991a), such as via sediment and water column by bottom-feeding flatfish, and suspended particulates and water column by filter-feeding bivalve molluscs such as the common mussel (Mytilus edulis L.). The uptake of organic compounds and metals is largely a passive process determined by physico-chemical principles, the rate of uptake increasing with external bioavailable concentration of the chemical, and its hydrophobicity in the case of organic compounds (Zaroogian, Heltshe & Johnson, 1985; Hawker & Connell, 1986). In contrast, rates of metabolism of fat-soluble organic contaminants to water-soluble products and their subsequent removal to the environment are intrinsic to the animal, and depend on their levels of biotransformation enzymes and effectiveness of excretory mechanisms, which are generally significantly greater overall in vertebrates such as fish than in invertebrates such as mussels (Livingstone et al., 1992; Livingstone, 1996a). These differences result in different patterns of bioaccumulation of organic contaminants in the two groups of organisms, with readily metabolized compounds, such as PAHs, reaching highest tissue concentrations near the bottom of food chains in mussels, and poorly metabolized contaminants, such as many PCB congeners, accumulating to highest tissue concentrations in fish, towards the top of food chains (Livingstone, 1993, 1996b). Differences are also seen for metals, with specialized mechanisms of sequestration and storage resulting in very high tissue levels in particular types of molluscs such as some gastropods (Livingstone & Pipe, 1992).

Because of their marked bioaccumulation of chemicals, the analysis of bivalve tissues has, for many years, been used in pollution monitoring as a measure of environmental contamination. Mussel species in particular have been used extensively in so-called 'Mussel Watch' monitoring programmes because of their filter-feeding and sessile habit, geographical distribution, available numbers and resistance to general stress (Widdows & Donkin, 1992). Such programmes have been carried out on the coasts and inland waters of North and South America, Europe, Asia and Australia (Livingstone, 1991a; Livingstone & Pipe, 1992; Rodriguez-Ariza et al., 1992; Porte & Albaigés, 1993). The species of marine and freshwater mussel used have included M. edulis, Mediterranean mussel (Mytilus galloprovincialis), American mussel (Mytilus californianus), horse mussel (Modiolus modiolus), swan mussel (Anodonta cyngea) and green-lipped mussel (Perna viridis). Similarly, many species of marine, brackish and freshwater teleost and elasmobranch fish from all types of aquatic habitats have been used in pollution monitoring (Lemaire & Livingstone, 1993; Bucheli & Fent, 1995; Livingstone, 1996b), including, for example, very deep-water species far from any obvious areas of human activity, such as the rattail (Coryphaenoides armatus) in the North Atlantic Sea (Stegeman, Kloeper-Sams & Farrington, 1986) and the roundnose grenadier (*Coryphaenoides rupestris*) in the Skagerrak, North Sea (Förlin *et al.*, 1996*a*).

6.2 Molecular biomarkers

The need to detect and assess the impact of pollution on environmental quality, particularly for low concentrations of increasingly complex mixtures of chemicals, has led to the development of molecular markers of biological effect of contaminants on organisms: variously called 'stress indices' or similar descriptions in aquatic organisms in the past, but now termed *biomarkers* in both ecotoxicology (McCarthy & Shugart, 1990; Huggett *et al*, 1992; Livingstone, 1993; Schlenk, 1996) and human toxicology (Timbrell, 1996). Exact definitions of biomarkers vary, but a typical one is 'measurements of body fluids, cells, or tissues that indicate in biochemical or cellular terms the presence of contaminants or the magnitude of the host response' (McCarthy & Shugart, 1990). Different categories of biomarkers have been identified variously, such as biomarkers of exposure, response and susceptibility, but a key distinction in ecotoxicology is between *general biomarkers* which respond to most types of environmental stress and often provide a quantitative measure of animal performance or fitness, such as physiological 'scope for growth' (i.e. energy available for growth) in mussels (Widdows & Donkin, 1992), and *specific biomarkers* which respond only, or mainly, to particular groups of chemical contaminants and therefore are diagnostic of exposure to these particular groups of chemical contaminants (Livingstone, 1993). Molecular biomarkers fall predominantly into the latter category, and much effort in recent years has been devoted to refining the specificity, reliability and ease-of-use of such measurements in widely employed monitoring organisms such as fish and mussels, particularly with respect to the development of specific gene and specific enzyme probes (Livingstone, 1996*b*). The application of specific biomarkers is dependent on a thorough mechanistic understanding of the processes underlying gene induction by the particular type of contaminants, which not surprisingly is considerably more advanced in fish than mussels, given the greater global commercial importance and more immediate public impact of the former compared to the latter. Additionally, the transfer of mechanistic understanding between animal groups is limited by phylogenetic differences in biochemistry, particularly with respect to diverse evolving multi-gene families such as the cytochrome P450 biotransformation enzymes (Livingstone, 1994, 1996*b*; Stegeman & Hahn, 1994; Nelson *et al.*, 1996).

Molecular biomarkers have been used extensively in environmental monitoring as part of integrated programmes comprising analysis of contaminants in biota and environment and both general and specific biomarkers (Bayne *et al.*, 1988; Hodson *et al.*, 1992; Soimasuo *et al.*, 1995; Hylland *et al.*, 1996; Schlenk *et al.*, 1996; Spies *et al.*, 1996). The reasons for using biomarkers have been discussed extensively, but they include that they (i) provide a temporally and spatially integrated measure of bioavailable contaminants; (ii) demonstrate causality through mechanistic understanding of the underlying processes; (iii) identify the importance of different routes of exposure by application to organisms from different habitats and different trophic levels; (iv) detect exposure to readily metabolizable contaminants such as PAHs and organophosphates; and (v) have the potential through integration into a suite of measurements at different levels of biological organization (molecular through to community) to be predictors of long-term ecological effects, i.e. they are prognostic of events to come if avoidance action is not taken (McCarthy & Shugart, 1990). Biomarkers thus detect both known (measured) and unknown contaminants, and provide a sensitive, early warning that a sublethal effect on the organism has occurred. Monitoring programmes can use sentinel species, such as *M. edulis*, where the health of the organism is taken to reflect the health of the environment, or any species of commercial or ecological interest. Potential field applications of molecular biomarkers include routine surveillance, hazard and risk assessment at specific sites, enforcement of regulatory environmental standards, and monitoring of the effectiveness of remediation actions (McCarthy & Shugart, 1990; Schlenk, 1996). With respect to the ecological risk assessment of new chemicals, effluents, etc. produced by man, they form an important link between the univariate and multivariate toxicity testing database of laboratory exposures and the multifaceted interactive situation of the field. Molecular biomarkers can also change in response to other environmental and biological factors, but such changes are generally far less marked than the induction caused by the contaminants. However, this 'background noise' has to be taken into account in the design of monitoring strategies and sampling programmes, and should be characterized for each new biomonitoring species employed (Livingstone, 1993; Goksøyr, 1995; Schlenk, 1996).

6.3 Cytochrome P450 IAI (CYPIAI): biomarker of exposure to organic contaminants (PAHs, coplanar PCBs, PCDDs, PCDFs, other compounds)

6.3.1 Mechanistic basis

Cytochrome P450 (EC1.14.14.1) is the terminal component of the mixed-function oxygenase (MFO) system (also called the cytochrome P450 mono-oxygenase system) which catalyses a wide range of monooxygenation reactions, including epoxidation, hydroxylation dealkylation and desulphuration. It has been found in virtually all animal groups examined to date, including both vertebrates and invertebrate phyla (Livingstone, 1991a; Stegeman & Hahn, 1994), which is not surprising given its very ancient origin; particular forms being present in animals, fungi and plants (Nelson *et al.*, 1996). The enzyme exists in many forms (isoenzymes) as products of a multi-gene family, the different isoenzymes having different functions in endogenous and xenobiotic metabolism. To date, over 480 cytochrome P450 genes have been identified, mainly in mammalian systems (Nelson *et al.*, 1996). The form cytochrome

P450 1A1 (CYP1A1) is a biotransformation enzyme involved in the metabolism of a wide range of organic xenobiotics, including contaminants such as PAHs. The nomenclature of the different forms is based on the degree of sequence similarity of the protein: thus, the first number is the family, the letter is the subfamily, and the last number is the individual gene or isoenzyme, e.g. CYP1A1 (isoenzyme) or *CYP1A1* gene (the convention is that the gene is written in italics).

The regulation of the *CYP1A1* gene has been characterized extensively in mammalian systems (Nebert & Gonzalez, 1987; Whitlock, 1993; Poellinger, 1995). It is rapidly induced (within hours) by exposure to many of the compounds that it metabolizes, including PAHs, coplanar PCB congeners, PCDDs, PCDFs and chemicals of similar planar structure. Selective induction occurs via binding of the xenobiotic to a soluble protein complex comprising the 'aromatic hydrocarbon receptor' (AhR) protein and the so-called heat-shock protein 90 (hsp 90), the latter having the dual function of both repressing AhR function and possibly being required for efficient binding of the xenobiotic ligand to the AhR (Poellinger, 1995). Following subsequent release of the hsp 90, the AhR–xenobiotic complex binds to the 'aryl hydrocarbon nuclear transferase' enzyme (ARNT) and is transferred to the cell nucleus where binding of ARNT to the 'xenobiotic regulatory element' (XRE) of the DNA permits access of transcription factors to the promotor region of the *CYP1A1* gene. This results in stimulation of *CYP1A1* gene transcription rate, resulting in increased levels of CYP1A1 mRNA, and appropriate protein with characteristic catalytic activity. This selective induction forms the basis of the use of CYP1A1 as a biomarker for impact by organic contaminants. Additionally, CYP1A1 can activate particular xenobiotics (such as particular PAHs) to mutagenic metabolites, and therefore its increased synthesis may have consequences for carcinogenicity and animal health (Stegeman, 1995).

6.3.2 Use of CYP1A1 as a biomarker in fish

The properties, gene regulation and biomarker application of CYP1A1 in fish have been reviewed extensively (Stegeman, 1989, 1995; Goksøyr & Förlin, 1992; Huggett *et al.*, 1992; Livingstone, 1993; Stegeman & Hahn, 1994; Addison, 1995; Bucheli & Fent, 1995; Buhler, 1995; Goksøyr, 1995). The *CYP1A1* gene has been sequenced in seven species of teleost fish: rainbow trout (*Oncorhynchus mykiss*), scup (*Stenotomus chrysops*), plaice (*Pleuronectes platessa*), tomcod (*Microgadus tomcod*), red sea bream (*Pagrus major*), toadfish (*Opsanus tau*), sea bass (*Dicentrarchus labrax*), four-eye butterfly fish, and ice cod (Nelson *et al.*, 1996). The inducible gene or its protein has also been detected or indicated in 60 or more species of freshwater and marine fish from the presence of DNA and RNA hybridizing to *CYP1A1* nucleic acid probes, CYP1A1-immunopositive protein recognized by antibodies to CYP1A1, and/or the enzyme's characteristic catalytic activity, 7-ethoxyresorufin-*o*-deethylase (EROD) (for species list see Livingstone, 1996*b*). Recent additional species from around the world in which the enzyme (CYP1A1) has been found include the Alaskan sculpin (*Cottus aleuticus* and *C. cognatus*) (Hein

& Kennish, 1996), American rainbow surfperch (*Hypsurus caryi*), rubberlip surfperch (*Rachochlius*) (Spies *et al.*, 1996) and striped bass (*Morone saxatilis*) (Washburn *et al.*, 1996), Arctic charr (*Salvelinus alpinus*) (Wolkers *et al.*, 1996), Australian sand flathead (*Platycephalus bassensis*) (Brumley *et al.*, 1995), European three-spined stickleback (*Gasterosteus aculeatus*) (Holm *et al.*, 1994) and grayling (*Thymallus thymallus*) (Monod, Boudry & Gillet, 1996), Atlantic salmon (*Salmo salar*) (Vignier, Vandermeulen & Mossman, 1996), Japanese medaka (*Oryziates latipes*) (Miller *et al.*, 1996), middle eastern safi fish (*Siganus canalicatus*) (Raza, Otaiba & Montague, 1995), and the tropical mudfish (*Clarias anguillaris*) and tilapia (*Oreochromis niloticus*) (Gadagbui, Addy & Goksøyr, 1996; Pathiratne & George, 1996). If the sequence of the enzyme has not been fully established, then it is recommended that the terminology CYP1A be used (Stegeman, 1992).

In common with many other cytochrome P450 forms, CYP1A is present in highest levels in the liver, although it is found in other tissues such as intestines (Veld, 1990). Its catalytic properties and gene regulation (inducibility) appear similar to those of the orthologous mammalian enzyme. Significant similarity in *CYP1A1* genes is seen between fish species (*M. tomcod*, *O. mykiss*, *P. platessa*) and mammals in terms of organization, nucleotide sequence and amino acid sequence, e.g. all have seven exons and six introns of similar relative length (Roy *et al.*, 1995). The AhR has been detected in the liver of several fish species (Hahn *et al.*, 1994), and a 700 bp cloned cDNA fragment obtained by reverse transcription–polymerase chain reaction (RT–PCR) from killifish (*Fundulus heteroclitus*) has been shown to share significant sequence identity (62–64%) with rodent and human AhRs, revealing conservation of AhR structure between mammals and fish (Karchner & Hahn, 1996). Experimental induction of hepatic CYP1A in fish has been demonstrated with a wide range of compounds, including both single and mixed model, or contaminant chemicals such as various PAHs, PCDDs, PCB congeners and other organochlorines (Bucheli & Fent, 1995; Parrott, Hodson & Dixon, 1995; Sleiderink *et al.*, 1995a; Huuskonen *et al.*, 1996; Sleiderink & Boon, 1996), and environmental mixtures such as river water, carbonaceous pitch extract, crude oils, sediment extracts, creosote and bleached kraft mill effluents (Goksøyr, 1995; Hylland *et al.*, 1996; Livingstone, 1996b; Miller *et al.*, 1996). In addition to adults and juveniles, experimental induction of CYP1A by organic xenobiotics has been observed in early life stages of fish, including embryos, eleutereoembryos and larvae (Peters & Livingstone, 1995; Monod *et al.*, 1996).

Induction of hepatic CYP1A has been used successively as a specific biomarker of exposure to organic contaminants in over 55 species of fish from all types of aquatic ecosystems (freshwater, brackish and marine, shallow and deep-sea) and in most parts of the world, including Europe, USA and Australia (Bucheli & Fent, 1995; Livingstone, 1996b). Most studies have used fish caught at the areas of interest, employing animals from local relatively uncontaminated sites or minimally induced conditions as the control (Table 6.1). An alternative approach has been to use farm-reared or locally caught fish from clean sites placed in cages for a fixed

Table 6.1. *Types of point contaminant sources and geographical areas studied using induction of hepatic cytochrome P4501A in indigenous feral fish as a biomarker of organic pollution*

Area of pollution	Type of pollution or monitoring area	References
Point source	Chemical plants, incineration plants, industrial complexes, landfill sites, oil industry, oil spills, natural oil seeps, pulp mills, sewage	Bucheli & Fent (1995); Förlin *et al.*, (1995); George *et al.* (1995a); Huuskonen & Lindström-Seppä (1995); Livingstone (1996*b*); Spies *et al.* (1996)
Diffuse area	Bays, bights, estuaries, fjords, gulfs, harbours, lakes, offshore areas, river systems	Balk *et al.* (1996); Bucheli & Fent (1995); Förlin *et al.*, (1996*a*); Livingstone (1996*b*); Schlenk *et al.* (1996); Sleiderink & Boon (1995)

Adapted from Tables 4 and 5 of Bucheli and Fent (1995).

period of time at the sites of interest (Table 6.2). The caging or transplant strategy has the advantage of being a controlled situation which uses fish of uniform size, single sex and known history, and observes induction directly over a time period, but this strategy has the possible disadvantages of cost, animal stress and mortality, and is not suitable for all fish species or locations. Induction of hepatic CYP1A in fish has been used to evaluate a wide range of both point source and more widespread contamination (Tables 6.1 and 6.2). Most of these studies have shown increasing induction of fish hepatic CYP1A with increasing organic pollution: an evaluation of 76 fish field studies (37 marine and 39 freshwater) revealed that CYP1A levels were either elevated relative to an uncontaminated reference site or along a contaminant gradient (66% of studies), or positively correlated significantly with contaminant levels (27%). With very few studies (7%), there was no relationship with contaminant levels (Bucheli & Fent, 1995).

Early studies measured induction of hepatic CYP1A through elevation of benzo[a]pyrene (BaP) hydroxylase catalytic activity, which is catalysed predominantly by CYP1A1 in fish and other vertebrates (Stegeman & Hahn, 1994). However, the standard and most widely used measurement of choice now is EROD activity (Table 6.3) because it is specific for CYP1A, is a readily accessible assay technique requiring standard biochemical equipment and a spectrofluorometer, and does not use a carcinogenic substrate such as BaP. More recent studies have complemented EROD activity with measurement of CYP1A-protein (immunorecognition Western blot or ELISA assay using antibodies to fish hepatic CYP1A) and to a lesser extent of CYP1A-mRNA (Northern or slot blot assay using cDNA to fish hepatic *CYP1A*) (Table 6.3). The antibody and cDNA probes for the two types of

Table 6.2. *Examples of induction of hepatic cytochrome P450 1A (CYP1A) as a biomarker of organic pollution using caged fish*

Fish species[a]	Environment[b]	Exposure period	CYP1A measurements[c,d]	References
Cod (*Gadus morhua*)	Sørfjorden fjord, Norway (PAHs, PCBs)	4 weeks	EROD ($\times 4$), CYP1A protein ($\times 2$)	Goksøyr et al. (1994)
Whitefish (*Coregonus lavaratus*)	Lake Saima, Finland (BKME)	4 weeks	EROD ($\times 13$)	Soimasuo et al. (1995)
Rainbow trout (*Oncorhynchus mykiss*)	Lake Saima, Finland (BKME)	3 weeks	EROD ($\times 7$), BPH ($\times 4$)	Lindström-Seppä & Oikari (1988)
O. mykiss	Lake Kallavesi, Finland (UKME)	3 weeks	EROD ($\times 2$)	Lindström-Seppä et al. (1992)
O. mykiss	Lake Võrtsjärv and River Suur, Emajõgi, Estonia (urban)	3 weeks	EROD ($\times 5$), BPH ($\times 3$)	Tuvikene et al. (1996)
O. mykiss	River Po, Italy (PAHs, PCBs)	4 weeks	EROD ($\times 2$), BPH ($\times 2$)	Viganò et al. (1994)
Largemouth bass (*Micropterus salmoides*)	Kinnickinnic river, Great Lakes, USA (PCBs)	1 week	EROD activity ($\times 5$)	Haasch et al. (1992)
Atlantic tomcod (*Microgadus tomcod*)	Miramichi river, New Brunswick, Canada (BKME)	2 weeks	CYP1A mRNA ($\times 11$)	Courtenay et al. (1993)
Tilapia (*Oreochromis niloticus*)	Volta river, Ghana (textiles)	3 weeks	EROD ($\times 21$), CYP1A protein ($\times 21$)	Gadagbui & Goksøyr (1996)

[a]Fish were either caught locally from a clean site (e.g. tomcod) or farm-reared juveniles (cod, whitefish, rainbow trout); [b]polynuclear aromatic hydrocarbons (PAHs), polychlorobiphenyls (PCBs), bleached kraft pulp and paper mill effluent (BKME), unbleached kraft pulp mill effluent (UKME); [c]7-ethoxyresorufin o-deethylase (EROD), cytochrome P450 1A (CYP1A), benzo[a]pyrene hydroxylase (BPH); [d]maximum fold induction observed relative to control site ($\times 5$) ($\times 11$) ($\times 21$), respectively.

Table 6.3. *Numbers of field studies measuring induction of hepatic CYP1A in fish as a biomarker of organic pollution at the levels of catalytic (EROD) activity, enzyme protein, and mRNA*

EROD activity[a]	CYP1A protein[b]	CYP1A mRNA[c]
80 (98%)	36 (44%)	4 (5%)

The studies are from Tables 6.1 and 6.2, and the number of studies using each measurement as a percentage of the total number of studies carried out (82) is given in parenthesis. [a]7-ethoxyresorufin *o*-deethylase; [b]measured by Western blot or ELISA using monoclonal and polyclonal antibodies to cod (*G. morhua*), perch (*P. fluviatilis*), rainbow trout (*O. mykiss*) or scup (*S. chrysops*) hepatic CYP1A; [c]measured by Northern or slot blot using cDNA to *O. mykiss CYP1A*.

measurement are now increasingly becoming available, either commercially or in repository, and the use of the two techniques in addition to EROD activity is becoming routine and recommended (see below). Good conservation of the fish hepatic CYP1A structure is indicated from cross-species probe (Haasch *et al.*, 1989; Goksøyr *et al.*, 1991*a*) and sequencing studies: 72% similarity for the deduced amino acid sequence of *M. tomcod, O. mykiss* and *P. platessa* (Roy *et al.*, 1995), indicating that the probes can be used to assay CYP1A in many if not all fish species; although best results will be obtained where the probes are derived from the species being analysed. Immunoquantitation by ELISA can be less quantitative than the EROD assay, but has the advantage that it can be applied to poor quality (denatured) samples (Goksøyr, Larson & Husøy, 1991*b*). Automation, permitting greater sample throughput, is becoming increasingly important as these catalytic and probe assays become more used in routine monitoring programmes. Multi-sample microplate reader-based procedures have been developed for EROD and CYP1A ELISA assays (Goksøyr, 1991; Grzebyk & Galgani, 1991; Eggens & Galgani, 1992; Burgeot *et al.*, 1994*a,b*). Standardisation of the EROD assay and other methodologies is being addressed in order to maintain quality control and uniformity in monitoring programmes (Stagg, 1991; Goksøyr, 1995).

Non-pollutant factors can also affect the status of CYP1A, and it is important that they should be considered and/or characterized prior to the use of any new fish species. They include temperature, natural xenobiotics, diet, season/reproductive condition, animal condition, sex, species differences and migration (Goksøyr, 1995; Yang & Smith, 1995; Schlenk *et al.*, 1996). Induction of CYP1A1 by hyperoxia has also been recently identified in mammals (Okamoto *et al.*, 1993). Examples of such effects in fish include inverse correlations of EROD activity and CYP1A protein levels with environmental temperature (Goksøyr, 1995): also the impairment of induction responses to contaminants at certain short periods of the seasonal cycle due to the animal's reproductive condition (Elskus, Pruell & Stegeman, 1992). For the latter reason, the use of male fish only has been recommended as a cautionary or preferred option in monitoring (Goksøyr, 1995). In some studies, factorial analysis has been used to identify positive correlations between CYP1A and contaminant levels despite seasonal and sex differences (Vindimian & Garric, 1989), whereas in others temperature has been the dominant influence (Sleiderink *et al.*, 1995*b*). Induction of fish hepatic CYP1A has been seen following exposure to natural xenobiotics such as algal toxins (Washburn *et al.*, 1996) and microbial products (Schlenk, 1994). Of particular importance is the observed inhibition of CYP1A (EROD or BaP hydroxylase) catalytic activity by particular PCB congeners (Boon *et al.*, 1992; Huuskonen *et al.*, 1996), hepatotoxins (Oikari & Jimenez, 1992), metals such as Cd (Fair, 1986), and components in pulp mill effluents (Croce *et al.*, 1995; Huuskonen & Lindström-Seppä, 1995). Because the CYP1A may be induced but with its catalytic activity impaired, measurement of at least both EROD activity and CYP1A protein is recommended in field studies and routine pollution monitoring (Bucheli & Fent, 1995; Goksøyr, 1995). The specific down-regulation of hepatic CYP1A1 and its impaired inducibility have also been seen in *O. mykiss* following prolonged exposure to PCBs (Celander & Förlin, 1995; Celander, Stegeman & Förlin, 1996), which may partly explain similar field observations in fish from very heavily PCB contaminated sites in North America and Europe (Wirgin *et al.*, 1992; Förlin & Celander, 1995; Eggens *et al.*, 1995). Despite these problems, and because maximal induction by organic contaminants is of the order of 100-fold or more compared to generally only several-fold for other biotic and abiotic factors, fish hepatic CYP1A has become one of the most robust and successfully used biomarkers in field application today. It has been employed in a number of national and international monitoring programmes, including the National Status and Trends Programme, USA, the North Sea Task Force Biological Effects Monitoring Programme, the National Observation Network programme, France, and UNESCO-MURST studies of Venice Lagoon, Italy (Livingstone, 1996*b*). It has also been used in laboratory systems to assess river water quality (Melacon, Yeo & Lech, 1987; Jedamski-Grymlas, Lange & Karbe, 1994) and in the field to monitor impact and recovery from individual pollution incidents, such as the release of oil from the stranded ships M/S Eira in Vaasa Archipelago, Gulf of Bothnia, Finland (Lindström-Seppä, 1988), Exxon Valdez in Alaska, USA (Collier *et al.*, 1992*a*), and MV Braer in the Shetlands Isles, UK (George, Wright & Conroy, 1995*a*) and along the coastal area of Kuwait to Qatar following the 1991 Gulf War (Beyer & Goksøyr, 1993). Similarly, it has been used to monitor the effect of the installation of secondary treatment systems on the BKME released into Lake Superior, Canada (Munkittrick *et al.*, 1992). Other recent developments include preliminary studies to incorporate the fish *CYP1A1* gene into yeast to produce catalytically active heterologous expression systems for testing procarcinogen chemicals and other uses in aquatic toxicology (George, Scott & Ellis, 1995*b*).

Establishing the links between CYP1A induction, resultant mechanisms of observed toxicity, and higher order consequences for animal fitness is important because it improves the prognostic application of the biomarker and provides insight into the likely consequences of such changes at the whole animal level. The relationship between exposure to organic contaminants, such as PAHs and PCBs, and hepatic cancers and other pathologies in fish has been demonstrated both experimentally and in the field (see Section 6.4.2). Various organic contaminants, such as BaP, are activated by CYP1A to reactive (mutagenic) species, resulting in the formation of DNA-adducts, and such processes have been implicated in the aetiology of chemically caused carcinogenesis in fish (Livingstone, Förlin & George, 1994). Both species and population differences in susceptibility to contaminant-caused hepatic cancer related to CYP1A and other biotransformation enzymes have also been identified. The greater susceptibility of English sole (*Parophrys vetulus*), compared to starry flounder (*Platichthys stellatus*), has been related to higher CYP1A and lower epoxide hydrolase (EC 4.2.1.64) and glutathione *S*-transferase (GST; EC 2.5.1.18) activities (Collier *et al.*, 1992*b*), whereas the cancer-prone susceptibility of a Hudson river population of *M. tomcod* has been linked to a polymorphism in CYP1A (Roy *et al.*, 1995). Correlative, rather than mechanistic, links have also been established between the induction of hepatic CYP1A in fish and other higher-order effects such as reproduction. Thus, in studies on the effects of BKME on fish in Scandinavian and North American waters, induction of hepatic CYP1A has been correlated with aspects of deteriorating health, including altered blood cell counts, reduced gonad size, reduced survival rates of larvae and adults, and altered patterns of growth (Andersson *et al.*, 1988; Lindström-Seppä & Oikari, 1990; Munkittrick *et al.*, 1991). Thus, the extensive data sets produced from the pulp mill and other studies indicate that CYP1A induction in fish can be used as an early warning of pollutant impact at higher levels of biological organization. However, in contrast, in analyses of fish field data, use of neural networks showed minimal marginal ability to predict growth from EROD activity (Adams, Jaworska & Ham, 1996), and inverse relationships were found between EROD activity and a health index based on morphological and physiological observations (Schlenk *et al.*, 1996).

6.3.3 Use of CYP1A-like protein or enzyme as a biomarker in mussel

Although a great many cytochrome P450 genes have been sequenced, and schemes for the phylogenetic presence of the gene families and subfamilies constructed, relatively little of this information relates to marine invertebrates (Nelson *et al.*, 1996). Compared to fish, much less is known of the properties, regulation and existence of a contaminant-inducible CYP1A-like enzyme in molluscs such as mussel (Livingstone, 1991*a*,*b*, 1994, 1996*b*). Although the MFO system contains the same basic components (cytochromes P450 and b_5; cytochromes P450 reductase and b_5 reductase), differences in aspects of its functioning are indicated, e.g. similar activities with NADH or NADPH as the source of reducing equivalents for molluscs and crustaceans compared to much higher activity with NADPH for vertebrates (Lemaire *et al.*, 1993). Unique properties are also seen for the cytochromes

P450 of bivalve molluscs compared to other marine invertebrate phyla: metabolism of BaP predominantly to diones with fewer dihydrodiols and phenols compared to the reverse pattern for echinoderms and crustaceans (Livingstone, 1991*a*; Michel *et al.*, 1992; Den Besten, Lemaire & Livingstone, 1994; Porte *et al.*, 1995). Characterizing the regulation and induction of cytochrome P450 by organic contaminants, and the consequences of this for higher-order effects such as carcinogenicity, are necessary for the confident application of MFO induction in mussels as a robust biomarker of organic pollution (Livingstone, 1991*b*).

Total cytochrome P450 levels and MFO activities in mussels and other molluscs are highest in the digestive gland (Livingstone, 1991*a*). Multiple forms of cytochrome P450 are indicated in marine invertebrates from enzymological, immunorecognition and molecular biological studies (Livingstone, 1996*b*), including the presence of CYP1A-epitopes or proteins both in *Mytilus* sp. (see below) and in less evolved marine invertebrate phyla: several species of sea anemone (phylum: Cnidaria); although in the latter case the apparent molecular weights of the proteins recognized by antibodies to fish hepatic CYP1A were about 70 kDa compared with the vertebrate 50 to 60 kDa range (Heffernan *et al.*, 1996). Unique forms of cytochrome P450 have also been found in aquatic invertebrates compared to vertebrates: CYP10 in the snail *Lymnaea stagnalis* (Teuissen *et al.*, 1992). In contrast to fish, EROD activity has rarely been detected in molluscs (Yawetz, Mandelis & Fishelson, 1992) or other marine invertebrates, whereas BaP hydroxylase activity is widespread (Livingstone, 1991*a*). Apparent induction of the MFO system in marine invertebrates is much less marked and more variable than in fish (one- to three-fold compared to 100-fold), but nevertheless increases in MFO components and/or MFO activities with exposure to organic xenobiotics have been seen or indicated for most types of molluscs, including chitons (Schlenk & Buhler, 1989), bivalves (Livingstone, Kirchin & Wiseman, 1989; Yawetz *et al.*, 1992; Michel *et al.*, 1993: Solé, Porte & Albaigés, 1995*a*; Weinstein, 1995), gastropods (Livingstone *et al.*, 1989; Yawetz *et al.*, 1992) and cephalopods (Cheah *et al.*, 1995). Field studies with mussels (*Mytilus* sp.) have shown correlations between organic contaminants and higher levels of BaP hydroxylase activity (Narbonne *et al.*, 1991; Michel *et al.*, 1994; Förlin *et al.*, 1996*a*), total cytochrome P450 content (Solé *et al.*, 1996) and the '418-peak' (putative denatured cytochrome P450) (Livingstone *et al.*, 1989), but as yet no single parameter has emerged as a widely used biomarker for exposure to organic pollution in molluscs. Evidence for an AhR-type mechanism of induction has also been obtained with the detection of dioxin-specific binding proteins in tissues of the clams *Mya arenaria* and *Mercenaria* sp., although their apparent molecular weights were 28 to 39 kDa compared with 105 to 145 kDa in fish (Brown, Van Beneden & Clark, 1995; Brown *et al.*, 1996).

Recently, evidence has been obtained for a *CYP1A*-like gene and enzyme in digestive gland of mussel and other molluscs, although as yet no sequence information exists to confirm this, and alternatively it could be a member of a unique molluscan gene family. For example, *CYP2L* is an unique crustacean gene but epitopes of the protein are indicated in fish and mammals from antibody cross-reactivity studies (Boyle & James, 1996). Expression of a *CYP1A*-like gene in *Mytilus* sp. has been demonstrated from Northern blotting and RT-PCR studies using a cDNA probe to *O. mykiss* CYP1A (Wootton *et al.*, 1995, 1996). Using oligonucleotide primers to amplify a sequence around the conserved haem-binding cysteine region of hepatic *CYP1A1* of *O. mykiss*, several cDNA bands were resolved by electrophoresis, including a major one of about 280 bp (compared to the predicted size of this band for *O. mykiss* of 208 bp), which was recognized on Southern blotting with the cDNA probe to *O. mykiss CYP1A1*. Immunorecognition studies using polyclonal antibodies to fish hepatic CYP1A indicated the presence of a CYP1A-like epitope or protein in digestive gland of the chiton *Cryptochiton stelleri* and *Mytilus* sp. that were elevated following exposure to the classical CYP1A-inducers β-naphthoflavone or PCBs, respectively (Schlenk & Buhler, 1989; Porte *et al.*, 1995; Livingstone *et al.*, 1997). Evidence also exists from reconstitution (Porte *et al.*, 1995), induction (Livingstone *et al.*, 1996) and seasonal (Wootton *et al.*, 1996) studies to indicate that this CYP1A-like protein is, at least in part, responsible for the catalysis of BaP metabolism.

Field studies using the antibody and cDNA probes to fish hepatic CYP1A have indicated induction of a CYP1A-like enzyme in digestive gland of *Mytilus* sp. with exposure to PAHs, PCBs and other contaminants. Increases in levels of CYP1A-like mRNA, CYP1A-immunopositive protein and microsomal BaP metabolism were seen in mussels from Venice Lagoon compared with a cleaner site in the Adriatic Sea, Italy (Livingstone *et al.*, 1995; Livingstone, 1996b). In contrast, increases in levels of microsomal CYP1A-immunopositive protein, but not BaP hydroxylase activity, were seen in mussels following the oil spill from tanker the *Aegean Sea* off northern Spain (Solé *et al.*, 1996). The difference in results between these two studies, combined with the low levels of inducibility of the MFO system relative to such background effects as seasonal changes (Kirchin, Wiseman & Livingstone, 1992; Solé, Porte & Albairgés, 1995b; Weinstein, 1995), illustrate the need for greater mechanistic understanding of the molluscan MFO system and the development of molluscan-specific antibody and cDNA probes before it can be used as a more reliable and robust biomarker in the field. A prognostic capability for the biomarker is indicated from studies showing the formation of mutagens (Michel *et al.*, 1992), DNA-adducts (Section 6.4.2) and chemically caused cancer in *Mytilus* sp. and/or other bivalves (Gardner, Pruell & Malcolm, 1992). Additionally, studies on the gonadal tumours of *M. arenaria* and *Mercenaria* sp. have revealed the presence of transforming genes (Van Beneden *et al.*, 1993) and differentially expressed genes related to cell growth and proliferation (Rhodes & Van Beneden, 1996).

6.4 Examples of other molecular biomarkers

Many other types of gene responses have been proposed as molecular biomarkers for pollution monitoring and used to varying degrees of success in fish and mussels (McCarthy & Shugart, 1990; Huggett *et al.*, 1992; Livingstone, 1993). Some are now used routinely in monitoring programmes, such as metallothioneins and, increasingly, DNA-adducts, whereas others are in various stages of development and assessment. Some major examples are given below.

6.4.1 Metallothioneins (MTs): biomarker of exposure to heavy metals

MTs are widely distributed, low molecular weight, cysteine-rich, metal-binding protein products of a multigene family (Heuchel, Radtke & Schaffner, 1995) present in the tissues of most, if not all, animals, including fish and marine invertebrates such as mussels (Livingstone, 1993). MTs bind various transition metals via the cysteinyl residues, and usually contain displaceable metals such as Zn and Cu. Their functions include detoxication of excess levels of both endogenous metals such as Zn and Cu and contaminant metals such as Cd, Hg and Ag. Induction of MTs is thought to occur via metal-mediated transcriptional activation of MT genes, involving interaction with upstream regulatory sequences, termed metal responsive elements (MREs) (Heuchel et al., 1995). Increased synthesis of MTs occurs in response to a wide range of metals, including Cd, Cu, Zn, Co, Ni, Bi and Ag, and this induction forms the basis of its use as a biomarker for metal exposure (Huggett et al., 1992). Varying levels of MT synthesis can also be induced by other agents, including hormones and secondary messengers, inflammatory agents and cytokines, particular vitamins and cytotoxic agents, and stress-producing conditions such as UV-radiation (Heuchel et al., 1995). Induction of MTs by metal contaminants has been demonstrated both by laboratory exposure and in the field for a number of fish and mussel species (Kille et al., 1992; Livingstone, 1993); recent examples including sea bass (Dicentrarchus labrax) (Cattani et al., 1996), turbot (Scophthalmus maximus) (George, Todd & Wright, 1996) and P. viridis exposed to Cd (Yang & Thompson, 1996). MT induction has been measured mainly in terms of levels of MT protein by various metal analysis, chromatographic, radiometric and polarographic techniques, but more recently by antibody and cDNA quantitation of respectively MT protein and mRNA (Kille et al., 1992; George et al., 1996). A high degree of conservation of MT structure in different fish species is seen, indicating that the antibody and cDNA probes will be widely applicable for fish MT quantitation by ELISA, RIA and Northern analyses (Kille et al., 1992). Recent studies have shown that all six MREs in the promoter of the MT-A gene of O. mykiss are necessary for maximal inducibility (Kling et al., 1996). Structural differences are seen for mussel compared with fish MTs, the former containing less cysteine and sometimes being referred to as MT-like proteins.

6.4.2 DNA-adducts – biomarker of exposure to organic contaminants

The covalent binding of organic contaminants to DNA to form DNA-adducts can occur directly, or metabolically via activation of the organic contaminant by CYP1A (and other biotransformation enzymes) to reactive electrophilic species. DNA-adduct formation reflects the integration of the effects of contaminant uptake, metabolism and macromolecular repair, and is the initial event in contaminant-caused carcinogenesis. DNA-adduct formation and subsequent measurement can thus act as biomarkers of both contaminant exposure and biological damage, and these are increasingly used in human occupational and animal environmental monitoring (Livingstone, 1993). Levels of DNA-adducts of up to 1 in 10^9 normal bases can be detected by a variety of fluorescence, immunochemical, ^{32}P-postlabelling or mass spectroscopy methods (Livingstone, 1993). The relationship between exposure to contaminants such as PAHs, DNA-adduct formation (Maccubbin, 1994), oncogene activation and tumour suppressor gene inactivation (Van Beneden, 1993; Van Beneden & Ostrander, 1994; Rotchell, Stagg & Craft, 1995; Torten et al., 1996), and neoplasia (Bailey et al., 1994; Moore & Myers, 1994) has been studied extensively in fish. Less is known of the processes in mussels and other marine invertebrates, but in addition to contaminant-caused neoplasia (see Section 6.3.3), a genotoxic disease syndrome has been proposed linking DNA damage to a range of deleterious molecular, cellular and whole animal effects (Kurelec, 1993). Field correlations between levels of contaminants and DNA-adducts have been seen for a number of fish species (Livingstone, 1993). More recently, 20-fold greater levels of DNA-adducts were found in early life stages of cod (*Gadus morhua*) from the Baltic Sea compared to the Barents Sea, which correlated with higher mortalities and poorer reproductive success of the former (Ericson et al., 1996), and evidence was obtained that exhaust from two-stroke outboard motors may contribute to DNA-adduct formation in feral fish (Tjärnlund et al., 1996). Juveniles, in addition to adults and larvae, have also been shown to form DNA-adducts; e.g. *S. maximus* exposed to BaP (Peters et al., 1996). In laboratory studies of *P. vetulus*, the persistence of hepatic BaP-DNA-adducts, together with increases in their levels with exposure to successive doses of BaP, indicate that such adducts can be used as molecular dosimeters of relatively long-term exposure to genotoxic PAHs (Stein et al., 1993). Dose-dependent DNA-adduct formation has also been demonstrated in gills of *M. galloprovincialis* exposed to BaP (Venier & Canova, 1996). In both fish and invertebrate species, the occurrence of apparently endogenous adducts has been identified as a possible background factor in biomarker application (Livingstone, 1993).

6.4.3 *Other enzyme and protein biomarkers*

Cytochrome P450 4A1 (CYP4A1) of particular mammals is induced by peroxisome proliferators, such as phthalate ester plasticisers, and a similar phenomenon has recently been indicated in some fish species: bluegill (*Lepomis macrochirus*) and catfish (*Ictalurus punctatus*), but not others, e.g. *O. mykiss*, offering the possibility of a biomarker for this group of contaminants (Haasch, 1996). CYP4A has been indicated in *Mytilus* sp. by Northern blotting (Wootton et al., 1995), but induction by peroxisome proliferators has not been seen (Michel et al., 1994). Hepatic phase II biotransformation enzymes, such as glutathione S-transferases (EC 2.5.1.18; GST) and UDP-glucuronyl transferase (EC 2.4.1.17), have been employed as biomarkers of exposure to organic contaminants in fish, but the responses are generally much less marked compared to CYP1A (Van Veld et al., 1991; Viganò et *al.*, 1994; Brumley *et al.*, 1995; Huuskonen & Lindström-Seppä, 1995; Huuskonen *et al.*, 1996). However, recent studies have indicated that changes may also occur in GST isoenzyme patterns, which could have biomarker potential (Martínez-Lara *et al.*, 1996). GST induction has been proposed as a biomarker in mussels (Sheehan *et al.*, 1995), but this has not proved reliable to date (Livingstone *et al.*, 1995; Looise, Holwerda & Foekema, 1996). Inhibition of cholinesterase activities as a biomarker of organophosphate and carbamate pesticide exposure has been used successfully in a number of freshwater and marine fish species (Livingstone, 1993; Yawetz, Mandelis & Fishelson, 1992) and is being adapted for use in mussels (C. Porte, *pers. commun.*). Pro-oxidant and antioxidant measurements in fish and mussels offer potential as biomarkers of contaminant-mediated oxidative stress and free radical damage (Livingstone *et al.*, 1994; Pedrajas, Peinado & López-Barea, 1995; Bainy *et al.*, 1996; Förlin *et al.*, 1996*b*; Palace *et al.*, 1996; Regnoli, Sacucci & Principato, 1996). Finally, two groups of non-catalytic proteins which have attracted considerable biomarker attention in fish and mussels are stress proteins (Sanders, 1993; Luft *et al.*, 1996; Schlenk *et al.*, 1996) and the multi-xenobiotic transport proteins (Kurelec, 1992; Cornwall *et al.*, 1995; Galgani *et al.*, 1996; Minier & Moore, 1996): e.g. in *Mytilus* sp., the former (hsp70) were induced by experimental exposure to TBT (Steinert & Pickwell, 1993), and the latter were indicated to be higher in animals from polluted field sites (Kurelec, Krca & Lucic, 1996).

Acknowledgements

Grateful thanks are expressed for the discussions with coworkers and collaborators. The review was written partly under the auspices of grant EVSV-CT94-0550 (BIOMAR) from the European Community to DRL.

References

Adams, S. M., Jaworska, J. S. & Ham, K. D. (1996). Influence of ecological factors on the relationship between MFO induction and fish growth: bridging the gap using neural networks. *Marine Environmental Research*, 42, 197–201.

Addison, R. F. (1995). Monooxygenase measurements as indicators of pollution in the field. In *Molecular Aspects of Oxidative Drug Metabolizing Enzymes: Their Significance in Environmental Toxicology, Chemical Carcinogenesis and Health*, ed. E. Arinç, J. B. Schenkman & E. Hodgson, NATO ASI Series H: Cell Biology, Vol. 90, pp. 549–65.

Andersson, T., Förlin, L., Härdig, J. & Larsson, Å. (1988). Physiological disturbances in fish living in coastal water polluted with bleached kraft mill effluents. *Canadian Journal of Fisheries and Aquatic Sciences*, 45, 1525–36.

Bailey, G. S., Loveland, P. M., Pereira, C., Pierce, D., Hendricks, J. D. & Groopman, J. D. (1994). Quantitative carcinogenesis and dosimetry in rainbow trout for aflatoxin B1 and aflatoxicol, two aflatoxins that form the same adduct. *Mutation Research*, 313, 25–38.

Bainy, A. C. D., Saito, E., Carvalho, P. S. M. & Junqueira, V. B. C. (1996). Oxidative stress in gill, erythrocytes, liver and kidney of Nile tilapia (*Oreochromis niloticus*) from a polluted site. *Aquatic Toxicology*, 34, 151–62.

Balch, G. C., Metcalfe, C. D. & Huestis, S. Y. (1995). Identification of potential fish carcinogens in sediment from Hamilton Harbour, Ontario, Canada. *Environmental Toxicology and Chemistry*, 14, 79–91.

Balk, L., Larsson, Å. & Förlin, L. (1996). Baseline studies of biomarkers in the female feral perch (*Perca fluviatilis*) as tools in biological monitoring of anthropogenic substances. *Marine Environmental Research*, 42, 203–8.

Bayne, B. L., Addison, R. F., Capuzzo, J. M., Clarke, K. R., Gray, J. S., Moore, M. N. & Warwick, R. M. (1988). An overview of the GEEP workshop. *Marine Ecology Progress Series*, 46, 235–43.

Beyer, J. & Goksøyr, A. (1993). Cytochrome P450 observations in gulf fish. *Marine Pollution Bulletin*, 27, 293–6.

Boon, J. P., Everaarts, J. M., Hillebrand, M. T. J., Eggens, M. J., Pijnenburg, J. & Goksøyr, A. (1992). Changes in levels of hepatic biotransformation enzymes and hemoglobin levels in female plaice (*Pleuronectes platessa*) and after oral administration of a technical polychlorinated biphenyl mixture (Clophen A40). *The Science of the Total Environment*, 114, 113–33.

Boyle, S. M. & James, M. O. (1996). Cross-reactivity of an antibody to spiny lobster P450 2L with microsomes from other species. *Marine Environmental Research*, 42, 1–6.

Brown, R., Van Beneden, R. J. & Clark, G. C. (1995). Identification of two binding proteins for halogenated aromatic hydrocarbons proteins in the hard-shell clam, *Mercenaria mercenaria*. *Archives of Biochemistry and Biophysics*, 319, 217–24.

Brown, R., Clark, G. C., Gardner, G. R. & Van Beneden, R. J. (1996). Identification of dioxin-specific binding proteins in marine bivalves. *Marine Environmental Research*, 42, 7–11.

Brumley, C. M., Haritos, V. S., Ahokas, J. T. & Holdway, D. A. (1995). Validation of biomarkers of marine pollution exposure in sand flathead using Arochlor 1254. *Aquatic Toxicology*, 31, 249–62.

Bucheli, T. D. & Fent, K. (1995). Induction of cytochrome P450 as a biomarker for environmental contamination in aquatic ecosystems. *Critical Reviews in Environmental Science and Technology*, 25, 201–68.

Buhler, D. R. (1995). Cytochrome P450 expression in rainbow trout: an overview. In *Molecular Aspects of Oxidative Drug Metabolizing Enzymes: Their Significance in Environmental Toxicology, Chemical Carcinogenesis and Health*, ed. E. Arinç, J. B. Schenkman & E. Hodgson, NATO ASI Series H: Cell Biology, Vol. 90, pp. 159–80.

Burgeot, T., Bocquéné, G., Pingray, G., Godefroy, D., Legrand, J., Dimeet, J., Marco, F., Vincent, F., Hencocque, Y., Oger Jeanneret, H. & Galgani, F. (1994*a*). Monitoring biological effects of contamination in marine fish along French coasts by measurement of ethoxyresorufin-O-deethylase activity. *Ecotoxicology and Environmental Safety*, 29, 131–47.

Burgeot, T., Bocquéné, G., Truquet, P., Le Dean, L. & Galgani, F. (1994*b*). Induction of EROD activity in red mullet (*Mullus barbatus*) along the French Mediterranean coasts. *The Science of the Total Environment*, 142, 213–30.

Cattani, O., Serra, R., Isani, G., Raggi, G., Cortesi P. & Carpené, E. (1996). Correlation between metallothionein and energy metabolism in sea bass, *Dicentrarchus labrax*, exposed to cadmium. *Comparative Biochemistry and Physiology*, 113C, 193–9.

Celander, M. & Förlin, F. (1995). Decreased responsiveness of the hepatic cytochrome P450 1A1 system in rainbow trout (*Oncorhynchus mykiss*) after prolonged exposure to PCB. *Aquatic Toxicology*, 33, 141–53.

Celander, M., Stegeman, J. J. & Förlin, L. (1996). CYP1A1-, CYP2B- and CYP3A-like proteins in rainbow trout (*Oncorhynchus mykiss*) liver: CYP1A1-specific down-regulation after prolonged exposure to PCB. *Marine Environmental Research*, 42, 283–6.

Cheah, D. M. Y., Wright, P. F. A., Holdway, D. A. & Ahokas, J. T. (1995). *Octopus pallidus* cytochrome P-450: characterisation and induction studies with β-naphthoflavone and Arochlor 1254. *Aquatic Toxicology*, 33, 201–14.

Collier, T. K., Connor, S. D., Eberhart, B. L., Analacion, B. F., Goksøyr, A. & Varanasi, U. (1992a). Using cytochrome P450 to monitor the aquatic environment: initial results from regional and national surveys. *Marine Environmental Research*, 34, 195–9.

Collier, T. K., Singh, S. V., Awasthi, Y. C. & Varanasi, U. (1992b). Hepatic xenobiotic metabolizing enzymes in two species of benthic fish showing different prevalences of contaminant–associated liver neoplasms. *Toxicology and Applied Pharmacology*, 113, 319–24.

Cooper, K. R. (1989). Effects of polychlorinated dibenzo-*p*-dioxins and polychlorinated dibenzofurans on aquatic organisms. *Reviews in Aquatic Sciences*, 1, 227–42.

Cornwall, R., Toomey, B. H., Bard, S., Bacon, C., Jarman, W. M. & Epel, D. (1995). Characterization of multixenobiotic/multidrug transport in the gills of the mussel *Mytilus californianus* and identification of environmental substrates. *Aquatic Toxicology*, 31, 277–96.

Courtenay, S., Grunwald, C., Kreamer, G-L., Alexander, R. & Wirgin, I. (1993). Induction and clearance of cytochrome P4501A mRNA in Atlantic tomcod caged in bleached kraft mill effluent in the Miramichi river. *Aquatic Toxicology*, 27, 225–44.

Croce, B., Stagg, R. M. & Smith, M. (1995). Effects of exposure to a combination of β-naphthoflavone and resins acids on biotransformation enzymes in Atlantic salmon (*Salmo salari*). *Aquatic Toxicology*, 32, 161–76.

Den Besten, P. J., Lemaire, P. & Livingstone, D. R. (1994). NADPH-, NADH- and cumene hydroperoxide-dependent metabolism of benzo[a]pyrene by pyloric caeca microsomes of the sea star, *Asterias rubens* L. (Echinodermata: Asteroidea). *Xenobiotica*, 24, 989–1001.

Eggens, M. L. & Galgani, F. (1992). Ethoxyresorufin 0-deethylase (EROD) activity in flatfish: fast determination with a fluorescence plate-reader. *Marine Environmental Research*, 33, 213–21.

Eggens, M., Bergman, A., Vethaak D., Van der Weiden, M., Celander M. & Boon, J. P. (1995). Cytochrome P4501A indices as biomarkers of contaminant exposure: results of a field study with plaice (*Pleuronectes platessa*) and flounder (*Platichthys flesus*) from the southern North Sea. *Aquatic Toxicology* 32, 211–25.

Elskus, A. A., Pruell, R. & Stegeman, J. J. (1992). Endogenously-mediated pretranslational suppression of cytochrome P4501A in PCB-contaminated flounder. *Marine Environmental Research*, 34, 97–101.

Ericson, G., Åkerman, G., Liewenborg, B. & Balk, L. (1996). Comparison of DNA damage in the early life stages of cod, *Gadus morhua*, originating from the Barents Sea and Baltic Sea. *Marine Environmental Research*, 42, 119–213.

Fair, P. II. (1986). Interaction of benzo(a)pyrene and cadmium on GSH-transferase and benzo(a)pyrene hydroxylase in the black sea bass *Centropristis striata. Archives of Environmental Contamination and Toxicology*, 15, 257–63.

Fent, K. (1996). Ecotoxicology of organotin compounds. *Critical Reviews in Toxicology*, 26, 1–117.

Förlin, L. & Celander, M. (1995). Studies of the inducibility of P4501A in perch from the PCB-contaminated Lake Järnsjön in Sweden. *Marine Environmental Research*, 39, 85–8.

Förlin, L., Andersson, T., Balk, L. & Larsson, Å. (1995). Biochemical and physiological effects in fish exposed to bleached kraft mill effluents. *Ecotoxicology and Environmental Safety*, 30, 164–70.

Förlin, L., Livingstone, D. R., Magnusson, K., Peters, L. D., Solé, M., Sjölin, A. & Granmo, Å. (1996a). Molecular investigations into pollutant impact on roundnose grenadier (*C. rupestris*) and transplanted common mussel (*M. edulis*) in Skagerrak, the North Sea. *Marine Environmental Research*, 42, 209–12.

Förlin, L., Blom, S., Celander, M. & Sturve, J. (1996b). Effects on UDP-gluronosyl transferase, glutathione transferase, DT-diaphorase and glutathione reductase activities in rainbow trout liver after long-term exposure to PCB. *Marine Environmental Research*, 42, 213–16.

Fu, P. P. (1990). Metabolism of nitro-polycyclic aromatic hydrocarbons. *Drug Metabolism Reviews*, 22, 209–68.

Fujiwara, K., Ushiroda T., Takeda K., Kumamoto Y., & Tsubota, H. (1993). Diurnal and seasonal distribution of hydrogen peroxide in seawater of the Seto inland sea. *Geochemical Journal*, 27, 103–15.

Gadagbui, B. K. M. & Goksøyr, A. (1996). Biomarker studies in tilapia (*Oreochromis niloticus*) caged in, and in mudfish (*Clarias anguilaris*) exposed to sediment from a polluted river in Ghana, west Africa. *Marine Environmental Research*, 42, 275–6.

Gadagbui, B. K. M., Addy, M. & Goksøyr, A. (1996). Species characteristics of hepatic biotransformation enzymes in two tropical freshwater teleosts, tilapia (*Oreochromis niloticus*) and mudfish (*Clarias anguilaris*). *Comparative Biochemistry and Physiology*, 114C, 201–11.

Galgani, F., Cornwall, R., Toomey, B. H. & Epel, D. (1996). Interaction of environmental xenobiotics with a multixenobiotic defense mechanism in the bay mussel *Mytilus californianus* from the coast of California. *Environmental Toxicology and Chemistry*, 15, 325–31.

Gardner, G. R., Pruell, R. J. & Malcolm, A. R. (1992). Chemical induction of tumors in oysters by a mixture of aromatic and chlorinated hydrocarbons, amines and metals. *Marine Environmental Research*, 34, 59–63.

George, S. G., Wright, J. & Conroy, J. (1995a). Temporal studies of the impact of the Braer oilspill on inshore feral fish from Shetland, Scotland. *Archives of Environmental Contamination and Toxicology*, 29, 530–4.

George, S. G., Scott, J. & Ellis, S. W. (1995b). Genetically engineered fish cytochromes P-450 from yeasts for aquatic toxicological studies. *Journal of Marine Biotechnology*, 3, 220–3.

George, S. G., Todd, K. & Wright, J. (1996). Regulation of metallothionein in teleosts: induction of MTmRNA and protein by cadmium in hepatic and extrahepatic tissues of a marine flatfish, the turbot (*Scopthalmus maximus*). *Comparative Biochemistry and Physiology*, 113C, 109–15.

Goksøyr, A. (1991). A semi–quantitative cytochrome P4501A1 ELISA: simple method for studying the monooxygenase induction response in environmental monitoring and ecotoxicological testing of fish. *The Science of the Total Environment*, 101, 255–62.

Goksøyr, A. (1995). Use of cytochrome P450 1A (CYP1A) in fish as a biomarker of aquatic pollution. *Archives of Toxicology*, Supplement 17, 80–95.

Goksøyr, A. & Förlin, L. (1992). The cytochrome *P*-450 system in fish, aquatic toxicology and environmental monitoring. *Aquatic Toxicology*, 22, 287–311.

Goksøyr, A., Andersson, T., Buhler, D. R., Stegeman, J. J., Williams, D. E. & Förlin, L. (1991*a*). Immunochemical cross-reactivity of β-naphthoflavone-inducible cytochrome P450 (P450IA) in liver microsomes from different fish species and rat. *Fish Physiology and Biochemistry*, 9, 1–13.

Goksøyr, A., Larsen, H. E. & Husøy, A-M (1991*b*). Application of a cytochrome P-450 1A1-ELISA in environmental monitoring and toxicological testing of fish. *Comparative Biochemistry and Physiology*, 100C, 157–60.

Goksøyr, A., Beyer, J., Husøy, A-M., Larsen, H. E., Westerheim, K., Wilhelmsen, S. & Klungsøyr, J. (1994). Accumulation and effects of aromatic and chlorinated hydrocarbons in juvenile Atlantic cod *(Gadus morhua)* caged in a polluted fjord (Sørfjorden, Norway). *Aquatic Toxicology*, 29, 21–35.

Granmo, Å, Ekelund, R., Magnusson, K. & Berggren, M. (1989). Lethal and sublethal toxicity of 4-nonylphenol to the common mussel (*Mytilus edulis* L.). *Environmental Pollution*, 59, 115–27.

Grzebyk, D. & Galgani, F. (1991). Measurement of the effect of organic pollution on marine organisms: rapid determination with a fluorescence plate-reader. *Aquatic Living Resources*, 4, 53–9.

Haasch, M. L. (1996). Induction of anti-trout lauric acid hydroxylase immunoreactive proteins by peroxisome proliferators in bluegill and catfish. *Marine Environmental Research*, 42, 287–91.

Haasch, M. L., Wejksnora, P. J., Stegeman, J. J. & Lech, J. J. (1989). Cloned rainbow trout liver P_1450 complementary DNA as a potential environmental monitor. *Toxicology and Applied Pharmacology*, 98, 362–8.

Haasch, M. L., Quardokus, E. M., Sutherland, L. A., Goodrich, M. S., Prince, R., Cooper, K. R. & Lech, J. J. (1992). CYP1A1 protein and mRNA in teleosts as an environmental bioindicator: laboratory and environmental studies. *Marine Environmental Research*, 34, 139–45.

Hahn, M. E., Poland, A., Glover, E. & Stegeman, J. J. (1994). Photoaffinity labeling of the Ah receptor: phylogenetic survey of diverse vertebrate and invertebrate species. *Archives of Biochemistry and Biophysics*, 310, 218–28.

Hawker, D. W. & Connell, D. W. (1986). Bioconcentration of lipophilic compounds by some aquatic organisms. *Ecotoxicology and Environmental Safety*, 11, 184–97.

Heffernan, L. M., Ertl, R. P., Stegeman, J. J., Buhler, D. R. & Winston, G. W. (1996). Immuno-detection of proteins by cytochrome P450 antibodies in five species of sea anemones. *Marine Environmental Research*, 42, 353–7.

Hein, N. J. & Kennish, J. M. (1996). Cytochrome P4501A1 induction as a biochemical indicator of pollutant exposure in *Cottus* spp. *Marine Environmental Research*, 42, 276–7.

Hetherington, L. H., Livingstone, D. R. & Walker, C. H. (1996). Two- and one-electron-dependent *in vitro* reductive metabolism of nitroaromatics by *Mytilus edulis*, *Carcinus maenas* and *Asterias rubens*. *Comparative Biochemistry and Physiology*, 113C, 231–9.

Heuchel, R., Radtke, F. & Schaffner, W. (1995). Transcriptional regulation by heavy metals, exemplified at the metallothionein genes. In *Inducible Gene Expression*, Vol. 1, *Environmental Stresses and Nutrients, Progress in Gene Expression*, ed. P. A. Baeuerle, pp. 206–40. Boston: Birkhäuser.

Hodson, P. V., McWhirter, M., Ralph, K., Gray, B., Thivierge, D., Carey, J. H., Van der Kraak, G., Whittle, D. M. & Levesque, M. C. (1992). Effects of bleached kraft mill effluent on fish in the St Maurice river, Quebec. *Environmental Toxicology and Chemistry*, 11, 1635–51.

Holm, G., Lundström, J., Andersson, T. & Norrgren, L. (1994). Influences of halogenated organic substances on ovarian development and hepatic EROD activity in the three-spined stickleback, *Gasterosteus aculeatus*, and rainbow trout, *Oncorhynchus mykiss*. *Aquatic Toxicology*, 29, 241–56.

Huggett, R. J., Kimerle, R. A., Mehrle P. M. Jr. & Bergman, H. L. (eds). (1992). In *Biomarkers. Biochemical, Physiological, and Histological Markers of Anthropogenic Stress*. Boca Raton, Florida: Lewis Publishers.

Huuskonen, S. & Lindström–Seppä, P. (1995). Hepatic cytochrome P4501A and other biotransformation activities in perch (*Perca fluviatilis*): the effects of unbleached pulp mill effluents. *Aquatic Toxicology*, 31, 27–41.

Huuskonen, S., Lindström–Seppä, P., Koponen, K. & Roy, S. (1996). Effects of non-*ortho*-substituted polychlorinated biphenyls (congeners 77 and 126) on cytochrome P4501A and conjugation activities in rainbow trout (*Oncorhynchus mykiss*). *Comparative Biochemistry and Physiology*, 113C, 205–13.

Hylland, K., Sandvik, M., Skåre, U., Beyer, J., Egaas, E. & Goksøyr, A. (1996). Biomarkers in flounder (*Platichthys flesus*): an evaluation of their use in pollution monitoring. *Marine Environmental Research*, 42, 223–7.

Jedamski-Grymlas, J., Lange, U. & Karbe, L. (1994). Induction of the hepatic biotransformation system of the golden ide (*Leuciscus idus* (L.)) after exposure in the river Elbe. *Ecotoxicology and Environmental Safety*, 28, 35–42.

Karchner, S. I. & Hahn, M. E. (1996). A reverse transcription–polymerase chain reaction (RT–PCR) approach for cloning Ah receptors from diverse vertebrate species: partial sequence of an Ah receptor from the teleost *Fundulus heteroclitus*. *Marine Environmental Research*, 42, 13–17.

Khan, M. A. Q., Al-Ghais, S. M. & Al-Marri, S. (1995). Petroleum hydrocarbons in fish from the Arabian Gulf. *Archives of Environmental Contamination and Toxicology*, 29, 517–22.

Kille, P., Kay, J., Leaver, M. & George, S. (1992). Induction of piscine metallothionein as a primary response to heavy metal pollutants: applicability of new sensitive molecular probes. *Aquatic Toxicology*, 22, 279–86.

Kirchin, M. A., Wiseman, A. & Livingstone, D. R. (1992). Seasonal and sex variation in the mixed-function oxygenase system of digestive gland microsomes of the common mussel, *Mytilus edulis* L. *Comparative Biochemistry and Physiology*, 101C, 81–91.

Kling, P., Erkell, L. J., Kille, P. & Olsson, P.-E. (1996). Metallothionein induction in rainbow trout gonadal (RTG-2) cells during free radical exposure. *Marine Environmental Research*, 42, 33–6.

Kurelec, B. (1992). The multixenobiotic resistance mechanism in aquatic organisms. *Critical Reviews in Toxicology*, 22, 23–43.

Kurelec, B. (1993). The genotoxic disease syndrome. *Marine Environmental Research*, 35, 341–8.

Kurelec, B., Krca, S. & Lucic, D. (1996). Expression of multixenobiotic resistance mechanism in a marine mussel *Mytilus galloprovincialis* as a biomarker of exposure to polluted environments. *Comparative Biochemistry and Physiology*, 113C, 283–9.

Lech, J. J., Lewis S. K. & Ren, L. (1996). *In vivo* estrogenic activity of nonylphenol in rainbow trout. *Fundamental and Applied Toxicology*, 30, 229–32.

Lemaire, P. & Livingstone, D. R. (1993). Pro-oxidant/antioxidant processes and organic xenobiotic interactions in marine organisms, in particular the flounder *Platichthys flesus* and the mussel *Mytilus edulis*. In *Trends in Comparative Biochemistry and Physiology*, Vol. 1, pp. 1119–50. Trivandrum, India: Research Trends.

Lemaire, P., Den Besten, P. J., O'Hara, S. C. M. & Livingstone, D. R. (1993). Comparative metabolism of benzo[a]pyrene by digestive gland microsomes of the shore crab *Carcinus maenas* L. and the common mussel *Mytilus edulis* L. *Polycyclic Aromatic Compounds*, 3 (Supplement), 1133–40.

Lindström–Seppä, P. (1988). Biomonitoring of oil spill in a boreal archipelago by xenobiotic biotransformation in perch (*Perca fluviatilis*). *Ecotoxicology and Environmental Safety*, 15, 162–70.

Lindström-Seppä, P. & Oikari, A. (1988). Hepatic xenobiotic biotransformation in fishes exposed to pulpmill effluents. *Water Science and Technology*, 20, 167–70.

Lindström-Seppä, P. & Oikari, A. (1990). Biotransformation activities in feral fish in waters receiving bleached pulp mill effluents. *Environmental Toxicology and Chemistry*, 9, 1415–24.

Lindström-Seppä, P., Huuskonen, S., Pesonen, M., Muona, P. & Hänninen O. (1992). Unbleached pulp mill effluents affect cytochrome P450 monooxygenase enzyme activities. *Marine Environmental Research*, 34, 157–61.

Livingstone, D. R. (1991a). Organic xenobiotic metabolism in marine invertebrates. In *Advances in Comparative and Environmental Physiology*, ed. R. Gilles, Vol. 7, pp. 45–185. Berlin: Springer-Verlag.

Livingstone, D. R. (1991b). Towards a specific index of impact by organic pollution for marine invertebrates. *Comparative Biochemistry and Physiology*, 100C, 151–5.

Livingstone, D. R. (1992). Persistent pollutants in marine invertebrates. In *Persistent Pollutants in Marine Ecosystems*, ed. C. H. Walker & D. R. Livingstone, SETAC Special Publication, pp. 3–34. Oxford: Pergamon Press.

Livingstone, D. R. (1993). Biotechnology and pollution monitoring: use of molecular biomarkers in the aquatic environment. *Journal of Chemical Technology and Biotechnology*, 57, 195–211.

Livingstone, D. R. (1994). Recent developments in marine invertebrate organic xenobiotic metabolism. *Toxicology and Ecotoxicology News*, 1, 88–95.

Livingstone, D. R. (1996a). The fate of organic xenobiotics in aquatic ecosystems: quantitative and qualitative differences in biotransformation by invertebrates and fish. *Comparative Biochemistry and Physiology Part C*, submitted.

Livingstone, D. R. (1996b). Cytochrome P450 in pollution monitoring. Use of cytochrome P4501A (CYP1A) as a biomarker of organic pollution in aquatic and other organisms. In *Environmental Xenobiotics*, ed. M. Richardson, pp. 143–60. London: Taylor & Francis Ltd.

Livingstone, D. R. & Pipe, R. K. (1992). Mussels and environmental contaminants: molecular and cellular aspects. In *The Mussel Mytilus: Ecology, Physiology, Genetics and Culture*, ed. E. Gosling. *Developments in Aquaculture and Fisheries Science,* Vol. 25, pp. 425–64. Amsterdam: Elsevier Science Publishers.

Livingstone, D. R., Kirchin, M. A. & Wiseman, A. (1989). Cytochrome P-450 and oxidative metabolism in molluscs. *Xenobiotica*, 19, 1041–62.

Livingstone, D. R., Donkin, P. & Walker, C. H. (1992). Pollutants in marine ecosystems: an overview. In *Persistent Pollutants in Marine Ecosystems*, ed. C. H. Walker & D. R. Livingstone, SETAC Special Publication, pp. 235–63. Oxford: Pergamon Press.

Livingstone, D. R., Förlin, L. & George, S. D. (1994). Molecular biomarkers and toxic consequences of impact by organic pollution in aquatic organisms. In *Water Quality and Stress Indicators in Marine and Freshwater Systems: Linking Levels of Organisation*, ed. D. W. Sutcliffe, pp. 154–71. Ambleside, UK: Freshwater Biological Association.

Livingstone, D. R., Lemaire, P., Matthews, A., Peters, L. D., Porte, C., Fitzpatrick, P. J., Förlin, L., Nasci, C., Fossato, V., Wootton, N. & Goldfarb, P. (1995). Assessment of the impact of organic pollutants on goby (*Zosterisessor ophiocephalus*) and mussel (*Mytilus galloprovincialis*) from the Venice Lagoon, Italy: biochemical studies. *Marine Environmental Research*, 39, 235–40.

Livingstone, D. R., Nasci, C., Solé, C., Da Ros, L., O'Hara, S. C. M., Peters, L. D., Fossato, V., Wootton, A. N. & Goldfarb, P. S. (1997). Apparent induction of a cytochrome P450 with immunochemical similarities to CYP1A in digestive gland of the common mussel (*Mytilus galloprovincialis* L.) with exposure to 2,2′,3,4,4′,5′-hexachlorobiphenyl and Arochlor 1254. *Aquatic Toxicology*, 38, 205–24.

Looise, B. A. S., Holwerda, D. A. & Foekema, E. M. (1996). Induction of glutathione S-transferase in the freshwater bivalve *Spaerium corneum* as a biomarker for short-term toxicity tests? *Comparative Biochemistry and Physiology*, 113C, 101–7.

Luft, J. C., Wilson, M. R., Bly, J. E., Miller, N. W. & Clem, L. W. (1996). Identification and characterization of a heat shock protein 70 family member in channel catfish (*Ictalurus punctatus*). *Comparative Biochemistry and Physiology*, 113B, 169–74.

Maccubbin, A. E. (1994). DNA adduct formation analysis in fish: laboratory and field studies. In *Aquatic Toxicology. Molecular, Biochemical, and Cellular Perspectives*, ed. D. C. Malins & G. K. Ostrander, pp. 241–65. Boca Raton, Florida: Lewis Publishers.

Martínez-Lara, E., Toribio, F., López-Barea, J. & Bárcena, J. A. (1996). Glutathione-S-transferase isoenzyme patterns in the gilthead seabream (*Sparus aurata*) exposed to environmental contaminants. *Comparative Biochemistry and Physiology*, 113C, 215–20.

McCarthy, J. F. & Shugart, L. R. (eds). (1990). *Biomarkers of Environmental Contamination*. Boca Raton, Florida: Lewis Publishers.

Melacon, M. J., Yeo, S. E. & Lech, J. J. (1987). Induction of hepatic microsomal monooxygenase activity in fish by exposure to river water. *Environmental Toxicology and Chemistry*, 6, 127–35.

Michel, X. R., Cassand, P. M., Ribera, D. G. & Narbonne, J. F. (1992). Metabolism and mutagenic activation of benzo[a]pyrene by subcellular fractions from mussel (*Mytilus galloprovincialis*) digestive gland and sea bass (*Dicentrarchus labrax*) liver. *Comparative Biochemistry and Physiology*, 103C, 43–55.

Michel X. R., Suteau, P., Roberston, L. W. & Narbonne, J. F. (1993). Effects of benzo(a)pyrene, 3,3′,4,4′-tetrachlorobiphenyl and 2,2′,4,4′,5,5′-hexachlorobiphenyl on the xenobiotic-metabolizing enzyme in the mussel (*Mytilus galloprovincialis*). *Aquatic Toxicology*, 27, 335–44.

Michel, X., Salaun, J. P., Galgani, F. & Narbonne, J. F. (1994). Benzo(a)pyrene hydroxylase activity in the marine mussel *Mytilus galloprovincialis*: a potential marker of contamination by polycyclic aromatic hydrocarbon-type compounds. *Marine Environmental Research*, **38**, 257–73.

Miller, M. R., Stanley, R. M., Stansberry, P. G., Stamm, S. C. & Stiller, A. H. (1996). Induction of CYP1A in Japanese medaka exposed to carbonaceous pitches via water. *Marine Environmental Research*, **42**, 235–9.

Minier, C. & Moore, M. N. (1996). Induction of multixenobiotic resistance in mussel blood cells. *Marine Environmental Research*, **42**, 389–92.

Monod, G., Boudry, M.-A. & Gillet, C. (1996). Biotransformation enzymes and their induction by β-naphthoflavone during embryolarval development in salmonid species. *Comparative Biochemistry and Physiology*, **114C**, 45–50.

Moore, M. J. & Myers, M. S. (1994). Pathobiology of chemical-associated neoplasia in fish. In *Aquatic Toxicology. Molecular, Biochemical, and Cellular Perspectives*, ed. D. C. Malins & G. K. Ostrander, pp. 327–86. Boca Raton, Florida: Lewis Publishers.

Munkittrick, K. R., Portt, C. B., Van der Kraak, G. J., Smith, I. R. & Rokosh, D. A. (1991). Impact of bleached kraft mill effluent on population characteristics, liver MFO activity, and serum steroid levels of a Lake Superior white sucker (*Catostomus commersoni*) population. *Canadian Journal of Fisheries and Aquatic Sciences*, **48**, 1371–80.

Munkittrick, K. R., Van der Kraak, G. J., McMaster, M. E. & Portt, C. B. (1992). Response of hepatic MFO activity and plasma sex steroids to secondary treatment of bleached kraft pulp mill effluent and mill shutdown. *Environmental Toxicology and Chemistry*, **11**, 1427–39.

Narbonne, J. F., Garrigues, P., Ribera, D., Raoux, C., Mathieu, A., Lemaire, P., Salaun, P. & Lafaurie, M. (1991). Mixed–function oxygenase enzymes as tools for pollution monitoring: field studies on the French coast of the Mediterranean Sea. *Comparative Biochemistry and Physiology*, **100C**, 37–42.

Nebert, D. W. & Gonzalez, F. J. (1987). P-450 genes: structure, evolution and regulation. *Annual Review of Biochemistry*, **56**, 945–93.

Neff, J. M. (1979). *Polycyclic Aromatic Hydrocarbons in the Aquatic Environment. Sources, Fates and Biological Effects.* London: Applied Science Publishers.

Nelson, D. R., Koymans, L., Kamataki, T., Stegeman, J. J., Feyereisen, R., Waxman, D. J., Waterman, M. R., Gotoh, O., Coon, M. J., Estabrook, R. W., Gunslus, I. C. & Nebert, D. W. (1996). P450 superfamily: update on new sequences, gene mapping, accession numbers and nomenclature. *Pharmacogenetics*, **6**, 1–42.

Nimrod, A. C. & Benson, W. H. (1996). Environmental estrogenic effects of alkylphenol ethoxylates. *Critical Reviews in Toxicology*, **26**, 335–64.

Oikari, A. & Jimenez, B. (1992). Effects of hepatotoxicants on the induction of microsomal monooxygenase activity in sunfish liver by β-naphthoflavone and benzo[a]pyrene. *Ecotoxicology and Environmental Safety*, **23**, 89–102.

Okamoto, T., Mitsuhashi, M., Fujita, I., Sindhu R. K. & Kikkawa, Y. (1993). Induction of cytochrome P450 1A1 and 1A2 by hyperoxia. *Biochemical and Biophysical Research Communications*, **197**, 878–85.

Palace, V. P., Dick, T. A., Brown, S. B., Baron, C. L. & Klaverkamp, J. F. (1996). Oxidative stress in lake sturgeon (*Acipenser fulvescens*) orally exposed to 2,3,7,8-tetrachloro-dibenzofuran. *Aquatic Toxicology*, **35**, 79–92.

Parrott, J. L., Hodson, P. V. & Dixon, D. G. (1995). Rainbow trout hepatic mixed–function oxygenase induction by polychlorinated dibenzo-*p*-dioxins (PCDDs) as a function of time and tissue concentration. *Journal of Toxicology and Environmental Health*, **46**, 301–16.

Pathiratne, A. & George, S. (1996). Comparison of xenobiotic metabolizing enzymes of *Tilapia* with those of other fish species and interspecies relationships between gene families. *Marine Environmental Research*, **42**, 293–6.

Pedrajas, J. R., Peinado, J. & López-Barea, J. (1995). Oxidative stress in fish exposed to model xenobiotics. Oxidatively modified forms of Cu, Zn-superoxide dismutase as potential biomarkers. *Chemico-Biological Interactions*, **98**, 267–82.

Peters, L. D. & Livingstone, D. R. (1995). Studies of cytochrome P4501A in early life stages of turbot (*Scophthalmus maximus* L.). *Marine Environmental Research*, **39**, 5–9.

Peters, L. D., Morse, H. R., Waters, R. & Livingstone, D. R. (1996). Responses of hepatic cytochrome P450 1A and formation of DNA-adducts in juveniles of turbot (*Scophthalmus maximus* L.) exposed to water-borne benzo[a]pyrene. *Aquatic Toxicology*, in press.

Poellinger, L. (1995). Mechanism of signal transduction by the basic helix-loop-helix dioxin receptor. In *Inducible Gene Expression*, Vol. 1, *Environmental Stresses and Nutrients*, Progress in Gene Expression, ed. P. A. Baeuerle, pp. 177–205. Boston: Birkhäuser.

Porte, C. & Albaigés, J. (1993). Bioaccumulation patterns of hydrocarbons and polychlorinated biphenyls in bivalves, crustaceans, and fishes. *Archives of Environmental Contamination and Toxicology*, **26**, 273–81.

Porte, C., Lemaire, P., Peters, L. D. & Livingstone, D. R. (1995). Partial purification and properties of cytochrome P450 from digestive gland microsomes of the common mussel, *Mytilus edulis* L. *Marine Environmental Research*, **39**, 27–31.

Price, D., Worsfold, P. J. & Mantoura, R. F. C. (1992). Hydrogen peroxide in the marine environment: cycling and methods of analysis. *Trends in Analytical Chemistry*, **11**, 379–84.

Rainio, K., Linko, R. R. & Ruotsila, L. (1986). Polycyclic aromatic hydrocarbons in mussel and fish from the Finnish Archipelago Sea. *Bulletin of Environmental Contamination and Toxicology*, **37**, 337–43.

Rand, G. (ed.) (1995). *Fundamentals of Aquatic Toxicology. Effects, Environmental Fate, and Risk Assessment*. London: Taylor and Francis.

Raza, H., Otaiba, A. & Montague, W. (1995). β-naphthoflavone-inducible cytochrome P4501A1 activity in liver microsomes of the marine safi fish (*Siganus canaliculatus*). *Biochemical Pharmacology*, **50**, 1401–6.

Regnoli, F., Sacucci, F. & Principato, G. (1996). Mussel glyoxylase I as a possible marker for ecotoxicological studies: preliminary characterization. *Comparative Biochemistry and Physiology*, **113C**, 313–17.

Rhodes, L. D. & Van Beneden, R. J. (1996). Application of differential display polymerase chain reaction to the study of neoplasms of feral marine bivalves. *Marine Environmental Research*, **42**, 81–5.

Rodriguez-Ariza, A., Abril, N., Navas, J. I., Dorado, G., López-Barea, J. & Pueyo, C. (1992). Metal, mutagenicity, and biochemical studies on bivalve molluscs from Spanish coasts. *Environmental and Molecular Mutagenesis*, **19**, 112–24.

Rotchell, J. M., Stagg, R. M. & Craft, J. A. (1995). Chemically-induced genetic damage in fish: isolation and characterization of the dab (*Limanda limanda*) *ras* gene. *Marine Pollution Bulletin*, **31**, 457–9.

Routledge, E. J. & Sumpter, J. P. (1996). Estrogenic activity of surfactants and some of their degradation products assessed using a recombinant yeast screen. *Environmental Toxicology and Chemistry*, 15, 241–8.

Roy, N. K., Kreamer, G.-L., Konkle, B., Grunwald, C. & Wirgin, I. (1995). Characterization and prevalence of a polymorphism in the 3′ untranslated region of cytochrome P4501A1 in cancer-prone Atlantic tomcod. *Archives of Biochemistry and Biophysics*, 322, 204–13.

Sanders, B. M. (1993). Stress proteins in aquatic organisms: an environmental perspective. *Critical Reviews in Toxicology*, 23, 49–75.

Schlenk, D. (1994). The effects of 2-methylisoborneol on cytochrome P450 expression in the channel catfish (*Ictalurus punctatus*). *Aquaculture*, 120, 33–44.

Schlenk, D. (1996). The role of biomarkers in risk assessment. *Human and Ecological Risk Assessment*, 2, 251–6.

Schlenk, D. & Buhler, D. R. (1989). Determination of multiple forms of cytochrome P-450 in microsomes from digestive gland of *Cryptochiton stelleri*. *Biochemical and Biophysical Research Communications*, 163, 476–80.

Schlenk, D., Perkins, E. J., Layher, W. G. & Zhang, Y. S. (1996). Correlating metrics of fish health with cellular indicators of stress in an Arkansas bayou. *Marine Environmental Research*, 42, 247–51.

Sheehan, D., McIntosh, J., Power, A. & Fitzpatrick, P. J. (1995). Drug metabolizing enzymes of mussels as bioindicators of chemical pollution. *Biochemical Society Transactions*, 23, 419–22.

Sleiderink, H. M. & Boon, J. P. (1995). Cytochrome P450 1A response in North Sea dab, *Linanda limanda*, from offshore and coastal sites. *Marine Pollution Bulletin*, 30, 660–6.

Sleiderink, H. M. & Boon, J. P. (1996). Temporal induction pattern of hepatic cytochrome P450 1A in thermally acclimated dab (*Limanda limanda*) treated with 3,3′,4,4′-tetrachlorobiphenyl (CB77). *Chemosphere*, 32, 2335–44.

Sleiderink, H. M., Everaarts, J. M., Goksøyr, A. & Boon, J. P. (1995a). Hepatic cytochrome P450 1A induction in dab (*Limanda limanda*) after oral dosing with the polychlorinated biphenyl mixture Clophen A40. *Environmental Toxicology and Chemistry*, 14, 679–87.

Sleiderink, H. M., Beyer, J., Scholtens, E., Sleiderink, H. M., Nieuwenhuize, J., Van Liere, J. M., Everaarts, J. M. & Boon, J. P. (1995b). Influence of temperature and polyaromatic contaminants on CYP1A levels in North Sea dab (*Limanda limanda*). *Aquatic Toxicology*, 32, 189–209.

Soimasuo, R., Jokinen, I., Kukkonen, J., Petänen, T., Ristola, T. & Oikari, A. (1995). Biomarker responses along a pollution gradient: effects of pulp and paper mill effluents on caged whitefish. *Aquatic Toxicology*, 31, 329–45.

Solé, M., Porte, C. & Albaigés, J. (1995a). The use of biomarkers for assessing the effects of organic pollution in mussels. *The Science of the Total Environment*, 159, 147–53.

Solé, M., Porte, C. & Albaigés, J. (1995b). Seasonal variation in the mixed-function oxygenase system and antioxidant enzymes of the mussel *Mytilus galloprovincialis*. *Environmental and Toxicology and Chemistry*, 14, 157–64.

Solé, M., Porte, C., Biosca, X., Mitchelmore, C., Chipman, J. K., Livingstone, D. R. & Albaigés, J. (1996). Effects of the 'Aegean Sea' oil spill on biotransformation enzymes, oxidative stress and DNA-adducts in digestive gland of the mussel (*Mytilus edulis* L.). *Comparative Biochemistry and Physiology*, 113C, 257–65.

Speer, K., Steeg, E., Horstmann, P., Kühn, Th. & Montag, A. (1990). Determination and distribution of polycyclic aromatic hydrocarbons in native vegetable oils, smoked fish products, mussels and oysters, and bream from the River Elbe. *Journal of High Resolution Chromatography*, **13**, 104–11.

Spies, R. B., Stegeman, J. J., Hinton, D. E., Woodin, B., Smolowitz, R., Okihiro, M. & Shea, D. (1996). Biomarkers of hydrocarbon exposure and sublethal effects in embiotocid fishes from a natural petroleum seep in the Santa Barbara channel. *Aquatic Toxicology*, **34**, 195–219.

Stagg, R. M. (1991). North Sea task force biological effects monitoring programme. *Water Science Technology*, **24**, 87–98.

Stegeman, J. J. (1989). Cytochrome P-450 forms in fish: catalytic, immunological and sequence similarities. *Xenobiotica*, **19**, 1093–110.

Stegeman, J. J. (1992). Nomenclature for hydrocarbon-inducible cytochrome P450 in fish. *Marine Environmental Research*, **34**, 133–8.

Stegeman, J. J. (1995). Diversity and regulation of cytochrome P450 in aquatic organisms. In *Molecular Aspects of Oxidative Drug Metabolizing Enzymes: Their Significance in Environmental Toxicology, Chemical Carcinogenesis and Health*, ed. E. Arinç, J. B. Schenkman & E. Hodgson, NATO ASI Series H: Cell Biology, Vol. 90, pp. 135–58.

Stegeman, J. J. & Hahn, M. E. (1994). Biochemistry and molecular biology of monooxygenases: current perspectives on forms, functions, and regulation of cytochrome P450 in aquatic species. In *Aquatic Toxicology. Molecular, Biochemical, and Cellular Perspectives*, ed. D. C. Malins & G. K. Ostrander, pp. 87–206. Boca Raton, Florida: Lewis Publishers.

Stegeman, J. J., Kloeper-Sams, P. J. & Farrington, J. W. (1986). Monooxygenase induction and chlorobiphenyls in the deep-sea fish *Coryphaenoides armatus*. *Science*, **231**, 1287–9.

Stein, J. E., Reichert, W. L., French, B. & Varanasi, U. (1993). ^{32}P-postlabeling analysis of DNA adduct formation and persistence in English sole (*Pleuronectes vetulus*) exposed to benzo[a]pyrene and 7H-dibenzo[c,g]carbazole. *Chemico-Biological Interactions*, **88**, 55–69.

Steinert, S. A. & Pickwell, G. V. (1993). Induction of HSP70 proteins in mussels by ingestion of tributyltin. *Marine Environmental Research*, **35**, 89–93.

Stohs, S. J. & Bagchi, D. (1995). Oxidative mechanisms in the toxicity of metal ions. *Free Radical Biology and Medicine*, **18**, 321–36.

Teuissen, Y., Geraerts, W. P. M., Van Heerikhuizen, H., Planta, R. J. & Joosse, J. (1992). Molecular cloning of a cDNA encoding a member of a novel cytochrome P450 family in the mollusc *Lymnaea stagnalis*. *Journal of Biochemistry*, **112**, 249–52.

Timbrell, J. A. (1996). Editorial: *Biomarkers*, **1**, 1–2.

Tjärnlund, U., Ericson, G., Lindesjöö, E., Petterson, I., Åkerman, G. & Balk, L. (1996). Further studies of the effects of exhaust from two-stroke outboard motors on fish. *Marine Environmental Research*, **42**, 267–71.

Torten, M., Liu, Z., Okihiro, M. S., The, S. J. & Hinton, D. E. (1996). Induction of *ras* oncogene mutations and hepatocarcinogenesis in medaka (*Oryzias latipes*) exposed to diethylnitrosamine. *Marine Environmental Research*, **42**, 93–8.

Tuvikene, A., Huuskonen, S., Roy, S. & Lindström-Seppä, P. (1996). Biomonitoring of south Estonian waters by means of xenobiotic metabolism of rainbow trout (*Oncorhynchus mykiss*) liver. *Comparative Biochemistry and Physiology*, **114C**, 171–7.

Van Beneden, R. J. (1993). Oncogenes. In *Biochemistry and Molecular Biology of Fishes*, Vol. 2 *Molecular Biology Frontiers*, ed. P. W. Hochachka & T. P. Mommsen, pp. 113–36. Amsterdam: Elsevier.

Van Beneden, R. J. & Ostrander, G. K. (1994). Expression of oncogenes and tumor suppression genes in teleost fish. In *Aquatic Toxicology. Molecular, Biochemical, and Cellular Perspectives*, ed. D. C. Malins & G. K. Ostrander, pp. 295–325. Boca Raton, Florida: Lewis Publishers.

Van Beneden, R. J., Gardner, G. R., Blake, N. J. & Blair, D. G. (1993). Implications for the presence of transforming genes in gonadal tumors in two bivalve mollusc species. *Cancer Research*, 53, 2976–9.

Van der Oost, R., Opperhuizen, A., Satumalay, K., Heida, H. & Vermeulen, N. P. E. (1996). Biomonitoring aquatic pollution with feral eel (*Anguilla anguilla*). I. Bioaccumulation: biota-sediment ratios of PCBs, OCPs, PCDDs and PCDFs. *Aquatic Toxicology*, 35, 21–46.

Van Veld, P. A. (1990). Absorption and metabolism of dietary xenobiotics by the intestine of fish. *Reviews in Aquatic Sciences*, 2, 185–203.

Van Veld, P. A., Ko, U., Vogelbein, W. K. & Westbrook, D. J. (1991). Glutathione S-transferase in intestines, liver and hepatic lesions of mummichog (*Fundulus heteroclitus*) from a creosote-contaminated environment. *Fish Physiology and Biochemistry*, 9, 369–76.

Varanasi, U. (ed.) (1989). *Metabolism of Polycyclic Aromatic Hydrocarbons in the Aquatic Environment*. Boca Raton, Florida: CRC Press.

Varanasi, U., Stein, J. E., Reichert, W. I., Tilbury, K. L., Krahn, M. M. & Chan, S. L. (1992). Chlorinated and aromatic hydrocarbons in bottom sediments, fish and marine mammals in US coastal waters: laboratory and field studies of metabolism and accumulation. In *Persistent Pollutants in Marine Ecosystems*, ed. C. H. Walker & D. R. Livingstone, SETAC Special Publication, pp. 83–115. Oxford: Pergamon Press.

Venier, P. & Canova, S. (1996). Formation of DNA adducts in the gill tissue of *Mytilus galloprovincialis* treated with benzo[a]pyrene. *Aquatic Toxicology*, 34, 119–33.

Viganò, L., Arillo, A., Bagnasco, M., Bennicelli, C. & Melodia, F. (1994). Time course of xenobiotic biotransformation enzyme activities of rainbow trout caged in the River Po. *The Science of the Total Environment*, 151, 37–46.

Vignier, V., Vandermeulen, J. H. & Mossman, D. (1996). Assay conditions and basal activity of CYP1A-dependent mixed-function oxidase in parr and smolt of Atlantic salmon. *Comparative Biochemistry and Physiology*, 113C, 325–30.

Vindimian, E. & Garric, J. (1989). Freshwater fish cytochrome P450-dependent enzymatic activities: a chemical pollution indicator. *Ecotoxicology and Environmental Safety*, 18, 277–85.

Walker, C. H. & Livingstone, D. R. (eds.) (1992). *Persistent Pollutants in Marine Ecosystems*, SETAC Special Publication. Oxford: Pergamon Press.

Washburn, B. S., Vines, C. A., Baden, D. G., Hinton, D. E. & Walsh, P. J. (1996). Differential effects of brevetoxin and β-naphthoflavone on xenobiotic metabolizing enzymes in striped bass (*Morone saxatilis*). *Aquatic Toxicology*, 35, 1–10.

Weinstein, J. E. (1995). Seasonal responses of the mixed-function oxygenase system in the American oyster, *Crassostrea virginica* (Gmelin 1791), to urban-derived polycyclic aromatic hydrocarbons. *Comparative Biochemistry and Physiology*, 112C, 299–307.

Whitlock, J. P. Jr. (1993). Mechanistic aspects of dioxin action. *Chemical Research and Toxicology*, 6, 754–63.

Widdows, J. & Donkin, P. (1992). Mussels and environmental contaminants: bioaccumulation and physiological aspects. In *The Mussel Mytilus: Ecology, Physiology, Genetics and*

Culture, ed. E. Gosling, *Developments in Aquaculture and Fisheries Science,* Vol. 25, pp. 383–424. Amsterdam: Elsevier Science Publishers.

Wirgin, I. I., Kreamer, G. L., Grunwald, C., Squibb, K., Garte, S. J. & Courtenay, S. (1992). Effects of prior exposure history on cytochrome P4501A mRNA induction by PCB congener 77 in Atlantic tomcod. *Marine Environmental Research,* **34,** 103–8.

Wolkers, J., Jørgensen, E. H., Nijmeijer, S. M. & Witkamp, R. F. (1996). Time-dependent induction of two distinct hepatic P4501A catalytic activities at low temperatures in Arctic charr (*Salvelinus alpinus*) after oral exposure to benzo(a)pyrene. *Aquatic Toxicology,* **35,** 127–38.

Wootton, A. N., Herring, C., Spry, A. J., Wiseman, A., Livingstone, D. R. & Goldfarb, P. S. (1995). Evidence for the existence of cytochrome P450 gene families (*CYP1A1,* 3A, 4A1, 11A1) and modulation of gene expression (*CYP1A1*) in the mussel *Mytilus* sp. *Marine Environmental Research,* **39,** 21–6.

Wootton, A. N., Goldfarb, P. S., Lemaire, P., O'Hara, S. C. M. & Livingstone, D. R. (1996). Characterisation of the presence and seasonal variation of a CYP1A-like enzyme in digestive gland of the common mussel, *Mytilus edulis. Marine Environmental Research,* **42,** 297–301.

Yang, C. S. & Smith, T. J. (1995). Modulation of xenobiotic metabolism and toxicity by dietary chemical. In *Molecular Aspects of Oxidative Drug Metabolizing Enzymes: Their Significance in Environmental Toxicology, Chemical Carcinogenesis and Health,* ed. E. Arinç, J. B. Schenkman & E. Hodgson, NATO ASI Series H: Cell Biology, Vol. 90, pp. 249–59.

Yang, M. S. & Thompson, J. A. J. (1996). Binding of endogenous copper and zinc to cadmium-induced metal-binding proteins in various tissues of *Perna viridis. Archives of Environmental Contamination and Toxicology,* **30,** 267–73.

Yawetz, A., Mandelis, R. & Fishelson, L. (1992). The effects of Arochlor 1254 and petrochemical pollutants on cytochrome P-450 from the digestive gland of four species of Mediterranean molluscs. *Comparative Biochemistry and Physiology,* **103C,** 607–14.

Yawetz, A., Mandelis, R. & Gasith, A. (1993). Cholinesterase enzymatic profiles and the exposure of fish to organophosphorous and carbamate pesticides in Israel. *Water Science Technology,* **27,** 465–72.

Zaroogian, G. E., Heltshe, J. F. & Johnson, M. (1985). Estimation of bioconcentration in marine species using structure–activity relationships. *Environmental Toxicology and Chemistry,* **4,** 3–12.

Part II
Ecotoxicology and bioremediation

7

Use of non-indigenous organisms for bioremediation: the promise and concern

R. R. Colwell

7.1 Introduction

Bioremediation offers the most realistic approach for dealing with waste management and waste problems, problems that will only increase as the world population grows (currently six billion people, projected to be ten billion at the end of the next century) and as societies become more technology based. Until the start of the industrial revolution, our species produced little waste, and most of it was biodegradable. However, after the industrial revolution began, manufacturing and mass production and marketing (toxic pollution sources) resulted in increased types and amounts of toxic waste materials, many of them aromatic compounds (Field *et al.*, 1995). These aromatic compounds, most of them anthropogenic in origin, form a major class of recalcitrant toxic wastes with which we must cope, but other waste products (biomass, gaseous air pollutants, heavy metals, hydrocarbons, plastics, and fertilizers, etc.) are also accumulating, causing harm to our planet and representing a threat to public health (Lean & Hinrichsen, 1994).

The Chemical Manufacturers Association (CMA) has published figures indicating that its member companies reduced environmental toxic release through waste management by approximately 49% between 1987 and 1993 (Ember, 1995). This is a step in the right direction, but the figure does not include releases by non-CMA member companies and by end-users: using *all* its waste products to produce electricity is a positive and even attainable goal, but, we're a long way from reaching that goal.

Methods used historically to handle wastes have created problems of their own. Incineration pollutes the air, burial at sea pollutes the oceans, and landfills and underground burial have been found to be sources of toxic gases and groundwater pollution.

For example, one of New York City's landfills, a 2200-acre site, has been in use since 1948 and releases approximately one million gallons per day of leachate (Fig.

Fig. 7.1. A New York City landfill.

7.1) containing ammonia, metals and organic material, into surface water (NYC Reports, 1994). Asia has some of the world's most polluted river systems, with pollution resulting from industrial, agricultural, human, and animal wastes. Some of Malaysia's rivers are so polluted they are considered to be 'biologically dead' (Lean & Hinrichsen, 1994). Oil slicks cover the oceans and seas surrounding North America, Africa, Europe and much of Asia, and there are deep-sea dump sites off the coasts of western Europe, north-eastern North America, Japan and South Africa (Lean & Hinrichsen, 1994).

The more that is learnt about the effects of profligate methods of chemical use and disposal, the more urgent it becomes to devise ecologically sound alternatives. For example, recent reports indicate that PCBs (polychlorinated biphenyls) are more dangerous to human physiology than was suspected, potentially lowering sperm counts through alteration of thyroid hormone function (Stone, 1995). Other reports indicate that increased methylbromide (CH_3Br, MeBr) in the atmosphere, resulting in part from 'large-scale biomass burning', and fumigation of the soil with MeBr, may be one of the many factors contributing to loss of the Earth's ozone layer (Yagi et al., 1995).

Problems left to future generations to solve include ocean-dumped wastes. Recent work at a dump site off New York City, DW 106, shows the residual effect of sludge dumping at this deep-sea site. Even at 2500 m, the material reaches bottom and remains recalcitrant.

Today's newspapers, contain accounts of environmental crises, but any discussion of biological means to remediate the vast pollution problems is left to the experts: we have a responsibility to educate the public.

7.2 Natural bioremediation processes overwhelmed

The natural processes of bioremediation, if left alone to deal with the problems, are overwhelmed by the rate of production of toxic and waste products. For example, in 1994, the world output of thermoplastic resins, which include low-density polyethylene, polyvinylchloride (PVC) and copolymers, high-density polyethylene, polystyrene, and polypropylene, reached c. 50 billion pounds weight (Kirschner, 1995). Although not necessarily toxic, most of these polymers are recalcitrant to bacterial or fungal degradation (Alexander, 1994).

Micro-organisms, the janitors of the Earth, cannot do their jobs unassisted, although we historically have expected them to do so (Atlas, 1995). As research continues, we have found many surprises and many not-so-surprising facts. Naturally occurring organisms are capable of detoxifying some of our most dangerous or recalcitrant materials. *Pseudomonas* spp. can completely degrade nitroaromatics, such as 2,6-dinitrophenol (DNP) or 2,4,6-trinitrotoluene (TNT), after removal of the nitro group in the presence of oxygen. Other species of *Pseudomonas* spp. will completely mineralize 2-, 3-, or 4-nitrobenzoate (NBA) after removal of the nitro group via reduction through addition of NADPH (Marvin-Sikkema & de Bont, 1994).

Acinetobacter spp. can destroy highly chlorinated PCBs, although often they may do so only through the first mineralization steps. *Arthrobacter* spp. mineralizes both naphthalene and hexadecane dissolved in a non-aqueous phase liquid (NAPL) by attaching to the interface between the NAPL and water. *Arthrobacter* spp. also inactivate the herbicide, isopropyl *N*-phenylcarbamate (Alexander, 1994).

o- and *p*-toluidines, by-products of TNT manufacturing, can be completely mineralized aerobically by species of *Rhodococcus* and *Pseudomonas* (Gorontzy *et al.*, 1994). *Rhodococcus chlorophenolicus* can mineralize pentachlorophenol (PCP) (Alexander, 1994).

Among the fungi, the white rot fungus, *Phanerochaete chrysosporium*, can degrade lignin, a complex, stereochemically irregular, structural polymer found in wood (not a source of carbon for the fungus) in an extracellular process, via lignin peroxidases. As a result of the non-specificity of this process, this fungus may be used to degrade many toxic environmental pollutants, including the polycyclic aromatic hydrocarbons (PAHs), chlorinated aromatics, pesticides, munition-chemicals, cyanides, azides and other compounds (Barr & Aust, 1994). The fungus, *P. sordida*, is capable of biodegrading PCP and PAHs (Lamar & Glaser, 1994). *P. chrysosporium*, two other species of white-rot fungi (*Pleurotus ostreatus* and *Trametes versicolor*) and the brown-rot fungus, *Gleophyllum trabeum*, can break down a lignin/styrene copolymer and a polystyrene homopolymer (Milstein *et al.*, 1994). Even protozoa, which tend to affect bacterial biodegradation negatively because they feed upon the bacteria, conversely have been found to assist in the degradative activity of some bacteria. For example, some of the ciliates and flagellates excrete P or N, enriching the bacterial medium (Alexander, 1994).

7.3 Micro-organisms work in consortia

In nature, micro-organisms do not generally work alone, but in consortia, with different species carrying out different metabolic processes. Among our best hopes for alleviating some of the Earth's pollution problems are judicious use of naturally occurring and artificially constructed microbial consortia. In order to best utilize these consortia, we must elucidate how they function together, particularly in the field. It is now proved that augmentation of bacteria with oxygen and nutrients can be successful. However, the degradative metabolic pathways used by these organisms must be elucidated for optimum utilization.

One of the important factors that must be considered in setting up microbial consortia for bioremediation of toxic chemicals is the energetics of the degradative reaction. Field *et al.* (1995) offer the example of the energetics of the degradation of benzoate. Aerobic reduction and anaerobic nitrate and iron reduction produce the greatest energy yields available to the micro-organisms. The energy yields are dependent upon the terminal electron receptor. Thus, electron receptors may determine the degree of bacterial colony growth. The methanogenic dechlorination of 3-chlorobenzoate is carried out via a consortium of microbes that includes *Desulfomonile tiedjeii*, which carries out reductive dechlorination but is dependent upon H_2 transfer by another species of bacteria capable of oxidation of benzoate to acetate, hydrogen, and CO_2 (Field *et al.*, 1995).

Recent metabolic studies have shown that anaerobic degradation of aromatic compounds such as phenylacetic acid, phenol and toluene, proceeds to production of benzoyl-CoA, which, in turn, will undergo anaerobic degradation (Morris, 1994). The reactions require microbial consortia.

Unfortunately, not enough is known about functions within consortia. The bioenergetics and metabolic needs of the organisms involved must be studied in order to increase the likelihood of optimum activity of the consortia (Alexander, 1994). For example, toxins present in the environment in small quantities may be especially difficult to destroy microbially because the substrate may not contain enough of a given nutrient, such as C or P, to be utilized for colony growth. Although the micro-organisms may utilize the toxic material as a source of nutrition, they do so at a rate that may be undetectable and that may result in no net growth of biomass of the microbial colony. Once the microbial colony receives enough nutrients to allow for reproduction of bacterial cells and growth of colony biomass, increased degradation will ensue. Nevertheless, increased understanding of the nutritional needs of these consortia is required to control the amounts of nutrients (allowing for colonial increase).

Morris proposes that consortia be 'precustomized', with addition of specialized microbes into granular masses of bacteria for bioremediation (Morris, 1994). Other methods of 'precustomization' include introduction of members of the hyper-thermophilic *Archaea* spp., or enzymes from the *Archaea* spp., into consortia used in high-temperature transformations.

Biotechnology-based methods may be used to good advantage to improve biodegradative processes. Biofilms with immobilized communities of micro-organisms offer a mechanism for introduction of biodegradative micro-organisms to a site for remediation. In biofilters, such as those used to scrub fouled air, biofilms are wet layers formed on the packing material where micro-organisms attach. These biofilters may contain soil, compost, wood chips, or other supporting surface areas for the micro-organisms (Saberiyan *et al.*, 1994). In trickling filters, polluted water may be run through a bioreactor that is supplemented with nutrients (Alexander, 1994). Often, in bioremediation, *in situ*, the naturally occurring microbial flora need assistance in the form of addition of oxygen or other nutrients to break down the pollutants. In these cases, especially with polluted groundwater, the nutrients are introduced into the subsurface water, which is then pumped through a biofilter at the surface.

7.4 Genetic manipulation of organisms

Although naturally occurring organisms have a myriad of uses in bioremediation, genetic manipulation of organisms may render biormediation more efficient by allowing insertion of genes for production of specific enzymes or a wider range of environmental tolerance into the micro-organism to be used. The key phrase here is alteration of metabolic pathways. By altering pathways, bioremediation may become more efficient and faster, and will prevent build-up of inhibitory by-products.

Genetic engineering of micro-organisms is actually a form of forced, rapid evolution. Selection may take the form of altering substrates to select for micro-organisms within a culture that have the capability of mineralizing recalcitrant substances by: transferring genetic material *in vivo* using transformation, transduction, and conjugation to alter an organism's genetic makeup; or cloning specific genes *in vitro* for transfer to another micro-organism (Timmis, Rojo & Ramos, 1988). Technically, selection of organisms that do not undergo human-mediated genetic engineering for optimum functioning on a particular substrate may not be considered to be genetic engineering. In the US, for example, field use of such selected organisms is not controlled by the Environmental Protection Agency (EPA).

Genetically engineered micro-organisms (GEMs) hold great promise, especially for remediation of recalcitrant compounds or those that are naturally degraded only *via* co-metabolism. Genetic constructs can be used effectively to model organisms with the capacity to metabolize carbon in a pollutant and utilize products of co-metabolism for growth. They also can establish metabolic pathways that prevent the build-up of by-products that impede bacterial growth and function (Washington report, 1993).

An Organization for Economic Co-operation and Development (OECD) report (1994) suggest that the best use for GEMs is in chlorinated hydrocarbon degradation or biopolymer formation. Transformation of recalcitrant aromatics is another field

GENE SEQUENCE DEFINING
ABILITY TO SURVIVE IN THE
PRESENCE OF HEAVY METALS

GENE SEQUENCE DEFINING
ABILITY TO DEGRADE PCBs

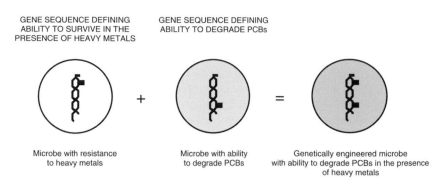

Microbe with resistance
to heavy metals

Microbe with ability
to degrade PCBs

Genetically engineered microbe
with ability to degrade PCBs in the presence
of heavy metals

Fig. 7.2. Genetic engineering concept (after P. H. Pritchard).

in which GEMs may be applied. These aromatics may be degraded by naturally occurring organisms, but the degradation is likely to occur more rapidly and efficiently with use of GEMs.

GEMs that carry out biotransformations of aromatics have been produced. Toluene mono-oxygenase encoding genes from *Pseudomonas mendocina* were cloned into *Escherichia coli* K-12 expression vectors. These genes are important for the breakdown of toluene to *p*-cresol, acetanilide to acetaminophen, fluorobenzene to fluorophenol, methylphenylacetate to hydroxyphenylacetate, and ethylbenzene to ethylphenol. Genes encoding for the enzyme, naphthalene dioxygenase (NDO), have been cloned in *E. coli*. These genes are regulated by temperature: the promoter turns on the genes when temperature in the fermentative system reaches 12 °C, but it took significant manipulation of the system to achieve optimal production of all products: indole and thence indigo (US Department of Energy Report, 1993).

Thus, with proper engineering, in some cases, fewer species of GEMs could be used within a microbial consortium in the field. GEMs also can be engineered to survive under conditions adverse to growth of most micro-organisms. For example, as has been demonstrated, a bacterium can be engineered both to break down a toxic material and to survive in conditions with high levels of heavy metals (see Fig. 7.2; Atlas, 1995). Insertion of genes from the hyperthermophilic *Archaea* spp. may extend bacterial survival in extremely hot temperatures, and recent identification of *Archaea* spp. in extremely cold water could lead to identification of genes that allow for survival in that environmental extreme (see Fig. 7.3; Watanabe, 1994).

To increase the numbers of GEMs available for bioremediation, however, it is mandatory that the bacterial genes regulating enzyme production, taxis and bacterial motility, for example, be fully understood, both genetically and physiologically (Timmis *et al.*, 1988). Engineered micro-organisms will not only produce enzymes for proper degradative functioning in the field but will also be able to detect, i.e. 'sense', target molecules and move directly to those locations within a cleanup site containing pollutant molecules to be metabolized.

EXPAND THE CAPABILITIES OF
BIOREMEDIATION BY:

Targeting wastes not degradable naturally

Addressing conditions where naturally
occurring bacteria cannot survive

Providing faster or more complete degradation

Fig. 7.3. Genetic engineering: potential role in bioremediation.

7.5 Problems

Although GEMs hold great promise, there are scientific, social and political problems with use of these organisms. Scientific obstacles include time and cost of engineering organisms for survival and/or flourishing in environmental extremes. Organisms functioning optimally to remediate an oil spill in the Arctic will, most likely, not function as effectively on the Equator or in a desert. Is the organism safe? Will it overwhelm the natural bacterial flora in a region, changing the ecosystem (Mooney & Drake, 1990)? How do we monitor released organisms (Colwell *et al.*, 1988)?

These are not insurmountable problems. To date, research indicates that the majority of GEMs cannot compete well against the natural microbial flora (Dwyer & Timmis, 1990). But to allay fears and ensure safety, antibody or nucleic acid-based probes to monitor the presence of the micro-organism in the environment can be produced. Furthermore, GEMs can be engineered with 'kill' genes or genes that inactivate their functions (Dwyer & Timmis, 1990).

Social problems include public perception. How much proof will the public require to judge these organisms as safe? Recent surveys in Europe show that as many as 87% of the public support the concept of biotechnology research to improve the environment; however, in some European countries there is strong opposition to recombinant DNA technology (OECD Report, 1994). Short of including a 'kill' gene in each GEM, only recently (1996), was it possible to release GEMs wholesale into the environment in a controlled study in the United States (Saylor, personal communication). Many countries still forbid release of GEMs into the environment and, when GEMs may be released, the permitting process is both complex and costly (Atlas, 1995). Even if such organisms may not be readily released into the environment, they can be used in biofilters and scrubbers, from which they do not become disseminated. As research on GEMs progresses, scientists must work together with the media to educate the public on

R. R. Colwell

▨ Still in developmental stages

▨ Public acceptance needs to be
    cultivated through education

▨ Limited to contained use

▨ Concern over releases and fate of
    genetically engineered micro-organisms

Fig. 7.4. Genetic engineering: current limitations.

the potentially positive role of GEMs in the environment; but also limitations (see Fig. 7.4).

Political problems include the regulatory climate. Although strict regulation will control safety, it often increases R&D costs. More important to the development of GEMs, however, is the political climate in which we must work. Current political attitudes in the US stress alleviation of environmental controls and regulations. This, with the significant cuts (in real dollars) available for scientific R&D funding that lie ahead, will produce a climate that will not be conducive to intensive research on GEMs or any other new technologies to remediate environmental problems. Although the United States Environmental Protection Agency (EPA) 1995 R&D budget increased from 1994, there were real losses in R&D funds for hazardous waste disposal and toxic substances, while the budget for evaluating bioremediation of oil spills remained the same as in 1994 (Fox, 1994). The 1996 budget, after much legislative turmoil, held steady for EPA. This double-edged sword, however, could accede to the wishes of industry to moderate regulation of environmental release of GEMs, (Miller, 1994) in the United States.

Although field studies of GEMs are highly regulated in the US, this does not appear to be a major roadblock to achieving EPA approval for field testing or use of GEMs in bioreactors (Glass, 1994).

There are also serious questions about the efficacy of using GEMs when so many of the naturally occurring micro-organisms (many of which could function in some manner in bioremediation) are yet to be discovered, many of which may be more effective tools of bioremediation than we now have.

7.6 Not only micro-organisms

Bioremediation is not carried out solely by micro-organisms. Phytoremediation relies on plants to concentrate toxic materials, especially heavy metals. Members of the genus *Brassica* have been used to concentrate heavy metals such as lead (Atlas, 1995). The common wetland weed, *Phragmites*, which is highly pollution tolerant, has been used in sewage treatment (Kiviat, 1994). The micro-organisms attached to the soil around the plant roots (the rhizosphere) form a rich consortium for destroying toxic materials found in the soil in which the plant stands (Alexander, 1994). Species of bivalve molluscs, especially clams, have the ability not only to concentrate toxins within the water, but to break them down (Hutchinson, 1994).

Bioremediation is an attractive method for cleaning up environmental contamination because there is not one set method for carrying it out: it can be done *in situ* and *ex situ*, using various techniques, including bioreactors, addition of nutrients, air sparging, etc. Because remediation *in situ* obviates the large costs of transportation of contaminated soil and other material, it is considered by some to be cost-effective and preferable to other means of cleanup (Atlas, 1995): and because GEMs can be contained within biofilters at remediation sites, it may render use of such organisms acceptable from the standpoint of ecological safety.

7.7 Marketable end-products

Because, in many cases, bioremediation results in an end-product that can be marketed, such as electricity, gasohol, single-cell protein, or methane gas, its cost may be offset by profit, making it a holistic process palatable to legislators and the general public (Fig. 7.5). But, in order for this to occur, fundamental changes are required in the way we look at the results of bioremediation.

For example, cogeneration of electricity from municipal sewage treatment plants or other waste treatment facilities is a fact. Cogeneration plants dot the country. The Anacostia sewage treatment plant in Washington, District of Columbia, USA, generates electricity used to light the plant. Also, New Jersey's PSE&G maintains a massive cogen plant a few miles from New York City, but regulations that forced power companies to buy the electricity from cogen plants and other generating facilities at above-market prices were removed by the United States Federal Energy Regulatory Commission, resulting in a reluctance by power companies to purchase this electricity (Salpukas, 1995). A better solution, perhaps, would be use of the electricity or fuels generated by power-selected areas near the plants.

Short-chain fatty acids and alcohols are products of fermentations by *Clostridium acetobutylicum*. This specific fermentation represents the first industrial use of a micro-organism, for production of acetone. The products of these reactions, however, are toxic to the microbe, so genetic engineering of a bacterium with greater tolerance to such products may again lead to cost-effective commercialization (Morris, 1994).

Biogas generation through methanogenic waste digestion also holds much promise. Although heavily promoted in Asia and developing nations, this approach could be utilized world-wide and would decrease our reliance upon fossil fuels, which, themselves, pollute our environment.

		$ MILLIONS	
		1990	1995
	BIOREMEDIATION OF CONTAMINATED SITES	50	150
	BIOREMEDIATION OF HAZARDOUS WASTE	460	570
	BIOREMEDIATION FOR TOTAL ENVIRONMENTAL MARKET	830	1000

Fig. 7.5. Markets: 1990–95 market potentials (from a survey by a private company)

7.8 Great expectations

Despite the obstacles to be overcome and the massive amounts of research needed (Miller & Poindexter, 1994), GEMs carry the expectation of improved wastewater treatment, removal of toxic heavy metals from our waterways, treatment of radioactive wastes, military base clean-up, more efficient treatment of oil spills, improved degradation of pesticides and herbicides, degradation of plastics, removal of deadly carbon monoxide, cleansing of dangerous carbon dioxide and sulphur from the air we breathe, and clean-up of numerous toxic chemicals, e.g., PCBs, formaldehyde, hydrazine, and naphthalene. Remediation of toxic effluents from manufacturing processes, such as those produced by the paper and pulp industry, also can be achieved.

7.9 Market growth

The first step in determining the market for bioremediation is the promulgation of legislation recognizing the problem and establishing a mechanism to report it, classify it and remediate it.

Although this has been done in the US and Western Europe, areas such as Eastern Europe and parts of the former Soviet Union may be slower to do this. None the less, the international market for bioremediation is growing at a rapid pace and is expected to continue to expand for the foreseeable future. In the US, recent reports predict clean-up of underground storage tank sites will yield *c.* $375 million per year over the next two years (Howard & Fox, 1994). Hazardous site clean-up is projected to increase from $100 million in 1995 to nearly $200 million by the year 2000 in the US alone (Kreeger, 1995). Western European nations spend a total of as much as $6.5 billion annually for bioremediation, with the greatest expenditures by far by Germany ($3–6 billion per year) (Porta, Young & Molron, 1994). Total bioremediation estimates for Western Europe range as high as more than $250 billion! OECD members (Australia, Austria, Belgium, Canada, Denmark, Finland, France, Germany, Greece, Iceland, Ireland, Italy, Japan,

Luxembourg, Mexico, the Netherlands, New Zealand, Norway, Portugal, Spain, Sweden, Switzerland, Turkey, the UK and the US) are projected to spend $300 billion for bioremediation (as much as $160 billion of this for solid waste treatment) by the year 2000 (OECD Report, 1994).

Despite the growth, there were less than 20 technical bioremediation companies in the US in 1994 (Howard & Fox, 1994), and three-quarters of Europe's bioremediation companies are equipment suppliers (OECD Report, 1994). More than 50% of the money spent for environmental remediation will go for air pollution remediation (OECD Report, 1994).

This does not include the massive amount of money that will be spent to clean up former military bases in Eastern Europe.

The US bioremediation industry was fuelled by the identification of contaminated 'Superfund' sites. Although we do not expect additional 'Superfund' sites within the US (Easterbrook, 1995), unusual situations (such as the hidden 250 000 gallons of contaminated sludge on a rotting barge (Hevesi, 1995)) may result in incidents that will require clean-up.

The need for bioremediation in Asia, especially for the fouled waterways, is urgent, but recent reports suggest that little or no progress is being made there (Anon, 1995a). Japan, however, remains an exception and is actively pursuing R&D in bioremediation, focusing on air quality through removal of sulphur from emissions, and removal of CO_2 from air and incorporating the carbon into polymers or other potentially useful products (Atlas, 1995).

7.10 The future

We have not even scratched the surface in our discovery of potentially useful micro-organisms. Because only a minute fraction (approximately less than 1%) of naturally occurring bacteria can be cultured on media (Angert et al., 1993), new techniques must be used to identify, maintain, and utilize the Earth's massive numbers of microbial species. Researchers are combing the soil, probing deep within the earth, in and under the oceans, and in areas around volcanoes, hot vents and hot springs, to find potentially useful, hitherto unidentified microbial species (Gold, 1992).

Thus, bioremediation technologies have enormous potential to expand, direct and focus bioremediation (Fig. 7.6) and although current technologies may not suggest it is possible at present, the goal is to achieve 'green' industries with zero discharge. Governments and intergovernmental agencies support this ecologically friendly research. The US National Science Foundation, along with the US EPA, published a request for proposals for projects aimed at stimulating 'green' process chemistry and materials-manufacturing in order to minimize or prevent the generation of wastes (NSF/EPA Report, 1995). The executive director of the United Nations Environmental Programme (UNEP) has called on governments to support 'ecologically appropriate technologies' to protect the environment (Dowdeswell, 1995).

R. R. Colwell

Company	1993 Reveue ($ millions)	Projects completed	Number of years in industry
Cytoculture Point Richmond, CA	0.6	10	8
ENSR Houston, TX	10.0	20	12
Envirogen, Inc. Lawrenceville, NJ	5.0	75	6
IT Corp. Knoxville, TN	20.0	70+	14
OHM Corp. Findlay, OH	6.0	60	16
RETEC Tuscon, AZ	8.0	30	9
Total market	200.0		

Fig. 7.6. Market figures for representative bioremediation companies.

Industry is responding to the call. A pilot plant for continuous biocatalytic disulphurization of petroleum fuel streams has been constructed in St Louis, Missouri (Anon, 1995*b*), a patented process called 'Nite-de-Nite' is treating waste waters with high ammonia concentrations in a steel plant in Utah (Howard & Fox, 1994); a company has placed an *in situ* bioreactor in a Redwood City, California shopping centre to treat petrol-contaminated water (Howard & Fox, 1994). Projects ranging from pilot stage to industrial scale for soil or water treatment are being pursued in Europe, notably in Germany and the Netherlands (Porta *et al.*, 1994); and there are many other examples. Thus, the outlook is highly promising for bioremediation. Although only a small portion of the information necessary to render bioremediation both economically and environmentally successful is currently available, the promise is evident.

Acknowledgements

The excellent technical assistance of Myrna Watanabe is gratefully acknowledged.

References

Alexander, M. (1994). *Biodegradation and Bioremediation*, p. 229. San Diego, CA: Academic Press.
Angert, E. R., Clements, K. D. & Pace, N. R. (1993). The largest bacterium. *Nature*, 362, 239–41.
Anon. (1995*a*). Review of biotechnology in Asia, 1994: An interview with Michael Hsu and Robert Yuan. *Genetic Engineering News*, Jan. 15.
Anon. (1995*b*). Biodesulfurization pilot plant complete. *Applied Genetics News*, 15(7), 3.
Atlas, R. (1995). Bioremediation. *Chemical and Engineering News*, 73, 32–42.

144

Barr, D. P. & Aust, S. D. (1994). Mechanisms white rot fungi use to degrade pollutants. *Environmental Science and Technology*, **28**, 79A–87A.

Colwell, R. R., Somerville, C., Knight, I. & Straube, W. (1988). Detection and monitoring of genetically-engineered micro-organisms. In *The Release of Genetically-Engineered Micro-Organisms*, ed. M. Sussman, C. H. Collins, F. A. Skinner & D. E. Stewart-Tull. pp. 47–60. London: Academic Press.

Committee on *In Situ* Bioremediation, Water Science and Technology Board, Commission on Engineering and Technical Systems, National Research Council. (1993). In Situ *Bioremediation: When Does It Work?* Washington, DC: National Academy Press.

Dowdeswell, E. (1995). Speech at World Summit for Social Development, Copenhagen, Denmark, 7 March.

Dwyer, D. & Timmis, K. N. (1990). Engineering microbes for function and safety in the environment. In *SCOPE 44. Introduction of Genetically Modified Organisms into the Environment*, ed. H. A. Mooney & G. Bernardi. pp. 79–98. Chichester: John Wiley.

Easterbrook, G. (1995). Good news from planet Earth. *USA Weekend*, April 14–16, pp. 4–6.

Ember, L. (1995). Pollution prevention: study says chemical industry lags. *Chemical and Engineering News*, **73**(12), 6–7.

Field, J. A., Stams, A. J. M., Kato, M. & Schraa, G. (1995). Enhanced biodegradation of aromatic pollutants in cocultures of anaerobic and aerobic bacterial consortia. *Antonie van Leeuwenhoek*, **67**, 47–77.

Fox, J. L. (1994). Is Clinton increasing biotech R&D spending? *Bio/Techology*.

Glass, D. J. (1994). Obtaining regulatory approval and public acceptance for bioremediation projects with engineered organisms in the United States. In *Applied Biotechnology for Site Remediation*, ed. R. E. Hinchee, D. B. Henderson, B. Anderson, F. B. Metting, Jr. & G. D. Sayles. pp. 256–67. Boca Raton, FL: Lewis Publishers.

Gold, T. (1992). The deep, hot biosphere. *Proceedings of the National Academy of Sciences, USA*, **89**, 6045–9.

Gorontzy, T., Drzyzga, O., Kahl, M. W., Bruns-Nagel, D., Breitung, J., von Loew, E. & Blotevogel, K.-H. (1994). Microbial degradation of explosives and related compounds. *Critical Reviews in Microbiology*, 20, 265–84.

Hevesi, D. (1995). 4 acquitted in conspiracy over sludge. *New York Times* April 5, B7.

Howard, J. & Fox, S. (1994). Review of current research projects and innovations in bioremediation. *Genetic Engineering News*. October 1.

Hutchinson, P. J. (1994). Remediation of aqueous-phased xenobiotic contamination by freshwater bivalves. In *Applied Biotechnology for Site Remediation*, ed. R. E. Hinchee, D. B. Anderson, F. Metting, Jr. & G. D. Sayles, pp. 21–35. Boca Raton, FL: Lewis Publishers.

Kirschner, E. (1995). Polymer production jumped 7.2% in 1994. *Chemical and Engineering News*, **73**(15), 20–2.

Kiviat, E. (1994). Reed, sometimes a weed. *News from Hudsonia*, **10**(3), 4–6.

Kreeger, K. Y. (1995). Growing bioremediation industry presents a potential boom in jobs for life scientists. *The Scientist*, **9**(2), 1, 8–9.

Lamar, R. T. & Glaser, J. A. (1994). Field evaluations of the remediation of soils contaminated with wood-preserving chemicals using lignin-degrading fungi. In *Bioremediation of Chlorinated and Polycyclic Aromatic Hydrocarbon Compounds*, ed. R. E. Hinchee, A. Leeson, L. Semprini & S. K. Ong. pp. 239–47. Boca Raton, FL: Lewis Publishers.

Lean, G. & Hinrichsen, D. (1994). *WWF Atlas of the Environment*, 2nd edn. New York: Harper Perennial.

Marvin-Sikkema, F. D. & de Bont, J. A. M. (1994). Degradation of nitroaromatic compounds by microorganisms. *Applied Microbiology and Biotechnology*. **42**, 499–507.

Miller, H. I. (1994). Administration's technology rhetoric is belied by its policy actions. *The Scientist*, **8**(23), 12.

Miller, R. V. & Poindexter, J. S. (1994). Strategies and Mechanisms for Field Research. In *Environmental Bioremediation: A Call for a National Environmental Bioremediation Field Research Program*. Washington, DC: American Academy of Microbiology, 20 pp.

Milstein, O., Gersonde, R., Huttermann, A., Chen, M. J. & Meister, J. J. (1994). Rotting of thermoplastics made from lignin and styrene by white-rot basidiomycetes. In *Applied Biotechnology for Site Remediation*, ed. R. E. Hinchee, D. B. Anderson, F. B. Metting, Jr. & G. D. Sayles. pp. 129–42. Boca Raton, FL: Lewis Publishers.

Mooney, H. A. & Drake J. A. (1990). The release of genetically designed organisms in the environment: lessons from the study of the ecology of biological invasions. In *SCOPE 44. Introduction of Genetically Modified Organisms into the Environment*, ed. H. A. Mooney & G. Bernardi. pp. 117–29. Chichester: John Wiley & Sons.

Morris, J. G. (1994). Obligately anaerobic bacteria in biotechnology. *Applied Biochemistry and Biotechnology*, **48**, 75–106.

National Science Foundation/Environmental Protection Agency (1995). Interagency announcement of opportunity. NSF 95–48 (New).

New York City Dept. of Sanitation (1994). Fresh Kills landfill leachate mitigation/corrective measures assessment. *DOS Fact Sheet*, **1**(6); March.

New York City Dept. of Sanitation (1994). New York City Fresh Kills landfill. Pamphlet. Dec.

Organisation for Economic Co-operation and Development. (1994). *Biotechnology for a Clean Environment: Prevention, Detection, Remediation*. Paris, France.

Porta, A., Young, J. K. & Molton, P. M. (1994). *In situ* bioremediation in Europe. In *Applied Biotechnology for Site Remediation*, ed. R. E. Hinchee, D. B. Anderson, F. B. Metting, Jr. & G. D. Sayles. pp. 1–20. Boca Raton, FL: Lewis Publishers.

Saberiyan, A. G., Wilson, M. A., Roe, E. O., Andrilenas, J. S., Esler, C. T., Kise, G. H. & Reith, P. E. (1994). Removal of gasoline volatile organic compounds via air biofiltration: a technique for treating secondary air emissions from vapor-extraction and air-stripping systems. In *Hydrocarbon Bioremediation*, ed. R. E. Hinchee, B. C. Alleman, R. E. Hoeppel & R. N. Miller. pp. 1–11. Boca Raton, FL: Lewis Publishers.

Salpukas, A. (1995). 70's dreams, 90's realities: renewable energy: A luxury now. A necessity later? *New York Times*, April 11, D1, D8.

Stone, R. (1995). Environmental toxicants under scrutiny at Baltimore meeting. *Science*, **267**, 1770–1.

Timmis, K. N., Rojo, F. & Ramos, J. L. (1988). Prospects for laboratory engineering of bacteria to degrade pollutants. In *Environmental Biotechnology: Reducing Risks from Environmental Chemicals through Biotechnology*, ed. G. S. Omenn. pp. 61–79. New York: Plenum Press.

US Dept. Energy, Office of Energy Research, Office of Program Analysis (1993). *Fossil Energy Biotechnology: A Research Needs Assessment Final Report*. Nov. 302 pp. Available from: NTIS, US Dept. Commerce, Springfield, VA 22161, USA.

Watanabe, M. (1994). Hot-vent microbes: looking backward in evolution for future uses. *The Scientist*, **8**(11), 14–15.

Yagi, K., Williams, J., Wang, N.-Y. Cicerone, R. J. (1995). Atmospheric methyl bromide (CH_3Br) from agricultural soil fumigations. *Science*, **267**, 1979–81.

8

Bioremediation: case studies

Ronald M. Atlas

8.1 Overview

In many cases there is a strong intrinsic bioremediation potential for the biodegradation of petroleum hydrocarbon pollutants that contaminate marine ecosystems. Oil spillages that do not contaminate shorelines are not treated and have not been documented to cause ecological damage. In the case of the *Ixtoc-I* well blowout, hydrocarbons in the water column were rapidly degraded and did not contaminate US shorelines. Surface from that spillage, however, formed a thick emulsion that resisted biodegradation and some of that oil contaminated Mexican and US shorelines. In the case of the *Amoco Cadiz* oil spill where high concentrations of oil contaminated the shorelines it took approximately 3 years for the indigenous micro-organisms to remove the biodegradable hydrocarbons.

Biodegradation of oil from the *Amoco Cadiz* was aided by high energy wave action which maintained aerobic conditions and by the influx of nitrogen and phosphorus nutrients from agricultural runoff. There was greater biodegradation of n-alkanes and low molecular weight aromatic hydrocarbons than for branched alkanes and methylated polynuclear aromatics. Micro-organisms along the coast of France are well adapted for biodegradation of many hydrocarbons as evidenced by a three order of magnitude increase in numbers of hydrocarbon degraders within 24 hours following the wreck of the tanker *Tanio*.

Unlike the *Amoco Cadiz* oil spill where there were adequate nutrients to support intrinsic bioremediation, biodegradation of hydrocarbons from the *Exxon Valdez* spill in Prince William Sound, Alaska was severely nutrient limited. Indigenous micro-organisms were capable of degrading branched alkanes, such as pristane and phytane, when the nutrient limitation was removed. Addition of nitrogen and phosphorus fertilizers stimulated rates of biodegradation three to five times and hastened the recovery of the contaminated shorelines. The stimulation of micro-organisms by fertilizer application to treat the *Exxon Valdez* oil spill was the largest such project to date with hundreds of miles of shoreline treated during two summers; its success is largely responsible for a revitalized interest in bioremediation.

8.2 Introduction

The wreck of the *Torrey Canyon* in 1967 ushered in an era of repeated large marine oil spills with their images of dead sea birds washing up on shorelines, public calls for action, and authorities facing decisions about employing any of a number of technologies that have been developed for dealing with oil spills. With each oil spill, we have learned that action may cause more harm than leaving the oil to undergo natural degradation. As examples, we learned from the *Torrey Canyon* spill that the application of dispersants containing organic solvents in nearshore regions causes greater exposure of marine life to the oil and greater toxicity and damage to various marine biological populations. Thus, the use of dispersants in treating oil spills is limited to regions that are not ecologically sensitive and formulations of dispersants have been modified so as to eliminate toxic organic solvents. We learned from the *Torrey Canyon* spill that sinking oil increases its persistence because it tends to move the oil into anoxic zones where biodegradation of the oil is severely limited. We also learned from a variety of spills that physical removal of oil with heavy equipment can cause long-lasting ecological damage to vegetation so that recovery takes longer in treated areas than in those left to natural weathering of the oil and hydrocarbon biodegradation.

The scientific studies that followed the *Torrey Canyon* spill and continued throughout the 1970s established a high degree of scientific understanding of the fate of oil in the sea that has been summarized in several reviews (Atlas, 1981; Leahy & Colwell, 1990; Atlas & Bartha, 1992). One of the key findings of these studies is that naturally occurring marine micro-organisms have a high capacity for biodegrading petroleum hydrocarbons. In most cases, however, it was found that environmental conditions limited those biodegradative activities.

Many of the laboratory studies that followed the *Torrey Canyon* spill, as well as chemical analyses performed on environmental samples, established a series of principles about the fate of oil in the marine environment that would dominate this field of science for over a decade. These principles were that oil weathering was a sequential process, with physical and chemical processes occurring prior to biological weathering of the oil; biodegradation of oil was not considered a significant process for 2–3 weeks after an oil spill. Aliphatic hydrocarbons with 14–20 carbons, such as hexadecane, were considered to be more readily degraded than aromatics or other aliphatics. Branched alkanes, such as pristane and phytane, were thought to be biodegraded at exceedingly slow rates. Hydrocarbon biodegradation was considered to be exclusively an aerobic process; no hydrocarbon biodegradation was supposed to occur under anaerobic conditions.

Based upon the understanding of the natural fate of oil in the seas, ways were sought to overcome those factors that imposed rate limitations, including the selection or development of microbial strains with enhanced biodegradative capabilities and the development of methodologies for modifying environmental conditions to enhance the rates of petroleum biodegradation by the indigenous hydrocarbon-degrading micro-organisms: bioremediation emerged as a method for treating marine oil spills and has been applied in a variety of cases (Prince, 1993; Swannell, Lee & McDonagh, 1996).

8.3 *Amoco Cadiz* and *Tanio* spills: Brittany coastline

The supertanker *Amoco Cadiz* spilled approximately 223 000 metric tonnes of crude oil into the English Channel in March 1978, making it one of the world's largest oil spills. The spill contaminated over 100 miles of shoreline of the Brittany coast of France. Studies were conducted on the fate of the spilled oil (Gundlach *et al.*, 1983). Of the total oil spilled, approximately 13.5% was incorporated into the water column and moved offshore, 28% washed into the intertidal zone, 30% evaporated, 8% was deposited in subtidal sediments, about 4.5% was biodegraded in the water column while the oil was moving toward shore; the fate of the rest of the oil remains unknown.

Analyses of the residual hydrocarbons showed that biodegradation began rapidly after the oil entered the water. Depressed concentrations of oxygen in the water column beneath the oil showed that biodegradation was occurring even as the oil was moving to the shore; during biodegradation, molecular oxygen is incorporated into hydrocarbons to form oxygenated intermediates that are subsequently converted to carbon dioxide and water. Rates of biodegradation of low, and higher molecular weight alkanes in the oil indicated that physical and chemical weathering did not occur prior to the onset of significant biodegradation. Rather, biodegradation proceeded as fast as or faster than chemical evaporation and dispersal of oil into the water column. The indigenous micro-organisms appear to have been very well adapted to hydrocarbon biodegradation, presumably from extensive exposure to hydrocarbons in ballast waters released by tankers moving through the region. Microbial oil-degrading populations increased by several orders of magnitude following the *Amoco Cadiz* and *Tanio* spills (Fig. 8.1). In the case of the *Tanio* spill, an increase of three orders of magnitude in concentrations of hydrocarbon degraders occurred within 24 hours of oil reaching the shorelines.

The indigenous micro-organisms rapidly degraded straight chain aliphatics and aromatics with up to three rings (Fig. 8.2). Branched alkanes, including pristane and phytane were degraded but at significantly lower rates than observed for the n-alkanes. Hopanes did not appear to be attacked.

Based upon measurements of hydrocarbon biodegradation potentials and generation times of the indigenous micro-organisms, it was estimated that 8 tonnes of oil per day were biodegraded within the impacted shorelines. These extrapolated rates of oil biodegradation indicated that the intrinsic biodegradation potential would remove all the biodegradable components of the oil from most contaminated sites

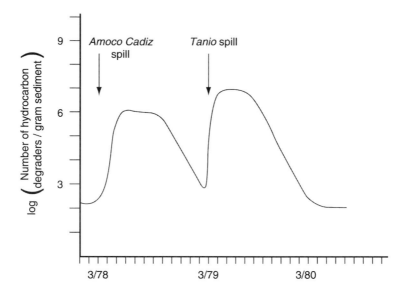

Fig. 8.1. Changes in populations of oil-degrading micro-organisms in intertidal sediments off the Brittany coast impacted by the *Amoco Cadiz* and *Tanio* oil spills between March 1978 and March 1980.

within 3 years. Monitoring of representative sites along the Brittany coast confirmed the accuracy of this prediction. The high rates of oil biodegradation in the impacted sediments indicated a lack of environmental limitations that characterize many oil spills.

The lack of nutrient limitation for biodegradation of hydrocarbons in the marine environment is very unusual. In most marine environments, availability of nitrogen and phosphate that can be used to support microbial hydrocarbon degradation metabolic activities, severely limits the rates of hydrocarbon bio-degradation. In some cases oxygen also limits the rates of hydrocarbon biodegradation. The high energy waves impacting the Brittany coast, which had driven the oil on-shore, continuously supplied oxygen-rich water and dispersed the oil so that it mixed with the available nutrients. The nitrogen and phosphate needed to support extensive microbial biodegradation activities came in large part from agricultural runoff. Liquid ammonia and other fertilizers are added in excess to farms on the highlands above the oiled shorelines. Thus, optimal environmental conditions and adapted microbial populations coexisted in the oil-contaminated shorelines, facilitating the rapid biodegradation of oil from the *Amoco Cadiz* and *Tanio* spills without additional seeding or fertilizer treatment.

While most of the oil from the *Amoco Cadiz* and *Tanio* spills impacted well-aerated shorelines, some of the oil became stranded in the supratidal zone and some entered anaerobic sediments and soils. Microbial attack of the oil was severely limited in

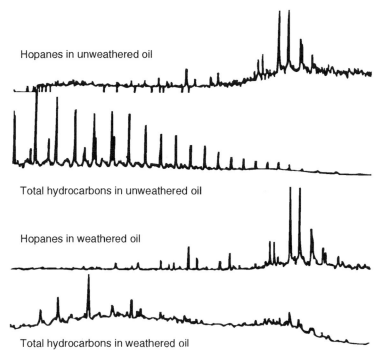

Hopanes in unweathered oil

Total hydrocarbons in unweathered oil

Hopanes in weathered oil

Total hydrocarbons in weathered oil

Fig. 8.2. Gas chromatographic–mass spectral analyses of hopanes and total hydrocarbons in unweathered oil collected shortly after the *Amoco Cadiz* oil spill and weathered oil collected a few months after the spill. Both have similar concentrations of hopanes. The weathered oil is depleted of alkanes and aromatics that have been biodegraded.

those environments, largely due to the lack of oxygen. Oil in those regions persisted longer than 3 years. While it had previously been believed that no hydrocarbon degradation would occur under strictly anaerobic conditions, careful studies of the anaerobic sediments oiled by the *Amoco Cadiz* spill showed that anaerobic biodegradation of hydrocarbons was occurring but at rates that were much slower than occurred under aerobic conditions. Anaerobic hydrocarbon degradation occurred at rates of only about 1–5% of those that occurred under aerobic conditions. Also, there was preferential degradation of low molecular weight (one ring) aromatics over alkanes and higher molecular weight aromatic hydrocarbons, under anaerobic conditions.

8.4 *Ixtoc-I* well blowout: Gulf of Mexico

The *Ixtoc-I* well blowout in the Bay of Campeche in 1979 initiated a flow of oil into the Gulf of Mexico that lasted for 10 months before the well could be capped. This incident created the world's largest oil spill to date with approximately three

R. M. Atlas

million barrels of oil entering the marine environment. The spill was unusual in that the oil was injected at depth as a vortex under high pressure. Some of the oil dissolved in the water column but most of the oil formed a water in oil emulsion called mousse (with greater than 60% hydrocarbon) that floated on the surface.

After the spill there was a significant elevation of several orders of magnitude in the numbers of hydrocarbon-utilizing micro-organisms found in association with the mousse and in the water column impacted by the flow of oil. Rates of hydrocarbon degradation of the dissolved hydrocarbons, principally low molecular weight aromatics such as benzene, toluene, ethyl benzene and xylene, were very rapid. However, the hydrocarbons in the mousse were not attacked rapidly even though elevated numbers of hydrocarbon degraders were present. The mousse was extremely stable and even addition of dispersants failed to break the emulsion. Addition of fertilizers also failed to stimulate rates of biodegradation of the emulsified hydrocarbons; the physical form of the mousse protected the hydrocarbons against microbial attack.

8.5 *Exxon Valdez* spill: Prince William Sound, Alaska shorelines

The *Exxon Valdez* spilled approximatley 41 000 cubic metres of oil into Prince William Sound in March 1989. Although much smaller than the *Amoco Cadiz* and *Ixtoc I* oil spill incidents, the *Exxon Valdez* oil spill was the worst marine pollution incident in the United States and impacted ecologically very sensitive regions of Alaska. Much of the spilled oil washed onto shorelines of islands, contaminating over 2 000 km of coastline. Some of the shorelines, which predominantly were rocky, were heavily oiled; in some cases oil contaminated the subsurface to a depth of about 1 metre.

Despite exhaustive and costly attempts to wash shorelines physically with high pressure water, oil would resurface and extensive oil contamination persisted months after the spill. This forced examination of alternate clean-up methods that included bioremediation (Pritchard & Costa, 1991; Bragg *et al.*, 1994). Seeding was not considered an option because of concerns about introducing non-indigenous micro-organisms. Rather, bioremediation testing consisted of examining a variety of fertilizers for their abilities to enhance rates of biodegradation without causing unacceptable ecotoxicological reactions. Oleophilic, slow release and rapid release fertilizer formulations were considered. Toxicity tests were conducted, especially on the oleophilic formulation EAP-22, to determine safe concentrations that would not cause adverse effects on fish or invertebrates, including sensitive larval stages. Field tests were conducted to establish the efficacy of fertilizer application with regard to the rate of oil biodegradation stimulation that could be achieved. This turned into the largest bioremediation-demonstration project ever conducted. It was performed jointly by numerous Exxon scientists, EPA scientists from several laboratories, the Alaska Department of Environment Conservation, consultants and university scientists.

152

The ecotoxicological test programme showed that the primary toxicity was associated with ammonia, regardless of the nitrogen fertilizer source. This was predicted, as ammonia is known to be toxic to fish and marine invertebrates. Concentrations of nitrogen below those that caused toxicity, well within the range routinely applied to local Alaskan streams to increase fish productivity, supported enhanced rates of oil biodegradation. Assessing the actual rates of enhancement by fertilizer application in field experiments proved very difficult because of the patchy distribution of oil. Advanced statistical treatments were necessary to establish confidence in the efficacy of fertilizer application for enhancing rates of oil biodegradation. Reliance had to be placed on a relatively non-degradable compound within the oil to act as an internal standard and reduce the variability to the point where the data could be interpreted. Pristane and phytane, which had been used as internal standards in most previous studies, proved inadequate choices as internal standards because they were biodegraded relatively rapidly. The indigenous micro-organisms appear to be adapted to terpene biodegradation which has a similar structure to the branched alkanes found in petroleum; thus, these micro-organisms were able to degrade rapidly pristane and phytane. They additionally could degrade two- and three-ring aromatics. They were, however, unable to degrade hopanes, and concentrations of specific hopanes in the residual oil therefore could be used as an internal standard for normalization and reduction of variability in statistical analyses.

Chemical analyses indicated that there was an accumulation of polar compounds during oil biodegradation especially when fertilizer was applied (Fig. 8.3). This was unexpected as the rate-limiting step in hydrocarbon biodegradation generally is the initial incorporation of oxygen. Once hydroxylated, the rate of degradation is usually rapid with carbon dioxide and water as the end products. The accumulation of polar compounds, presumably partially oxygenated intermediary metabolites or products of cometabolism, raised concern about potential ecotoxicological impacts of bioremediation. Toxicity testing of water collected from bioremediated sites, however, indicated no increase in toxicity to fish or invertebrates. Analyses of mussels that were suspended in cages just offshore from bioremediated sites also showed no increase in toxicity and no increase in hydrocarbon accumulation compared to mussels in non-bioremediated regions.

Statistical analyses of chemical oil residues normalized to hopane indicated that fertilizer addition using nitrogen concentrations well below those that cause toxicity stimulated oil biodegradation in the field three to five times above the intrinsic rates of hydrocarbon biodegradation (Fig. 8.4). Thus, if the oil would have persisted for a decade, the application of fertilizer to stimulate biodegradation would reduce the persistence of biodegradable oil components to 2–3 years. Greater stimulation could have been achieved by applying higher concentrations of nitrogen but concern about ecotoxicity prevented attempts to achieve higher rates of oil removal (Fig. 8.5). Based upon the field demonstrations that established the efficacy of fertilizer application for stimulating oil biodegradation, full-scale

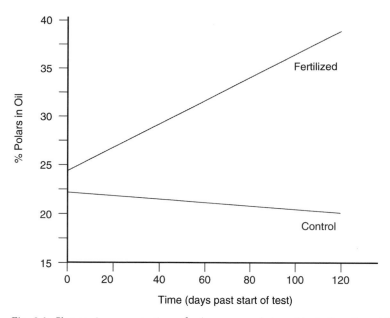

Fig. 8.3. Changes in concentrations of polar compounds in residual oils collected from intertidal sediments impacted by the *Exxon Valdez* spill. Much greater concentrations of polars occurred when bioremediation was carried out.

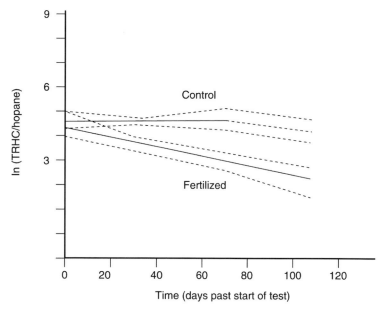

Fig. 8.4. Statistical analyses with confidence limits showing changes in concentrations of total resolvable hydrocarbons relative to concentrations of hopanes in bioremediated and control shorelines impacted by the *Exxon Valdez* spill. Note that the control was fertilized at 72 days leading to an increased rate of oil biodegradation.

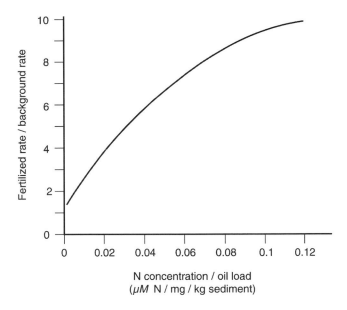

Fig. 8.5. Relative rates of biodegradation stimulation obtainable by applying different concentrations of nitrogen to sediments impacted by the *Exxon Valdez* spill.

bioremediation was carried out with hundreds of miles of shoreline treated with a combination of the oleophilic fertilizer Inipol EAP-22 and the slow release fertilizer Customblen. This was a highly effective use of bioremediation.

8.6 Discussion

Whenever there is a major marine oil spill, there is an immediate public outcry to save the birds and to clean up the oil. However, it is not always clear now best to respond in order to minimize ecological damage and to facilitate long-term ecological recovery. In many cases of marine oil spills, especially in Europe, the only treatment is to physically remove excessive surface accumulations of oil from impacted shorelines and to rely on natural microbial biodegradation activities. The reliance on natural biodegradation is called intrinsic bioremediation treatment within the context of integrated oil spill cleanup measures. Intrinsic bioremediation consists of watching, in some cases with monitoring measurements, the course of natural degradation of petroleum hydrocarbons. This approach worked well in the *Amoco Cadiz* and *Tanio* spills where adapted microbial populations and favourable environmental conditions that included agricultural runoff carrying nitrogen fertilizers favoured rapid oil biodegradation. In other cases, such as the *Exxon Valdez* spill, the application of fertilizers is useful for overcoming environmental constraints that limit the natural rates of oil biodegradation. Bioremediation of the *Exxon Valdez* oil spill showed the effectiveness of bioremediation for treatment of oil spills.

References

Atlas, R. M. (1981). Microbial degradation of petroleum hydrocarbons: an environmental perspective. *Microbiological Reviews*, 45, 180–209.

Atlas, R. M. & Bartha, R. (1992). Hydrocarbon biodegradation and oil spill bioremediation. *Advances in Microbial Ecology*, 12, 287–338.

Bragg, J. R., Prince, R. C., Harner, E. J. & Atlas, R. M. (1994). Effectiveness of bioremediation for the *Exxon Valdez* oil spill. *Nature*, 368, 413–18.

Gundlach, E. R., Boehm, P. D., Marchand, M., Atlas, R. M., Ward, D. M. & Wolfe, D. A. (1983). The fate of the *Amoco Cadiz* oil. *Science*, 221, 122–9.

Leahy, J. G. & Colwell, R. R. (1990). Microbial degradation of hydrocarbons in the environment. *Microbiological Reviews*, 54, 305–15.

Prince, R. C. (1993). Petroleum spill bioremediation in marine environments. *Critical Reviews in Microbiology*, 19, 217–42.

Pritchard, P. H. & Costa, C. F. (1991). EPA's Alaska oil spill bioremediation project. *Environmental Science and Technology*, 25, 372–9.

Swannell, R. P. J., Lee, K. & McDonagh, M. (1996). Field evaluations of marine oil spill bioremediation. *Microbiological Reviews*, 60, 342–65.

9

Utilization of biocatalysts in cellulose waste minimization

Jonathan Woodward and Barbara R. Evans

9.1 Introduction

Cellulose, a polymer of glucose, is the principal component of biomass and, therefore, a major source of waste that is either buried or burned. Examples of biomass waste include agricultural crop residues, forestry products and municipal wastes. Recycling of this waste is important for energy conservation as well as for waste minimization and there is some probability that, in the future, biomass could become a major energy source and replace fossil fuels that are currently used for fuels and chemicals production (Woodward, 1987; Woodward, Wyman & Goodman, 1993). It has been estimated that, in the United States, between 100 and 450 million dry tonnes of agricultural waste are produced annually, approximately 6 million dry tonnes of animal waste (Kitani & Hall, 1989), and of the 190 million tonnes of municipal solid waste (MSW) generated annually, approximately two-thirds is cellulosic in nature and over one-third is paper waste (Setterholm, 1991). Interestingly, more than 70% of MSW is landfilled or burned; however, landfill space is becoming increasingly scarce. On a smaller scale, important cellulosic products such as cellulose acetate also present waste problems; an estimated 43 thousand tonnes of cellulose ester waste are generated annually in the United States (Gedon & Fengl, 1993). Biocatalysts could be used in cellulose waste minimization (Table 9.1) and this chapter describes their characteristics and potential in bioconversion and bioremediation processes.

9.2 Cellulases

9.2.1 Bioconversion of cellulosic wastes to energy

The cellulosic content of municipal waste, at least 40–50%, could be used to produce liquid fuels, such as ethanol, instead of burying or burning it. The energy

Table 9.1. *Biocatalysts in cellulose waste minimization*

Biocatalyst	Bioprocess
Cellulases	Enzymatic hydrolysis of cellulose to glucose; de-inking of paper
Cellulose oxidase (redox group added)	Simultaneous oxidation of lignin and hydrolysis of cellulose
Xylanases	Bleaching of pulp wastes
Xylan oxidase (redox group added)	Enhanced bleaching
Esterases	De-esterification of cellulose ester wastes
Glucose dehydrogenase/hydrogenase	Oxidation of glucose/molecular hydrogen production

content of cellulosic waste (4×10^{-9} quads per ton; 1 quad = 10^{15} Btu) can be released by burning it, but cellulose incineration is environmentally unacceptable because it releases toxins into the environment and, as yet, no device has been developed to control toxic emissions from cellulose incinerators adequately or economically (Armson, 1985). Another way to produce energy from cellulosic waste is to employ cellulases to hydrolyse cellulose to glucose. The glucose can then be converted to fuels and chemicals using appropriate fermentations. For example, if currently generated newspaper waste were hydrolysed enzymatically to glucose and subsequently fermented to ethanol using yeast, over 2 billion gallons (70 million cubic metres) of fuel could be generated annually.

The enzymatic hydrolysis of cellulose to glucose requires the action of three enzymes, namely cellobiohydrolase, CBH, (EC 3.2.1.21), endoglucanase, EG, (EC 3.2.1.4) and β-glucosidase, BG, (EC 3.2.1.21) (Goyal, Ghosh & Eveleigh, 1991). There are two major fungal cellobiohydrolases (CBH I and II) comprising 80% of the total secreted protein and at least three endoglucanases (EG I, II, and III) comprising 15% of the protein. An understanding of how these cellulases effect the degradation of cellulosic waste materials is necessary for their efficient utilization.

In its native state, crystalline cellulose is composed of parallel or antiparallel fibril chains that are held together in tight bundles by hydrogen bonds. Cellulose is completely insoluble in aqueous media, but acid treatment or a chemical modification render it non-crystalline, or amorphous. In 1950, Reese, Siu & Levinson (1950) observed that two groups of cellulase-producing fungi exist, differing in their hydrolysis abilities. Both groups were found to produce the cellulase enzyme that can hydrolyse glycosidic bonds in amorphous cellulose, e.g. carboxymethylcellulose (CMC). However, Reese observed that only a limited number of fungi (e.g. *Trichoderma reesei, Trichoderma koningi, Fusarium solani, Penicillium funiculosum, Sporotrichum pulverulentum,* and *Talaromyces emersonii*) produce cellulase enzymes that can hydrolyse naturally occurring crystalline celluloses, such as cotton. This discovery prompted Reese to propose his C_1–C_x hypothesis to explain the difference. Basically, the hypothesis states that cellulases capable of hydrolysing naturally occurring cellulose require a factor (C_1) that renders cellulose susceptible to the hydrolytic action of C_x that results in glucose formation. The role of C_1 would be to separate individual cellulose chains from bundles of crystalline cellulosic fibres so that they could be hydrolysed by C_x. Reese proposed that those cellulases unable to hydrolyse naturally occurring cellulose, lack C_1. His hypothesis was the primary impetus for the next four decades of cellulase research, dedicated to understanding the mechanism by which cellulases catalyse the hydrolysis of naturally occurring cellulosic materials to glucose.

In the third decade after Reese's C_1 factor hypothesis, the purification and characterization of cellulase components led to the knowledge that those cellulases capable of complete degradation of crystalline cellulose to glucose required the three types of cellulase activity. The work of Wood and McCrae was significant because it showed that neither the CBH nor EG components alone were capable of significant cotton solubilization but that, in combination, they acted synergistically to effectively solubilize cotton (Wood & McCrae, 1978): C_1 was not therefore a discrete non-enzymatic entity but rather a cellulase component (CBH), without which little degradation of cellulose occurred. For a review on synergy in cellulase systems, see Woodward (1991). This would seem to be supported by a recent report of Evans *et al.* (1992) which indicated an EG with an alkaline pH optimum, and a mass of 24 kD, was essential for the degradation of crystalline cellulose. During the latter part of the fourth decade after Reese's original hypothesis, knowledge about the molecular architecture of several cellulases from both fungal and bacterial sources became available. In light of this development, many cellulases are now known to be composed of a two-domain architecture: a catalytic domain and a cellulose-binding domain, CBD (Henrissatt, 1994). The proposed structure of the CBD from *T. reesei* CBH I is that it is wedge-shaped and that it has one hydrophilic face containing three tyrosines which interact with the cellulose surface (Kraulis *et al.*, 1989). The fact that proteolytic removal of the CBD from cellulases reduces their activity on crystalline cellulose and the possibility that such a wedge could be involved in disrupting non-covalent interactions in the cellulose structure suggested that the CBD component of cellulases might be Reese's C_1 factor. Evidence for this is based upon the work of Din *et al.* (1991, 1994), which showed the CBD of an *Cellulomonas fimi* endoglucanase (Cen A) was capable of disrupting cotton fibres and releasing small insoluble particles from the fibre surface. Both the intact enzyme and the CBD were capable of fibre disruption, whereas the catalytic domain of Cen A smoothed or polished the fibre surface. Therefore, in the fifth decade after Reese originally proposed that a non-enzymatic factor (C_1) was necessary to render crystalline cellulose susceptible to enzymatic degradation, it seemed possible that C_1 could be an integral part of the CBH or EG molecular architecture and that catalytic activity was not necessary for this initiator role.

We have been interested in determining the function of the CBD of *T. reesei*

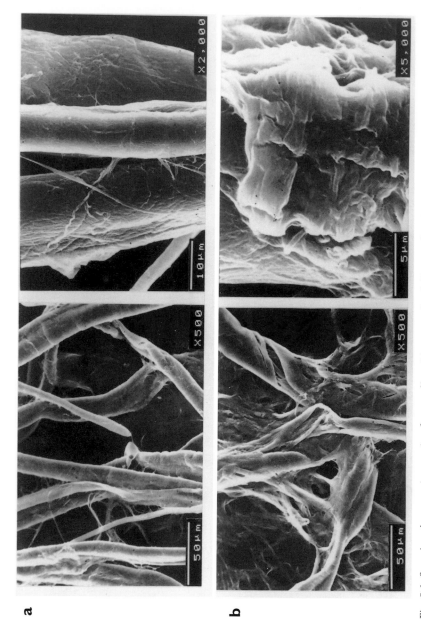

Fig. 9.1. Scanning electron micrographs of cotton fibres (a) untreated and (b) treated with CBH I. Reprinted by permission from *Bioresource Technology*. Copyright Elsevier Science Ltd., 1996.

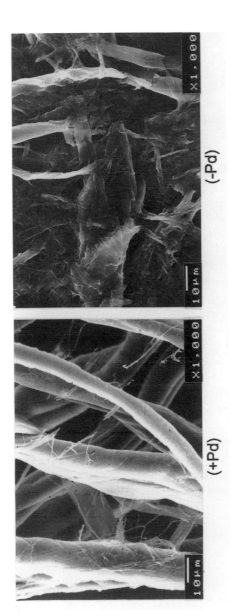

Fig. 9.2. Scanning electron micrographs of cotton fibres treated with CBH II/EG II in the presence and absence of ammonium hexachloropalladate. Reprinted by permission from *Bioresource Technology*. Copyright Elsevier Science Ltd., 1996.

cellulase components for cellulose processing and, in particular, that of CBH I, the major component comprising 60% of the total cellulase protein.

Our approach to examining the effect of the CBD of CBH I was to inactivate CBH I catalytically without affecting its ability to bind to cellulose. The inactivation, without affecting binding, was achieved by using palladium complexes (Shultz *et al.*, 1995; Lassig *et al.*, 1995), and the effect of palladium-inactivated CBH I and other cellulase components on the surface of cellulose fibres was observed by SEM and AFM (Lee *et al.*, 1996).

Scanning electron micrographs (SEM) of industrial native cotton linter fibres and those treated with active CBH I are shown in Fig. 9.1a. The fibres treated with Pd-inactivated CBH I had the same appearance of native fibres, whereas those fibres shaken with active CBH I exhibited surface disruption and loss of structural integrity (Fig. 9.1b). Hoshino *et al.* (1993) showed that an exo-type cellulase from *Irpex lacteus* caused deep transverse cracks in cotton fibres, and such cracks can also be observed in Fig. 9.1b. The effect of CBHII/EG II on the cotton linters is shown in Fig. 9.2. In the presence of Pd, there was clearly no effect on the morphology of the fibres; in the absence of Pd, however, the CBH II/EG II combination resulted in fibre disruption and loss of structural integrity. These data suggest that major structural changes to the cotton fibre structure are not obvious when catalytically inactive cellulase components from *T. reesei* bind to the fibre surface. However, it cannot be completely discounted that structural changes to cotton fibres at higher magnification would be observed upon binding of inactive cellulase components.

The cotton fibre samples were, therefore, examined by atomic force microscopy (AFM). Figures 9.3a and 9.3b show the surface of a control cotton fibre in a $2 \times 2\,\mu m$ and $300 \times 300\,nm$ scan respectively. Parallel microfibrils (Hon, 1994) are clearly obvious throughout the surface. Figure 9.4a shows the structural integrity of the surface of the CBH I-treated fibre to be destroyed with no parallel microfibrils being obvious. At the higher magnification ($300 \times 300\,nm$), fibre-like structures could be seen throughout the surface of native cotton fibres (Fig. 9.3b), whereas randomly shaped structures were observed on the CBH I-treated fibre surface (Fig. 9.4b). At lower magnification ($2 \times 2\,\mu m$), the surface of the Pd-inactivated CBH I-treated fibre looked similar to the control untreated fibre (Fig. 9.5a). However, at the higher magnification (Fig. 9.5b), small holes could be seen throughout the surface of the Pd-inactivated CBH I-treated fibre. These slightly elongated holes had their long axis aligned along the direction of the fibre-like structures. The long axis ranged from 25–75 nm, the short axis ranged from 15–26 nm, and the depth ranged from 4–12 nm. Since Pd-inactivated CBH I is capable of adsorbing on to the surface of cellulose fibres (Lassig *et al.*, 1995), it is possible that these holes were caused by inactivated CBH I molecules on the surface of the fibre which, upon removal by washing, removed part of the fibre surface. The holes observed in the microfibrils after washing the fibres treated with the inactivated enzyme could represent images of CBH I molecules, and the shape and dimension of the smaller holes would not be incompatible with those

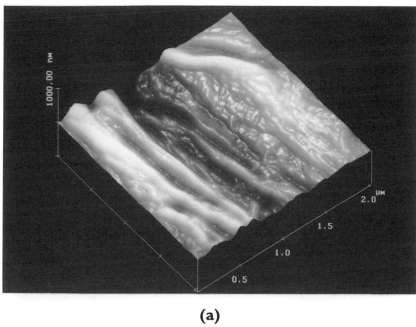

(a)

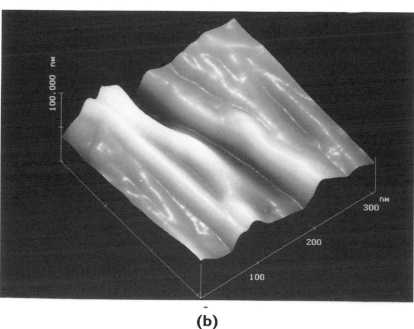

(b)

Fig. 9.3. Atomic force microscope images of native cotton linter fibres in (a) 2 × 2 μm and (b) 300 × 300 nm scans. Reprinted by permission from *Bioresource Technology*. Copyright Elsevier Science Ltd., 1996.

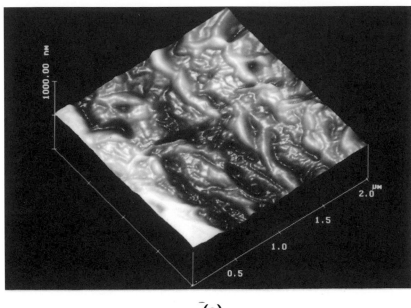

(a)

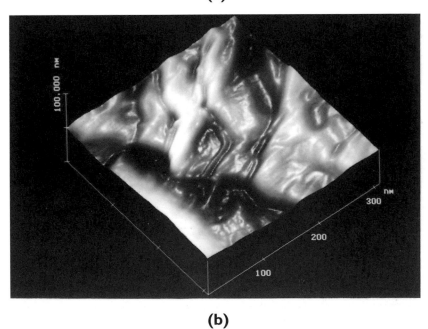

(b)

Fig. 9.4. Atomic force microscope images of CBH I-treated cotton linter fibres in (a) 2 × 2 μm and (b) 300 × 300 nm scans. Reprinted by permission from *Bioresource Technology*. Copyright Elsevier Science Ltd., 1996.

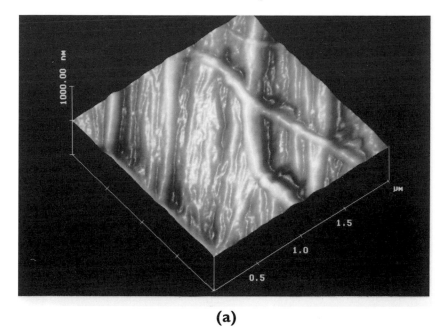

(a)

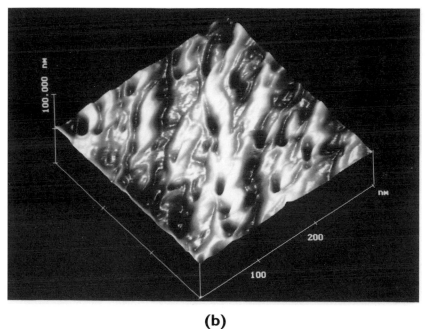

(b)

Fig. 9.5. Atomic force microscope images of Pd-inactivated CBH I-treated cotton linter fibres in (a) 2 × 2 μm and (b) 300 × 300 nm scans. Reprinted by permission from *Bioresource Technology*. Copyright Elsevier Science Ltd., 1996.

determined for this enzyme by small-angle X-ray scattering (Esterbauer *et al.,* 1991). It would appear, therefore, that at least for the fungal CBH and EG components of cellulase, disruption of the cellulosic fibre structure by CBD does not occur and that catalytic activity is required.

9.2.2 Cellulases in wastepaper recycling

The recycling of wastepaper is important for energy conservation and waste minimization. As forests (for harvesting) dwindle, the recycling of all forms of paper, e.g. old newspaper (ONP), magazines, telephone directories, printing and writing paper, tissue and cartons will increase in importance.

Approximately 15 million tonnes of ONP are available in the United States for recycling annually, and currently 8 million tonnes are actually recycled (Heitmann & Joyce, 1991/92). Prior to recycling, ONP and other forms of wastepaper must be de-inked. Current methods for de-inking paper have recently been reviewed (Borchardt, 1993; Shrinath, Szewchzak & Bowen, 1991), and involve pulping the paper in the presence of a mixture of chemicals, i.e. caustic sodium hydroxide, diethylenetriaminepentaacetic acid, sodium silicate and a surfactant. The released ink is removed by washing and air flotation techniques, and the recovered pulp fibres are bleached with hydrogen peroxide to give the desired brightness. The wastewater generated must also be rendered harmless prior to its discharge into the environment. Water-based inks (currently used for only 15–20% of newspapers) present a recovery problem because of their aqueous solubility. The use of water-based, as opposed to oil-based, inks is preferable, however, from an environmental point of view.

For these reasons, there has been interest recently in developing alternate technology for the de-inking of wastepaper. Basically, the use of cellulase (Woodward, 1987) and hemicellulase (Wong & Saddler, 1992) enzymes instead of chemicals to de-ink wastepaper has been proposed, coupled with the usual washing and flotation procedures (Heitmann & Joyce, 1991/92; Kim & Eom, 1991; Pommier, 1990). The action of these enzymes on wastepaper such as ONP results in the loosening or release of ink from the surface of the pulp fibre by unknown mechanisms.

We have developed a novel process for the separation of uninked from inked fibres in old newspaper (Woodward *et al.,* 1994). The process consists of two connected batch reactors in which ONP is pulped in one with enzyme (cellulase). After several hours, uninked pulp fibres are retained in one vessel by means of a plastic mesh screen while inked fibres migrate with the liquid flow to the other vessel where they are also retained (Fig. 9.6). The uninked fibres were shown to be high-quality secondary fibres, based on their strength and length, and possessed similar brightness to chemically de-inked wastepaper. Because the process does not use traditional de-inking chemicals, it does not produce a waste water effluent that needs to be rendered harmless before being discharged into the environment, i.e. an example of 'clean technology'. In addition, preliminary estimates suggest that its use could result in significant energy savings for industry employing traditional chemical de-inking facilities.

Fig. 9.6. Bioreactor configuration for the separation of uninked and inked fibres in ONP. Reprinted with permission from *Bio/Technology*. Copyright Nature Publishing Company, 1994.

Finally, a comparison of the chemical analysis of the uninked and inked fibres from ONP is shown in Table 9.2. The major differences between the composition of the uninked and inked fibres appears to be in lignin content (22% and 34%, respectively) and cellulose content (50% and 37%, respectively). The uninked fibres appear to have the same composition as wood pulp.

9.3 Lignocellulose oxidase; cellulase lignin-oxidase, a constructed enzyme

The cellulose in lignocellulosic materials is generally slow (and difficult) to hydrolyse without extensive pretreatment, due largely to the protective effect of the associated lignin and the insolubility of the crystalline cellulose (Walker & Wilson, 1991). In nature, organisms such as the white rot fungus *Phanerochaete chrysosporium* slowly degrade lignin in lignocellulose by means of flavin or protohaem-containing oxidoreductases via aryl cation or other intermediate carbon-centred free radical formation (Tien & Kirk, 1984). It was wondered whether the enzymatic hydrolysis of cellulose or lignocellulose could be enhanced by conferring upon cellulase, oxidoreductase activity, through the attachment of penta-

Table 9.2. *Chemical composition of uninked and inked fibres from ONP*

Component	Uninked fibres	Inked fibres
Glucose	50.15 (52.8[a])	37.2 (39.2[a])
Xylose	8.21	7.0
Galactose	1.68	2.72
Arabinose	1.98	1.98
Mannose	11.49	8.64
Klason lignin	22.32	33.85
Acid-soluble lignin	0.31	0.61
Ash	0.57	1.51
Total	96.71 (99.36[a])	93.51 (95.51[a])

ONP values are % dry weight of fibres, average of duplicate determinations.
[a]Value obtained for glucose calculated by a glucose analyser.
Reprinted from *Bio/Technology*. Copyright Nature Publishing Company, 1994.

ammineruthenium(III). Such a chemically modified cellulase, it was hypothesized, might oxidize and degrade lignin and lead to subsequent enhanced hydrolysis of the exposed glycosidic bonds in cellulose. The rationale for such a modification was based on the findings of Stanbury *et al.* who showed that a series of ruthenium(II) amines catalysed the reduction of O_2 to H_2O_2 and that during this reaction, superoxide (O_2^-) and perhydroxyl (HO_2^-) free radical intermediates were formed (Stanbury, Hass & Taube, 1980). Also, pentaammineruthenium(III) has been attached to histidine groups of various metalloproteins (Che *et al.*, 1987) and would be likely to attach to cellulases through a similar mechanism.

9.3.1 Conferring oxidase activity on cellulase

Pentaammineruthenium (III) was covalently attached to CBH I, the major component of *T. reesei* cellulase, resulting in 0.7 mol ruthenium/mol CBH I and an electrode potential of +95 mV (Evans *et al.*, 1993). An absorption peak appears at 360–364 nm in the UV-visible absorption scan of modified CBH I (Fig. 9.7). This modification endowed CBH I with novel oxidoreductase activity! The modified enzyme was able to carry out hydrogen peroxide-dependent oxidation of veratryl alcohol, a substrate for lignin peroxidase, at a rate of 0.148 μmol substrate oxidized $min^{-1} \mu mol^{-1}$ enzyme (Fig. 9.8). The 'optimal temperature' was determined to be 45 °C, and the optimum pH was 4.3. The K_m and V_{max} for veratryl alcohol were determined to be 3.5 mM and 52 $\mu mol^{-1} min^{-1}$, respectively. (For details see Evans, Margalit & Woodward, 1994.)

9.3.2. Effects on hydrolytic activity

Examination of the hydolytic activity of pentaammineruthenium(III)-CBH I on several cellulosic substrates indicated that no appreciable loss of activity was

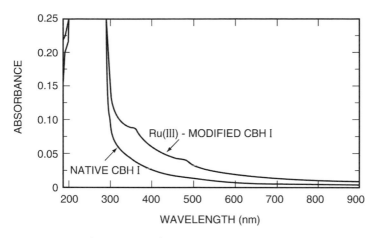

Fig. 9.7. UV-visible spectrum of pentaammineruthenium(III)-CBH I and native CBH I. Reprinted with permission from *Archives of Biochemistry and Biophysics.* Copyright Academic Press, 1994.

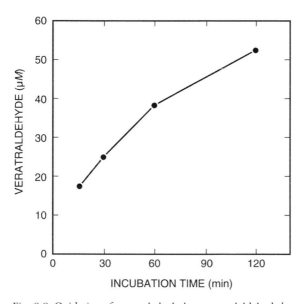

Fig. 9.8. Oxidation of veratryl alcohol to veratrylaldehyde by pentaammineruthenium(III)-CBH I at 45 °C pH 4.3. Reprinted with permission from *Archives of Biochemistry and Biophysics.* Copyright Academic Press, 1994.

caused by the modification with pentaammineruthenium (Table 9.3). Fractionation of the modified enzyme by chromatofocusing resulted in the isolation of fractions that had exhibited enhanced activity toward cellulosic substrates (Fig. 9.9) (Evans *et al.,* 1993).

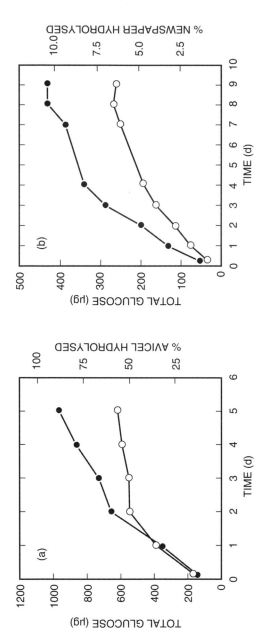

Fig. 9.9. Comparison of the hydrolysis of pure microcrystalline cellulose (avicel) (a) and newspaper (b) by native and fractionated pentaammineruthenium(III)-modified CBH I. Reprinted with permission from *Biochemical and Biophysical Research Communications*. Native —○—; fractionated —●—. Copyright Academic Press, 1993.

Table 9.3. *Initial rates of hydrolysis of various substrates by pentaammineruthenium (III)-modified and native CBH I*

| | | Activity (μmol mg^{-1} min^{-1}) | |
| | | Ru(NH$_3$)$_5$-CBH I | Native CBH I |
Substrate	Conditions		
Filter paper	pH 4.3, 42 °C, 60 min	0.218	0.226
Newsprint	pH 4.3, 42 °C, 360 min	0.0347	0.0345
CMC	pH 4.3, 45 °C, 60 min	0.841	0.872
10 mM PNPC	pH 4.3, 55 °C, 60 min	0.268	0.295
10 mM PNPC	pH 4.3, 23 °C, 120 min	0.0499	0.0575

All substrate concentrations were 1% (w/vol), except for PNPC (*p*-nitrophenyl β-cellobioside). Activities are calculated as μmol cellobiose (mg CBH I)$^{-1}$ min^{-1} produced at the incubation times indicated, using the dinitrosalicylic acid reagent to assay reducing sugar, except for the PNPC assays. In the PNPC assays, μmol *p*-nitrophenol (mg CBH I)$^{-1}$ min^{-1} was determined by measuring the absorbance at 402 nm of an aliquot of reaction added to 1 M sodium carbonate.
Reprinted from *Archives of Biochemistry and Biophysics.* Copyright Academic Press, Inc., 1994.

A cellulase enzyme fraction was also separated from *T. reesei* Pulpzyme HA™, and its characteristics suggested that it was composed mainly of cellobiohydrolase II (CBH II). The covalent attachment of pentaammineruthenium(III) to this enzyme resulted in three-fold and four-fold enhancements of its hydrolytic activity on carboxymethyl cellulose (CMC) and barley β-glucan, respectively, as well as endowing it with veratryl alcohol oxidase activity (Evans, Margalit & Woodward, 1995). The specific activities of native and modified CBH II on various substrates are shown in Table 9.4.

9.4 Xylanase and xylan oxidase (a constructed enzyme)

Xylanases (xyn) are used to decrease the amount of chemicals required in the bleaching of wood pulp and pulp wastes for paper manufacture (Senior & Hamilton, 1992). Improved efficacy of xylanase pretreatment would further decrease the use of bleaching chemicals and improve the results for 'totally chlorine-free' bleaching. Hardwood xylans, such as birchwood xylan, are composed of acetyl-4-o-methyl-glucuronoxylan with a degree of polymerization (DP) of about 200, and with one in ten of the β-D-xylopyranoside backbone units having a 1,2-linked 4-o-methylglucuronic acid moiety. The xylan found in cereals, such as oat-spelt xylan (and other grasses), is arabino-4-methyl-glucuronoxylan with a DP of about 70 and with L-arabinofuranosyl side chains (Coughlan & Hazelwood, 1993). The differences between the two types of xylan can affect the bleaching of different wood pulps (Kantelinen *et al.*, 1993). The xylanase pretreatment aids the removal

Table 9.4. *Specific activities of native and pentaammineruthenium(III)-modified CBH II*

Substrate	Native CBH II	Pentaammine-ruthenium(III)-CBH II
Veratryl alcohol	ND	0.0240
Carboxymethyl cellulose	0.916 ± 0.404	2.50 ± 0.14
	($n = 4$)	($n = 5$)
Barley β-glucan	1.43 ± 0.40	5.56 ± 0.84
	($n = 3$)	($n = 3$)
Birchwood xylan	1.16 ± 0.24	1.38 ± 0.04
	($n = 2$)	($n = 2$)
Cellobiose	0.0268	0.0257
	($n = 1$)	($n = 1$)
ρ-Nitrophenyl β-cellobioside	0.00170	0.00594
	($n = 1$)	($n = 1$)

Activities are in μmol min^{-1} mg^{-1} for production of veratraldehyde from veratryl alcohol; production of reducing sugar from carboxymethyl cellulose, barley β-glucan and birchwood xylan; production of glucose from cellobiose; and production of ρ-nitrophenol from ρ-nitrophenyl β-cellobioside. ND = not detected; n = number of trials; values are mean of the values from n trials ± SD. Reprinted from *Applied Biochemistry and Biotechnology*. Copyright The Humana Press, 1995.

of lignin from the wood pulp by hydrolysing the xylan backbone of the hemicellulose to which the lignin is covalently attached. If the xylanase were equipped additionally with a redox group (as has been shown with cellulases – see above), the bifunctional enzyme thus designed might be able to directly attack and depolymerize the lignin in a manner similar to that employed by lignin peroxidases. A bifunctional *Bacillus pumilus* xylanase with hydrolytic and oxidative activity was obtained by attachment of pentaammineruthenium groups (Evans *et al.*, 1996). A substantial loss of activity in hydrolysis of birchwood and oat-spelt xylans was observed for xynA modified with pentaammineruthenium. Loss of activity was reduced when xynA was modified in the presence of 0.10 M xylose to protect the active site of the enzyme (Table 9.5). Veratryl alcohol oxidase activity was higher for xynA modified without xylose.

As mentioned above, treatment of wood pulps with xylanases to reduce the amount of chemicals required for bleaching is a method that is currently being investigated and is of great interest to the pulp and paper industries (Viikari *et al.*, 1991). In one experiment that was carried out, bleaching pretreatment of kraft pulps using xylanases modified with pentaammineruthenium was shown to reduce the requirement for chlorine dioxide to a greater degree than pretreatment with native xylanases (Evans *et al.*, 1996). Further investigation and application of these

Table 9.5. *Comparison of native and pentaammineruthenium-modified xylanase xynA*

Xylanase preparation	Specific activity[a]		
	Birchwood xylan	Oat spelt xylan	Veratryl alcohol
Native enzyme	194 ± 12 (*n* = 4)	137 ± 11 (*n* = 5)	ND
Modified enzyme	19.8	14.5	0.0115
Enzyme modified in presence of xylose	148 ± 1.7 (*n* – 2)	86.1 ± 4.2 (*n* = 3)	0.00938

[a]Specific activities for catalytic activities on the indicated substrates in μmol (mg protein)$^{-1}$ min^{-1}. (*n* = number of trials). Reprinted from *Enzyme and Microbial Technology*. Copyright Elsevier Science, Inc., 1996.

results could result in improvement of the quality of paper while reducing the requirement for bleaching-chemicals, thus decreasing the amount of halogenated organic compounds that would have to be removed from paper mill effluents. Pentaammineruthenium and pentammineruthenium-modified proteins have been reported to produce reactive oxygen species (ROS) and to carry out oxidation of organic compounds (Stanbury *et al.*, 1980). Xylanases with attached redox groups such as pentaammineruthenium could, therefore, also be used to solubilize pulp residues and depolymerize lignin in the treatment of effluent streams.

9.5 Esterases for utilizing cellulose ester waste

The acetyl, butyryl and propionyl esters of cellulose are widely used in the production of fibres, plastics, films and coatings. These esters are prepared from α-cellulose derived from wood pulp or cotton. As cotton linters are relatively expensive, about $1000 per metric tonne, wood pulp is often used as an industrial source of α-cellulose. Wood is composed of about 40–50% cellulose, a polysaccharide of D-glucose; 20% is hemicellulose, a polysaccharide consisting of D-xylose with branching side chains of other sugars; and the remaining 30% is lignin, a polymer of various hydroxy phenyl propane units. The long fibres of cellulose are the components that possess the desirable qualities for the manufacture of paper. The branched chains of hemicellulose contribute to the mechanical strength of the paper through inter-fibre binding. The aromatic polymer (lignin) provides structural strength and helps protect the wood from microbial attack. Lignin is the component that reacts with pulping chemicals and with air in the presence of light, causing undesirable dark colours in the pulp. Preparation of α-cellulose from wood pulp requires the removal of lignin and hemicellulose by chemical pulping and bleaching, thus generating the waste streams typical of those processes. The cellulose is dried, and then swollen in acetic acid. Acetic anhydride, or propionic or butyric acid, and a catalytic amount of sulphuric acid are added to esterify the cellulose. Water is added to hydrolyse the product, cellulose triacetate, to the desired degree of substitution. The final product is isolated as precipitated flakes from the aqueous solution. The organic acids used in the esterification are recovered and recycled: the waste stream still contains small particles and soluble fragments of cellulose acetate of assorted chain lengths and degrees of substitution. Production of cellulose acetate fibres in the United States was 225 million pounds in 1994, with the wastes generated amounting to 5% of this weight.

The presence of an acetyl esterase in citrus peel that removes acetyl groups from pectin had been reported in 1947 (Jansen, Jang & MacDonnel, 1947). The citrus acetyl esterases were able to deacetylate a number of synthetic substrates such as triacetin (glycerol triacetate) and xylitol pentaacetate. The acetyl esterase from Valencia orange peel has been partially purified and characterized. The natural substrate of the enzyme is pectin, a polysaccharide that contains 2,3-O-acetylated galacturonic acid. Despite the reported activity of the citrus acetyl esterase on various acetylated substrates and the availability of citrus peel as a by-product of the food industry, the application of this enzyme to deacetylation of cellulose acetate or acetylated xylans does not appear to have been investigated thoroughly. Published reports show a preference for fungal acetyl esterases in the treatment of cellulosic materials intended for saccharification. Cellulolytic fungi such as *Aspergillus niger* and *T. reesei* have been found to produce enzymes that remove acetyl groups from the acetylated xylan portion of the hemicellulose (Linden *et al.*, 1994; Poutanen & Sundberg, 1998). Simultaneous saccharification and fermentation was carried out on cellulose that was first acetylated in order to solubilize it, then treated with cellulase and acetyl esterase enzymes from *Pestalotiopsis westerdijkii* or yeast (Downing, Ho & Zabriski, 1987).

It has been found that a commercial preparation of partially purified acetyl esterase (orange peel, *Citrus sinensis*, Sigma) is capable of removing acetate from triacetin and β-D-glucose pentaacetate. In the case of the model substrate, β-D-glucose pentaacetate, after treatment with acetyl esterase the substrate could not be phosphorylated by hexokinase, an enzyme that phosphorylates glucose specifically at the carbon 6-hydroxyl position. As the natural substrate, pectin is reported to be acetylated only at carbon positions 2 and 3 of its galacturonyl residues, it appears likely that the esterase may only remove acetyl groups from certain positions on glucose pentaacetate and cellulose acetate (B. R. Evans & J. Woodward, unpublished data). Lime peel acetyl esterase may also have potential in deacetylating cellulose ester wastes, since it has recently been found that this enzyme also deacetylates glucose pentaacetate. These esterases may also prove useful in the manufacture of cellulose esters which are selectively substituted at one or more positions. Such stereoregular cellulose esters could have novel properties and, as such, provide valuable materials for the manufacture of plastics.

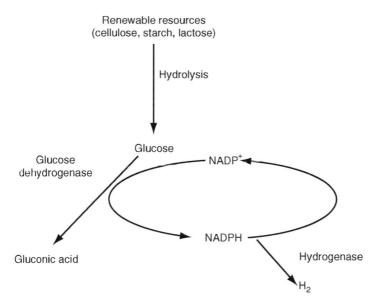

Fig. 9.10. Enzymatic pathway for the conversion of renewable resources to hydrogen. Reprinted with permission from *Nature Biotechnology.* Copyright Nature Publishing Company, 1996.

9.6 Glucose dehydrogenase and hydrogenase

Cellulosic waste also represents a vast untapped source of hydrogen. For example, current annually available waste newspaper in the United States comprises 7.26 million tonnes of cellulose (Woodward *et al.*, 1994), which, theoretically, could yield 37.5 billion standard ft^3 (1.06 trillion dm^3) of hydrogen or 12.2 trillion Btu (assuming standard gas conditions at 15.6 °C and 1.033 kg cm^2, where 1 g mol hydrogen is equivalent to 23.7 dm^3). This volume of hydrogen could serve 37 cities with gas demands equivalent to that of Oak Ridge, a city with a population of approximately 27 000 and a natural-gas consumption of 30.6 billion dm^3 for the fiscal year ending April 1995. These calculations are based upon a new enzymatic pathway for the conversion of glucose to molecular hydrogen that we recently demonstrated (Woodward *et al.*, 1996). The pathway, depicted in Fig. 9.10, is based on a combination of glucose dehydrogenase and hydrogenase that could be used to generate molecular hydrogen from glucose, which in turn could be derived from sources such as cellulose, starch, and lactose, all of which are abundant and renewable. Continuous regeneration and recycle of NADP, in addition to enzyme stability, would be essential for prolonged hydrogen generation. The data in Fig. 9.11 show that cellulose was converted to hydrogen when cellulase was present in the reaction mixture. Under the experimental conditions, the maximum rate of hydrogen evolution was approximately 325 nmol/h, and after 22 h the stoichiometric

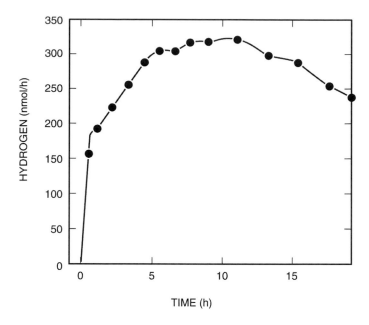

Fig. 9.11. Hydrogen production from microcrystalline cellulose. Hydrogen was generated from cellulose in a reaction mixture containing three enzymes: *Humicola insolens* cellulase, *Thermoplasma acidophilum* glucose dehydrogenase, and *Pyrococcus furiosus* hydrogenase together with the cofactor NADP⁺. Reprinted with permission from *Nature Biotechnology*. Copyright Nature Publishing Company, 1996.

yield of hydrogen was approximately 2.6%. These values compare to 8 μmol/h and a 100% yield of hydrogen if glucose is the starting substrate. Thus, the rate-limiting step in this reaction was the rate of glucose formation from cellulose. The only other product of this reaction is gluconic acid, an important industrial chemical used by major industries for sequestration and chelation.

Acknowledgements

The authors thank Laura Wagner for secretarial assistance. This work was supported by the Offices of Basic Energy Sciences and Energy Efficiency and Renewable Energy, US Department of Energy. Oak Ridge National Laboratory is managed by Lockheed Martin Energy Research Corporation for the US Department of Energy under contract DE-AC05-96OR22464.

The submitted manuscript has been authored by a contractor of the US Government under contract DE-AC05-96OR22464. Accordingly, the US Government retains a non-exclusive, royalty-free licence to publish or reproduce the published form of this contribution, or allow others to do so, for US Government purposes.

References

Armson, R. (1985). Turning rubbish to heat and electricity. *New Scientist*, 7 November, 33–6.

Borchardt, J. K. (1993). Paper de-inking technology. *Chemical Industry*, 8, 273–76.

Che, C-M., Margalit, R., Chiang, H-J. & Gray, H. B. (1987). Ruthenium modified proteins. Reactions of *cis*-[Ru(NH$_3$)$_4$(OH$_2$)$_2$]$^{2+}$ with azurin, myoglobin and cytochrome c. *Inorganica Chimica Acta*, 135, 33–5.

Coughlan, M. P. & Hazelwood, G. P. (1993). β-1, 4-D-xylan-degrading enzyme systems: Biochemistry, molecular biology and application. *Applied Biochemistry and Biotechnology*, 17, 259–89.

Din, N., Gilkes, N. R., Tekant, B., Miller, R. C., Jr., Warren, R. A. J. & Kilburn, D. G. (1991). Non-hydrolytic disruption of cellulose fibers by the binding domain of a bacterial cellulose. *Bio/Technology*, 9, 1096–9.

Din, N., Damude, H. G., Gilkes, N. R., Miller, R. C., Jr., Warren, R. A. J. & Kilburn, D. G. (1994). C$_1$–C$_x$ revisited: intramolecular synergism in a cellulase. *Proceedings of the National Academy of Sciences, USA*, 91, 11 383–7.

Downing, K. M., Ho, C. S. & Zabriski, D. W. (1987). Enzymic production of ethanol from cellulose using soluble cellulose acetate as an intermediate. *Biotechnology and Bioengineering*, 29, 1086–96.

Esterbauer, H., Hayn, M., Abuja, P. M. & Claeyssens, M. (1991). Structure of cellulytic enzymes. In *ACS Symposium Series*, ed. G. F. Leatham & M. E. Himmel. Vol. 460, pp. 301–12. Washington, DC: American Chemical Society.

Evans, E. T., Wales, D. S., Bratt, R. P. & Sagar, B, F. (1992). Investigation of an endoglucanase essential for the action of the cellulase system of *Trichoderma reesei* on crystalline cellulose. *Journal of General Microbiology*, 138, 1639–46.

Evans, B. R., Margalit, R. & Woodward, J. (1993). Attachment of pentaammineruthenium(III) to *Trichoderma reesei* cellobiohydrolase I increases its catalytic activity. *Biochemical and Biophysical Research Communications*, 195, 497–503.

Evans, B. R., Margalit, R. & Woodward, J. (1994). Veratryl alcohol oxidase activity of a chemically modified cellulase protein. *Archives of Biochemistry and Biophysics*, 312, 459–66.

Evans, B. R., Margalit, R. & Woodward J. (1995). Enhanced hydrolysis of soluble cellulosic substrates by a metallocellulase with veratryl alcohol-oxidase activity. *Applied Biochemistry and Biotechnology*, 51/52, 225–39.

Evans, B. R., Lane, L. M., Margalit, R., Hathaway, G. M., Ragauskas, A. & Woodward J. (1996). Comparison of the properties of native and pentaammineruthenium(III) modified xylanase. *Enzyme and Microbial Technology*, 19, 367–73.

Gedon, S. & Fengl, R. (1993). Cellulose ester, organic–inorganic. In *Kirk–Othmer Encyclopedia of Chemical Technology*, 4th edn, Vol. 5, pp. 496–540. New York: John Wiley and Sons, Inc.

Goyal, A., Ghosh, B. & Eveleigh, D. (1991). Characteristics of fungal cellulases. *Bioresource Technology*, 36, 37–50.

Heitmann, J. A., Jr. & Joyce, T. W. (1991/92). Paper recycling: state of the art and future directions. Chapter 1: *AIChE Magazine for Students*, 6, 19–23.

Henrissat, B. (1994). Cellulases and their interaction with cellulose. *Cellulose*, 1, 169–96.

Hon, D. N.-S. (1994). Cellulose: a random walk along its historical path. *Cellulose*, 1, 1–25.

Hoshino, E., Sasaki, Y., Mori, K., Okazaki, M., Nisizawa, K. & Kanda, T. (1993). Electron microscopic observation of cotton cellulose degradation by exo- and endo-type cellulases from *Irpex laxteus*. *Journal of Biochemistry*, 114, 236–45.

J. Woodward and B. R. Evans

Jansen, E. F., Jang, R. & MacDonnel, L. R. (1947). Citrus acetylesterase. *Archives of Biochemistry*, 15, 415–31.
Kantelinen, A., Hortling, B., Sundquist, J., Linko, M. & Viikari, L. (1993). Proposed mechanism of the enzymatic bleaching of kraft pulps with xylanases. *Holzforschung*, 47, 318–14.
Kim, S.-W. & Eom, T.-J. (1991). Enzymatic de-inking method of wastepaper. In *Proceedings of Tappi Pulping Conference*, Orlando, Book 2, 1023–7.
Kitani, O. & Hall C.W. (eds) (1989). *Biomass Handbook*. New York: Gordon and Breach Science Publishers.
Kraulis, P. J., Clore, G. M., Nilges, M., Jones, T. A., Pettersson, G., Knowles, J. & Gronenborn, A. M. (1989). Determination of the three dimensional structure of the C-terminal domain of cellobiohydrolase I from *Trichoderma reesei*. *Biochemistry*, 28, 7241–57.
Lassig, J. P., Shultz, M. D., Gooch, M. G., Evans, B. R. & Woodward, J. (1995). Inhibition of cellobiohydrolase I from *Trichoderma reesei* by palladium. *Archives of Biochemistry and Biophysics*, 322, 119–26.
Lee, I., Evans, B. R., Lane, L. M. and Woodward, J. (1996). Substrate–enzyme interactions in cellulase systems. *Bioresource Technology*, 58, 163–9.
Linden, J., Samara, M., Decker, S., Johnson, E., Boyer, M., Pecs, M., Adney, W. & Himmel, M. (1994). Purification and characterization of an acetyl esterase from *Aspergillus niger*. *Applied Biochemistry and Biotechnology*, 45–46, 383–93.
Pommier, J. C. (1990). Biotechnology in papermaking: Dream or impending reality. *ATIP*, 44, 125–32.
Poutanen, K. & Sundberg, M. (1988). An acetyl esterase of *Trichoderma reesei* and its role in the hydrolysis of acetyl xylans. *Applied Microbiology and Biotechnology*, 28, 419–24.
Reese, E. T., Siu, R. G. H. & Levinson, H. S. (1950). The biological degradation of soluble cellulose derivatives and its relationship to the mechanism of cellulose hydrolysis. *Journal of Bacteriology*, 59, 485–97.
Senior, D. J. & Hamilton, J. (1992). Biobleaching with xylanases brings biotechnology to reality. *Pulp and Paper*, September 1992, 111–14.
Setterholm, V. C. (1991). Recycling wood fiber in municipal solid wastes: opportunity for government-industry partnership. *Tappi Journal*, 74, 79–84.
Shrinath, A., Szewchzak, J. T. & Bowen, I. J. (1991). A review of ink-removal techniques in current de-inking technology. *Tappi Journal*, 74, 85–93.
Shultz, M. D., Lassig, J. P., Gooch, M. G., Evans, B. R. & Woodward, J. (1995). Palladium – a new inhibitor of cellulase activities. *Biochemical and Biophysical Research Communications*, 209, 1046–52.
Stanbury, D. M., Hass, O. & Taube, H. (1980). Reduction of oxygen by ruthenium(II) ammines. *Inorganic Chemistry*, 19, 518–24.
Tien, M. & Kirk, T. K. (1984). Lignin-degrading enzyme from *Phanerochaete chrysosporium*: purification, characterizaton and catalytic properties of a unique H_2O_2-requiring oxygenase. *Proceedings of the National Academy of Sciences, USA*, 81, 2280–4.
Viikari, L., Kanteline, A., Rättö, M. & Sundquist, J. (1991). Enzymes in pulp paper processing. *ACS Symposium Series*, 460, 12–21.
Walker, L. P. & Wilson, D. B. (1991). Enzymatic hydrolysis of cellulose: an overview. *Bioresource Technology*, 36, 3–14.

Williamson, G. (1991). Purification and characterization of pectin acetylesterase from orange peel. *Phytochemistry*, 30, 445–9.

Wong, K. K. Y. & Saddler, J. N. (1992). *Trichoderma* xylanases, their properties and application. *Critical Reviews in Biotechnology*, 12, 413–35.

Wood, T. M. & McCrae, S. I. (1978). The cellulase of *Trichoderma koningii*. *Biochemical Journal*, 171, 61–72.

Woodward, J. (1987). Utilisation of cellulose as a fermentation substrate: problems and potential. In *Carbon Substrates in Biotechnology*, ed. J. D. Stowell, A. D. Beardsmore, C. W. Keevil & J. R. Woodward, pp. 45–65. Oxford: IRL Press.

Woodward, J. (1991). Synergism in cellulase systems. *Bioresource Technology*, 36, 67–75.

Woodward, J., Wyman, C. E. & Goodman, B. J. (eds) (1993). Fourteenth symposium on biotechnology for fuels and chemicals. *Applied Biochemistry and Biotechnology* 39/40. Totowa, New Jersey: The Humana Press.

Woodward, J., Stephan, L. M., Koran, L. J., Jr, Wong, K. K. Y. & Saddler, J. N. (1994). Enzymatic separation of high-quality uninked pulp fibers from recycled newspaper. *Bio/Technology*, 12, 905–8.

Woodward, J., Mattingly, S. M., Danson, M., Hough, D., Ward, N. & Adams, M. (1996). *In vitro* hydrogen production by glucose dehydrogenase and hydrogenase. *Nature Biotechnology*, 14, 872–4.

10

Sensors for nitrogen removal monitoring in wastewater treatment

K. Gernaey, H. Bogaert, P. Vanrolleghem, L. Van Vooren and W. Verstraete

10.1 Introduction

An overview of sensors and techniques for monitoring of nitrogen removal processes is presented and some recent evolutions in this area are discussed in detail. The overview is not limited to a description of sensors for the on-line collection of ammonium, nitrate and nitrite concentration data but also covers sensors and techniques that can be used to measure nitrification and denitrification activities of activated sludge. Sensors were subdivided into three categories: direct probes (DO, pH, ORP), indirect probes (e.g. on-line NH_4^+ and NO_3^- analysers) and biosensors (e.g. RODTOX, NITROX, DECADOS, BRAM . . .). Finally, the application of activity measurements for influent nitrification toxicity monitoring is discussed, both in technical and cost/benefit terms.

Biological nitrogen removal is one of the most important and most intensively studied wastewater treatment processes. The growing attention to biological nitrogen removal was favoured by the more stringent effluent criteria for nitrogen that have been imposed on new and existing treatment plants (Nyberg *et al.*, 1992; Wacheux, Da Silva & Lesavre 1993), and by the fact that biological nitrogen removal is, in most cases, the most economical way to reduce the concentration of nitrogen compounds in wastewater (EPA, 1993). Biological nitrogen removal requires two reaction steps: in a first aerobic phase, nitrification (the biological oxidation of ammonium to nitrite and nitrate) takes place; in a second anoxic phase, denitrification occurs. During denitrification, oxidized nitrogen species are used as electron acceptors by micro-organisms in the presence of sufficient biodegradable COD, resulting in the conversion of nitrate and nitrite into dinitrogen gas that escapes from the mixed liquor.

Different reactor configurations (e.g. completely mixed systems, plug flow reactors, sequencing batch reactors . . .) have been developed to obtain biological nitrogen removal (Randall, 1992). A general characteristic of all systems is that mixed liquor is cycling through aerobic and anoxic conditions to obtain nitrification and denitrification. When facing the daily, weekly and seasonal influent load variations to the treatment plant, it was a tradition for many years to design oversized wastewater treatment plants, to guarantee a good effluent quality without much process adjustment. Nowadays, increased loads at many existing treatment plants and more stringent effluent discharge limits have strongly stimulated research and development (R&D) in this domain. The resulting improved understanding of the actual treatment processes for biological nitrogen removal allows many plants to attain advanced treatment objectives by implementing better control of the treatment plant. The latter is based on on-line monitoring of relevant process parameters as, e.g. the NH_4^+-N or NO_3^--N concentration, and oxidation–reduction potential (ORP) in the mixed liquor: such treatment plant optimization is more advantageous in terms of required efforts than extending the existing treatment plant capacity by constructing additional reactor volume (Thornberg, Neilson & Andersen, 1993).

This chapter concentrates on sensors for monitoring biological nitrogen removal processes in activated sludge plants. In the field of traditional sensor equipment (DO, pH, ORP, NH_4^+-N, NO_3^--N), the general measuring principles of the sensors are briefly discussed together with some applications and recent advances in this field. In a separate section, some recently developed biosensors for nitrification and denitrification monitoring are presented and compared to existing technology.

10.2 Sensors

The sensors used for monitoring nitrogen removal processes can be subdivided into three main categories. Direct probes (DO, pH and ORP electrodes-see below) are physico-chemical sensors that have direct contact with the wastewater or the mixed liquor. Indirect probes (on-line NH_4^+-N and NO_3^--N analysers) are generally operating near to the measuring point but the sample is transported to the measuring device. Connection between measuring point and analyser is obtained by a sampling (pretreatment) unit. Biosensors have an active biology directly involved in the measurement.

10.2.1 Direct probes

DO, pH and ORP probes have in practice proved their robustness, reliability and limited maintenance demand. For several years, there has been a trend to extract as much information as possible from the raw data provided by these sensors when submerged in the mixed liquor. As a logical consequence of these efforts, especially DO but also pH and ORP electrodes are used as the robust sensor element in respirometers, nitrification-activity meters and denitrification-activity meters, (Vanrolleghem & Coen, 1995).

Dissolved oxygen (DO)

DO electrodes are applied in aerobic stages of wastewater treatment processes. The general measuring principle of the electrode is based on the diffusion of O_2 molecules through a gas-permeable membrane, followed by the electrochemical reaction of the O_2 in an amperometric (current) or polarographic (voltage) measuring cell.

Application of DO electrodes is widespread due to the high cost of aeration in wastewater treatment plants and the cost reduction that can be obtained by DO-based aeration control. One of the most common problems is the choice of a representative measuring point in the aeration tank (Harremoës *et al.*, 1993). Electrode fouling is a well-known operational problem (Sasaki *et al.*, 1993; Watts & Garber, 1993). DO electrodes need frequent cleaning and calibration, because absolute values are used for control purposes. Maintenance of the electrode can be limited by automatic cleaning of the electrode with a brush, with an air or liquid stream, in combination with automatic calibration of the electrode and a continuous check of the quality of the DO data with appropriate software (Watts & Garber, 1993).

DO electrodes are generally applied for keeping a fixed DO setpoint in the aeration tank, to minimize aeration costs. The intensity of the aeration is adjusted based on the DO measurement in the mixed liquor. An example of the application of such a control strategy is presented in Fig. 10.1, where some parameters recorded during the aerobic phase of a sequencing batch reactor cycle are shown (Demuynck *et al.*, 1994). The combination of a fixed DO setpoint (setpoint = 2 mg/1, dead-band = 0.5 mg/1) with an on/off aeration system for a nutrient-removal sequencing batch reactor, results in typical DO profiles. Additional information can be extracted from the recorded DO profile. It can be seen that aeration is switched on frequently at the beginning of the aerobic phase, indicating that the biological activity is high at that moment. The aeration intensity decreases after about 90 minutes, due to the complete oxidation of all NH_4^+-N, as indicated by the N species concentration data also presented in Fig. 10.1. The slope of the decreasing DO curves obtained when aeration is off allows us to estimate the oxygen uptake rate (OUR) of the mixed liquor. This information can be useful to check the actual state (or the completeness) of the respiration processes in the aeration tank. In Fig. 10.1, a clear decrease of the OUR can be observed when nitrification is finished (see below for further discussion of Fig. 10.1).

Over the years, more complex control systems using on-line DO measurements have been developed, yielding more additional information about ongoing processes in the aeration tank. An example is the simultaneous on-line estimation of both oxygen mass transfer characteristics and biological oxygen uptake in the aeration tank (Holmberg, Olsson & Andersson, 1989; Declercq, 1993).

In exceptional cases, DO electrodes are also applied for anoxic processes. For predenitrification systems, they are sometimes used to check whether or not recirculation rates are set properly. Measurable DO concentrations indicate that

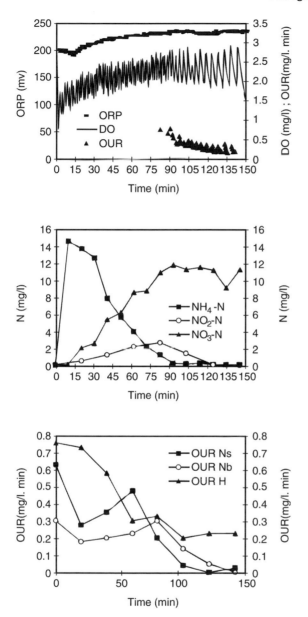

Fig. 10.1. Oxidation–reduction potential (ORP), dissolved oxygen (DO) and oxygen uptake rate (OUR) (top); NH_4^+, NO_2^- and NO_3^--N (middle); nitrification step 1 (OUR Ns), nitrification step 2 (OUR Nb) and heterotrophic OUR (OUR H) (bottom) during a typical aeration phase of a sequencing batch reactor cycle (Demuynck *et al.*, 1994). For the differentiation of different OUR types, see text below.

the anoxic respiration is too low and that the recirculation ratio can be decreased (Teichgräber, 1993).

pH

pH measurements are common in wastewater treatment plants. Nevertheless, electrode fouling can give trouble (Sikow & Pursiainen, 1995); but longer periods without maintenance of the electrode can be obtained by providing an automatic hydraulic (water spray), mechanical (brush), chemical (rinsing with cleaning agent) or ultrasonic cleaning system (Vanrolleghem & Verstraete, 1993a).

During nitrification, aerobic conditions are necessary and protons are produced, as can be seen from equation (1):

$$NH_4^+ + 2\ O_2 \rightarrow NO_3^- + H_2O + 2\ H^+ \tag{1}$$

The proton production can lead to acidification and subsequent process failure. When the buffer capacity of the mixed liquor is too low to compensate for the proton production due to nitrification, a pH measurement system coupled to a dosing system can be applied for pH adjustment in nitrifying activated sludge units (Teichgräber, 1993). Teichgräber (1990) proposed to perform alkalinity measurements instead of pH measurements to control the dosage of alkali during nitrification. However, the alkalinity measurement is more complicated and expensive than operating a pH probe.

Denitrification, however, requires a source of readily biodegradable substrate (RBS) and anoxic conditions for it to occur. Contrary to nitrification, alkalinity is produced. The denitrification reaction with acetate is shown in equation (2).

$$CH_3COO^- + 0.84\ NO_3^- + 1.84\ H^+ \rightarrow 1.16\ CO_2$$
$$+ 0.17\ C_5H_7O_2N + 0.34\ N_2 + 1.83\ H_2O \tag{2}$$

Recently, a series of titrimetric sensors to be applied in nitrogen removal activated sludge plants have been described (Aivasidis et al., 1992; Massone et al., 1995; Vanderhasselt, 1995; Van Vooren et al., 1995). In these applications, which will be discussed below, the proton production or consumption is used to characterize nitrifying and denitrifying populations, respectively. Al-Ghusain et al. (1994) showed that well-defined control points on pH profiles, recorded during an alternating aerobic-anoxic process, were related directly to the alternating nitrification and denitrification reactions in the process. Moreover, the pH control points were consistent with bending points identified on simultaneously recorded ORP profiles. Control strategies were developed using fixed pH setpoints and dynamic pH variations. However, Al-Ghusain et al. (1994) do not mention anything about the influence of influent alkalinity variations on the pH measurements. It can be expected that the proposed pH control system will fail partly or completely for mixed liquors with a high buffer capacity, especially when using fixed pH setpoints.

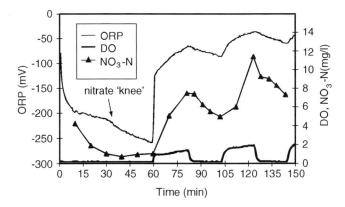

Fig. 10.2. ORP, nitrate and DO profiles recorded during subsequent anoxic and aerobic phases in a sequencing batch reactor. The knee obtained after about 35 minutes coincides with the disappearance of nitrate from the mixed liquor (Demuynck *et al.*, 1994).

Oxidation–reduction potential (ORP)

ORP electrodes provide a general indication of the oxidative status of the monitored system. ORP electrodes, in contrast to DO electrodes, also provide information about the biological processes occurring under anoxic and anaerobic conditions. From a technical point of view, the ORP measurement can be considered accurate and unproblematic (Harremoës *et al.* 1993).

Interpretation of ORP measurements is based on the detection of breakpoints or 'knees' in ORP profiles. The knees indicate the appearance or disappearance of a redox buffer system, comparable to a pH buffer system in acid/base titrations. The most well-known ORP breakpoints are the DO breakpoint and the NO_3^- breakpoint (de la Ménardière *et al.*, 1991; Wareham, Hall & Mavinic, 1993; Wouters-Wasiak *et al.*, 1993; Al-Ghusain *et al.*, 1994). The DO breakpoint indicates the disappearance of NH_4^+ during the aerobic phase (end of nitrification). The NO_3^- breakpoint indicates the disappearance of NO_3^- during the anoxic cycle (end of denitrification). An example is shown in Fig. 10.2 for a nutrient-removal sequencing batch reactor. The nitrate knee occurs after 35 minutes in the anoxic phase, indicating that all NO_3^- is denitrified, as indicated also by the NO_3^- measurements presented in Fig. 10.2. After the detection of the knee, aeration could be started again.

The absolute ORP values fluctuate with the actual load and also depend on the surface treatment and maintenance procedure for the electrode (Charpentier *et al.*, 1988; Heduit & Thevenot, 1992; Heduit, Martin & Thevenot, 1994): interferences with other redox buffers and slow changes on the electrode surface also affect the absolute values. However, because the applied control methods depend on the shape of the ORP curve rather than on absolute ORP values, ORP electrodes do not require as strict a maintenance as DO and pH electrodes (Sasaki *et al.*, 1993).

However, because it is better to monitor relative ORP changes, it is essential to impose varying conditions on the process such as, for instance, in sequencing batch reactors, intermittent aeration systems or alternating activated sludge plants (Vanrolleghem & Verstraete, 1993*a*). Different authors presented control strategies for sequencing batch reactors based on the different bending points of the recorded ORP curve (Sasaki *et al.*, 1993; Wareham *et al.*, 1993; Plisson-Saune *et al.*, 1995). It was shown that control strategies based on ORP bending points are more advantageous than strategies based on absolute ORP values (Plisson-Saune *et al.*, 1995). Methods for knee detection were recently evaluated by Vanrolleghem and Coen (1995). They found that a knee detection method based on absolute differences between two slopes (Wareham, Hall & Mavinic 1993) was somewhat slower but more reliable than a method based on the ratio of two slopes (Sasaki *et al.*, 1993).

10.2.2 Indirect probes

On-line NH_4^+ and NO_3^- analysers have been developed for nitrogen removal monitoring and process control. Basically, the on-line analysers make use of known laboratory measuring principles. However, it is important to note that the measuring principles have often been modified (simplified) compared to the standard laboratory method when applied to on-line analysers.

Operation of on-line NH_4^+ and NO_3^- analysers requires sample pretreatment for most applications in biological process tanks (Harremoës *et al.*, 1993). Sample pretreatment techniques will be discussed separately.

At a nitrogen removal treatment plant, basically three different measuring points can be distinguished: the inlet to the treatment plant or the biotransformation unit, the mixed liquor tanks and the outlet of the treatment plant. Measurement of NH_4^+ in the inlet enables us to monitor the load entering the treatment plant, but on-line NH_4^+ measurements are not always representative of the actual N load because a significant part of the N can be incorporated in organic compounds that have not (or only partly) been hydrolysed by the inlet of the treatment plant. An on-line NO_3^- measurement is generally not applied because most influents contain little or no oxidized N compounds.

For N-removal process control, measurements in the mixed liquor are the best because the immediate effect of control actions on plant performance can be detected this way. Measurement at the outlet of the treatment plant is suitable for effluent quality monitoring, but is less useful for process control because the signal will be smoothened and delayed.

Sample pretreatment

Most of the available NH_4^+ and NO_3^- analysers require a sample stream that is free of suspended solids, which necessitates the use of a membrane filter sampling system. Up to 32% of the total costs for the installation of an on-line analyser can be due to the installation of a sampling system (Schlegel & Baumann, 1995). A submerged pump pumps the sludge through the sampling system. The pump is to be equipped with a shredding device for the destruction of threads and ropes. The choice of the correct pump and the use of low-angle pipe bends and smooth narrowings in the pipe diameter give a stable sampling system for most applications. The sampling itself is carried out by means of crossflow filters. A schematic presentation of a sampling system is given in Fig. 10.3. Only a small sample flow free of suspended solids (a few litres per hour) is going to the analysers, while large volumes (several m^3/h) are pumped through the filter. The high flow and the resulting shear forces prevent the deposition of small particles on the membrane surface (Thomsen & Nielsen, 1992).

For most applications, ultrafiltration (UF) membranes with a molecular weight cut-off of 20 000 are applied. Several analysers can be connected to one sampling system. Wacheux et al. (1993) selected a sintered polyethylene crossflow filter with a pore size of 15 μm. Application of a gauze filter equipped with a compressor for automatic cleaning of the filter with air is reported (Sikow & Pursiainen, 1995). For effluent measurements, this simplified type of pretreatment was satisfactory, except for UV absorbance NO_3^- measurements where installation of an UF unit was necessary. For operation on presettled influent, operation of the gauze filter system was not satisfactory because frequent manual cleaning was needed.

Normally, the filters have to be cleaned every 1 to 4 weeks (Thomsen & Nielsen, 1992; Vanrolleghem & Verstraete, 1993a). In practice, a set-up with two parallel UF units is preferred to maintain a continuous sample flow to the analysers (Teichgräber, 1993), as shown also in Fig. 10.3. While cleaning the first UF unit, the second one is used for sampling. Built-in filtrate flow meters or pressure drop measurements automatically switch off the active unit and activate the cleaning program. Cleaning is obtained by an air blow or a hypochlorite chemical treatment (Vanrolleghem & Verstraete, 1993a). For influent sampling, daily manual cleaning of the UF units can be necessary (Schlegel & Baumann, 1995). The life-time of a crossflow filter is about 1 year (Thomsen & Nielsen, 1992).

The maximum allowable total response time of the measurement (pretreatment included) should preferably be less than 15 minutes for on-line control of alternating biological wastewater treatment plants in which phase changes from aerobic to anoxic or vice versa may occur as often as every 30 minutes (Thomsen & Nielsen, 1992; Thomsen & Kisbye, 1995). For effluent monitoring, response times can be longer because effluent concentrations vary rather slowly. Thomsen and Nielsen (1992) found a response time of 3–9 minutes for an UF sampling system.

Only recently, on-line colorimetric analysers were developed for immediate installation in the mixed liquor tanks without any need for a separate sampling and filtration unit, thereby reducing the total response time of the analyser system to less than 5 minutes (Lynggaard-Jensen et al., 1995). Sampling is done by enrichment of a carrier liquid with ions passing through a membrane that acts as an ion sieve (membrane thickness = 50 μm, molecular weight cut-off = 100). The carrier (clean water) is pumped on one side of the membrane, while the other side is immediately exposed to the mixed liquor/wastewater. The lifetime of the membrane is estimated

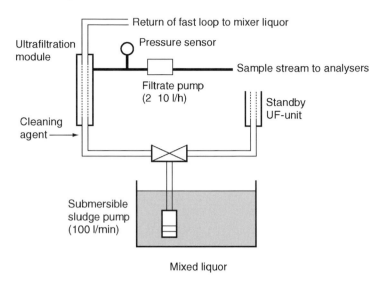

Fig. 10.3. Diagram of a typical ultrafiltration module (Vanrolleghem & Verstraete, 1993*a*).

to be more than 1 month. One drawback associated with this type of meter is that it is impossible to couple more than one measuring point to one meter analyser. UF units allow us to use one meter analyser for several parallel UF units connected to different sampling points.

NH_4^+-analysers

The measuring principle of most on-line NH_4^+-analysers is based on ion-selective electrodes or colorimetric reactions. Well-known control applications of on-line NH_4^+-analysers installed on the activated sludge tanks are the endpoint detection of nitrification in alternating activated sludge processes and the increase of the DO setpoint in the aeration tank at increased NH_4^+ concentrations (Balslev, Lynggaard-Jensen & Nickelsen, 1995). The increase of the DO setpoint will result in a higher nitrification rate in the aeration tank, because oxygen is a limiting substrate for nitrification under normal operating conditions. For alternating activated sludge processes, endpoint detection with an NH_4^+-analyser is believed to allow slightly higher overall process rates compared to ORP or DO measurements (e.g. Fig. 10.1). The on-line analysers allow us to stop the aerated phase before all substrate (in this case NH_4^+) is oxidized completely, resulting in both a low effluent NH_4^+ concentration and an optimal use of the available reactor volume.

When using an ion-selective electrode, the pH of the sample typically is increased to 11, thereby converting all NH_4^+ into NH_3. The NH_3 is subsequently detected by the gas-sensitive electrode. Ion-selective electrodes are preferred for the measurement of NH_4^+ for their low reagent consumption, the almost complete absence of chemical interference and the short response time of the analyser (less than 10 minutes) (Thomsen & Nielsen, 1992; Wacheux *et al.*, 1995). However, a good temperature compensation system is necessary (Thomsen & Nielsen, 1992; Wacheux *et al.*, 1995). Some problems were reported with gas bubble retention under the electrode tip (Andersen and Wagner, 1990), hydroxide poisoning of the electrode (Aspegren, Nyberg & Andersson, 1993) and electrode drifting (Patry & Takacs, 1995; Bogaert, personal communication). Aspegren *et al.* (1993) reported rather frequent clogging problems when performing on-line NH_4^+ measurements on presettled wastewater with an ion-selective electrode without any sample pretreatment.

For colorimetric NH_4^+ determinations, all NH_4^+ is also converted into NH_3 before it is transformed into a blue (phenate method) or a yellow (nesslerization method) azo dye. Colorimetric NH_4^+ analysers have a higher reagent consumption (Thomsen & Nielsen, 1992) and are sensitive to sample temperature variations (Wacheux *et al.*, 1995). Most traditional colorimetric NH_4^+-analysers suffer from a too-long response time of about 20 minutes (Wacheux *et al.*, 1995). Pedersen Kümmel & Soeberg (1990) solved this problem by using a flow injection analysis (FIA) system with a response time of about 1 minute. After conversion of NH_4^+ into NH_3 under alkaline conditions and diffusion of NH_3 through a gas-permeable membrane into a weak pH buffer with a pH indicator, NH_3 could be quantified colorimetrically. However, the high maintenance need (e.g. the gas diffusion membrane had to be replaced once every week, and this needed a well-trained technician) is a serious drawback for on-line application. Continuous technological improvements (reported in Isaacs & Soeberg, 1995) have resulted in a gas diffusion membrane with a life time of about 6 months. A standard calibration of the FIA system is performed frequently as a validity check for the analyser system (Isaacs & Soeberg, 1995). Recently, a prototype of an FIA-based auto-calibrating colorimetric NH_4^+-analyser operational in the 0–25 mg NH_4^+-N/1 concentration range was developed with a response time of less than 5 minutes (Lynggaard-Jensen *et al.*, 1995). The response time could be limited because, on the one hand, the analyser could immediately be placed in the mixed liquor and, on the other hand, because colour reactions did not have to completely come to an end for a reliable concentration restimation. This reliable measurement was obtained by the development of a system with a very high 'repeatability' enabling the photometer detection to take place always at exactly the same time during the development of a detectable colour (indophenol blue). Although the analyser is operated continuously, reagent consumption is limited to less than 3 litres per month through use of semi-micro continuous flow analysis. Wacheux *et al.* (1995) reported that this type of analyser is sensitive to interferences of chemicals, e.g. S^{2-} and ethanolamine. At present, no long-term experience with this kind of submerged analyser is available. A low response time of about 3 minutes is reported for UV absorption NH_4^+-analysers (Wacheux *et al.*, 1995). However, this measurement is also sensitive to temperature variations.

Van Vooren *et al.* (1995) presented an automatic buffer capacity sensor for

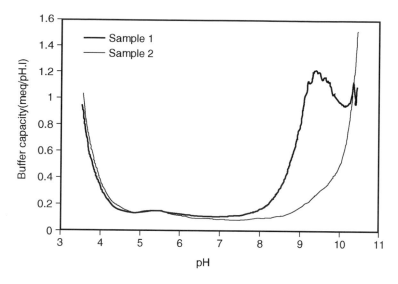

Fig. 10.4. Buffer capacity curves obtained from two different surface waters. Sample 1 = 9.6 mg NH_4^+-N/l; Sample 2 = 1.0 mg NH_4^+-N/l (Van Vooren *et al.*, 1995).

effluent and surface water quality monitoring capable of estimating effluent NH_4^+ concentrations. The sampling is followed by a pH adjustment to pH 2 and a short aeration of about 5 minutes to strip the dissolved CO_2. After the sample pretreatment, a titration curve is obtained by stepwise base addition to the sample. From this titration curve, the buffer capacity in each point is calculated as the derivative of the amount of base needed (in meq/1) for a pH increase of one pH unit. The buffer capacity (meq/1 pH) as a function of the pH is called the buffer capacity profile. A particular component will give its maximum buffer capacity around the pK_a of that component. From the buffer capacity curve, estimates of the different buffering components (e.g. o-PO_4-P; NH_4^+-N) can be computed using a mathematical model, by separating the buffer capacity curve into its components. An example of a buffer capacity curve recorded for two surface water samples is presented in Fig. 10.4. The effect of increasing NH_4^+-N (pK_a = 9.0–9.5) concentrations on the shape of the buffer capacity curves is very clear.

NO_3^--analysers

The measuring principle of on-line NO_3^--analysers is based on ion-selective electrodes, colorimetric reactions or UV absorption. The best results are obtained with UV absorption NO_3^--analysers (Thomsen & Nielsen, 1992; Wacheux *et al.*, 1993; Sikow & Pursiainen, 1995). The measurement is based on the UV absorption of NO_3^- and NO_2^- at 210 nm. The UV absorption NO_3^--analysers are highly appreciated for their low maintenance requirement (Thomsen & Nielsen, 1992; Sikow & Pursiainen, 1995) and short response time of about 10 seconds (Wacheux *et al.*, 1993). Moreover, addition of chemicals is not needed to complete the analysis. However, because particles interfere with the UV absorption measurement, filtered samples must be supplied to the analyser which affects the total response time of the measuring system (analyser + crossflow UF pretreatment system) considerably. In some cases, interference by UV-absorbing organic matter may influence the measurements (Thomsen & Nielsen, 1992; Teichgräber, 1993; Wacheux et al., 1993). Teichgräber (1993) installed a granular activated carbon filter between UF unit and analyser to remove interference due to soluble organic matter. However, no activated carbon could be selected which removed sufficient organic matter without retaining any NO_3^-. For some applications, UV absorption NO_3^--analysers were reported to have a moving baseline, but this can be solved by a frequent automatic zero-calibration (Andersen & Wagner, 1990). Aspegren et al. (1993) reported that the analyser was sometimes calibrated at an erroneous zero level.

Analysers with ion-selective NO_3^- electrodes are advantageous for their low chemical consumption and little or no sample pretreatment, resulting in a short response time of the analysers (Thomsen & Nielsen, 1992). However, the system is sensitive to contamination of the electrode (Wacheux et al., 1993; Sikow & Pursiainen, 1995), electrode drift (Andersen & Wagner, 1990; Wacheux et al., 1993) and interference of ions as, e.g. HCO_3^- (Sikow & Pursiainen, 1995) and Cl^- (APHA, 1992). Limited lifetime of the electrode can also cause trouble (Sikow & Pursiainen, 1995).

Sample pretreatment, frequent automatic calibration and availability of a spare electrode can partly alleviate such problems, but negatively affects the response time of the system, increases the operational costs and limits the real measuring time of the analyser (total operational time of the analyser minus time needed for calibration and maintenance).

Colorimetric NO_3^- analysers (NO_3^- + NO_2^- analysers) first convert the NO_3^- to NO_2^-. The reduction of NO_3^- to NO_2^- is mostly obtained by passing the NO_3^- over a Cd column. In a following step, an azo dye (that can be measured optically) is formed with NO_2^-. This explains why NO_2^-, originally present in the sample, is also measured with this procedure. Lynggaard-Jensen et al. (1995) describe an on-line colourimetric NO_3^- analyser with a response time of less than 5 minutes. In this case, the analyser was placed immediately in the mixed liquor. However, the operational range of the analyser was limited to the 0–10 mg N/1 concentration range. An FIA system for NO_3^- measurements has a comparable response time but allows us to perform NO_3^- concentration measurements at different sampling points with the same analyser (Isaacs & Soeberg, 1995). A separate colorimetric on-line NO_2^- measurement can be carried out by just bypassing the Cd reduction step from the colorimetric NO_3^- determination method (Pedersen et al. 1990; Teichgräber, 1993).

10.2.3 Biosensors

Characterization of substrate and biomass in biological wastewater treatment systems is important. Simple microbial activity measurements can give information about the biodegradability of a substrate, the actual process rates (nitrification, denitrification, carbon oxidation), toxicity of a wastestream or a chemical. This information can be obtained by operating a biosensor. An example of an important application for biosensors is on-line detection of influent toxicity, especially for treatment plants receiving only industrial (or a mixture of industrial and municipal) wastewater. Two groups of biosensors for nitrification–denitrification monitoring are used: respirometric and titrimetric biosensors.

Respirometry

Biodegradation processes in the aerobic stage of activated sludge plants consume oxygen. Respirometry is the measurement of the oxygen uptake rate (OUR or the respiration rate) of activated sludge. The measurement device itself is called a respirometer. The oxygen consumption can be monitored either volumetrically using pressure transducers and CO_2 stripping, or by specific oxygen sensing devices either in the liquid phase, i.e. DO probes, or in the gas phase using fuel cells or paramagnetic oxygen analysers (Spanjers, 1993; Vanrolleghem & Spanjers, 1994). Most respirometric methods that have been proposed rely on DO probes to monitor the OUR of the sludge.

Two main respirometric principles can be distinguished: batch and continuous respirometers (Spanjers, 1993; Vanrolleghem & Spanjers, 1994). Batch respirometers can be either closed or open. The closed respirometer is operated by withdrawing a sample of activated sludge from a plant, transferring it into a small vessel and then monitoring the decline of DO concentration with time following a short aerated phase. Use of closed batch respirometers is restricted because of the danger of oxygen limitation. On the contrary, most open respirometers are aerated continuously and have the advantage that higher sludge concentrations can be used, because there is a continuous input of oxygen, and oxygen limitation is unlikely. In this case, the oxygen mass transfer coefficient and the saturation DO concentration have to be known to calculate the respiration rate. Batch respirometers can be automated to operate in a semi-continuous way, i.e. the respirometer carries out a repeated batch experiment. An open batch respirometer, the RODTOX (rapid oxygen demand and toxicity tester) has been developed in our laboratory. Its operating principle is discussed in detail by Vanrolleghem *et al.* (1994). Continuous flow-through respirometers measure the DO concentration at both the inlet and the outlet of a closed respiration chamber. Aerated sludge is pumped continuously through the respiration chamber. The OUR is calculated by making an oxygen mass balance over the respiration chamber, using the input and output DO concentration and the residence time in the vessel.

For nitrogen removal systems, respirometric measurements are useful for monitoring purposes. Among other uses, respirometry can be applied successfully to the measurement of the nitrifying sludge activity, due to the high oxygen consumption for nitrification. The main problem to be solved before nitrification activities can be determined is to separate the nitrification oxygen uptake from the oxygen uptake for carbon substrate oxidation and endogenous metabolism. Different methods are applied in practice to obtain this separation.

Batch experiments for the determination of the nitrifying capacity of a sludge are normally performed using an endogenously respiring sludge sample. During the experiment a limited amount of NH_4^+ is injected. The respirogram obtained in this way allows us to estimate kinetic nitrification parameters (Brouwer & Klapwijk, 1995; Spanjers & Vanrolleghem, 1995). A procedure for the simultaneous characterization of carbon oxidation and nitrification was also proposed using an appropriate mixture of a readily biodegradable carbon source and NH_4^+ (Vanrolleghem & Verstraete, 1993b). An example of raw OUR data obtained from such an experiment is shown in Fig. 10.5. During the first minutes (data not shown), a transient phenomenon occurs that provides no reliable data on the biokinetics. The high OUR measured during the first 15 minutes represents the activity of both the nitrification and carbon oxidation. After about 15 minutes, the OUR is due only to nitrification of the remaining NH_4^+-N. By using appropriate models, nitrification and carbon substrate oxidation kinetic parameters can each be estimated.

Kong et al. (1996) applied this procedure for the simultaneous estimation of the effect of toxic compounds on carbon oxidation and nitrification. An example is shown in Fig. 10.6: here the oxygen uptake for nitrification and carbon substrate oxidation can be clearly distinguished for the second substrate injection (calibration: no cyanide added). Injection of increasing cyanide concentrations inhibits both the nitrification and the carbon substrate oxidation: the OUR for carbon substrate oxidation and nitrification decreases with increasing toxicant concentrations. The OUR data show that nitrification is more sensitive to cyanide intoxication, e.g. nitrification is already completely inhibited at 0.788 mg cyanide/l, while the OUR for carbon substrate oxidation is still measurable, even for a concentration of 1.588 mg cyanide/l.

Respirometric methods with endogenously respiring activated sludge cannot be applied to the estimation of the actual nitrification rate in a treatment plant, because wastewater entering the plant is providing fresh substrate continuously for both carbon oxidation and nitrification. Selective nitrification inhibitors are helpful to solve this practical problem, as illustrated in Fig. 10.7. A double experiment is performed and a differential analysis made. After measuring the total OUR of the sludge, a nitrification inhibitor is added to the sludge sample and a second OUR is measured. The nitrification rate can be determined by subtraction of the second OUR from the first OUR.

Respirometry is frequently used for on-line influent toxicity detection in wastewater treatment plants. Specific applications in this field using nitrifying bacteria as indicator organisms for toxicity are studied intensively. Here too, use of specific nitrification inhibitors allows us to distinguish nitrification oxygen uptake from heterotrophic oxygen uptake. An indication of the toxicity of wastewater towards nitrifying bacteria can be obtained also with bacteria of a specific nitrifying

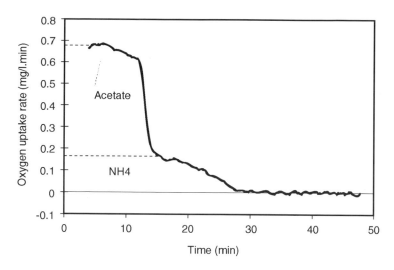

Fig. 10.5. Raw OUR data obtained after an injection of a mixture of acetate (16 mg COD/l) and NH_4^+-N (1.0 mg/l) into the RODTOX respirometer (Vanrolleghem & Verstraete, 1993*b*). After about 15 minutes, all acetate is degraded and the OUR is only due to nitrification of the remaining NH_4^+-N.

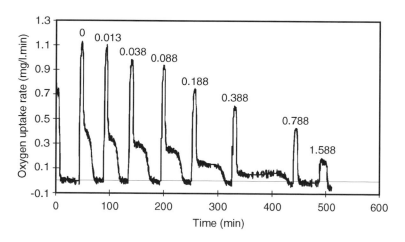

Fig. 10.6. OUR data obtained after the injection of a mixture of acetate (20 mg COD/l) and NH_4^+-N (2 mg/l) in the RODTOX respirometer for increasing CN^- concentrations (Kong *et al.*, 1996). For the first peak only acetate was injected. For the other peaks, a mixture of acetate and NH_4^+-N was used. The figures indicate the CN^- concentrations (mg/l) in the mixed liquor sample.

enrichment culture that contains little or no heterotrophic bacteria (Aivasidis *et al.*, 1992; Arbuckle & Alleman, 1992). In this case, the OUR measured in the presence of a wastewater sample is mainly due to nitrification and the use of specific nitrification inhibitors is unnecessary.

The NITROX (nitrification toxicity tester) was developed in our laboratory as a respirometric on-line toxicity detection system that combines a high sensitivity with a short response time (Verschuere, Gernaey & Verstraete, 1995). The measuring principle is that of a closed batch respirometer. It is based on the measurement of the activity of the nitrifiers (OUR_n) as the difference between the total activity (OUR_{tot}) of a mixed culture (nitrifiers and heterotrophs) and the activity of the heterotrophs after inhibiting the nitrification (OUR_{atu}) by the addition of a selective inhibitor, allylthiourea (ATU) (Stensel, McDowell & Ritter, 1976; Sato, Sekine & Nakano, 1990; Kroiss *et al.*, 1992; Surmacz-Gorska *et al.*, 1996). The presence of the toxicant will be indicated by a decrease of OUR_n where $OUR_n = OUR_{tot} - OUR_{atu}$.

The actual operation of the NITROX biosensor basically consists of the measurement of the nitrifying activity of a sludge after mixing it with a potentially toxic wastewater sample. The detailed operating procedure consists of two main phases: contact phase and a measuring phase. During the contact phase an amount of sludge is mixed with a fixed volume of wastewater. Excess NH_4^+-N (5–10 mg NH_4^+-N/1) is added to the mixture, to ensure zero-order nitrification kinetics; however, without causing substrate inhibition effects. The mixture is aerated for a few minutes. Then, aeration is stopped and the suspension is mixed only. First the total oxygen uptake rate (OUR_{tot}) is determined. After addition of ATU the oxygen uptake rate is determined a second time (OUR_{atu}). The oxygen uptake rate representing the nitrifying activity of the mixture is obtained as $OUR_n = OUR_{tot} - OUR_{atu}$. One measuring cycle is presented in Fig. 10.7.

The toxicity of a sample is determined by comparing the nitrifying activity obtained from a wastewater sample with unknown toxicity ($OUR_{N,sample}$) with that obtained from a reference cycle ($OUR_{N,ref}$), as shown in equation (3).

$$\%\text{inhibition} = \frac{OUR_{N,ref} - OUR_{N,sample}}{OUR_{N,ref}} \times 100 \tag{3}$$

Tap water is used as a non-toxic reference solution. A reference cycle is normally performed once every 2 or 3 hours. The simple measuring principle and design of the NITROX biosensor results in a low cost apparatus that can be used also for small wastewater treatment plants.

Nitrification is a two-step reaction. Surmacz-Gorska *et al.* (1996) recently took the above-mentioned approach a step further and presented a more sophisticated respirometer that allows us to monitor the activity of both nitrification steps separately. The method also provides information about the oxygen uptake for carbon oxidation or endogenous metabolism of the biomass. The measurement is

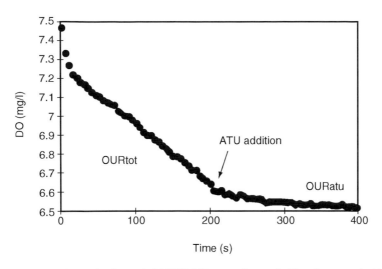

Fig. 10.7. Example of a typical NITROX measuring cycle (Verschuere *et al.*, 1995).

based on the subsequent addition of specific inhibitors for the two nitrification steps to the sludge sample. The separate activities can be calculated by subtracting the different OUR values, as illustrated in Fig. 10.8. Results obtained using this method during the aerobic phase of a sequencing batch reactor cycle are presented in Fig. 10.1 (see above). From Fig. 10.1, it can be seen that the measured nitrification step 1 activity sharply decreases after about 90 minutes, because NH_4^+ has been oxidized almost completely. This decreasing nitrification activity coincides with the decrease of the OUR measured in the sequencing batch reactor. Nitrification step 2 activity drops to zero after about 120 minutes when all NO_2^+ is converted into NO_3^-. During the nitrification phase some NO_2^- build-up was observed. Dosing with both $NaClO_3$ and ATU gives extra value to respirometric methods. When applied on a nitrifying activated sludge system, the method should, for instance, allow us to detect the presence of NO_2^--N in the mixed liquor. These data could be used to optimize the activated sludge process in such a way that NO_2^--N is converted completely to NO_3^--N. For the specific case of the sequencing batch reactor, the activity measurements with this method could be used to optimize the reactor performance, resulting in aeration energy cost savings and a more constant effluent quality. Some examples are presented to illustrate this: the denitrification phase could be started immediately after the disappearance of NH_4^+, without completing the oxidation of NO_2^- to NO_3^-, because NO_2^- can be used also as a substrate for denitrification; in the case of high nitrogen loads, the aeration period could be prolonged to complete the NH_4^+-N removal.

Respirometric applications for nitrogen removal processes are not limited to the estimation of nitrification rates only. Applications of respirometry for the estimation of the concentration of nitrifiable nitrogen present in the influent of a wastewater

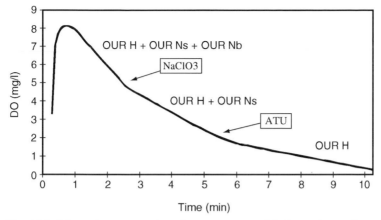

Fig. 10.8. Schematic representation of a measurement with the respirometric method of Surmacz-Gorska *et al.* (1996). In a first phase, total OUR is measured. After addition of NaClO$_3$, nitrification step 2 (OUR Nb) is inhibited. Addition of ATU inhibits nitrification step 1 (OUR Ns). The remaining OUR H is the heterotrophic and endogenous OUR.

treatment plant were reported recently (Brouwer & Klapwijk, 1995; Spanjers & Vanrolleghem, 1995). Initial substrate concentrations could be calculated from the surface under the respirogram. An example of measurements with a respirogram is given in Fig. 10.5.

A respirometric biosensor for monitoring NH$_4^+$-N concentrations in river water and effluents of wastewater treatment plants was developed by Tanaka *et al.* (1993). The biosensor consisted of *Nitrosomonas europaea* bacteria that were immobilized between two acetylcellulose membranes on the surface of a DO electrode. A correlation was found between the oxygen consumption of the immobilized bacteria and NH$_4^+$-N concentration (measurement range = 0–20 mg N/1). However, the need for prefiltered samples to prevent clogging of the measuring system, together with the necessity for accurate pH and temperature control to obtain reliable measurements, are serious drawbacks of the measuring system.

Respirometric methods fail completely under anoxic conditions. Characterization of denitrifying populations under anoxic conditions can be done by the determination of the NO$_3^-$ uptake rate (NUR) of activated sludge (Kristensen, Jorgensen & Henze, 1992). Samples are taken at regular times and analysed off-line for NO$_x^-$-N (= NO$_3^-$ + NO$_2^-$). On-line analysers with a short response time open perspectives for on-line estimation of the denitrification rate *in situ* in alternating activated sludge systems (Lynggaard-Jensen *et al.*, 1995). For completely mixed reactor systems, performing a batch experiment with a mixed liquor sample allows us to do the same. For the calculation of the NH$_4^+$ uptake rate associated with nitrification, a similar technique with off-line NO$_x^-$-N measurements was reported (Kristensen *et al.*, 1992; Arvin *et al.*, 1994), NO$_x^-$-N being the product formed during nitrification. In this case, parallel NH$_4^+$-N measurements can be used as a check for the NO_x^--N production curve. Lynggaard-Jensen *et al.* (1995) estimated nitrification rates in batch experiments using submerged on-line NH_4^+ and NO_3^- analysers.

Titrimetric biosensors

Taking into account the stoichiometric relationship between the amount of oxidized NH_4^+-N and the number of protons formed during nitrification (see equation (1) above), a titration unit can be used as a pH controller and record the amount of base needed to neutralize the protons produced in a mixed liquor sample. Aivasidis *et al.* (1992) presented a titrimetic biosensor for toxicity detection. The nitrifying biomass was immobilized in a flow-through reactor and the wastewater suspected to contain toxic chemicals was supplied continuously. The nitrification rate was calculated based on the base addition rate necessary to keep the pH in the reactor vessel at a constant level.

Biological residual ammonium monitor (BRAM)

In the biological residual ammonium monitor (BRAM), the stoichiometric conversion of NH_4^+ to 2 H^+ is used to measure the residual NH_4^+-N concentration in mixed liquor samples (Massone *et al.*, 1995). For each measurement of the biosensor, activated sludge taken from a nitrifying wastewater treatment plant is transferred to the reactor vessel of a titrator, and a batch experiment is performed. Base is added to maintain the pH within the '$pH_{setpoint} \pm \Delta pH$ interval'. During the measurement, the total amount of base (meq) added to the measuring vessel is recorded. The result of a typical test is presented in Fig. 10.9. During the first part of the experiment, base is added at the maximum rate (steepest slope of the cumulative base addition curve) and most of the alkali is used to increase the pH of the solution because the $pH_{setpoint}$ has not been reached yet ($pH_{setpoint} = 8.2 \pm 0.02$), as can be seen from the pH profile (Fig. 10.9). After this phase, the slope of the base addition curve decreases (segment P_1–P_2), and base addition is closely related to the actual NH_4^+-N removal velocity, unless aerobic acidifying/alkalifying microbial populations other than nitrifiers are active. The levelling of the cumulative base addition curve after about 20 minutes indicates the end of the measurement. An important advantage of this measuring technique compared to most existing chemical NH_4^+-N analysers is that no filtration of the mixed liquor sample is needed; the measurement is carried out on the mixed liquor itself. Another benefit of this method is that, besides the NH_4^+-N concentration the nitrifying activity of the mixed liquor is also obtained, by simple interpretation of the raw titration data (i.e. the slope of segment P_1–P_2 in Fig. 10.9 is a measure of the nitrification activity). Evidently, the response time of the sensor is dependent on the nitrification rate of the sludge and the NH_4^+-N concentration initially present in the mixed liquor. As for the respirometric methods, all organic N that is converted into NH_4^+-N during a titration will be measured too.

Titration data related to the first 5 minutes of the line P_1–P_2 are regressed linearly and the slope, which is proportional to the nitrification rate, is calculated.

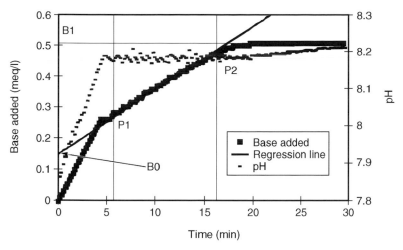

Fig. 10.9. Titration and pH data obtained during a BRAM test. T = 25 ± 0.5 °C; pH = 8.2 ± 0.02; V = 1 l; aeration = 60 l/h; injection of 3 mg N at t = 0 (Massone *et al.*, 1995). The meaning of the symbols B0, B1, P1 and P2 is explained in the text.

The NH_4^+-N concentration present in a mixed liquor sample at the beginning of the titration is obtained by extrapolation of the above determined line, to time zero, and by subsequent calculation of the total amount of base needed to neutralize the oxidized NH_4^+-N, i.e. $(B_1-B_0)/2$. To verify the recovery efficiency of the BRAM, a range of NH_4^+-N concentrations (0.5–4 mg N/l) was added to mixed liquors free of NH_4^+-N. NH_4^+-N concentrations measured by the BRAM compared well with the input concentrations. All standard deviations were in the 1% to 8% range. Nitrification rate per unit volume and NH_4^+-N removal rates per unit biomass (q) were found to be $(r_v =)$ 8.4 mg N/l h and $(q =)$ 4.2 mg N/g VSS h, respectively.

Denitrification carbon source dosage system (DECADOS)

DECADOS (denitrification carbon source dosage system; patent pending) (Vanderhasselt, 1995) is a biosensor for denitrification control in activated sludge plants. It is based on simple and 'robust' probes (pH and ORP) and, as for the BRAM (see above), requires no filtration of the mixed liquor. It provides relevant information concerning the kinetics and stoichiometry of the denitrification process and, in some instances, the concentration of nitrate.

The concept is that of a 'titration' of the nitrate with a readily biodegradable substrate (RBS) as carbon source. Carbon source is added until all nitrate has been respired. The use of pH for monitoring the denitrification process was already suggested by Al-Ghusain *et al.* (1994) and this can be supported by equation (2) (see above) describing a typical denitrification process. DECADOS consists of a 1 litre vessel equipped with a pH electrode placed in a flow-through cell (to prevent

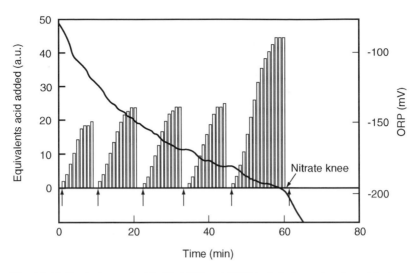

Fig. 10.10. Equivalents of acid added (□) and ORP (—) during a titration with the DECADOS biosensor (Vanderhasselt, 1995). The arrows indicate RBS additions.

fouling). The pump that circulates the mixed liquor over this measuring cell provides also for the mixing in the reactor. Two computer-controlled dosing pumps add acid and base, respectively, for the pH control. A third one is used for the carbon source addition.

A sample of activated sludge mixed liquor is pumped into the vessel and the titration with carbon source is started. The carbon source is added discontinuously as discrete aliquots. A new aliquot is added when the previous one has been consumed, as indicated by the pH controller. The ORP and pH profiles of a typical run are plotted on Fig. 10.10, which refers to an initial nitrate concentration of 20 mg N/1. Each arrow indicates a COD addition (COD concentration = 20 mg/1 after the addition). The first aliquot of carbon results in a sharp response of the pH controller. The acid addition rate drops to zero after a few minutes. This indicates that all the carbon is consumed and the denitrification rate has fallen back to the endogenous level. Adding a new pulse of carbon compound results again in a controller response. The pH controller does not respond upon a sixth RBS addition, indicating that all nitrate has been converted. This is confirmed by the ORP knee occurring at the end of the consumption of the fifth RBS substrate pulse. One observes that the subsequent addition of small RBS aliquots disturbs an adequate ORP knee detection. As a result of the titration, the amount of RBS needed to obtain complete denitrification is determined.

The pH controller is implemented on the sensor in order to 'tune' the RBS-to-nitrate ratio. The DECADOS biosensor uses a pH controller to distinguish between endogenous and exogenous denitrification. The amount of acid added to keep the pH of the reactor vessel constant is proportional to the exogenous denitrification rate. Therefore, the pH controller enables us to control the RBS addition rate. If the rate is too slow, denitrification in the sensor's reactor will be limited by the RBS concentration and the fraction of nitrate reduced by endogenous respiration will be significant. The RBS requirement will be underestimated. If, however, the dosing rate is too high, RBS will accumulate after all nitrate has been respired and the determination of the latter will be overestimated. The ORP, on the contrary, provides insufficient information on the denitrification rate: it is difficult to distinguish endogenous from exogenous denitrification in the oxidation–reduction (ORP) profile.

10.3 Discussion

Control of biological nitrogen removal on wastewater treatment plants was limited largely by the availability of reliable on-line sensor equipment for the collection of the information necessary for optimizing plant performance (Harremoës *et al.*, 1993). Use of dissolved oxygen (DO) and pH probes is now accepted as being 'state-of-the art' in wastewater treatment. Also, ORP probes (in some process configurations), and on-line sensors for monitoring NH_4^+-N and NO_3^--N concentrations are increasingly considered for optimization of treatment plant performance (Nielsen & Önnerth, 1994). This changing attitude coincides with the ever-increasing quality of the available equipment. Intensive research and practical experience gained during the last 5 years have resulted in improved operational stability of the sensing equipment (Thomsen & Kisbye, 1995).

The choice of the appropriate analyser for a specific application is dependent on the wastewater composition (Thomsen & Kisbye, 1995). One measuring method may be suitable for one type of wastewater and not for another, due to interfering substances which give incorrect results. Initial tests prior to installation of the analyser are recommended. In general, the accuracy of the analysers can be expected to decrease with an increasing proportion of industrial wastewater (Thomsen & Kisbye, 1995). However, operational stability of the analysers can be expected to improve further with time due to the build-up of experience through the increasing use of on-line analysers. Experience and practical knowledge collected this way will be more and more helpful in the future when choosing an on-line analyser for a specific application.

For the installation of an on-line analyser, a cost/benefit analysis should be made for each plant separately. In Flanders, effluent levies are expressed as pollution units and calculated according to equation (4). Companies have to pay about US\$30 for every pollution unit (N) that has been discharged.

$$\text{Number of pollution units} = N1 + N2 + N3 \qquad (4)$$

In equation (4), N1, N2 and N3 are calculated, based on the COD, BOD and suspended solids (SS) concentration for N1, the heavy metal load for N2 and the concentration of the nutrients N and P for N3, respectively. For normal domestic wastewater, the reduced N compounds contribute for almost 30% of the total pollution, comparable to 44% for the COD and 20% for the SS, according to the standard primary settled domestic wastewater composition (260 mg COD/1; 160 mg SS/1; 25 mg N/1; 6 mg P/1) proposed by Henze *et al.* (1995). The costs for an on-line NH_4^+ or NO_3^- analysers are estimated to be 8000–35 000 US$, with an additional investment for the sample preparation unit of 3000–15 000 US$ (Thomsen & Kisbye, 1995). Maintenance costs are estimated to be 500–2500 US$/year for the analyser and 1500–2500 US$/year for the sample preparation unit. If the savings obtained by installing an on-line analyser combined with better process control (fewer pollution units are discharged) are higher than the installation costs of the analyser, it is feasible to make the extra investment for the analyser. The same cost/benefit analysis should be made for the installation of a biosensor, e.g. for influent toxicity detection.

Research is now concentrating on the development of biosensors, i.e. sensors that can give on-line information about both the concentration of relevant process parameters (e.g. NH_4^+, NO_3^-) and the activity of microbial populations responsible for specific processes in the mixed liquor (nitrification, denitrification). This evolution started with the development of respirometric methods. Originally, respirometry was used for the estimation of influent COD load and toxicity, and later also for the characterization of heterotrophic and autotrophic activated sludge populations and substrates.

Today, the development of biosensors that specifically monitor the activity of nitrifying and denitrifying activated sludge populations is an important research topic, as shown by the examples outlined above. A most promising application seems to be the development of toxicity biosensors that use nitrifying bacteria as indicator organisms for the detection of increased acute toxicity of the wastewater. The interest in nitrifying bacteria as indicator organisms for toxicity detection can be explained by the higher sensitivity of nitrifiers for all kinds of toxic compounds, compared to heterotrophs (Blum & Speece, 1991). Most of the existing biosensors are able to detect acute toxicity caused by toxic shock loads adequately. Grüttner *et al.* (1994) demonstrated that both acute and chronic effects can inhibit nitrification in activated sludge. Research should concentrate also on finding reliable detection methods for chronic toxic effects and, closely related with this, how to remediate in case of nitrification problems. Some options that should be studied thoroughly are the benefits of (i) the addition of quenching agents as, e.g. powdered activated carbon or bio-supplements (Vansever *et al.*, 1995), and (ii) storage and use of surplus sludge to reduce the impact of toxic compounds on nitrification in case a toxic shock load is detected.

10.4 Conclusions

Optimization of biological nitrogen removal processes is possible through use of efficient control strategies. The strategies are, however, strongly dependent on the availability of stable on-line measurements of the relevant process variables (i.e. NH_4^+, NO_3^-, DO, ORP, pH). For most applications, monitoring was once the weak part of the control system. Recent evolution and experiences in this field are helpful in solving many practical problems. Development of new biosensors leads to the availability of more relevant process information as, e.g. nitrification or denitrification rates.

Acknowledgements

The authors wish to thank everyone at the Laboratory for Microbial Ecology and BIOMATH involved in the research projects concerning development and application of new sensor technology. Special thanks to Alex Massone (Politecnico di Milano) and Alexis Vanderhasselt (Laboratory for Microbial Ecology). The authors are grateful to Aquafin (Aartselaar, Belgium), Biotim NV (Antwerp, Belgium), Hemmis NV (Kortrijk, Belgium), Kelma BVBA (Niel, Belgium) and Severn Trent Water (Birmingham, UK) for their co-operation and financial support.

Results described in this chapter were obtained as a part of the VLIM programme (Flemish Impulse Programme for Environmental Technology), initiated by the Flemish Minister responsible for the environment; a PhD scholarship funded by the Flemish Institute for the Improvement of Scientific–Technological Research in the Industry (IWT); a research project funded by Aquafin (Aartselaar, Belgium) and Severn Trent Water (Birmingham, UK).

References

Aivasidis, A., Hochscherf, H., Rottman, G., Hagen, T., Mertens, M. T., Reiners, G. & Wandrey, C. (1992). Neuere Konzepte zur Prozessüberwachung und -regelung bei der biologischen Stickstoffelimination. *Abwassertechnik*, 5, 48–55.

Al-Ghusain, I. A., Huang, J., Hao, O. J. & Lim, B. S. (1994). Using pH as a real-time control parameter for wastewater treatment and sludge digestion processes. *Water Science Technology*, 30(4), 159–68.

Andersen, K. L. & Wagner, P. (1990). Testing on-line monitors for ammonia, nitrate, orthophosphate and suspended solids in activated sludge sewage treatment plants. In *Proceedings 5th IAWPRC Workshop on ICA of Water and Wastewater Treatment and Transport Systems*, July 26–August 3, Yokohama/Kyoto (Japan), pp. 667–75.

APHA (1992). *Standard Methods for the Examination of Water and Wastewater*, 18th edn. Washington DC: American Public Health Association.

Arbuckle W. B. & Alleman, J. E. (1992). Effluent toxicity testing using nitrifiers and Mixrotox ™. *Water Environment Research*, 64, 263–7.

Arvin, E., Dyreborg, S., Menck, C. & Olsen, J. (1994). A mini-nitrification test for toxicity screening, *Minntoxicology Water Research*, 28, 2029–31.

Aspegren, H., Nyberg, U. & Andersson, B. (1993). Integration of on-line instruments in the practical operation of the Klagshamn wastewater treatment plant. *Mededelingen Faculteit Landbouwu. Universiteit of Gent*, 58, 2019–28.

203

Balslev, P., Lynggaard-Jensen, A. & Nickelsen, C. (1995). Nutrient sensor based real time on-line process control of a wastewater treatment plant using recirculation. In *Proceedings IAWQ Specialized Conference on Sensors in Wastewater Technology*, October 25–27, Copenhagen (Denmark).

Blum, D. J. W. & Speece, R. E. (1991). A database of chemical toxicity to environmental bacteria and its use in interspecies comparisons and correlations. *Research Journal of Water Pollution Control Federation*, 63, 198–207.

Brouwer, H. & Klapwijk, A. (1995). A method based on respirometry to calculate the aerobic nitrification volume of a nitrifying/denitrifying activated sludge plant. In *Proceedings Symposium 'Erfahrungen mit Analysen und Prozessmessgeräten in Abwasserreinigungs-anlagen'*, November 27, Ostfildern (Germany).

Charpentier, J., Godart, H., Martin, G. & Mogno, Y. (1988). Oxidation–reduction potential (ORP) regulation as a way to optimize aeration and C, N and P removal: experimental basis and various full-scale examples. *Water Science Technology*, 21(10/11), 1209–23.

Declercq, T. (1993). On-line parameterschatting en adaptieve proceskontrole van een aktief slib systeem. Engineers thesis. Fac. Agricultural and Applied Biological Sciences. University Gent, Belgium. pp. 149.

de la Ménardière, M., Charpentier, J., Vachon, A. & Martin, G. (1991). ORP as a control parameter in a single sludge biological nitrogen and phosphorus removal activated sludge system. *Water SA*, 17, 123–32.

Demuynck, C., Vanrolleghem, P. A., Mingneau, C., Liessens, J. & Verstraete, W. (1994). NDBEPR process optimization in SBRs: reduction of external carbon source and oxygen supply. *Water Science Technology*, 30(4), 169–79.

EPA (1993). *Manual Nitrogen Control*. US EPA, Washington, DC 20460.

Grüttner, H., Winther-Nielsen, M., Jorgensen, L., Bogebjerg, P. & Sinkjaer, O. (1994). Inhibition of the nitrification process in municipal wastewater treatment plants by industrial discharges. *Water Science Technology*, 29(9), 69–77.

Harremoës, P., Capodaglio, A. G., Hellström, B. G., Henze, M., Jensen, K. N., Lynggaard-Jensen, A., Otterpohl, R. & Soeberg, H. (1993). Wastewater treatment plants under transient loading–performance, modelling and control. *Water Science Technology*, 27(12), 71–115.

Heduit, A. & Thevenot, D. R. (1992). Elements in the interpretation of platinum electrode potentials in biological treatment. *Water Science Technology*, 26(5–6), 1335–44.

Heduit, A., Martin, B. & Thevenot, D. R. (1994). Preliminary study of surface treatments for platinum electrodes designed for oxidation–reduction potential determinations in activated sludge. *Water Science Technology*, 30(4), 239–42.

Henze, M., Gujer, W., Mino, T., Matsuo, T., Wentzel, M. C. & Marais, G. v. R. (1995). Wastewater and biomass characterization for the activated sludge model no. 2: Biological phosphorus removal. *Water Science Technology*, 31(2), 13–23.

Holmberg, U., Olsson, G. & Andersson, B. (1989). Simultaneous DO-control and respiration estimation. *Water Science Technology*, 21, 1185–95.

Isaacs, S. & Soeberg, H. (1995). Flow injection analysis for on-line monitoring of a wastewater treatment plant. In *Advanced Instrumentation, Data Interpretation and Control of Biotechnological Processes*, ed. J. Van Impe, P. Vanrolleghem & D. Iserentant. Dordrecht, The Netherlands: Kluwer Academic Publishers (in press).

Kong, Z., Vanrolleghem, P. A., Willems, P. & Verstraete, W. (1996). Simultaneous determination of inhibition kinetics of carbon oxidation and nitrification with a respirometer. *Water Research*, **30**, 825–36.

Kristensen, G. H., Jorgensen, P. E. & Henze, M. (1992). Characterisation of functional microorganism groups and substrates in activated sludge and wastewater by AUR, NUR and OUR. *Water Science Technology*, **25**(6), 43–57.

Kroiss, H., Schweighofer, P., Frey, W. & Matsche, N. (1992). Nitrification inhibition–a source identification method for combined municipal and/or industrial wastewater treatment plants. *Water Science Technology*, **26**(5–6), 1135–46.

Lynggaard-Jensen, A., Eisum, N. H., Rasmussen, I., Svankjaer, J. H. & Stenstrom, T. (1995). Description and test of a new generation of nutrient sensors. In *Proceedings IAWQ Specialized Conference on Sensors in Wastewater Technology*, October 25–27, Copenhagen (Denmark).

Massone, A., Gernaey, K., Rozzi, A., Willems, P. & Verstraete, W. (1995). Ammonium concentration measurements using a titrometric biosensor. *Mededelingen Faculteit Landbouww. Universiteit Gent*, **60**, 2361–8.

Nielsen, M. K. & Önnerth, T. B. (1994). State of the art. Control of activated sludge plants. In *Proceedings IAWQ International Specialized Seminar on Modelling and Control of Activated Sludge Processes*, August 22–24, Copenhagen (Denmark).

Nyberg, U., Aspegren, H., Andersson, B., Jansen, J. la C. & Villadsen, I. S. (1992). Full-scale application of nitrogen removal with methanol as carbon source. *Water Science Technology*, **26**(5–6), 1077–86.

Patry, G. G. & Takacs, I. (1995). Modelling, simulation and control of large-scale wastewater treatment plants: an integrated approach. *Mededelingen Faculteit Landbouww. Universiteit, Gent*, **60**, 2335–43.

Pedersen, K. M., Kümmel, M. & Soeberg, H. (1990). A real time measurement for an activated sludge wastewater treatment plant. In *Proceedings 5th IAWPRC Workshop on ICA of Water and Wastewater Treatment and Transport Systems*, July 26–August 3, Yokohama/Kyoto (Japan), pp. 171–8.

Plisson-Saune, S., Capdeville, B., Mauret, M., Deguin, A. & Baptiste, P. (1995). Real time control of nitrogen removal using three ORP bending-points: signification, control strategy and results. In *Proceedings IAWQ Specialized Conference on Sensors in Wastewater Technology*, October 25–27, Copenhagen (Denmark).

Randall, C. W. (1992). Introduction. In *Design and Retrofit of Wastewater Treatment Plants for Biological Nutrient Removal*, (ed) C. W. Randall, J. L. Barnard & H. D. Stensel. pp. 1–24. Lancaster: Technomic Publishing Company, Inc.

Sasaki, K., Yamamoto, Y., Tsumura, K., Hatsumata, S. & Tatewaki, M. (1993). Simultaneous removal of nitrogen and phosphorus in intermittently aerated 2-tank activated sludge process using DO and ORP-bending-point control. *Water Science Technology*, **28**(11–12), 513–21.

Sato, S., Sekine, T. & Nakano, T. (1990). Advanced control strategies for the activated sludge process by the ATU-r$_r$ meter. In *Proceedings 5th IAWPRC Workshop on ICA of Water and Wastewater Treatment and Transport Systems*, July 26–August 3, Yokohama/Kyoto (Japan), pp. 523–30.

Schlegel, S. & Baumann, P. (1995). Requirements with respect to on-line analyzers for N and P. In *Proceedings IAWQ Specialized Conference on Sensors in Wastewater Technology*, October 25–27, Copenhagen (Denmark).

K. Gernaey *et al.*

Sikow, M. & Pursiainen, J. (1995). Use and maintenance of on-line measurements at Suomenoja wastewater plant. In *Proceedings IAWQ Specialized Conference on Sensors in Wastewater Technology*, October 25–27, Copenhagen (Denmark).

Spanjers, H. (1993). Respirometry in activated sludge. PhD thesis, Landbouwuniversiteit Wageningen, The Netherlands, pp. 199.

Spanjers, H. & Vanrolleghem, P. (1995). Respirometry as a tool for rapid characterization of wastewater and activated sludge. *Water Science Technology*, 31(2), 105–14.

Stensel, H. D., McDowell, C. S. & Ritter, D. E. (1976). An automated biological nitrification toxicity test. *Journal of Water Pollution Control Federation*, 48, 2343–50.

Surmacz-Gorska, J., Gernaey, K., Demuynck, C., Vanrolleghem, P. & Verstraete, W. (1996). Nitrification monitoring in activated sludge by oxygen uptake rate (OUR) measurements. *Water Research*, 30, 1228–36.

Tanaka, H., Nakamura, E., Hoshikawa, H. & Tanaka, T. (1993). Development of the ammonia biosensor monitoring system. *Water Science Technology*, 28(11–12), 435–45.

Teichgräber, B. (1990). Alkalinity and pH-control in activated sludge plants with nitrification. In *Proceedings 5th IAWPRC Workshop on ICA of Water and Wastewater Treatment and Transport Systems*, July 26–August 3, Yokohama/Kyoto (Japan), 179–85.

Teichgräber, B. (1993). Control strategies for a highly loaded biological ammonia elimination process. *Water Science Technology*. 28(11–12), 531–8.

Thomsen, H. A. & Kisbye, K. (1995). N and P on-line meters: requirements, maintenance and stability. In *Proceedings IAWQ Specialized Conference on Sensors in Wastewater Technology*, October 25–27, Copenhagen (Denmark).

Thomsen, H. A. & Nielsen, M. K. (1992). Practical experience with on-line measurements of NH_4, NO_3, PO_4, redox, MLSS and SS in advanced activated sludge plants. *Hydrotop 92*, April 8–10, Marseille (France).

Thornberg, D. E., Nielsen, M. K. & Andersen, K. L. (1993). Nutrient removal, on-line measurements and control strategies. In *Proceedings 6th IAWQ Workshop on ICA of Water and Wastewater Treatment and Transport Systems*, June 17–25, Banff (Alberta)/Hamilton (Ontario) (Canada), pp. 548–59.

Vanderhasselt, A. (1995). Ontwikkelling van een on-line denitrifikatie sensor. Engineers thesis. Faculty of Agricultural and Applied Biological Sciences. University Gent, Belgium. 90 pp.

Vanrolleghem, P. & Coen, F. (1995). Optimal design of in-sensor-experiments for on-line modelling of nitrogen removal processes. *Water Science Technology*, 31(2), 149–60.

Vanrolleghem, P. A. & Spanjers, H. (1994). Comparison of two respirometric principles for the determination of short-term biochemical oxygen demand. In *Proceedings 49th Industrial Waste Conference*, May 9–11, Purdue University, West Lafayette (Indiana), pp. 177–88.

Vanrolleghem, P. & Verstraete, W. (1993*a*). On-line monitoring equipment for wastewater treatment processes: state of the art. In *Proceedings TI-KVIV Studiedag Optimalisatie van Waterzuiveringsinstallaties door Proceskontrole en -sturing*. 21 oktober, Gent (Belgium), 1–22.

Vanrolleghem, P. & Verstraete, W. (1993*b*). Simultaneous biokinetic characterization of heterotrophic and nitrifying populations of activated sludge with an on-line respirographic biosensor. *Water Science Technology*, 28(11–12), 377–87.

Vanrolleghem, P. A., Kong, Z., Rombouts, G. & Verstraete, W. (1994). An on-line respirographic biosensor for the characterization of load and toxicity of wastewaters. *Journal of Chemical Technology and Biotechnology*, **59**, 321–33.

Vansever, S., Van Der Zanden, J., Weytjens, D., Mingneau, C. & Verstraete, W. (1995). Improvement of activated sludge performance by the addition of Nutriflok S50. *Mededelingen Faculteit Landbouww. Universiteit Gent*, **60**, 2237–44.

Van Vooren, L., Willems, P., Ottoy, J. P., Vansteenkiste, G. C. & Verstraete, W. (1995). Automatic buffer capacity based sensor for effluent quality monitoring. In *Proceedings IAWQ Specialized Conference on Sensors in Wastewater Technology*, October 25–27, Copenhagen (Denmark).

Verschuere, L., Gernaey, K. & Verstraete, W. (1995). De NITROX: een snelle en gevoelige on-line toxiciteitsmeter voor water en afvalwater. *Water*, **14**, 163–8.

Wacheux, H., Da Silva, S. & Lesavre, J. (1993). Inventory and assessment of automatic nitrate analyzer for urban sewage works. *Water Science Technology*, **28**(11–12), 489–98.

Wacheux, H., Million, J.-L., Guillo, C. & Alves, E. (1995). NH_4 automatic analysers for WWTP: evaluation test at lab and field level. In *Proceedings IAWQ Specialized Conference on Sensors in Wastewater Technology*, October 25–27, Copenhagen (Denmark).

Wareham, D. G., Hall, K. J. & Mavinic, D. S. (1993). Real-time control of wastewater treatment systems using ORP. *Water Science Technology* **28**(11–12), 273–82.

Watts, J. B. & Garber, W. F. (1993). Instrument and system maintenance: a design and operational necessity. *Water Science Technology*, **28**(11–12), 447–56.

Wouters-Wasiak, K., Heduit, A., Audic, J. M. & Lefèvre, F. (1993). Oxidation reduction potential (ORP)-control of the aeration in a wastewater treatment plant: Nitrogen removal efficiency. A case study: the Benfeld activated sludge plant. *Mededelingen Faculteit Landbouww. Universiteit Gent*, **58**, 2107–12.

11

Nitrogen fertilizer and ecotoxicology: global distribution of environmental pollution caused by food production

H. Kawashima, K. Okamoto, M. J. Bazin and J. M. Lynch

11.1 Introduction

The world population has been increasing very rapidly in this century: in 1900, the world population was only 1.65 billion (Durand, 1967). It had reached 2.52 billion in 1950 and it is estimated that the world population will be 6.1 billion at the end of this century (World Bank, 1995). Such a growth in population is unprecedented in human history. The arable land area in the world has been almost constant in this century (Fig. 11.1) and it is about 1.45 billion ha currently (FAO, 1994). Modern agriculture has contributed to, and sustained this growth: the Green Revolution has contributed to crop increase. The crop yields per unit area have been increasing rapidly and this has contributed to food production in the world. The Green Revolution technologies have involved mainly the use of high-yield varieties and fertilizer. New crop varieties of wheat, rice and maize (having higher yield potentials) were developed through genetic improvements. The realization of their potential output required heavy applications of fertilizers because the availability of nutrients in the soil and from organic sources was not adequate to meet their requirements (Cooke, 1975). Without adequate dosages of fertilizers, the yield of high-yielding varieties achieved was generally lower than those of traditional varieties (Bumb, 1995).

There are three major nutrients for plant growth, i.e. nitrogen, phosphorus and potassium. Fertilizers containing phosphorus and potassium are made from mineral sources, while nitrogen fertilizer is made from air. The Haber and Bosch process was able to make ammonia and nitrogen fertilizer from the air. Nitrogen in the air was used as the nitrogen source of ammonia: a production of ammonia using industrially fixed nitrogen started in 1913: ammonia synthesis is unlimited if we use energy. Industrially fixed nitrogen fertilizer has contributed greatly to food production: if there had been no industrially fixed fertilizer, the world would not have been able to sustain the unprecedented increasing population on the globe. The world nitrogen fertilizer use was 15.3 million tonnes per year in 1965 and was

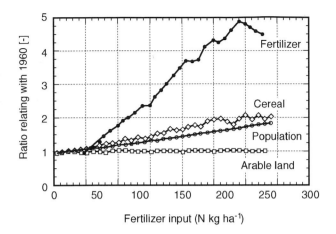

Fig. 11.1. The increase of the world population, arable land, cereal production and fertilizer consumption rate from 1960 to 1990. Fertilizer consumption rate is compared with the value in 1960. The values in 1960 are as follows. Cereal production: 936 million tonnes; population: 2982 million, arable land: 1405 million ha and fertilizer use: 15.3 million tonnes.

increased to 75.1 tonnes in 1992 (FAO, 1993) (Fig. 11.1). Fertilizer use had been increasing but began decreasing after 1990. Fertilizer uses in eastern Europe countries were decreased dramatically after 1989 (from 1989 to 1992, the former USSR 11.6 to 7.5 Tg y^{-1}; Hungary 0.65 to 0.29 Tg y^{-1}; Poland 1.52 to 0.62 Tg y^{-1}; Romania 0.74 to 0.27 Tg y^{-1}, respectively). Economic turmoil must be the cause of this decrease. Current fertilizer use in the world is relatively large in comparison to natural fixation by organisms (Jenkinson, 1990): the nitrogen fixed by organisms naturally in the terrestrial ecosystem is estimated to be 139 million tonnes (Paul & Clark, 1989). Approximately a further 50% amount of nitrogen fixed by natural ecosystem is added to the global ecosystem from other sources for food production.

However, excess use of nitrogen fertilizer results in environmental pollution, although nitrogen itself is not toxic. We must consider two types of ecotoxicology for nitrogen, i.e. direct and indirect ecotoxicology. Nitrate enriched in groundwater is important in direct ecotoxicology. Nitrous oxide generation from the fertilized field and eutrophication in lakes are significant in indirect ecotoxicology.

Nitrous oxide in the atmosphere has been increasing and this greenhouse gas is implicated in the destruction of the ozone layer. The increase of world fertilizer use has modified the global nitrogen cycle quantitatively and must be the cause of the nitrous oxide increase in the trophosphere (Kawashima, Bazin & Lynch, 1996). The destruction of the ozone layer increases the intensity of ultra-violet light reaching the ground: this increases the risk of development of skin cancer conditions initiated by body exposure to sunlight.

Nitrogen is also a key material for eutrophication in lakes. Low molecular weight organic matter is synthesized by some algae in eutrophic lakes, and this organic matter is readily converted tri-halomethane during the process of chlorination of drinking water. Drinking water that contains tri-halomethane can increase the risk of cancer.

11.2 Blue-baby syndrome: and also stomach cancer

Nitrate itself is not toxic. Nitrate becomes a problem only when it is converted into nitrite. We have to consider two problems: the blue-baby syndrome and stomach cancer. The blue-baby syndrome (methaemoglobinaemia), can occur in children less than about 1 year old. Nitrate contained in drinking water is converted to nitrite by body microflora. The oxidation of ferrous iron (to ferric iron) in haemoglobin occurs (normal haemoglobins contain iron in the ferrous form). As a result, the oxygen-carrying capacity of the blood is decreased, resulting in 'chemical suffocation': and in some very severe conditions it can prove fatal. Addiscott, Whitmore & Poulson (1991) describe the recent history of the 'blue-baby' syndrome. Fortunately, the 'blue-baby' syndrome (cyanosis) is extremely rare. The last death it caused in the UK was in 1950 (Ewing & Mayon-White, 1951) and the last confirmed case was in 1972. A world-wide survey (Sattelmacher, 1962) showed that, in all, only 1060 cases had been published, although many others had gone unreported. Others have occurred since, notably an outbreak in Hungary where 1353 cases occurred between 1976 and 1982 (Deak, 1985). Early authors reporting this condition used the term 'well-water methaemoglobinaemia' (Comly, 1945) and the death mentioned above was associated with water from a well.

Stomach cancer has also been associated with the concentration of nitrate in potable water. There are good theoretical reasons for proposing the association. Nitrite (produced from nitrate) by body microflora could react in the stomach with secondary amines, resulting in the production of an N-nitrous compound. Unfortunately, N-nitrous compounds can cause cancer because they are capable of modifying components of DNA. This suggested mechanism is only a hypothesis as yet, and needs to be tested further (Addiscott *et al.*, 1991).

11.3 World distribution of fertilizer use

Excess use of nitrogen can be the cause of environmental pollution and this is directly or indirectly toxic for humans. It is well known that excess use of nitrogen fertilizer is not good for the environment; however, man must use nitrogen fertilizer to sustain increasing population on the globe. The total amount of nitrogen fertilizer demand in the twenty-first century in the world was investigated in previous work (Kawashima *et al.*, 1997), but the distribution of population, economic status, and arable land was not considered. Population distribution is not uniform across the world, nor is the distribution of arable land use. The ratio of arable land to the whole land is high in Europe and Asia. Arable land per person is relatively large in the countries in Oceania and north America, but small in the countries in west Europe and east Asia. Fertilizer use is closely related to economic status (Kawashima et al., 1997). Currently, European, North American and Asian countries use large amounts of nitrogen fertilizer; small amounts are used in African countries. The current economic growth rates in the east Asian countries is high. This will affect the fertilizer use in Asia. The world distribution of nitrogen fertilizer demand in the twenty-first century is discussed below and outlines the potential nitrogen fertilizer use. The problem of food supply in Asian countries is associated with this nitrogen fertilizer use. It helps us to understand where the nitrogen pollution will occur in the world. This will give us the basic information for a developing strategy that can avoid environmental deterioration whilst supplying enough food to the people on the globe.

11.4 Mathematical approaches

There is a good relationship between economic status and meat protein uptake (when economic status is known the meat consumption rate per person can be estimated). When the population in future is estimated, the total demand of meat protein in future in each country can be calculated. Some livestock are fed on pasture: fish also contributes to protein production. Subtracting meat fed on pasture and fish from the whole meat protein demand, we can calculate the meat protein demand which must be produced by cereal feeding. About four times more cereal protein is needed to produce meat protein in farming (Halley & Soffe, 1988). The sum of the cereal demand for humans and the demand for feeding make up the total demand. There is a good relationship between nitrogen fertilizer input and nitrogen uptake by crops. Using this relationship, the nitrogen fertilizer demand in each country can be calculated.

11.5 Economic status and protein consumption rate

The relationship between economic status and protein consumption rate per capita per day in each country has been analysed (Kawashima et al., 1997). Economic status was represented by GNP (Gross National Product) per capita. The relationship between GNP and protein uptake in 54 countries whose population was over ten million in 1990 is summarized in Fig. 11.2. Vegetable protein represents the sum of cereal protein and pulse (bean) protein. The amount of protein is represented by nitrogen and the nitrogen amount multiplied by 6.25 equals the amount of protein (Jones, 1974). Economic status has little effect on vegetable protein uptake, but there is good correlation between meat protein uptake and GNP per capita. The vegetable protein uptake seems to be almost constant all over the world. People in advanced countries consume about 62.5 g per day (corresponding to 10 g nitrogen) of meat protein, while people in low-income economies consume under 31.25 g (5 g nitrogen).

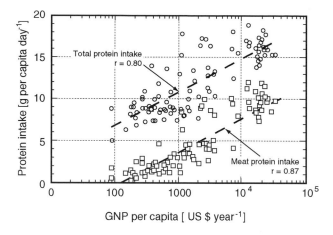

Fig. 11.2. Relationship between protein intake per capita per day and GNP per capita.

11.6 Nitrogen input and crop yield

We have investigated the nitrogen budgets for 65 countries, each with populations in excess of 10 million in 1990 (Kawashima *et al.*, 1997). There is a good relationship between nitrogen input and crop yield in the field. Nitrogen fertilizer input over 250 kg ha^{-1} is not common for cereal cultivation. A good linear correlation is observed within the range of nitrogen input under 250 kg ha^{-1}. The relationship is shown in Fig. 11.3. The correlation coefficient within this range is 0.93. We adopt this relationship to estimate fertilizer demand from the crop yield.

11.7 Arable land distribution

Matthews (1983) made the data set of cultivated intensity. The data set is based on existing maps of vegetation and satellite imagery, and it shows the percentage of each one degree square latitude/longitude grid cell that is under cultivation, versus the percentage of natural vegetation, including five classes. UNEP/GRID-Tsukuba (UNEP/GRID-Tsukuba 1994) provides the numerical world boundary data named 'WBDTEMP3.E00'. Using this boundary data, we calculated the cultivated land area in each country from the data set provided by Matthews, who classified the cultivated intensity into five classes. Assuming that each latitude/longitude grid is a trapezium, the cultivated area in each country is calculated using the following equation:

$$A_t = (0.9\ a_5 + 0.7\ a_4 + 0.5\ a_3 + 0.3\ a_2)\alpha \qquad (1)$$

where A_t represents the total cultivated area in each country. a_5 represents the area of the class 5, a_4 is for the class 4, a_3 is for the class 3 and a_2 for the class 2. It is

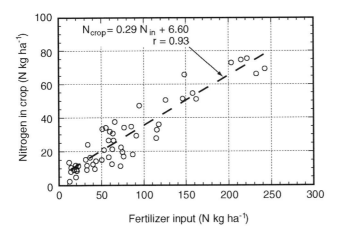

Fig. 11.3. Relationship between nitrogen fertilizer input and crop yield represented by nitrogen. The fertilizer use, arable area and cereal crop reported by FAO (1991) were adopted here.

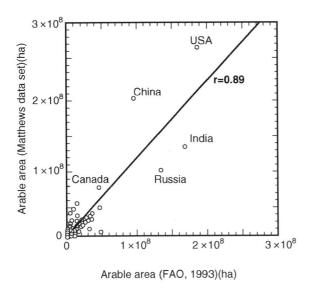

Fig. 11.4. Comparison between the arable area shown in the Matthews data set and the area reported by FAO (1993).

assumed that no cultivated land is in the class 1. (α [-] represents the coefficient for correction.) Assuming the coefficient for correction is 1.0, the cultivated area in each country was calculated. The calculated area was compared with the data compiled by FAO (FAO, 1994). The results are shown in Fig. 11.4. There is little difference between calculated area and the reported one. The value of α was adjusted in order to fit the calculated area to the reported one in each country.

11.8 Mathematical analyses

Recent trends suggest that arable land area in the world is almost constant (Fig. 11.1). The increase of crop production in the world depends on yield per unit arable land. Approximately five times more fertilizer was used to double cereal yield. In the past, nitrogen fertilizer has been applied in developed countries mainly. However, fertilizer will also be used in the developing countries to meet the demand for cereal crops.

Estimation of economic status in the developing countries in the 21st century is significant for the prediction of the cereal demand in the world. Economic status is represented by GNP per capita. We assumed the average growth rate from 1980 to 1993 (World Bank, 1995) will not change, and will continue in the twenty-first century. The world average growth rate from 1980 to 1993 was 1.2% per year. The World Bank divided the world into four groups, i.e. low-income economies with GNP per capita under US$ 700, low-middle-income economies where GNP is between US$ 700 and 3000, upper-middle-income economies where GNP is between US$ 3000 and 10 000 and high-income economies where GNP was over US$ 10 000. The average growth rate from 1980 to 1993 was negative in most of the low-income countries: but only the growth rates of Kuwait and United Arab Emirate are negative in the high income group. When we use the average growth rate from 1980 to 1993 directly to predict GNP per capita in the twenty-first century. It is predicted that GNP will continue to shrink in many developing countries. Probably, this is too pessimistic. There is another scenario, where the countries whose GNP growth rates were under 1.2% per year will grow at the rate of 1.2% per year into the twenty-first century. The countries whose growth rates are over 1.2% will continue to grow at the same rate. GNP was calculated for 132 countries. GNP per capita in 2025 and 2100 in the major 30 countries is shown in Table 11.1. The country is assumed to stop economic growth, when GNP per capita reaches US$ 30 000. This assumption is appropriate for estimating protein intake, because the protein intake rate reaches saturation in the range of GNP over US$ 30 000.

The population as estimated by the World Bank (World Bank, 1995) is shown in Table 11.2. Using the GNP and population in 2025 and 2100, the cereal demand can be calculated. The vegetable and meat protein demand per person from GNP per capita can be estimated (Fig. 11.1). From the population size in the twenty-first century in Table 11.2, the whole vegetable and meat protein demand in each country can be calculated. In order to produce meat protein in farming, approximately three to ten times more vegetable protein must be consumed. The conversion ratio from vegetable protein to meat protein is approximately ten times for beef, four times for pig meat and three times for chicken meat (Halley & Soffe,

Table 11.1. *GNP per capita estimated from the current growth rate*

Country	Growth rate	GNP	Scenario 1	Scenario 2	Scenario 1	Scenario 2
Year	1980–1993	1993	2025	2025	2100	2100
China	8.20	490	6 102	6 102	30 000	30 000
India	3.00	300	773	773	7 091	7 091
USA	1.70	24 740	30 000	30 000	30 000	30 000
Indonesia	4.20	740	2 761	2 761	30 000	30 000
Brazil	0.30	2 930	3 225	4 292	4 037	10 500
Pakistan	3.10	430	1 142	1 142	11 276	11 276
Mexico	−0.50	3 610	3 075	5 288	2 111	12 937
Japan	3.40	31 490	30 000	30 000	30 000	30 000
Russian Federation	−1.00	2 340	1 696	3 428	798	8 386
Nigeria	−0.10	300	291	439	270	1 075
Turkey	2.40	2 970	6 344	6 344	30 000	30 000
Bangladesh	2.10	220	428	428	2 033	2 033
Egypt	2.80	660	1 597	1 597	12 671	12 671
Thailand	6.40	2 110	15 361	15 361	30 000	30 000
Philippines	−0.60	850	701	1 245	446	3 046
South Africa	−0.20	2 980	2 795	4 365	2 405	10 679
Korea REP	8.20	7 660	30 000	30 000	30 000	30 000
Germany	2.10	23 560	30 000	30 000	30 000	30 000
Italy	2.10	19 840	30 000	30 000	30 000	30 000
UK	2.30	18 060	30 000	30 000	30 000	30 000
France	1.60	22 490	30 000	30 000	30 000	30 000
Algeria	−0.80	1 780	1 377	2 607	754	6 379

The average growth rate from 1980 to 1993 was assumed to be constant into the next century. The data compiled by the World Bank (1995) was adopted here.

1988). Farming on pasture can also produce meat protein. No cereal is consumed for farming on pasture. As a first attempt, it was assumed that 50% of the meat protein is produced from pasture and through feeding four times more cereal is needed to produce meat protein feeding. The demands in Africa, North America, South America, Asia, Europe and Oceania are shown in Fig. 11.5a. The demand in Asia is almost 60% of the total world demand. The average growth rate from 1980 to 1993 in China was 8.2% and in India was 3.0% per year (World Bank, 1995). Because most of the increase in demand will be from China and India, there is little difference in the demand between scenario 1 and scenario 2. Scenario 2 is used for the following discussion.

Fig. 11.4 shows that the area of arable land has been little changed in the past 35 years. It is assumed that the area of arable land will be constant into the next century. Then, more fertilizer will be required, especially in the developing

Table 11.2. *Population and cereal demand in the major 30 countries in the twenty-first century*

Country	Population	Population	Population	Demand	Demand	Demand
Year	1994	2025	2100	1994	2025	2100
China	1209	1471	1890	439	1037	1346
India	919	1370	1862	241	576	806
USA	261	323	317	172	231	225
Indonesia	195	265	360	56	156	215
Brazil	159	224	305	57	122	172
Pakistan	137	243	399	39	109	188
Mexico	92	136	184	44	86	120
Japan	125	124	114	66	79	70
Russian Federation	147	153	423	74	78	311
Nigeria	108	217	453	28	77	163
Turkey	61	92	120	22	66	90
Bangladesh	118	182	257	25	60	86
Egypt	62	86	120	29	55	78
Thailand	58	81	105	11	53	71
Philippines	66	115	137	20	45	55
South Africa	41	69	96	19	44	63
Korea REP	45	53	56	15	40	43
Germany	81	75	67	45	39	33
Italy	57	54	46	39	39	32
UK	58	61	61	30	38	38
France	58	63	62	32	37	36
Algeria	27	47	78	12	30	51

Population cited here is estimated by the World Bank (1995).

countries, to increase cereal production. When the cereal demand and the area of arable land are known, the yield which must be produced in twenty-first century in each country can be calculated.

Finally, as the yield is assumed, the fertilizer demand per unit area can be determined using the relationship in Fig. 11.3. The demand in each region is summarized in Fig. 11.5b. The nitrogen fertilizer use was 80 million tonnes per year in 1994. The nitrogen fertilizer demand will increase and be 120 million tonnes in 2025 and 200 million tonnes in 2100. Most of the increase will arise in Asia in the twenty-first century.

The amount of nitrogen emission (leaching plus gaseous evolution) from the field is calculated from the difference between nitrogen fertilizer input and nitrogen yield in crops. The distribution of nitrogen emission was calculated from the distribution of arable land and fertilizer input in each country. The result is shown in Fig. 11.6a,b,c. Cereal production and fertilizer use reported (FAO, 1994)

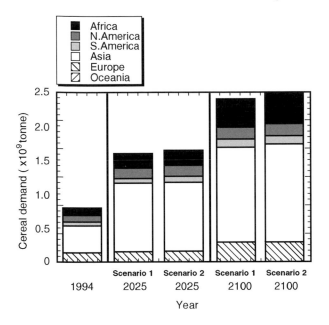

Fig. 11.5a. Cereal demand estimated from the economic situation and population growth in the twenty-first century. The growth rate from 1980 to 1993 will continue in scenario 1. No negative growth is assumed in scenario 2.

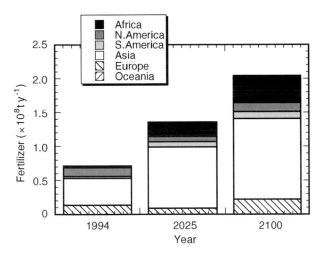

Fig. 11.5b. Fertilizer demand to meet cereal demand in the twenty-first century. Scenario 2 is adopted.

are used to calculate the value shown in Fig. 11.6a. Estimation of the amount of trade in twenty-first century is difficult (for the first attempt, the cereal trade is assumed to be zero all over the world). Self-sufficiency of cereal in each country is assumed for calculating nitrogen emission in the twenty-first century. Nitrogen emissions in 2025 and 2100 are shown in Fig. 11.6b and Fig. 11.6c. Nitrogen emission is relatively high in Europe and Asia in 1994. Nitrogen emission will increase in Asia in 2025. Nitrogen emission per unit area is over $100 \, kg \, ha^{-1}$ in the red zone. In this zone, over $132 \, kg \, ha^{-1}$ of nitrogen fertilizer is applied to the field. This value corresponds to a yield of $44.7 \, kg \, ha^{-1}$ nitrogen in the field. The cereal yield is 3.5 tonnes ha^{-1}, because nitrogen content in cereal is about 1.3%. Ground water pollution by nitrate and eutrophication in closed waters is a serious problem in these areas. The red area will spread to China, India and some Asian countries. There will be a problem in Mexico at the end of the next century. European and North and South American countries seem to be stable even in 2100. African and South American countries will still not be very polluted even in 2100.

Distribution of population and arable land is not uniform all over the world. Economic growth rate is not uniform either. Environmental pollution caused by nitrogen emitted from the field will be a serious problem in the East Asian countries. The Asian countries will face difficulties both in supplying sufficient protein, and in nitrogen pollution of the environment which will occur early in the next century.

11.9 Conclusions

The nitrogen fertilizer demand will increase to sustain the world population, but the demand will not rise uniformly. Arable land area per capita is relatively small in Asia and this will continue into the next century. As a consequence of the current economic growth, the demand for meat protein will rise especially in Asia. In order to meet meat protein demand, the cereal demand for feeding will increase. Asian countries will face environmental pollution by nitrogen if they continue a self-sufficient policy for food. To combat this, Asian countries will need to import large amounts of food from other regions of the world to prevent environmental deterioration.

Acknowledgements

This work was supported by the Co-operative Research Project on Biological Resource Management, Organization for Economic Co-operation and Development.

References

Addiscott, T. M., Whitmore, A. P. & Poulson, D. S. (1991). *Farming, Fertilizers and Nitrate Problem.* Wallingford, Oxon, UK: CAB International.

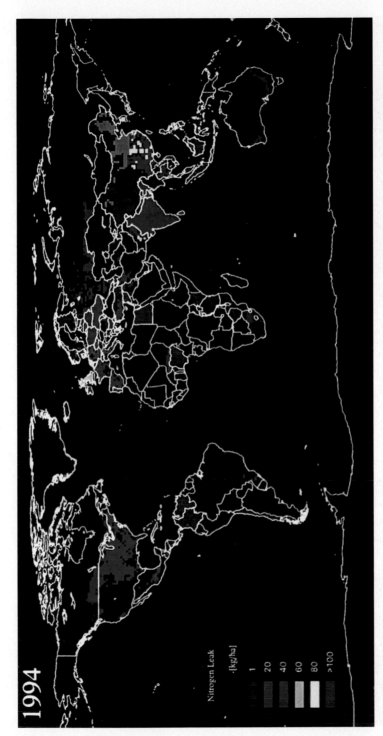

Figure 11.6a. Distribution of nitrogen load generating from the field in 1994. This shows the difference between nitrogen input in 1993 and nitrogen yield in crop in 1994.

Figure 11.6b. Distribution of nitrogen load generating from the field in 2025. No trade is assumed in this simulation.

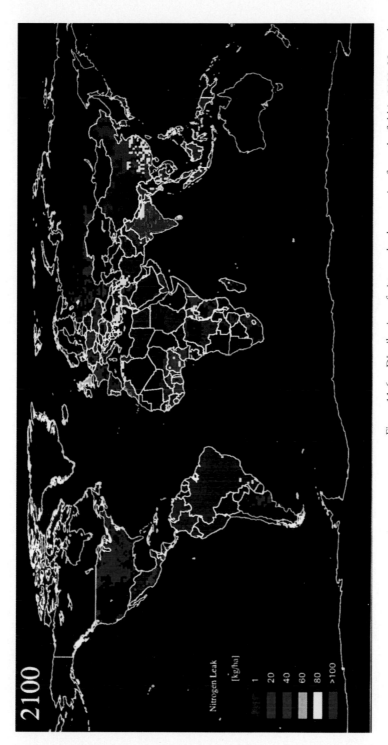

Figure 11.6c. Distribution of nitrogen load generating from the field in 2100. No trade is assumed in this simulation.

Bumb, B. L. (1995). World nitrogen supply and demand: an overview. In *Nitrogen Fertilizer*, ed. P. E. Bacon, pp. 1–35. Marcel Dekker, Inc.

Comly, H. H. (1945). Cyanosis in infants caused by nitrates in well-water. *Journal of the American Medical Association*, **129**, 112–16.

Cooke, G. W. (1975). *Fertilizing for Maximum Yield*, Granada Publishing Ltd.

Deak, S. (1985). Quoted in WHO meeting (1985). Health hazards from nitrates in drinking water. Report on WHO meeting. Copenhagen, 5–9 March, 1984.

Durand, J. D. (1967). The modern expansion of world population, *Proceedings of the American Philosophical Society*, **III**, 3.

Ewing, M. C. & Mayon-White, R. M. (1951). Cyanosis in infancy from nitrates in drinking water. *Lancet*, **260**, 931–4.

FAO (1991). *Food Balance Sheets*, Rome.

FAO (1993). *Yearbook, Fertilizer*, **43**, Rome, and earlier issues.

FAO (1994). *Yearbook, Production*, **48**, Rome, and earlier issues.

Halley, R. J. & Soffe, R. J. (1988). *The Agricultural Notebook*, 18th edn, Blackwell Scientific Publications.

Houghton, J. T., Meira Filho, L. G., Callander, B. A., Harris, N., Kattenberg, A. & Maskell, K. (eds) (1995). *Climate Change, Contribution of Working Group 1*, p. 88. Cambridge: Cambridge University Press.

Jenkinson, D. S. (1990). An introduction to the global nitrogen cycle. *Soil Use and Management*, **6**, (2), 56–61.

Jones, A. (1974). World Protein Resources. Lancaster, UK: Medical and Technical Publishing Co. Ltd.

Kawashima, H., Bazin, M. J. & Lynch, J. M. (1996). Global N_2O balance and nitrogen fertilizer. *Ecological Modelling*, **87**, 51–7.

Kawashima, H., Bazin, M. J. & Lynch, J. M. (1997). The world protein supply and nitrogen fertilizer demand in the 21st century. *Environmental Conservation*, in press.

Matthews, E., (1983). Global vegetation and land use: new high resolution data bases for climate studies. *Journal of Climate and Applied Meteorology*, **22**, 474–87.

Paul, E. A. & Clark, F. E. (1989). *Soil Microbiology and Biochemistry*, p. 176, Academic Press, Inc.

Sattelmacher, P. G. (1962). Methaemoglobinaemia durch nitrate in Trinkwasser. *Schriftenreie Verein, Wasser Boden Lufthyg. Berlin-Bahlen*, vol. 20, Stuttgart: Gustav Fischer Verlag.

Tisdale, S. & Werner, N. (1975). *Soil Fertility and Fertilizers*, 3rd edn, New York: Macmillan Publishing Co., Inc.

UNEP/GRID-Tsukuba (1994). *GRID Global Data Sets: Documentation Summaries*, Center for Global Environmental Research, National Institute for Environmental Studies, Tsukuba, Japan.

World Bank (1992). *World Development Report 1992*. Oxford: Oxford University Press.

World Bank (1995). *World Development Report 1995*. Oxford: Oxford University Press.

Part III
Biosafety regulations and economics

12

Risk perception, attitudes and defence strategies associated with toxic substances: the case of lead contamination in Hungary

Zsuzsanna Fuzesi, Laszlo Tistyan and Anna Vari

12.1 Background

Despite its decreasing volume, lead contamination has been one of the most important environmental health hazards in Hungary. Although the traffic lead emission continuously decreases in volume, in 1994 108 tonnes of lead was emitted into the air[1]. Of the sources of lead pollution, transportation is the most important (about 80% of the total emission is related to transportation), further sources include industry (e.g. glass manufacturing, battery production), and hazardous waste (e.g. lack of appropriate management of batteries and paints). The most endangered group include people living in heavy traffic areas or near to lead processing plants, and workers working with lead[2]. Children are especially at risk; according to estimates, 8–13% of the schoolchildren have blood lead levels above 10 μg/dl (Rudnai & Horvath, 1996; Groszmann, Hudak, & Naray, 1996).

In 1993, a project entitled 'A multi-sectoral approach to lead poisoning prevention in Hungary' was launched with the aim of developing and implementing a research and demonstration project to help prevent lead poisoning in Hungary and to raise public awareness related to lead contamination.

The first phase of the project was supported by a grant from the US Environmental Protection Agency to Tufts University (Boston, MA) and the second phase by a grant from the Social Insurance Fund of Hungary. The project was coordinated by the Fact Foundation (Pecs, Hungary).

In the initial phase of the project, among others[3], public perception, attitudes

[1] Traffic-origin lead emission was 637 t in 1980, and 387 t in 1991, and according to estimations, it will not reach 100 t in 1995. (Sources: Ministry for Environment and Regional Policy and Traffic Science Institute.)

[2] Among the 10 000 workers working with lead 400–600 acute cases of lead poisoning occur each year.

[3] Hungarian researchers with collaboration and technical assistance from American counterparts performed the following tasks in this phase of the project: obtained and reviewed existing scientific information on lead uses exposures and health effects in Hungary.

and individual prevention strategies associated with lead contamination were explored. The investigations were executed primarily to set a basis for the multi-faceted risk communication programme. A series of in-depth interviews was carried out with experts of government agencies and scientific institutions; representatives of local governments, environmental NGOs, and the media; and managers, union leaders, and work physicians of industrial plants endangered by lead exposure (88 persons in total). This was followed by a questionnaire survey conducted in May 1994 with samples of the most endangered groups. These included inhabitants from inner city regions[4] and people living near factories working with lead[5] (inhabitants' sample), and workers employed by these factories (workers' sample). The inhabitants' sample consisted of 308 persons while the workers' sample included 154 persons. Although because of the limited financial resources the samples were not representative, they were sufficiently large to provide an appropriate empirical basis for developing a communication strategy in the subsequent phases of the project.

In this chapter, the assumptions based on the findings of earlier empirical studies on environmental risk perception are first outlined. This is followed by the summary of the results of the survey conducted within the framework of the lead project.

12.2 Public perception on environmental risk in Hungary

The first study on risk perception by the Hungarian public was conducted in 1986 (Farago & Englander, 1987). The study investigated the perceived riskiness of 30 technologies and activities by Hungarian and US populations. The most important finding of the study was that the US group saw their environment about two times riskier than the Hungarian group, in spite of the fact that the real (statistical) hazards of most technologies and activities were higher in Hungary. These results were attributed primarily to the differences between media coverage on the risks and benefits of modern technologies in the two countries.

In 1992, Gallup International carried out an international comparative survey called 'The health of the planet survey', which included 22 countries (Gallup International, 1992). According to the survey results, less than 0.5% of the Hungarian respondents thought that environmental problems are among the most important ones in Hungary. With this result, Hungary came out last among the respondents. This 'insensitivity' is concomitant with the low activity level in the field of environmental protection. In Hungary, only 9% of the respondents believed that citizens and citizen groups can participate in solving environmental

---

[4] Inhabitants of the cities of Budapest and Pecs were included in the sample.

[5] The investigated plants did not allow their names to be published. The investigations were conducted in battery plants and glass factories which produce lead crystal as well. In some cases we could not gain entry to the factory; therefore, we used community surveys (the size of the settlement made it possible).

problems effectively: with this result, Hungary was also last in sequence order on this opinion.

In 1993, a survey was conducted with a representative sample of the residents of the city of Pecs on public opinion concerning environmental hazards, their impacts on health status, the main sources of hazards, and possibilities for prevention (Fuzesi & Tistyan, 1993). The interviewees considered the stressed lifestyle of the people as having the greatest impact on the deterioration of health status, but almost the same importance was attributed to environmental pollution. The importance attributed to environmental hazards is remarkable, because the connection between the harmful elements of lifestyle and the deterioration of health status had been discussed frequently in mass communication even in the past decade, while such effects of environmental contamination had hardly been mentioned earlier.

The respondents attributed the most important role in environment pollution to others (e.g. public transportation, industry, transportation of goods, private cars, and 'citizens in general'). At the other end of the scale of polluters, as 'the factor' which least pollutes the environment, stands the respondent him- or herself. The data indicate that respondents feel very little individual responsibility for the status of the environment.

12.3 Public perception on lead contamination

Based on the results of the former studies, the following questions were defined as the most important ones for setting the foundation for a risk communication project related to lead:

- What do people consider as hazardous for themselves?
- What do people know about lead as a health risk factor (health effects, endangered groups, etc.)?
- From what sources do people receive information about the issue of lead?
- Which factors are, in the opinion of the public, responsible for lead contamination?
- Where are the boundaries of the possibilities of individual activity and collective action for reducing the associated risks?

In the following, the main findings of the survey are summarized.

12.3.1 Factors endangering health status at place of residence and of work

First, data were collected on the extent to which the inhabitants are aware of environmental factors of health risk, and more specifically of lead as a risk factor. Figure 12.1 indicates that, of the factors affecting the state of health at the place of residence (giving answers to an open-ended question) 44% of the interviewees mentioned environmental problems in general. The second most frequently mentioned factor (emphasized by 41% of the respondents) was transportation-related air pollution (exhaust gases, petrol fumes) containing lead among other toxic

225

Z. Fuzesi, L. Tistyan and A. Vari

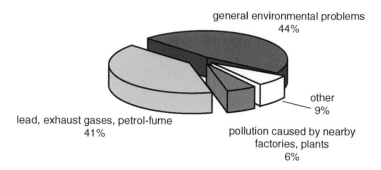

Fig. 12.1. Environmental hazards in the environment which affect health.

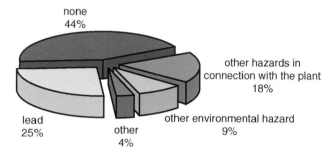

Fig. 12.2. Hazards affecting health at place of work (%).

substances. These data indicate that people are aware of environmental health risks, in general, and the risks of air pollution, in particular (Fig. 12.1).

The workers were asked a similar open-ended question about the most important factors affecting their health status in the work environment. According to 44% of the respondents, there are no hazardous factors at their workplace, and only 25% mentioned lead as a risk factor (Fig. 12.2). This data is remarkable as the only consideration in choosing the respondents was that they should work with lead in their job.

Next, the respondents were asked if they have already noticed the effects of environmental and occupational hazards on their own health. (Our question referred to the subjective perception of the health damages, and not to illnesses which were detected by a diagnosis already made.) The vast majority of the workers (87%), according to their own report, had not perceived any health effects of the mentioned factors yet (Fig. 12.3). However, in the case of the inhabitants, only 60% of the respondents claimed that they had not experienced any negative effects of the hazard factors on their health (Fig. 12.4).

12.3.2 The health effects of lead

Members of both the inhabitants and the workers sample were asked about the specific effects of lead exposure on human health. Figure 12.5 indicates that only

226

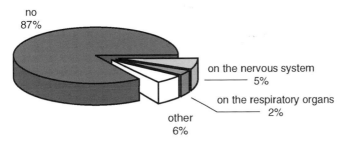

Fig. 12.3. 'Have you perceived any effects of hazardous factors on your state of health?' (workers).

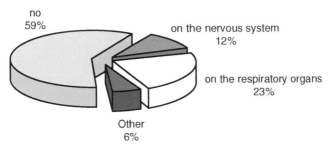

Fig. 12.4. 'Have you perceived any effects of hazardous factors on your state of health?' (inhabitants).

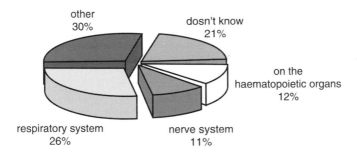

Fig. 12.5. Consequences of lead pollution on people's state of health (inhabitants).

about one-fifth of the inhabitants group was unable to answer the question on the health risks of lead contamination. The most frequently mentioned effects are those on the respiratory system (26%), haemopoietic organs (12%), and the nervous system (11%).

As far as the workers' group is concerned, it is remarkable that 57% of the respondents did not mention any consequential effects of lead exposure at all (Fig. 12.6).

The latter data may refer to the fact that the managers of industrial plants still pay little attention to creating awareness of particular jobs' health hazards. The

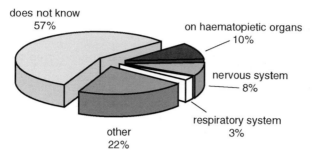

does not know
57%

on haematopietic organs
10%

nervous system
8%

respiratory system
3%

other
22%

Fig. 12.6. Consequences of lead pollution on the state of health (workers).

reason for this may be that such knowledge of workers would lead to the need to provide the necessary protection devices and equipment, and to compensation for the sustained damage to health. Purchases of equipment and good-quality respirators carry high costs. As explained in an interview with one of the factory managers, 'they would rather close down the factory than to undertake such great investments'. In the same settlement, an expert of the State Health and Medical Officer Service claimed that he does not go to the site, because he then would be obliged to close down the factory. This would increase the already high unemployment rate, which would further depress the standard of living of the people resident in the area. A peculiar explanation was given also by the physician of the plant: 'In my opinion, there is exaggeration in the literature in what is said about the harmful health effects of lead. This factory has been standing here in the city for a hundred years already, and people have been living here too. It is not a rare phenomenon in the factory that generations of the same family follow one another.'

It would be a simplified explanation to contribute the reasons for the previously given answers only as a lack of knowledge. Besides lack of knowledge, it is important that intensity of risk perception and recognition of personal involvement decrease in the case of those who have been living with the hazards and risks for a long time.[6]

Members of the population who are exposed to hazards for a longer period of time, in particular cases through generations, become accustomed to the hazards, and living together with the hazards will become natural for them. After a while, the hazards infiltrating into the lifestyle lose their 'hazardous' feature, and the individuals do not count them in creating their life strategies.[7] (An interesting result of the survey is that, for example, there is a relationship between the length

---

[6] 'Those who can, move out of the area polluted with lead. Unfortunately those who cannot, resign themselves to the situation.' 'People are fed up with the fact that we always talk about the environment causing illnesses, as this environmental pollution has been there for decades' (quotations from an interview with a leader of a green organization).

[7] 'The level of lead in the blood of those who come in from the street to be employed is the same as mine, so why should I care' (quoted from an interview with a worker).

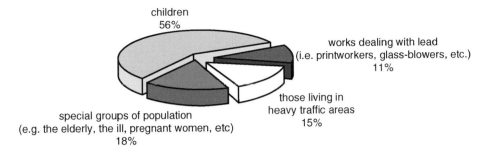

Fig. 12.7. '. . . Whose health is most affected by lead?' (inhabitants).

of employment and the application of the individual protection devices. That is, the longer has someone been working, the less he uses individual protection devices. Of the people who have been employed for more than 21 years, 23% use some kind of individual protection device, while 45% of those who have been working for a year or less do so.)

If risk awareness does not receive external support (employers, authorities, physicians, etc.), the workers do not protect themselves, and moreover, they accept the hazard as a natural concomitant to their work. Today, all factors in the economic and political sphere work against keeping up risk awareness, since it is assumed that high risk awareness would increase the likelihood of conflict between workers and management.

12.3.3 The most endangered groups

Members of both groups were asked to say in which groups the health is most affected by lead. About 56% of the respondents from the inhabitants' sample said that children are the most endangered group (Fig. 12.7).

It is especially important if workers are aware of the fact that lead is not only harmful to their own health but, by neglecting the compliance with rules of hygiene, they may endanger the health of their children as well. Regarding this issue, 20% of the interviewed workers did not know if lead has any effects on the health state of young children. The others were relatively well informed on what kind of consequences lead exposure may exert on children.

The workers are a lot less well informed on how children can be polluted by lead. It is remarkable that they have relatively little knowledge about the pollution they may cause. Some are aware that it is not 'healthy' for the little children to stay around the factories, but only a few know that they can carry home the pollution themselves (on clothes, hair, hands).

12.3.4 Sources of information about lead contamination

Both the inhabitants' and the workers' sample were asked about the main sources of information on the issue of lead contamination. In the inhabitants' sample, more

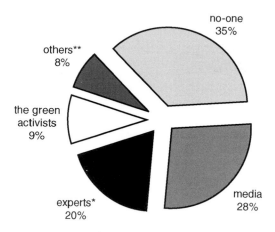

* Ministries, other
  authorities, doctors, etc

** Patients, victims,
   "good god", the opposition, etc

Fig. 12.8. 'Who do you trust concerning issues on the environment?'

than 50% of the respondents named the mass media (press, radio, television) as primary sources of information. The importance of media as communicators is followed in importance by that of acquaintances (17%). One's own experience as the source of information stands at third place (10%). Only about 5% of the respondents referred to official information sources, which include publications by authentic authorities, as their main source of information; so knowledge acquisition regarding lead pollution in the environment is rather occasional, and with respect to the communicators, it is often unprofessional.

In the workers' sample, 70% of the respondents, according to their statement, receive no information from anyone on the issue of lead pollution. Most others get information from within the plant (23%).

There is a particular degree of distrust towards announcements regarding the state of the environment and its lead pollution, and towards the communicators of this field. The data received on this issue are summarized in Fig. 12.8.

12.3.5 Ways of reducing lead pollution

As far as reducing lead pollution in the environment is concerned, more than one-third of the respondents in the inhabitants' group are very 'pessimistic' and do not see any chance to reduce this pollution. About half of the interviewees see the solution in measures[8] to be introduced in the field of traffic. Modernization of technologies were mentioned by 10% of the respondents. About the same percentage

---

[8] These measures include better organization of traffic, preference for unleaded petrol, a parking system which discourages driving into inner-city areas, etc.

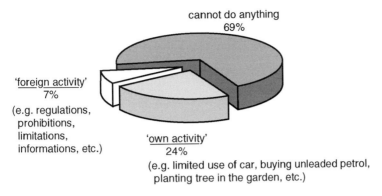

cannot do anything
69%

'foreign activity'
7%
(e.g. regulations,
prohibitions,
limitations,
informations, etc.)

'own activity'
24%
(e.g. limited use of car, buying unleaded petrol,
planting tree in the garden, etc.)

Fig. 12.9. 'How do you see your role in reducing lead pollution?' (inhabitants).

of respondents considered other ways that were effective in reducing lead pollution (e.g. planting trees, enforcing the compliance with the rules and standards).

With regard to the role of the interviewees themselves, the majority of the inhabitants' sample (69%) do not see any possibility that they could do anything about reducing the environmental hazards (Fig. 12.9). Only 24% of the interviewed people suggested solutions with the help of which they themselves could reduce environmental harms. This active attitude is rather characteristic of the younger members of the population, people with degrees and men (almost twice the number of women), and those living in large cities. Another 7% of the respondents expect others (authorities, local governments, etc.) to solve these problems. The essence of these solutions would be in regulations, bans, limitations, and only in few cases in providing information and education.

Workers are in a special situation because they are directly endangered through their work. Despite this, 50% of the workers' sample claimed that they do not protect themselves against the harmful effects of lead at all (Fig. 12.10). However, we can see great differences around the average value. It is characteristic of the older workers, those with the highest and with the lowest level of education, and those who have been employed for a longer period of time, that they do not use the means of protecting themselves, either because there are no such means or possibilities, or because they do not even want to.[9]

12.3.6 Possibilities for collective action for reducing lead contamination

Interviewees were asked (the inhabitants' sample as well as the workers) on ways to

[9] In the opinion of 40% of the workers, their workplaces do not provide them with any possibilities or means of individual protection, or at least they do not know of any of them. However, there are great differences behind the average between the workplaces. If someone does not use safety equipment, it depends on the particular factory what happens to the worker (he/she is warned, dismissed, etc.). It is understandable that, where there is not such safety equipment, they cannot sanction not using the non-existent. Besides, it seems that the factories are a lot more tolerant with their old workers than with the newcomers.

Table 12.1. *Where could you protest against the operation of a plant near you? (as %
of the answers)*

	Inhabitants	Workers
	(%)	
Could not do anything	35.0	32.0
Would try outside the plant altogether	58.0	21.0
local government	33.0	9.0
authorities	10.0	2.0
political parties	—	—
green activists press	7.0	4.0
physicians	5.0	2.0
other	2.0	1.0
	—	3.0
Would try within the plant altogether	4.0	40.0
boss		27.0
labour safety		7.0
person		2.0
work physician		2.0
union		2.0
Would move/quit job	2.0	5.0
Would do something else	1.0	2.0
Total	100.0	100.0

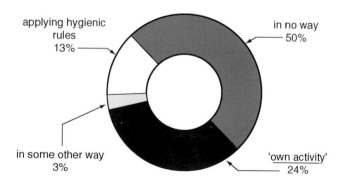

Fig. 12.10. 'How do you protect yourself from the harmful effects of lead?' (workers).

proceed in a hypothetical situation. The question was formulated the following
way (with either the workers or the inhabitants concerned): 'What could you do,
whom could you turn to if you were notified of any kind of serious health
consequences caused by the operation of a nearby plant?'

Table 12.2. *Would you close down the plant? (%)*

	Inhabitants	Workers
	(%)	
Yes	53.0	37.0
No	41.0	35.0
Could not decide/Insists on compromise	6.0	28.0
Total	100.0	100.0

Of the respondents in the inhabitants' sample, 35% said that they could not do anything. Of those who believed they could, 58% would try to find help outside the plant. Most of the people within this group would turn to the local government. Only 4% of the respondents would try to turn to the management of the plant (Table 12.1).

In the workers' sample, 32% of the respondents claimed that they would feel unable to act if the operation of the plant would impose considerable risk to the health of those working in it or living in its area. This rate is not far behind that experienced in the inhabitants' sample. About 40% of those who thought they would be able to act would try to find solutions within the plant, primarily by turning to their bosses, while 21% of them would find advisers outside the plant to solve their problems.

The hypothetical questions were continued by asking what would the respondent do if he/she 'had to decide on the fate of a plant which endangers not only the health of the workers but also that of the inhabitants living nearby'. In the hypothetical example, we emphasized that the plant employs several hundred people and there is no way of changing the production. Hence we offered only two alternatives, and did not even offer the 'don't know' option. In the group of inhabitants, 53% of the interviewed people would have decided to close down the plant, 41% to let it operate on, and 6% of them could not decide at all, or would have insisted on some kind of compromise (Table 12.2).

We found significant differences between the inhabitants' and the workers' samples concerning whether they would or would not close the plant. The closer someone is to being affected by the problem, the more difficult it is for him or her to make a decision, and he/she would decide on a possible closing down very unwillingly.

12.4 Conclusions

According to the results of the survey, people are generally and on a verbal level aware of the importance of environmental hazards (and their consequences on the

233

Z. Fuzesi, L. Tistyan and A. Vari

state of health). Recognizing the existence and consequences of the problems often does not include recognizing one's own personal involvement. It means that (using a citation from an interview) 'lead exposure is a very serious problem, it is very harmful to health, however, it affects others but not me'. Lack of recognizing personal involvement, and lack of interest deriving from it, results in low motivation level and weak inclination to act.

The inclination to act is further decreased by the logic according to which the pollution is generally caused by others, and thus those subjected to it from whose point of view we look at the problem, cannot do much.

As far as solutions to these types of issues are concerned, people are characterized by a particular feeling of being left on their own. They have very little confidence that the government or the authorities would do anything to solve this problem.

Comparing the two samples, it is observed that workers working with lead know less about the health effects of lead than the members of the population living in heavy traffic areas or in the vicinity of polluting plants. Due to their familiarity with the hazards and their interest in keeping their jobs, workers are also more likely to deny the health effects of lead than are the inhabitants. For the same reasons, workers are less willing to act against a polluting factory than people having no interest in maintaining its operation.

In this social environment, effective risk communication has to be a complex process. It is necessary to increase the knowledge and change the attitude of the most endangered groups, so that they would recognize the hazards, assess them properly, act to decrease them, and be able to protect themselves against the harmful effects more efficiently.

References

Farago, K. & Englander, T. (1987). The perception of risk: Comparative study with American and Hungarian groups. In *Risk and Society*, ed. A. Vari, pp. 34–56. Budapest: Akademiai Kiado. (In Hungarian.)

Fuzesi, Zs. & Tistyan, L. (1993). The relation of urban populations to environmental problems in Hungary. In *Environment and Public Health: City Conference. Book of Abstracts*. Antwerp, Belgium.

Gallup International (1992). *The Health of the Planet Survey*.

Groszmann, M., Hudak, A. & Naray, M. (1996). Blood lead concentrations of Hungarian children living in a suburban area surrounding a former lead processing plant. In *From Science to Action: The Lead Hazard in Hungary*, ed. Zs. Fuzesi, B. Levy & C. Levenstein. Pecs, Hungary: Fact Foundation.

Rudnai, P. & Horvath, A. (1996). Biological monitoring of environmental lead exposure in Hungary. In *From Science to Action: The Lead Hazard in Hungary*, ed. Zs. Fuzesi, B. Levy & C. Levenstein. Pecs, Hungary: Fact Foundation.

13

Risk, economics and legislation: risk assessment methodology

Brenda J. Nordenstam

13.1 Introduction

The use of quantitative analysis in the regulation of environmental hazards is a relatively new phenomenon. Risk-based decision-making is now used to balance costs and benefits of environmental policies, set standards for regulation, and most recently, to compare and rank environmental hazards so as to prioritize the spending of limited government resources. Diverse areas of study, including toxicology, epidemiology, engineering, psychology, statistics, and economics contribute to this rapidly growing area. Despite the young age of this research, the concept of risk has become central to environmental policy decisions in the past decade.

To the everyday person, 'risk' is a general word, used loosely and interchangeable with 'chance', 'gamble' or 'uncertainty' when describing potential outcomes dependent upon imperfect knowledge or variable conditions. However, within the environmental and health professions, 'risk' has become a highly technical term, referring to quantitative probability estimates derived from carefully constructed risk assessment models. Although risk assessment professionals have yet to achieve a unanimous consensus on the exact meaning of 'risk', it is often defined as:

Risk: 'The probability of the event multiplied by the magnitude of the event'.

There are three primary tributaries that have guided the interdisciplinary exploration of environmental risk topics. These three domains: risk analysis, risk management and risk appraisal, provide overlapping but sometimes conflicting approaches in assessing environmental hazards. Research in risk analysis investigates the identification, quantification and comparison of environmental risks; for example, quantifying human health risks from a specific air-emission source. Research in risk management includes the identification, selection, and implementation of policies to control risk; for example, regulating sulphur dioxide emissions by implementing a regional air credit trading programme. Research in risk-appraisal

Table 13.1. *Environmental risk approaches*

Risk analysis approach
Primary focus on technical aspects
The process of identifying, assessing and evaluating the risks associated with hazardous substances, processes, actions or events

Risk management approach
Primary focus on policy aspects
The process of identifying, selecting and implementing the policies to control environmental risks

Risk appraisal approach
Primary focus on social aspects
The process of identifying, evaluating and comparing the factors associated with individual and societal response to environmental risk

---

examines the sociopolitical context surrounding the identification, perception and evaluation of factors influencing individual and societal response to environmental risks; for example, a cross-national comparison of variables associated with tolerance of secondary cigarette smoke in the workplace (see Table 13.1).

13.2 Risk analysis approach

Ideally, the information derived from risk analysis should facilitate informed decisions regarding proposed or current events that affect our environment (Suter, 1993). Risk analysis is generally viewed to consist of three main stages: hazard identification, risk assessment and risk evaluation (Merkhofer, 1987), although it is also used more broadly to encompass elements of risk management (e.g. Davies, 1996). Hazard identification determines potential hazards and the conditions which result in adverse consequences; for example, identifying possible mechanisms by which genetically engineered organisms might escape from the laboratory. Risk assessment focuses on the description, measurement, and quantification of risks; for example, the probability of being killed in a plane crash based on number of miles flown each year. Risk evaluation utilizes comparisons and judgements to determine the magnitude and significance of environmental risks; for example, the ecological effects of two different pesticides (see Table 13.2).

13.3 Risk assessment approach

Risk assessment is the best known of the three stages of risk analysis. Ideally, this multi-step process should provide a systematic method for characterizing and quantifying the risks associated with hazardous substances, processes, actions or events (Covello & Merkhofer, 1993). Risk assessment is used widely by government and industry, and is often required as part of an environmental impact statement,

Table 13.2. *Three stages of risk analysis*

1. *Hazard identification*
Includes identifying potential risks and the conditions for adverse impacts

2. *Risk assessment*
Includes describing, estimating, and quantifying risks

3. *Risk evaluation*
Includes comparing and judging the magnitude and significance of risks

cost–benefit analysis, or forecasting report. The term is usually used to refer to the analytical method of describing, estimating and quantifying the probability and magnitude of risk. However, it has been expanded in scope to include related processes associated with the hazard identification stage, and/or processes within the evaluation stage of risk analysis (Nash, 1996).

Risk assessment models have been developed to assess a broad spectrum of health and environmental hazards (NRC, 1994). One of the most widely used models was proposed by the National Research Council of the US National Academy of Sciences (1983) primarily to assess human cancer risk from chemical exposure. This model treats hazard identification as part of the risk assessment process rather than a separate stage of risk analysis. The components of the NRC/NAS model include: hazard identification, dose-response assessment, exposure assessment and risk characterization. In comparison, Covello and Merkhofer (1993) proposed a generalized four-step model of risk assessment consisting of: release assessment, exposure assessment, consequence assessment and risk estimation. Because this model selects release assessment as the first step, a detailed quantification of the amount and probability of a risk release into the environment can be calculated. The inclusion of this step makes the Covello/Merkhofer model more applicable for the quantification of risk from large-scale release events, such as industrial accidents or ecological systems risk due to technological failure (see Table 13.3).

13.4 Uncertainty in risk assessment

Although the specification of uncertainty for utilization in risk management decisions is a relatively new procedure in health and environmental risk assessments, this approach has been utilized in water resource management for many years. As early as 1968 the National Academy of Sciences US produced a report on alternative methods of managing water resources in which they describe the possible sources of uncertainty in water flow estimates in the Colorado river (NRC, 1968). More recently, the inclusion of uncertainty analysis in hydrological models has been analysed in ground water models (Beck 1987; McKone & Bogen, 1991), urban

Table 13.3. *Four-step risk assessment model*

Step 1: Release assessment
The process of quantifying the potential of a given risk source to introduce risk agents into the environment. Includes research on risk sources; monitoring; accident investigation; failure-mode, fault-tree, event-tree and discharge models

Step 2: Exposure assessment
The process of quantifying the conditions and characteristics of exposure to risk agents released by a given risk source. Includes research on monitoring methods; controlled testing; atmospheric, watershed and multimedia exposure models

Step 3: Consequence assessment
The process of quantifying the relationship between specified exposures and the consequences of those exposures. Includes research on health effects; monitoring; animal and epidemiological studies; dose-response and pharmacokinetic models

Step 4: Risk estimation
The process of integrating the release, exposure and consequence assessment data to obtain quantified estimates of timing, nature, probability and magnitude of risk. Includes research on composite risk models, uncertainty analysis and risk indices

Source: Covello & Merkhofer, 1993.

runoff models (Griffin 1994) and remediation models (Dakins, Toll & Small, 1995).

The uncertainty surrounding a risk assessment endpoint is dependent on two types of errors, defined as parameter based and model based (Morgan & Henrion 1992). Depending on the degree of uncertainty associated with the final result, the risk assessment may contribute little useful information to the decision-making process. Uncertainty in relation to scientific knowledge has long been reviewed from a philosophical viewpoint (e.g. Polanyi, 1958), and provides a broader perspective on the significance of knowledge levels in shaping scientific inquiry. Table 13.4 is designed to present a qualitative typology of uncertainty, derived from several fields of study, providing a full spectrum of types and levels of knowledge encountered in environmental risk decisions.

In the environmental risk assessment area, the focus has been primarily on improving the ability to provide more accurate estimates of quantified risk (Level 4) and quantified uncertainty (Level 3). For example, if the processes associated with the risk are sufficiently well understood, a single-value analysis may be performed using best estimates as inputs for each variable, and the outcome is represented as a best-estimate or single-value (Covello & Merkhofer 1993). This would result in a risk assessment yielding a quantification of risk. Due to the relatively small number of parameters and the extensive and well-documented epidemiology data, a risk assessment conducted to assess the health consequences of cigarette smoking would be expected to result in a single-value estimate representing a quantifiable risk. However, if the processes associated with the risk

Table 13.4. *Type of uncertainty and level of knowledge*

Types of uncertainty
1. parameter, e.g. measurement error, systematic bias
2. model, e.g. relationship errors, oversimplification errors

Levels of knowledge
1. total ignorance
2. uncertainty (range only)
3. quantified uncertainty, e.g. probability distribution
4. quantified risk e.g. 1/1 000 000
5. probability, e.g. odds of dice throw
6. perfect knowledge

---

are poorly understood, the uncertainty of the input variables in addition to the outcome is characterized by a probability distribution, rather than a single value outcome (Covello & Merkhofer, 1993). This would result in a risk assessment giving a quantification of uncertainty. Because of the relatively large number of parameters and the insufficiency of empirical data, a risk assessment, for example, assessing the probability of sperm count deficiencies in bird populations exposed to sex hormone disrupter chemicals present in an aquatic ecosystems, would provide a probability distribution representing a quantifiable uncertainty.

13.5 Risk management approach

Risk management may be defined as the process of identification, selection and implementation of policies to control environmental risks, and to set priorities for government programmes. However, William D. Ruckelshaus, former administrator of the US EPA, paints a much richer picture of the field of risk management: 'risk management in its broadest sense means adjusting our environmental policies to obtain the array of social goods, environmental, health-related, social, economic and psychological, that forms our vision of how we want the world to be' (Ruckelshaus 1983). Most authors are somewhat more constrained, describing risk management as 'the process by which regulators decide where, to what degree, and by what means an outcome should be controlled, based on the probability and magnitude of its effects' (Nash 1996). Although some researchers place the process of evaluating, weighing and comparing the outcomes of different hazards within the domain of risk management, these activities are more properly designated under risk analysis. A generalized four-stage model of risk management has been proposed by Covello and Merkhofer (1993) that breaks down the risk management process into the stages of option generation, option evaluation, option selection, and option implementation and enforcement (see Table 13.5).

The uncertainty surrounding the endpoints used for setting regulatory standards is often discounted in the course of the risk management process. Decision-makers

B. J. Nordenstam

Table 13.5. *Four stages of risk management*

1. *Option generation*
Includes identifying alternatives for managing risk

2. *Option evaluation*
Includes appraising and comparing available options

3. *Option selection*
Includes selecting one or more alternatives for implementation

4. *Option implementation and enforcement*
Includes implementing, monitoring, and enforcing alternatives

Source: Covello & Merkhofer, 1993.

must improve the methods by which they identify and consider the total range of uncertainty inherent in the risk assessment when formulating environmental policies (Finkel, 1990; McKone & Bogen 1991; Carnegie Commission, 1993; NRC 1994). To address this issue, the Carnegie Commission on Risk and the Environment (1993) has suggested, following the recommendation of Graham, Green and Roberts (1988), that 'upper and lower risk estimates that a scientist believes are 80% likely to include the true yet unknown risk' be presented. Similarly, the National Research Council (1994) suggests that, in order to judge for themselves what action is appropriate, both 'risk managers and the public should be given the opportunity to understand the source of controversy' resulting from model-uncertainty in the risk assessment process. McKone and Bogen (1991) note that '. . . risk managers should be aware of the uncertainty in risk estimates and include this awareness in their decisions and their communications of risk to the public.'

One controversial outcome of risk analysis has been the development of tables ranking the risks from a variety of sources (see Table 13.6). Some risk managers believe that such objective measures of risk should be used as the basis of government standards, and as a risk communication tool to educate the public about risks. However, others expressed concern that such tables mixed the risks inappropriately, for example, by comparing voluntary and unvoluntary risks (e.g. smoking vs. industrial pollution, or by comparing known risks and unknown risks (e.g. car accidents vs. nuclear power plant explosion). Use of such tables as a risk communication tool often resulted in negative public reactions, and eventually spurred researchers to examine additional factors influencing public perception of risk beyond the ability to interpret numerical risk estimates (Nordenstam & DiMento 1990).

13.6 Risk appraisal approach

Risk appraisal is a contextual approach examining the processes of risk perception, comparison, and communication associated with individual and societal response

240

Table 13.6. *Activities estimated to increase risk of death in any year by one in a million*

Smoking 1.4 cigarettes
Spending 1 hour in a coal mine
Living 2 days in New York
Travelling 10 miles by bicycle
Flying 1000 miles by jet
Living 2 months in Denver
Eating 40 tablespoons of peanut butter
Drinking 30 cans of diet soda
Living 5 miles from a nuclear reactor for 50 years
Living 150 years within 20 miles of a nuclear power plant

Source: Wilson (1979).

Table 13.7. *Risk appraisal research methods*

1. *Expressed preference studies*
Direct assessment
Includes survey methods, such as opinion polls, to measure public views on environmental risk issues

2. *Revealed preference studies*
Indirect assessment
Includes content analysis methods, such as examination of historical data, to determine public preferences and views

3. *Cultural preference studies*
Comparative assessment
Includes comparative analysis methods, such as cross-nation survey of citizens regarding risk-based policy preferences and views

4. *Experimental studies*
Direct assessment
Includes quasi-experimental design methods, such as multiple framing effects, or controlled studies using student populations

to environmental risks. It is a fairly new paradigm which recognizes that environmental risks are embedded within a sociopolitical context influencing public reaction (Nordenstam, 1994; Krimsky & Plough, 1988). Several different research methods are utilized to study public appraisal of environmental risk. The research methodologies employed include expressed preference studies, revealed preference studies, cultural preference studies and experimental design studies (see Table 13.7).

The majority of early published reports on human response to environmental risk came from the field of cognitive psychology. Psychological research on risk

B. J. Nordenstam

Table 13.8. *Where's the 'BEEF'? Factors influencing public response to environmental risks*

1. *Beliefs* (individual or societal)
   Includes risk perception factors, environmental attitudes, world views, group norms, political ideology, and cultural beliefs

2. *Environment* (context of risk)
   Includes contextual framing effects, trust in government, industry or methods; political and cultural history of risk; uncertainty of information

3. *Economics* (individual or societal)
   Includes monetary and behavioural cost/benefit appraisal at individual, regional or national level; endowment effects; willingness to pay *versus* willingness to accept; tangible *versus* non-tangible environmental values

4. *Fairness* (distributive and procedural)
   Includes equity of risk distribution at individual, regional or national level; procedural fairness of risk distribution at individual, societal and national level

perception and communication included psychometric analysis of variables influencing public perception, and the most effective methods of communicating information about environmental risks. Slovic, Layman and Lichtenstein (1982) and Slovic, Fischoff and Lichtenstein (1985) were among the first researchers to identify characteristics of environmental risks that increase the perceived riskiness of the hazard. Factors that usually increase risk perception include: vividness of the risk (TV coverage), involuntary exposure to the risk (breathing air polluted from a neighbouring factory), unfairness of exposure to the risk (greater pollution in poor or minority communities), lack of control over the risk (industrial pollution) and catastrophic potential of the risk (nuclear power plant explosion).

The early emphasis on risk perception was driven initially by the assumption that most public opposition was primarily a result of cognitive bias and ignorance, and could be addressed by understanding and improving the risk-communication process. However, the results of risk-perception studies were insufficient in explaining the wide range of public reaction to environmental risk. Although risk perception is an important component of this process, the emphasis on measuring perceptual responses overlooked the role of other factors influencing public reaction to environmental risks. Contextual risk appraisal is an interdisciplinary approach incorporating research from psychology, sociology, political history and economics. For example, a recently developed contextual approach, the beliefs, environment, economics and fairness (BEEF) risk appraisal framework (Nordenstam, 1995) integrates research from several schools of social theory, including environmental psychology, micro-economics and equity analysis (Nordenstam, 1996; Zeiss, 1991; Tversky & Kahneman, 1981; Kahneman & Tversky, 1979; 1984; (see Table 13.8).

242

13.7 'Mad cow' disease: a contextual analysis of environmental risk

The public reaction to the recent 'mad cow' epidemic in Britain may be analysed by using the BEEF framework of public risk appraisal (see above). That is, by examining the historical and environmental context in which the 'mad cow' incident is embedded, one can conclude that, regardless of the extremely low objective risk of disease from eating British beef, public reaction to this threat is understandable, and in fact, reasonable from an individual micro-economic and socio-political perspective.

The term 'mad cow disease' refers to a variant of Creutzfeld–Jakob disease (CJD) acquired by eating beef from cattle infected with mad cow disease, also known as bovine spongiform encephalopathy or BSE. It has been linked to at least ten cases of a fatal human neurological disorder in Britain. The disease is characterized by a long incubation period, a relatively short course of symptoms, and a death rate of 100%. The disease was vividly described in newspaper accounts to 'eat away victims' brains', resulting in the formation of spongy holes in the brain, and to have no known cure (*Washington Post*, 24/1/96).

In March, 1996, British officials first announced the 'possibility' of a link between BSE and CJD. Despite assurances by the government that British beef was safe, this news resulted in a plummet in beef prices and sales, from which the British beef industry has still not recovered. Although officials continue to state that changes in the way dead cattle are rendered into food for other cattle has effectively blocked the disease's ability to infect other animals, and massive culling of sick cows has left Britain's herd cleaner than ever, public consumption of beef remains below normal (*Los Angeles Times*, 1/3/97). From an objective standpoint, this incident could be viewed a hysterical reaction by the public. However, if we examine a few of the socio-political issues in which this environmental controversy is embedded, the influence of factors outlined in the BEEF risk appraisal framework become apparent, and public reaction becomes more understandable.

Following the official announcement, there was widespread perception that some had been less than avid in its efforts to keep the food supply safe (*Washington Post*, 24/10/96). Scientists now believe that the outbreak in Britain was originally triggered by feeding sheep by-products infected with scrapie to cattle. An epidemic followed when carcasses of infected cattle were rendered into animal protein and fed to other cattle. Thirdly, the actions of other countries indicate that their governments believe the level of risk from eating British beef is sufficient to require precautionary measures. The US has banned British beef since 1985, and British cattle since 1989. A European Union ban remains in place as EU health groups, in addition to competing beef industries, continue to question the safety of British beef (*Wall Street Journal*, 2/1/97).

This account of the 'mad cow' controversy describes many of the characteristics listed under the BEEF risk appraisal framework. First, the historical and political components of this incident provide sufficient reason to cause the public to greatly mistrust the government, and to doubt its competency. Secondly, the uncertainties regarding the exact pathway of exposure created doubts about the accuracy of the risk assessment procedures. Thirdly, the vividness of the disease process (eating away at your brain) serves to heighten individual perception of the riskiness of this disease. Fourthly, from a fairness and equity perspective, the economic decision of the animal-rendering industry to place sheep by-products in cattle feed focused attention on the ability of one industry to place the entire British public at risk in order to increase their profit margin, thereby strengthening perceptions of injustice and unfairness within the involuntarily exposed populations. Fifthly, from a micro-economic perspective, there is little cost to the individual citizen, either economically or behaviourally, to buy fish, or chicken or pork instead of beef, and the pay-off from switching is potentially great, completely eliminating the risk of this very low probability but highly catastrophic disease. Governments rely on this type of public risk appraisal to sell lottery tickers (small cost/large but unlikely pay-off). The problem with this process occurs when we all make the same decision at once, as was the case with mad cow disease. Perhaps if information had been more forthcoming, this announcement would have generated less of a media event, resulting in fewer people making this decision at the same time.

This analysis of public response during the mad cow incident serves to highlight the utility of using a risk appraisal approach to aid risk management decisions. A starting point for expanding the scope of methods available to assess impacts that may be of greater importance to the public involves integrating other types of assessment techniques, including resource assessment, societal values assessment, response assessment, benefit assessment and community impact assessment into the risk evaluation process (Nordenstam, 1994; Soderbaum, 1987).

13.8 Conclusions

This chapter has presented a brief overview of the risk-based decision process, including risk assessment, variations in risk perceptions and public values, and policy considerations generated from risk management options. It is clear that risk assessment, which is increasingly employed in environmental policy-making to set standards and initiate regulatory controls, is a relatively young, complicated, and still-evolving science. The benefits of risk assessment methods are well known, and have helped to standardize evaluations used to address environmental hazards. However, both limitations of data and model are often ignored, and the uncertainty surrounding the risk estimate may prove difficult to translate into policy decisions. This chapter concludes that many environmental controversies surrounding the use of risk assessment methods are the result of three factors. First, the current level of inadequacy in the risk assessment process, particularly in the quantification of uncertainty; secondly, the public proclivity to include a much broader range of factors when appraising environmental risks; and thirdly, the inability of risk-based analysis to incorporate impacts beyond the calculated risk level into the assessment process. In order to improve risk-based environmental policies, further advances in risk assessment methodology are needed, and more importantly, policy-makers must develop better methods to integrate the social, political and contextual factors surrounding environmental risk issues into the decision-making process.

References

Beck, M. B. (1987). Water quality modelling: a review of the analysis of uncertainty. *Water Resource Research*, **23**, 1394–442.

Carnegie Commission (1993). *Risk and the Environment: Improving Regulatory Decision Making*. New York.

Covello, V. T. & Merkhofer, M. W. (1993). *Risk Assessment Methods: Approaches for Assessing Health and Environmental Risks*. New York: Plenum Press.

Dakins, M. E., Toll, J. E. & Small, M. J. (1995). Risk-based environmental remediation: decision framework and role of uncertainty. Dissertation, State University of New York, College of Environmental Science and Forestry, Syracuse, NY.

Davies, J. C. (ed.) (1996). *Comparing Environmental Risks: Tools for Setting Government Priorities*. Resources for the Future, Washington, DC.

Finkel, A. M. (1990). *Confronting Uncertainty in Risk Management: A Guide for Decision-Makers*. Resources for the Future, Washington, DC.

Graham, J. S. Green, L. C. & Roberts, M. J. (1988). *In Search of Safety: Chemicals and Cancer Risks*. Cambridge, Mass: Harvard University Press.

Griffin, C. (1994). *Effectiveness and feasibility of best management practices in reducing urban nonpoint sources of nitrogen: uncertainty and policy analysis*. Dissertation, State University of New York, College of Environmental Science and Forestry, Syracuse, NY.

Kahneman, D. & Tversky, A. (1979). Prospect theory: an analysis of decision under risk. *Econometrica*, **47**, 263–91.

Kahneman, D. & Tversky, A. (1984). Choices, values, and frames. *American Psychologist*, **39**, 341–50.

Krimsky, S. & Plough, A. (1988). *Environmental Hazards: Communicating Risk as a Social Process*. Dover, MA: Auburn House.

McKone, T. E. & Bogen, K. T. (1991). Predicting the uncertainties in risk assessment. *Environmental Science and Technology*, **25**(10), 1674–81.

Merkhofer, M. W. (1987). *Decision Science and Social Risk Management: A Comparative Evaluation of Cost–Benefit Analysis, Decision Analysis, and Other Formal Decision-Aiding Approaches*, ed. D. Reidel. Dordrecht, The Netherlands: Kluwer Press.

Morgan, M. G. & Henrion, M. (1992). *Uncertainty: A Guide to Dealing with Uncertainty in Quantitative Risk and Policy Analysis*. New York: Cambridge University Press.

Nash, J. A. (1996). Moral values in risk decisions. In *Handbook for Environmental Risk Decision Making*, ed. C. R. Cothern, pp. 195–212. NY: Lewis Publ.

National Research Council (1968). *Water and Choice in the Colorado Basin: An Example of Alternatives in Water Management*. Washington DC: National Academy of Sciences.

National Research Council (1983). *Risk Assessment in the Federal Government: Managing the Process*. Washington, DC: National Academy Press.

National Research Council (1994). *Science and Judgement in Risk Assessment*. Washington, DC: National Academy Press.

Nordenstam, B. J. (1994). When communities say NIMBY to their LULUs: factors influencing perceptions of environmental and social impact. Dissertation, University of California, Irvine.

Nordenstam, B. J. (1995). Where's the beef? Public perception of environmental risk issues. Paper presented at the Community Decision Making for Ash Recycling Municipal Solid Waste Ash Utilization Workshop, SUNY-ESF, March.

Nordenstam, B. J. (1996). The influence of environmental uncertainty on lay perceptions of risk and safety. In *Proceedings of the NATO Conference on Scientific Uncertainty and Its Influence on the Public Participation Process*, ed. V. Covello & V. Sublet. Dordrecht, The Netherlands: Kluwer Press.

Nordenstam, B. J. & DiMento, J. F. (1990). Right-to-know: implications of risk communication research for regulatory policy. *University of California, Davis Law Review*, 23(2), 333–74.

Polanyi, M. (1958). *Personal Knowledge: Towards a Post-Critical Philosophy*. Chicago, Illinois: University of Chicago Press.

Ruckelshaus, W. D. (1983). Science, risk, and public policy. *Science*, 221, 54–9.

Slovic, P., Layman, M. & Lichtenstein, S. (1982). Rating the risks: the structure of expert and lay perceptions. In *Risk in the Technological Society*. ed. C. Hohenemser & J. X. Kasperson. Boulder, Colorado: Westview Press.

Slovic, P. Fischoff, B. & Lichtenstein, S. (1985). Regulation of risk: a psychological perspective. In *Regulatory Policy and the Social Sciences*, ed. R. G. Noll. Berkeley: University of California Press.

Soderbaum, P. (1987). Environmental management: a non-traditional approach. *Journal of Economic Issues*, March, 223–56.

Suter, G. W. II. (1993). *Ecological Risk Assessment*. MI: Lewis Publishers.

Tversky, A. & Kahneman, D. (1981). The framing of decisions and the psychology of choice. *Science*, 211, 453–8.

Zeiss, C. (1991) Community decision-making and impact management priorities for siting waste facilities. *Environmental Impact Assessment Review*, 11, 231–55.

14

Environmental biomonitoring: legal problems world-wide

Stephen Battersby

14.1 Introduction

At the outset it should be pointed out that this chapter has not been written by a lawyer, but by someone with a background in enforcing environmental regulations and more recently in the development of environmental policy and management at both the company and governmental level. The perspective is, therefore, perhaps slightly different from that of a practising lawyer.

Environmental problems, concerns and priorities for action vary across the globe. Such differences may reflect the state of economic development in a country or region. In addition, political priorities may reflect economic concerns more than the environment; despite agreements at the UN Conference on Environment and Development (UNCED) in Rio de Janeiro in 1992. Law plays a key role in translating policy into practice, and environmental law is a system of rules to regulate human actions, providing institutional mechanisms, setting standards for environmental quality, providing guidelines for developments, governing public participation in decision making and providing a system for compensating victims of pollution and environmental impairment. The legal systems and the way they are used, or are allowed to be used, necessarily reflect governmental policy generally.

In the global context, economic growth, rising debt and priority in expenditure have been cited by Wee (1994) as common obstacles to environmentally desirable developments. Wee quoted Hurst (1990) in arguing that developing states must first be free of debt, and once free of debt they could increase investment in domestic industry and sustainable development. Certainly, debt burdens cause problems for many nations including those in Eastern Europe and prevent greater account being taken of the environment in the legal framework.

The globalization of trade, and worries that environmental controls might cause a company to shift its operations, or not establish itself at all in a country or region, can influence just what legal controls exist and more particularly how they are

S. Battersby

enforced. This paper examines some of the legal problems associated with these issues, including the effectiveness of law to deal with environmental problems.

Some of the issues can be summarized by considering, for any country, whether or not there is:

- a legal framework to address the environmental problems which exist;
- agreement on environmental standards;
- an adequate system of surveillance and monitoring, with free access to the information;
- adequately resourced regulatory agencies at the appropriate level; and
- a commitment to minimizing environmental impact by those who are regulated.

In any event, effective legal protection of the environment must now depend upon a general acceptance at global, national, regional and local levels that the environment can no longer be seen as a free-good to be exploited regardless of the consequences.

The legal framework which exists will depend upon the constitution of the country, even whether or not the country is a democratic state. The approach will reflect whether there is a Common Law system as in the UK and most of the countries which once comprised the British Empire, based on judicial interpretation of custom and precedent, as well as statute law, whether the system is a Civil Law system where the law is deliberately laid down as a complete codified system by means of statute. Legal problems may arise as the result of legislation failing to conform to the requirements of the constitution and whether it is federal or a unitary constitution, and whether it can be defined as diarchical or not (divisions of government competence between authorities other than on a geographical basis; De Smith & Brazier, 1990).

Not least of the problems is also the international nature of much pollution and environmental harm, which may also reflect the globalization of trade and the growth of multinational companies. Operations can be located or moved to areas where there are lesser environmental controls or away from those areas where environmental regulation is strong.

At the global level, there is also the matter of jurisdiction particularly with respect to effects on global air quality and climate, hence the exhortation to 'think globally but act locally'. International trade in hazardous waste may lead to environmental and health impacts far removed from the location of the waste arising, hence controls on transfrontier shipments. In the same way, releases of substances which deplete the ozone layer, increase global warming, or cause acidic deposition will have an effect far removed from the point of emission.

Implementation and enforcement of international conventions and agreements raise further and particular problems. As Wee (1994) concluded in the context of consideration of 'debt for nature swaps', compliance with agreements 'currently rests on the fear of political and economic reprisals, which may not be sufficient in the face of severe domestic economic and political pressures'.

It is also perhaps worth noting that Warren Christopher, then US Secretary of State, is reported, in his efforts to secure settlements to conflicts in the world, to have come to recognize that political or security problems often had a large environmental content; expanding populations and deforestation in Haiti for instance (*The Guardian*, 1996). He recognized the connection between sustainable economic growth, inflation rates, and commodity prices, all coming under strain from China's rapidly expanding need for grain and oil imports. With 22% of the world's population, that country only has 7% of its freshwater and cropland, 3% of its forests and 2% of its oil. At the same time, the new democracies of Eastern Europe are struggling with a legacy of environmental abuse. Poorly stored nuclear waste, for instance, poses a threat to human life, and one-sixth of the Russian land mass is so polluted as to be unfit even for industrial use.

14.2 Legal techniques

Turning to actual legal problems, it is useful to consider some of the techniques which are available or have been used to secure remedies for environmental pollution or seek to prevent adverse environmental impacts. An effective legal framework will include a range of techniques and instruments for securing acceptable environmental protection and clean-up. Various inter-related techniques have been developed to further the objectives of environmental law. As a supplement to, or substitute for, anti-pollution laws some states have enacted comprehensive codes regarding conservation and management of the environment and natural resources of the country. The techniques which are used in countries around the world and some of the problems are discussed in this section.

14.2.1 Prevention of damage

Preventative measures aim to avoid harm and reduce, or where possible eliminate, the risk of harm from activities.

Regulation
Standard setting

Four different categories of standards have been distinguished by Kiss and Shelton (1993). Quality standards fix the maximum permissible level of pollution of an environmental medium or receiving sector. Emission standards specify the quantity or concentration of pollutants that can be emitted from a source. Process standards have been typified as establishing specifications applicable to fixed installations, for instance, by requiring a particular production method. Product standards may include the setting of physical or chemical composition of substances, materials or other products, or may fix the handling and packaging of the product, or may fix the levels of pollutants the product can emit or resources it can consume during use. The difficulties surrounding standard setting depend upon whether a precautionary approach is adopted, whether the major concern is protection of long-term human health, or whether the agreed standard is that around which a political as well as scientific consensus can be reached.

Restrictions and prohibitions

Such techniques include listing restricted or banned products, processes or activities. It allows individualizing of situations and avoids too much technical detail, compared with standard setting where, for instance, the means of monitoring and measuring emissions for compliance with standards have to be prescribed. The French law on classified installations uses lists to regulate polluting activities. Zoning provides a means to locate activities which are potentially harmful to the environment in an area where the environment is less sensitive. Trade restrictions such as the 1973 Convention on International Trade in Endangered Species of Wild Fauna and Flora (CITES) uses trade restrictions and prohibitions as a means of protecting endangered species. Trade regulations also prohibit or regulate the transport and dumping of toxic and dangerous waste. The Basel Convention of 1989 regulates the transfer of dangerous wastes and requires the informed consent of the countries concerned prior to transfer.

Licensing

This is a widely used method of preventing harm, which involves a government authorization via a permit, certificate or licence before a new activity can be commenced. An operation which is considered to be environmentally hazardous is defined or listed and subject to licensing procedures.

Goals

In much of Europe, the permit process originated in a Napoleonic decree of 1810, the aim of which was to protect the immediate vicinity of a project. The aim may be to protect human beings, fauna and flora and all other things against any damage to the environment, in so far as such damage may be caused by installations subject to licensing, and to ensure protection against any significant danger, inconvenience or disturbance, such as in the German Emissions Control Act of 1974. The term 'significant' could be subject to much debate, and ultimately will involve value judgements beyond that which a purely scientific or mathematical approach may imply.

Scope

Whilst the scope of licensing may be broad, an initial and continuing requirement should be compliance with specific environmental standards. It also becomes problematic to apply a system to operations which existed when the licensing scheme was established. In general, laws are not given retroactive effect; exemption of older plant would not serve the purpose of protecting the environment. In some cases, as in the UK under Part I of the Environmental Protection Act 1990, licences for existing processes include a timetable for improvements to bring them up to new plant standards.

Procedures

Licensing systems operate on the basis of a list of activities necessitating a licence or lists of substances which, if released from a process, will necessitate a licence. The existence of different licensing systems whereby a single operation may require several licences means a fragmented approach, with similar procedures being implemented by different regulatory bodies. The determination of applications for licences may be exercised by central, regional or local bodies, each bringing their own perspectives and resources to examining and verifying information provided by the applicant. It is generally accepted that there should be some publicity surrounding the application, and this will require the licensing body to take account of any observations or objections from the local population.

Environmental assessment

This was first introduced in the USA in 1969 as a procedure to ensure that adequate and early information is available on the likely environmental consequences of development projects, possible alternatives and measures to mitigate adverse environmental impacts. Incorporation of formal environmental assessment into the development approval system has been required within the EU by way of Directive 85/337/EEC. In international law, EIA is required in a European transboundary context under the provisions of a treaty signed at Espoo, Finland in 1991. The treaty includes a model for further legislation as well as the general elements already found in domestic EIA legislation. Again, it is the developer who submits the Environmental Statement, which should include all the required information. It is up to the regulator and person granting the development consent to ensure that they are satisfied with that information and the mitigation measures. That regulatory agency may not have the expertise to make a proper evaluation of the environmental statement.

Something which can be required but which appears to be undertaken rarely, is the monitoring of the effectiveness of mitigation measures, and verification of predictions in statements so that the results can be used in future environmental assessments of similar developments or developments in similar environments.

14.2.2 Implementation measures

Implementation as well as the formulation of environmental law and policies must be based on the collection of reliable data and information, and on continuous assessment of that data and information. Environmental law can include requirements on surveillance, reporting and monitoring, surveillance being the acquisition of data on which further action such as monitoring may be based. The EC Directive 82/883/EEC sets out procedures for the surveillance and monitoring of environments concerned by waste from the titanium dioxide industry, and the surveillance requires sampling of the affected environments. Water samples, for instance, could be taken by individual enterprises, associations or by local or national authorities.

The information has to be sent to an appropriate agency who will assemble, organize and analyse it.

Monitoring, in turn, is the continuous assessment of information, comparing it to specified parameters, providing feedback on which future decisions can be made whether at the policy level or immediate emergency level. Whilst some countries have centralized their surveillance, monitoring and assessment in a single agency, in others there is a network of institutions coordinated by a national ministry or agency. The effectiveness of any system must depend upon the quality of information flow between those undertaking the monitoring and those being consulted and those making decisions. It should also be noted that licences may have conditions stipulating how the company will monitor discharges, with information obtained being made available to the regulatory agency who should verify the data.

Implementation measures can also be said to include environmental auditing. It is an increasingly popular control mechanism often linked to the market approach similar to the eco-label. It is also of importance in commercial transactions where the risk of environmental liabilities can have a bearing on negotiations and contracts. It provides a means of identifying any possible future environmental risks and legal liabilities, as the result of contamination of land, for example. Environmental audits are a means of evaluating procedures and work methods as they affect environmental performance, in a systematic way. Such audits will take account of compliance with legal regulations. Whilst the use of audits in transactions will prompt companies to take greater care with respect to the environment, and also provide a means of putting a value on good or bad environmental performance, of equal importance is the establishment of schemes which demonstrate that there are effective environmental management systems in place outside the considerations of any transaction. Council Regulation (EEC) 1836/93 establishes the system for allowing voluntary participation by companies in the industrial sector in a Community eco-management and audit scheme (EMAS).

Participation by companies in EMAS is entirely voluntary, although the scheme has been established by a Regulation, and participation and certification require compliance with the criteria of the scheme including the establishment of an environmental management system and publication of an environmental statement. It does not apply to a company as a whole, but rather to a particular site. However, as the scheme requires a commitment to demonstrable and continuous improvements in environmental performance regardless of the environmental merits of the product, it is an alternative way to reduce environmental pollution. It is, in effect, another market-based instrument as it is intended that the ability to publicize registration of a site will provide a marketing edge and thus encourage participation. It may also be that fulfilling the criteria for registration may also reduce the need for, or frequency of, regulatory visits from the appropriate enforcing agencies. It is also a way in which companies have recognized they can reduce waste, lower costs and increase efficiency. There has been some concern that participation in the scheme could lead to difficulties as the result of publication of environmental statements after each audit cycle, and which could be used against companies should they fail to make significant changes. Similarly, in the event of litigation against a company, registration indicates the extent of records and information held by the organization which in other circumstances may not have been available to a plaintiff. These fears may not be well founded, but have caused some concern.

14.2.3 Enforcement and remedial measures

Whatever preventative measures have been incorporated into environmental law, there will inevitably have been releases to the environment, and adverse impacts will occur whether as the result of neglect, mismanagement or accidents. The law seeks to act as a deterrent to wrongful acts and to remedy such wrongs and any harm caused. The law has to set out the appropriate enforcement actions and remedies, addressing questions as to the extent of harm that justifies legal actions, who is responsible for instituting proceedings, where legal actions should take place and what sanctions or compensation should exist. Procedures may be civil claims, administrative remedies and/or criminal prosecution.

Nature of liability

Wrongful acts, those which the law has set out as being contrary to behaviour acceptable to the society, may not lead to any measurable environmental harm; nevertheless this can still lead to legal sanctions. Public liability can be based on a risk of future harm which may incorporate the precautionary principle. On the other hand, harm may be defined in the legislation and be a requirement of any action, and may be serious or appreciable injury or defined as significant harmful effects. It may be that the notion of harm, discussed later in the context of contaminated land provisions in the UK, and the relevant level for action, may be negotiable, setting off or balancing conflicting interests equitably. However, this approach would lead to increased uncertainty or even possibly an unnecessarily bureaucratic approach involving protracted negotiations on what, if any, action is required.

Whilst in terms of environmental law the concept of harm may be seen as a property concept to which monetary value can be placed, particularly in civil claims, this becomes difficult when considering protection of a species, or habitat that is not economically exploited and has no market value. Measurement of harm for the purpose of damages awards poses considerable problems. Not least of these concerns, and one which the law has ignored, is the irreversibility of any harm which may be caused.

Scope of responsibility

Whilst anyone harming the environment may be held to be liable to those injured, or be subject to criminal or administrative sanctions sought by the state, the law may also extend this to include the principal owner or director of a polluting company where the pollution has resulted from their neglect or connivance. The law has to be clear as to who shall be responsible for any environmental harm. In the main, there has to be some fault, although some laws hold persons liable for all consequences of their actions even those that are accidental. There is growing pressure for strict (no fault) liability to apply in wider circumstances. Over the years it has been limited to operators of particularly hazardous operations but, in some countries including Germany, this is more widely applied. In Germany strict liability applies to a hundred installations listed in legislation.

Enforcement actions

Civil actions are started by those who have suffered as the result of the pollution. Enforcement of public laws is normally a matter for the state authorities or regulatory agency as specified in the law.

Civil liability

An individual who has suffered some damage to themselves or their property may bring a civil action against the operator of the installation that caused the damage based on concepts of tort or a legal wrong. Nuisance is the most frequent action in common law. Other bases for liability include trespass, strict liability and negligence. In France, the most common ground for holding polluting enterprises civilly liable is based on 'abnormal harm to the neighbourhood', and claims brought on this basis are subject to strict liability and negligence does not have to be shown, nor is compliance with government regulations a defence.

In any such actions, however, there are problems of locus (standing) to take legal action when this is based purely on property rights, and also the issue of remoteness of the damage or loss alleged to have been caused directly by the event. Of particular importance is the question of who can bring an action where harm is being caused to the environment. For instance, who brings an action on the part of the environment when the owner of land is causing adverse environmental impact such as the destruction of a habitat or species, but with no harm to any other human or land outside his/her ownership? What if there is no ownership of the area affected (the marine environment outside territorial waters, for instance) and no obvious or immediate harm to human health? Can environmental campaign groups have standing to bring actions in such circumstances if there is no government intervention? Environmental groups and citizens may have an 'interest' but how do they establish '*locus standi*' or legal interest in the courts? In Malaysia, for example, according to Azmi (1996), the issue of 'standing' is seen as the first (and usually successful) line of defence to any action. In Luxembourg and France, specific Acts recognize certain nature conservation associations which enjoy rights in administrative and judicial proceedings. Greenpeace has had a statutory right in Denmark since 1992 to challenge decisions affecting the marine environment. In the UK it is emerging that environmental associations which have existed for some time, are non-profit making, have articles of association which relate to environmental protection and whose geographical scope is determined and can prove a nexus between their objectives and the public interest on the point at issue will have standing according to Jewkes (1996), as is already the case in other member states. A national group with a general interest may have standing although, in the Greenpeace case, it was also argued that members lived in proximity to Sellafield (R v Secretary of State for the Environment and others *ex parte* Greenpeace and Lancashire County Council (High Court 4 March 1994)). The case was a challenge to the radioactive waste disposal authorizations related to the THORP reprocessing plant. Although the case was lost, the courts accepted that Greenpeace had sufficient standing to bring the case, despite strong opposition, reported by Macrory (1994), from British Nuclear Fuels Ltd (BNFL).

However, at the European level it is slightly different where Article 173 of the Treaty of the European Union is a form of judicial review or action to annul. The situation is different, not least because the majority of environmental measures are in the form of directives and therefore are not *prima facie* reviewable by private parties. They are limited by Article 173 to challenging decisions of direct and individual concern to them. In 1994, Greenpeace attempted to bring an action against the European Commission concerning the failure to require environmental assessment for a project in the Canary Islands to which ECU 40m had been awarded from the Structural Funds (Stichting Greenpeace Council and others v EC Commission). The application was dismissed by the Court of First Instance in 1995 and has now been appealed. The case turned on the question of whether an environmental association can ever have an individual concern. The Court of First Instance suggested that, because the class of applicants is not fixed, such groups can never prove an individual concern.

Jewkes (1996) has concluded it would make sense to harmonize the rules of standing as between member states, but given the different legal systems there are likely to be the same difficulties as were experienced in trying to harmonize the rules on civil liability. However, the proposed directive on Access to Justice in Environmental Matters recites the principle of subsidiarity with emphasis on national courts, although Jewkes believes that the European Court of Justice would offer a quicker prospect of opening up direct routes to justice on environmental matters.

Administrative procedures

Such procedures include injunctions, fines (which may be limited), and refusal, suspension, revocation or modification of licences or authorizations. Proceedings will be initiated by the authority or regulatory agency specified in the legislation. Appeals against such administrative actions may be to the next higher level of government such as a Minister sitting in a quasi-judicial capacity, rather than to the courts, which brings in the additional issue of politics.

Penal law

The function of penal law is to protect those persons and objects to which the society attach greatest value. It establishes and enforces penalties including custodial sentences. In many countries national law imposes criminal liability on those who pollute and whose actions damage the environment. The extent to which the penal law has been applied to the environment may reflect the importance attached to the environment.

Remedies

Civil remedies are normally compensatory, money damages, and injunctive, ordering that an activity cease and repairs be made. It is the function of the courts to assess what the damages should be and this can be problematic as to what costs to allow in any claim: for instance, should a claim for damage to the quality of life be allowed where there has been a large oil tanker spillage, and how would these be assessed? By comparison, restoration and clean-up costs for a harbour or coastline would be assessed relatively easily. Other sanctions can include denial of government contracts, or blacklisting of harmful products.

The issue then arises as to the standard of restoration, and if the object is to return the environment to the standard prior to the incident this implies complete knowledge of the particular ecosystem affected. The question is also in what time should that restoration be completed? It may be that expensive remedial measures will restore the environment quickly, but the ability for the environment to restore itself over a longer period of time with much less direct intervention could be cheaper. The calculation would then be based on some assessment as to the loss of enjoyment whilst this 'intrinsic remediation' was supposed to occur. This would become more problematic for the courts.

Remedies for transfrontier environmental harm

Whilst it is relatively straightforward to deal with matters where the polluter and the person affected are both within the jurisdiction of a single state, it becomes more complicated when harm occurs across state boundaries. Traditionally, such harm has been included in the idea that the state has responsibility for acts contrary to international law. Thus states may be held liable for pollution that causes damage to persons or property in another state. Principle 21 of the Stockholm Declaration, repeated in Principle 2 of the Rio Declaration, provides that states have responsibility to ensure that activities under their jurisdiction or control do not cause damage to the environment in other states or areas beyond national jurisdiction. Despite these agreements, few international liability claims have been presented.

In addition to the usual problems associated with litigation such as establishing fault, legal basis and locus (standing) to bring the action, inter-state procedures are lengthy and problems of proof will be exacerbated with more than one state and long distances involved. There is also the matter of the extent to which states can be held accountable for the actions of private parties under their jurisdiction, especially if the actions causing the pollution or harm were legal where they occurred. It seems that the state whose territory serves to support the activities causing environmental damage elsewhere is responsible for the resulting harm.

As far as compensation for victims of transfrontier pollution are concerned, the increasingly accepted solution according to Kiss and Shelton (1993) is to settle the issue on the inter-personal level within states as part of private law, rather than through public international law. An inhabitant of one state who suffers damage due to pollution originating in another state can file a civil action against the polluter. Jurisdiction to judge such a case can exist in the state of the victim or the polluter's state. There may sometimes be treaties between states to settle such jurisdictional matters. Within Europe, national law generally favours jurisdiction in the defendant's domicile. Whether this is right is open to some debate as it may give unfair advantage to the polluting defendant.

14.2.4 Economic and market devices

Apart from direct regulatory measures, legislators increasingly are enacting a range of economic incentives and disincentives to influence operations and their impact on the environment.

Taxation

In this area are such things as effluent charges, product charges, tax differentials, user charges and administrative charges. The intention is to tax more heavily those activities or products which are considered, at least initially on the basis of scientific evidence, to have greatest adverse impact on the environment. Whilst there may be easy decisions at the extremes, in some cases it may become more difficult to decide where the higher tax rate should fall.

Loans

In some countries such as France, government financial assistance and incentives can take the form of low-interest loans to aid the development and operation of less environmentally damaging installations and recycling systems.

Insurance

The use of insurance depends upon the development of the insurance market, and the laws governing insurance coverage of pollution-related claims vary from one jurisdiction to another. Insurance cover is normally only available for damage which is not caused by deliberate acts or omissions. Compulsory anti-pollution insurance is not required in every state, but the notion is that, where it is required, insurance companies will require operations to take stronger action to minimize emissions which cause environmental harm thereby reducing the risk of an insurance claim. This is true whenever environmental insurance is taken out, but until there is compulsion, or a fully developed market in environmental insurance, premiums may well be considered excessive compared with the risk of legal action or liability and the costs resulting from such liability.

S. Battersby

Grants and subsidies

Environmental funds, which have been created, often directly fund environmental protection measures. Turkey has such a fund. Its use is allocated through central government and is legislatively restricted to, among other things, projects of research, environmental clean-up, and education and training.

Negotiable permits

The USA and Germany have applied systems of negotiable permits under the 'bubble' concept. The total amount of pollution permissible within an area is fixed by the authorities. Each company obtains an emission permit, but companies investing in processes which emit lower levels of pollution than in the permit may exchange or sell the balance of the permitted pollution to another company located in the appropriate geographical area. In the USA this may even be in another state.

Deposits

This is a market mechanism aimed at reducing the amount of waste produced, by making it mandatory for deposits on plastic or glass containers, or other packaging to encourage their return or recycling.

Labelling

The 'ecolabel' is an incentive for environmental protection, moving away from regulation of processes, and encouraging consumers to purchase those products which have been assessed as causing less environmental harm throughout their life-cycle than other products, thereby using market forces to promote cleaner technology. This encourages pro-environmental purchasing on the part of the public and a precautionary approach on the part of the manufacturing industry.

The systems can be difficult to administer first by agreeing criteria which should be applied for a product range and the standards to apply. The system is further complicated by a lack of, or difficulties in agreeing, a protocol for life-cycle analysis of a product to assess its compliance with the criteria for awarding the ecolabel.

There is a range of legal techniques used in environmental law: some overlap, some may be more effective in some countries than others, certainly all can pose problems from the perspective of securing environmental protection.

14.3 Implementing international conventions

According to a UN study (Shand, 1992), less than half the 124 agreements and instruments surveyed are open to global membership, although several of the regionally restricted agreements do permit other States to join with the agreement of the original signatories. Incentives to participate in agreements by developing countries relate primarily to the availability of technical support to secure compliance. Participation is also dependent upon a combination of other factors including the availability of finance, parliamentary pressure, the activities of non-governmental organizations, industries, the press and the general public. Flexibility in the treaties, which allows temporary derogations, is also likely to have played a part in securing signatures.

Many international treaties and conventions are formulated in very general and abstract terms, making it difficult to assess whether objectives have been achieved. Measurable objectives including quantified targets and technical criteria for compliance are found in only a few and relate to standards for motor vehicles, aircraft and ships, although there are also biodegradability limits set in the 1968 European Agreement on the restriction of the use of certain detergents and quantified emission reductions laid down in protocols to the 1979 Convention on long-range transboundary air pollution and the 1985 Vienna Convention for the Protection of the Ozone Layer (and the subsequent Montreal and Copenhagen Protocols).

Agenda 21 of the Rio declaration (recommendations for future action) addressed the issue of international legal instruments and mechanisms. The basis for action recognized that the development of international law had to recognize the balance to be drawn between environmental and economic development concerns, the need to clarify the relationship between environmental agreements and relevant social and economic agreements (such as GATT), the need for all countries to participate in formulation and implementation of agreements, provide adequate technical assistance, and the requirement for proper codification of international law conducted on a universal basis.

Some of the proposed activities in Chapter 39 of Agenda 21 illustrate the difficulties which exist in implementing international law. These include the need to study ways of overcoming disputes between states, securing effective participation in international law-making by developing countries, including provision of assistance in building up expertise in this area, and to consider procedures and mechanisms to promote and review effective implementation.

Chapter 8 of Agenda 21 set out the pointers to providing an effective legal and regulatory framework, recognizing that laws and regulations 'suited to country-specific conditions are among the most important instruments for transforming environment and development policies into actions' and that 'much of the law-making in many countries is *ad hoc* and piecemeal or has not been endowed with the necessary institutional machinery and authority for enforcement and timely adjustment'. The UN survey (Shand, 1992) reported that there may be problems of compliance with international treaties, particularly with respect to the requirements on reporting legislative measures to implement these agreements. Agenda 21 includes the following activities for providing a more effective legal and regulatory framework for international treaties on the environment and development:

- making laws and regulations more effective, with governments, with the support of competent international organizations, assessing laws and regulations already enacted, and the administrative machinery established in the field of environment and sustainable development, including programmes to promote public awareness and specialized training;

- the establishment of judicial and administrative procedures for legal redress and remedy of actions causing environmental harm, providing access to individuals, groups and organizations with a recognized legal interest;
- the provision of legal information and support services and legal expert advice, establishing a co-operative training network for sustainable development law;
- the need for the establishment of a co-operative training network for sustainable development law using competent international and academic institutions;
- the development of effective national programmes for reviewing and enforcing compliance with national, state, provincial and local laws on the environment and which are enforceable in practice; and
- national monitoring of legal follow-up to international instruments, with contracting parties improving practices and procedures for information on legal and regulatory measures taken.

14.4 The legal process: evidence and proof

In all cases where a person is alleged to be responsible for environmental harm, there is a problem of proof. There has to be a causal link between the acts of the person or company alleged to be liable and the harm or damage which has occurred. In civil claims, that burden of proof may be less onerous than criminal cases, balance of probabilities as opposed to beyond reasonable doubt. Nevertheless, proof can be difficult where there may be multiple sources of a pollutant, a cumulative effect, diffuse pollution or the pollution has been rapidly carried away, down the river, for instance, so that effects are some distance from the alleged source. The degree of required proximity in time and space between the causes and harm have to be decided. This is important when deciding whether there is adequate evidence on which to base a prosecution.

The law itself can address some aspects of these issues, for example, should a lender be held liable for environmental damage caused by the use of funds by the borrower? If the lender's control of the borrower's activities is seen as direct, then a claim might be pursued in some countries such as the USA, because the causal link would be considered sufficiently strong. The question then becomes, who has the deepest pocket? This is the person against whom the action is then taken.

It should not be forgotten that gathering evidence can take some time; the legal process itself can be protracted whether it is action to bring an environmental offender to book, or to ensure that procedures to prevent pollution are properly implemented.

14.5 Resourcing regulators

Civil action is usually available only to those who have the resources to pursue legal action. For most of the citizenry, it is a matter of the governmental agencies enforcing the provisions of environmental law adequately on their behalf.

In the UK, the Environment Agency (which came into existence on 1 April, 1996, but which is not responsible for all environmental regulation), employs about 9000 people and will spend £500 million each year but 'will be under particularly close scrutiny to ensure it spends (this) wisely and deploys its workforce effectively' (Gallagher 1996). However, the vast majority of the staff have come from the former National Rivers Authority even though that body came to the Agency with 1200 fewer people than it planned to have 2 years ago. Almost 1000 additional technical staff were also recruited from local government who had been responsible for waste regulation, and these are having to be supported by the existing administrative structures from the NRA and Her Majesty's Inspectorate of Pollution which was the other major component body incorporated into the Agency. Furthermore, the budget of the Agency will be dependent upon the annual budget settlement agreed by the Treasury. It remains to be seen how long it is before there are staffing reductions and reduced budgets by the Agency, regardless of environmental problems or concerns.

Under this heading it might be appropriate to include the issue of deregulation which has been espoused by some governments including that of the UK, which is also introducing the idea of compliance cost assessment (CCA) to new regulatory proposals. This latter approach is controversial because it ignores the potential business benefits of environmental legislation and excludes environmental technology businesses from the CCA process (Anon, 1996*b*). Guidance even says that Government Departments should include in CCAs any extra costs which firms may incur by being forced by new regulations to comply with existing legislation with which they were not adhering.

In any event, the new Environment Agencies in Britain have been ordered to draw up codes of practice which are likely to burden them with red tape and discourage prompt action against polluters (Anon, 1996*a*). Thus, before any formal action can be taken, they will have to notify the person concerned that enforcement action is being considered, inviting representations against the proposed action.

14.6 An example of a legal problem: land and soil

Contaminated and polluted land and its clean-up has become a major environmental problem throughout Europe and the USA, in particular. The UN Food and Agriculture Organisation proclaimed a World Soil Charter in 1981 and, in 1982, the UN declared a World Soils Policy, recognizing the soil as a finite resource which is subject to ever-increasing demands. Source-based action included measures to control the shipment and disposal of hazardous waste. Soil Charters at the UN and European level have contained non-binding guidelines for action and basic principles, focusing on the need for land-use policies that create incentives for participation in soil conservation.

Contaminated land has been a particularly thorny problem. In the UK only now is there legislation to deal with the clean-up of contaminated land, and that is not yet in force. Until now, liability has been governed by the common law of tort. The particular concern in drafting legislation has often been the standard to which the land should be returned as the result of the remediation. The higher the standard of clean-up, the more expensive it becomes. Hence it was estimated that the average clean-up costs under the US Comprehensive Environmental Response, Compensation and Liability Act (CERCLA), more widely known as Superfund, was estimated to be $3 million, and as Varnum said 'this expense is no mere footnote to the purchase of a real estate parcel' (Varnum, 1990a). Under CERCLA, past and present owners and operators of property where a release of hazardous substance has occurred, are liable for remediation related to the release. It should be noted that CERCLA established a priority list of sites for remediation and not all contaminated sites fall within the scope of Superfund. In 1980, a $1.8 billion fund to finance the cost of necessary clean-ups was created. By 1991, it was estimated that the fund would be at least $25 billion. Yet, critics of Superfund suggest that too much of the costs end up as lawyers' fees rather than effective clean-up of land. This is because the costs of litigation in assigning responsibility come from Superfund, so reducing the money available for actual remedial work.

In a later article (Varnum, 1990b), it was reported how the US EPA and the State of Montana were holding the tiny Miners' Bank of Butte, Montana, responsible for the $10 million clean-up of an abandoned railroad tie (sleeper) creosoting plant which the bank owned for 3 months after the business failed. The bank relinquished title to the property as soon as it discovered the creosote contamination at the site. With working capital of only $2.5 million, the Bank was facing insolvency. The great concern was that a decision in United States v Fleet Factors Corporation found that a secured creditor might be liable under CERCLA. Varnum concluded that the Fleet standard of clean-up liability for lenders was too extreme to be practical.

There are millions of contaminated sites in the world with 427 500 in the USA in total, though only about 40 000 Superfund sites, and 1.5 million in the EU. The problem is that the contamination may have occurred under a previous ownership, may have been in legal compliance (if any relevant legislation even existed) and before there was great concern about the environment: now mere ownership can mean liability. Whether there is a requirement to secure clean-up, and who can be made to pay can, however, depend upon the phrasing of the legislation. There is a presumption in the legislation that responsibility can be correctly attributed. This is difficult where it is older contamination, and tracing the source of the contaminant is not always easy in any event as, after travelling some distance, it could be chemically different from the original contaminant.

In the UK, as far as the Environment Act 1995 is concerned, draft regulations and guidance indicate that the term 'contaminated land' will be defined quite narrowly so sites requiring remediation under the legislation will be fewer than the total number of contaminated sites. Contaminated land is defined as that where 'significant harm is being caused or there is significant possibility of such harm being caused' (Environment Act, 1995) or water pollution is being, or likely to be, caused. Although harm is defined in the Act as 'harm to the health of living organisms or other interference with the ecological systems of which they form part and, in the case of man, includes harm to his property', draft guidance circulated last year (DoE, 1995) suggested three types of harm to be taken into account when determining if land is contaminated:

- whether there is a risk of death, serious injury of clinical toxicity to human users or occupiers of a site;
- a significant change in a functioning of the ecosystems on statutorily protected wildlife sites; and
- harm to property whether continuing physical damage which cannot be put right without substantial works, or disease or other physical damage to crops or livestock causing loss in value.

A clear omission is any impacts on ecosystems outside statutorily protected sites.

Unlike the USA, the UK will only require clean-up fit for use, that is present or proposed next use. The standards of clean-up, will not, so far as can be gathered, take account of any possible future uses beyond that. In other countries, such as the Netherlands, they take a 'multi-functionality' approach which requires soils to be cleaned until their functional properties for humans, flora and fauna have been restored. As far as standards are concerned in the UK the Royal Commission on Environmental Pollution has argued for a 'best practicable environmental option' approach. That is, the standard of clean-up should be to the highest standard that can be reached without excessive cost and not merely the standard required for the use immediately intended (Royal Commission on Environmental Pollution, 1996).

When land is cleaned up, but not to a standard which fully restores its functional properties, there is a question as to whether the regulators can take future action on the same land, when a different next use is proposed which is more sensitive to the contamination which was left in the first place, when standards are improved or knowledge improves about the effects of the contamination which has been left. This would argue for some completion certificate, which would provide some protection against future action by the enforcing agency, but in all probability would throw the cost of any future further remediation on to the public authorities and public expenditure. In a country where a major policy is the reduction of public expenditure, such considerations become important. In the UK, public spending on contaminated land clean-up is less than £100 million per year. It is estimated that it will take a century at this rate to clean up all of Britain's contaminated land assuming this is about 100 000 hectares (ENDS Report, 1996b).

Conclusions

This chapter should be seen as a personal view of some of the problems associated with environmental law. The sums of money involved in legal action and implementing the law can be substantial whether to prevent pollution, protect environmental resources or secure remediation of damage, or in legal expenses. Legal processes world-wide can be slow, particularly where there are wealthy vested interests involved; in the meantime, environmental harm can continue to be caused. The question may be the extent to which the law is capable of securing environmental protection without fundamental changes to our economic systems and the way we account for impairment of our global environmental capital.

No direct reference has been made to the legal problems associated with particular techniques and methodologies in monitoring or remediation. For instance, the legal problems associated with intrinsic bioremediation, is understood to be almost akin to the old 'dilute and disperse' philosophy, and is a strategy for dealing with existing pollution plumes rather than a way of legitimizing further pollution of groundwaters. There must be some suspicion of companies who propose leaving contaminants in the ground relying on natural attenuation which has not been fully demonstrated, rather than the alternative, but more expensive, clean-up technologies. Certainly, without evidence that this approach works in a reasonable time frame, it will be difficult for a regulator to accept such an approach as an option for a clean-up strategy.

Vibhute (1995) has said in the context of the environment and development in India, development policies 'do not perceive the environment as an integral part of [the] development plan. It only treats environment as a "crucial guiding principle" in formulation of development policies'. Furthermore, Vibhute argues that, despite impressive laws on the statute books, there is a substantial gap between environmental policy reflected in those laws and what the laws achieve in action. He suggests such factors contributing to this as the absolute discretion the government has in staffing pollution control boards, and a lack of political will to ensure optimum structural and functional autonomy. He also concludes that environmental laws premised merely on deterrent philosophy and dominated by severe punitive sanctions have practical and theoretical limitations in achieving desired goals. He argues for a shift from a 'criminal law' model to a 'tort model' and from a punitive to a compensatory approach. It would seem that this could only be effective if the citizenry as a whole has adequate access to the judicial process, with the question of 'locus' or legal interest in bringing law suits being broadly interpreted. There also has to be full freedom of environmental information including emissions inventories and environmental monitoring data. These issues remain problems world-wide.

References

Anon (1996a). Deregulation of enforcement puts Agency at risk. *ENDS Report 252*, January. London: Environmental Data Services Ltd.
Anon (1996b). Deregulation stokes controversy on compliance cost, risk assessment. *ENDS Report 253*, February, p. 37. London: Environmental Data Services Ltd.
Anon (1996c). *ENDS Report 254*, March, London: Environmental Data Services Ltd.
Azmi, S. (1996). 'Issues of standing in Malaysian environmental law'. Paper 'Standing in Environmental Law Action', Conference, University of Central Lancashire, 12 June.

Department of the Environment, London (1995). Draft guidance on determination of whether land is contaminated land under the provisions of Part IIA of the Environmental Protection Act 1990, May 1995.

De Smith, S. & Brazier, R. (1990). *Constitutional and Administrative Law*. 6th edn. Penguin.

Gallagher, E. (1996). Framework for the future – first public briefing by the Environment Agency, 6 February, London.

The Guardian, May 1, 1996.

Hurst, P. (1990). *Rainforest Politics: Ecological Destruction in South East Asia*. London: Zed Books.

Jewkes, P. (1996). 'Developments in the EC: lessons for the future'. Paper to 'Standing in Environmental Law Actions' Conference, University of Central Lancashire, 12 June.

Kiss, A. & Shelton, D. (1993). *Manual of European Environmental Law*. Cambridge: Grotius Publications Ltd.

Macrory, R. (1994). 'Radioactive releases and Community Law'. *ENDS Report 230*, March, p. 43. London: Environmental Data Services Ltd.

Royal Commission on Environmental Pollution (1996). *19th Report Sustainable Use of Soil, Cm 3165*. London: HMSO.

Shand, P. H. (ed.) (1992). The effectiveness of international environmental agreements – a survey of existing legal instruments. Cambridge: UNCED, Grotius.

Varnum, J. (1990*a*). Hazardous waste and the purchase of real estate: a need for caution. *Environment Law Brief*, 1 (2).

Varnum, J. (1990*b*). Controversy heats up over hazardous waste clean-up liability of secured lenders, *Environment Law Brief*, 2 (1).

Vibhute, K. I. (1995). Environment, development and the law: the Indian perspective. *Journal of Environmental Law*, 7 (2), p. 137. OUP.

Wee, L. C. W. (1994). Debt for nature swaps, a reassessment of their significance in international environmental law. *Journal of Environmental Law*, 6 (1), OUP.

15

Bioremediation: an economic perspective

Simon Shohet

15.1 Introduction

The process by which new technologies replace existing ones involves a complex interplay of political, social, environmental and economic factors. The ability of a technology to deliver improved performance and profitability is an important prerequisite for replacement to occur, but not always sufficient in itself to displace another technology; even radical technologies such as microelectronics have taken several decades to diffuse widely. Diffusion rates of technologies may be influenced by a wide range of external factors, not least the presence of competing technologies, industrial standards, consumer resistance or, as has been the case with environmental control technologies, government regulation.

A perspective is provided below on the factors influencing the development of environmental biotechnology, and bioremediation in particular. This is an area where biotechnology has been slow to diffuse when compared to health and to agriculture sectors, and it is therefore useful to consider what might be some of the underlying economic causes of this slow diffusion rate.

15.1.1 Bioremediation: basic techniques and approaches

Bioremediation involves various biological agents (such as bacteria, fungi and enzymes) in combination with engineering techniques, to accelerate the decontamination of hazardous waste and pollutants. The techniques can be applied in various environments: contaminated ground water, soils, process waste streams, storage tanks, or contaminated rivers, coastlines or marine environments. The effectiveness depends on external conditions (such as pH and temperature) and on the types of contaminants: complex organic molecules such as aromatic hydrocarbons being more resistant to biodegradation than simple organic chain molecules. While substrates must be biodegradable, in some cases inorganics like heavy metals can be removed by selective accumulation by micro-organisms and plants. Genetically engineered micro-organisms (GEMs) could greatly increase the potential for degrading resistant chemical compounds, although, to date, their use has been limited because of strict regulations covering release of genetically altered organisms into the environment in most developed countries. Bioremediation *in situ* involves inoculation of a treatment site with contaminant-degrading bacteria and the addition of nutrients. In some cases, the site can be aerated to accelerate the degradation process. A further method involves removal or flushing of contaminants for treatment in an above-ground bioreactor into which micro-organisms, mutrients and oxygen are added. In contaminated soils, land farming techniques are practised, whereby soil is treated by adding water and nutrients and ploughed to increase aeration. In its simplest form, the process may rely on indigenous microbes for the degradation to occur. Aqueous contamination, e.g. of lakes and rivers frequently involves the addition of microbes and nutrients and powerful aeration, or the use of a separate bioreactor inoculated with bacteria. Processes such as sewage treatment (and composting) are examples of more traditional ways in which biodegradation is exploited, and the activated-sludge process especially relies upon gravel-immobilized mixed bacterial species.

Bioremediation represents one of several strategies for resolving contamination problems arising from industrial production and human consumption. While it may be desirable to avoid contamination in the first place, avoiding the production of all contaminants would involve major costs that almost certainly would not be outweighed by the social and environmental benefits. Furthermore, avoidance, as a strategy, provides no solution to removing contamination arising from past activities. One policy option is to permit the emission of contaminants and control outputs to an agreed level by treating effluents and emissions before they enter the environment.

While costly at the outset, the longer-term effect is to slow the accumulation of contaminants, and it is therefore an approach widely incorporated into integrated pollution control strategies.

Remediation and restoration are, however, the only options for resolving past contamination problems that remain resistant to natural degradation. The scale of these problems requires innovative technologies and the use of a range of techniques. Increasingly, it is being realized that biological remediation and restoration, rather than purely physical or chemical treatment, offer a number of benefits, notably relatively low energy inputs, relatively innocuous degradation products and potentially lower costs.

15.2 Bioremediation and the scale of contamination problems in developed countries

Cumulative contaminants create a stock of pollution in the environment (hence they are sometimes referred to as 'stock' pollutants) and, being resistant to natural degradation, they pose the greatest technological challenges. They may lead to a legacy of pollution where only later generations bear the costs of restoration.

Table 15.1. *Estimated contaminated sites in the US*

Type of site	Total number of sites	Likely to be remediated	Year of estimate
Designated under Superfund legislation[a]	36 814	1 235	1992
RCRA[b]	80 000	1 500 to 3 000	1993
Leaking underground storage tanks	1 500 000	200 000 to 600 000	1992
Defence Dept sites	24 446	7 313	1991
Energy Dept sites	n/a	4 000	1992

Source: Glass *et al.*, 1995*a*.

[a]The Superfund was established as a trust fund to pay for environmental clean-up enacted in the Comprehensive Emergency Response Compensation and Liability Act 1980, and is widely known as the Superfund law, see Burtraw and Portney (1991).

[b]Resource Conservation and Recovery Act 1976, designated to establish regulations on the generation, transportation, storage and disposal of hazardous and solid wastes. Leaking underground storage tanks were exempted in the 1976 law but included under amendments introduced in 1984.

Non-cumulative pollutants, on the other hand, can be assimilated in the environment (providing the pollutant's emission rate is low enough) and are sometimes referred to as 'fund' pollutants (see Tietenberg, 1995). Examples of fund pollutants include bio-organic effluents such as sewage, pulp and paper mill effluents and farm waste.

Stock pollutants can arise from a range of industrial activities such as the manufacture of chemicals, metal plating, wood preserving, petroleum refining. The types of chemicals include volatile organics such as trichloroethylene, tetrachlorethylene, BTEX compounds (benzene, toluene, ethylbenzene and xylenes) in addition to heavy metals such as lead, mercury and cadmium. Military and energy establishments pose additional problems with contamination by explosives, polychlorinated biphenyls (PCBs), pesticides and radioactive wastes. Over the last two decades, a number of countries have carried out extensive environmental assessment and auditing that has revealed a massive legacy of contaminated sites. Subsequently, legislation has been enacted in these countries to restore these sites to acceptable levels and to limit the release of future contamination and hazardous waste, driven in part by a public increasingly concerned about environmental contamination problems.

The large-scale nature of the problem is illustrated in Tables 15.1 and 15.2, which show the numbers of estimated sites in the US and a selection of European countries.

At present, bioremediation represents a small portion of the total treatment industry in most developed economies. US spending in 1993 on solid and hazardous waste management and on pollution control, consulting engineering

Table 15.2. *Hazardous waste sites known (or estimated) in selected European countries*

Country	Estimated number of sites	Year of estimate
Germany	150 000 to 200 000	1993
Netherlands	approx. 100 000	1993
Finland	10 000 to 25 000	1995
Denmark	6000 to 12 000	1991
Sweden	6000	1995
Norway	2000	1995

Source: Glass *et al.*, 1995*a*.

and analytical services has been estimated at between $100 and $134 billion, of which hazardous waste remediation comprised between 4 and 12 billion (averaging around 7% therefore), with bioremediation being a small percentage of this (Glass *et al.*, 1995*a*).

Similarly, in Europe, the 'biological portion' of the environmental market is valued at less than 5% of the 50 000 m ecu total environmental treatment market in Europe (Prieels, 1993). While there are estimated to be more than between 150 000 and 350 000 hazardous waste sites in western Europe (60 000 requiring urgent attention), a large number have yet to be documented in eastern Europe and in the former Soviet Union.

15.3 Factors influencing market entry and diffusion

The main focus of the remainder of this chapter is upon the factors influencing market entry and diffusion in the bioremediation sector. However, in general, there is scant economic analysis of this specialized area, and it is necessary to draw on the wider literature concerning environmental technologies and biotechnology, while making references to bioremediation where appropriate.

15.3.1 Regulation

The principle of 'polluter pays' is being broadly accepted by governments of many developed economies[1]. The justification is that pollution has costs to society and to the environment which commercial companies, rather than the rest of society, should bear. In the absence of any regulation, these companies have little incentive to abate their pollution when they are releasing it into common property resources (such as air or water). These resources are owned by no one, property rights are unclear, and the economically efficient mode of behaviour is to minimize costs and

---

[1] The principle is incorporated into the Single European Act of 1986, along with the principle that environmental policies should be integrated with others such as industrial policies.

to use the environment as a 'sink'. A company may gain little by unilaterally controlling its outputs (effluents) since this would limit its production and only favour competitors. Here, the market does not allocate resources efficiently from a welfare point of view and the task of regulators is to ensure that the outputs are curbed and/or that the appropriate share of the social costs (in the form of environmental damage) are carried by companies[2]. In most cases the objective of legislation, if sometimes only loosely stated, is to maximize the net benefits to society (see Luken & Fraas, 1993; Pearce & Brisson, 1994).

In western democratic systems, such as the US and Europe, and in Japan and elsewhere, where environmental regulation involves some form of social negotiation, the regulatory authority stands in-between groups and organizations with differing views on the extent to which polluters should bear these costs. This polarization has grown since the 1960s and has led to the rise of environmental movements in many developed and developing countries. Some of these groups, such as the Green Party in Germany, have gained political power and have been instrumental in pressuring for environmental legislation in Germany in problematic areas such as wastewater, landfill and chemicals manufacturing (although full implementation and public enthusiasm for these has subsequently been dampened by the costs of German reunification; see Smith (1995)).

Public pressure in the UK has been more muted, however: a key white paper[3] released in 1990 signalled a renewed approach to solving environmental problems, which led to the Environmental Protection Act of 1990 and subsequently the formation of an Environmental Agency.

The range of instruments which governments have to hand in order to control pollution and enforce remediation of damaged sites can be broadly divided between command and control approaches (where standards are set and enforced), and market-based mechanisms (such as pollution-taxes and fees). In the area of hazardous waste, command and control systems, based on standards, dominate US and European approaches, with regulations often containing detailed technical requirements (Russell, 1993).

The scope, and the specific phraseology and wording of regulations have an important impact on the subsequent development of abatement and treatment technologies. Much of recent environmental legislation in the US, the EU and in other developed countries such as Canada incorporates the principle of best available technology (BAT). The 'technology forcing' effect of regulation can be identified in a number of US environmental laws (Pearce & Brisson, 1994). Waxman (1991), in the context of the 1990 Amendments to the US Clean Air Act, explains that:

the rationale behind technology forcing is that by setting emission standards that are beyond the reach of conventional control methods, Congress creates a market incentive that can force the development and commercialisation of new technologies.

---

[2] See Hardin (1968). Economists have proposed various solutions to this problem such as the allocation of property rights and liability rules.

[3] This Common Inheritance: Britain's Environmental Strategy (HMSO, 1990).

Of more direct relevance to bioremediation are the principles under the Resource Conservation and Recovery Acts and Clean Air and Clean Water Acts which direct the US Environmental Protection Agency (USEPA) to seek permanent solutions to waste problems and to encourage volume and toxicity reduction at the point of generation (Markland-Day, 1993). Similar philosophies, which are aimed essentially at finding environmentally acceptable solutions to landfill and incineration practices, have been integrated into legislation of countries such as Germany, the Netherlands, Denmark and Sweden. Apart from legal instruments, a number of national agencies (such as USEPA and the German Bundesministerium für Forschung und Technologie (BFMT)) actively promote the use of bioremediation and other innovative technologies in waste treatment, e.g. through assessing the performance of bioremediation projects and by disseminating information and technical guidance to companies.

The 'command and control' label given to standards-based regulations reflects their need for strict enforcement through inspection agencies, normally empowered to use legislation to impose penalties on infringing companies. While the desired aim may be to promote the adoption of newer and better technologies, in practice there may be both negative and positive effects on incumbent firms and additional effects on the behaviour of firms which are contemplating market entry. These are summarized as follows:

- *Exit.* Some regulated companies eventually leave the industry because the long-run costs of meeting environmental standards exceed their revenues. This will occur if the company is unable to adapt or innovate perhaps because of the way the company is managed or structured, or because its capital assets cannot easily be switched to a new function. It also depends on how customers react to price increases (i.e. to the price elasticity of demand of the companies' products). One result may be an increase in the concentration of the industry, because only large companies which can gain from economies of scope and scale remain. A major perceived weakness of command and control regulations is that the regulators have to be highly informed to ensure that they do not set over-stringent standards. This could cause an excess of companies to exit from the industry, or impose higher than optimal costs on companies which would eventually be passed to customers.
- *Survival.* Regulated companies are able to bear the costs and remain in the industry in the long run. One reason may be that they are able to pass costs on to customers through price increases. Alternatively, the company may innovate and adapt to the regulatory requirements by carrying out in-house research and development or invest in new capital equipment.
- *Entry.* Alongside surviving regulated companies, new companies may be attracted to enter the market to supply ancillary goods and services (such as consultancy) to regulated companies.

It is difficult to find unequivocal evidence that companies have left the industry as a result of new environmental legislation. It is certainly the case that the compliance costs have risen sharply in the US, for example, from around 21 billion US$ in 1972 to 93 billion US$ in 1990 (in US$ 1990 currency) (USEPA, quoted by Luken

& Fraas, 1993). This is equivalent to a rise in annualized costs from 0.9 to 2.1 % of GDP during this period.

In relation to survival (see above), there is strong, albeit circumstantial, evidence that regulation has provided an incentive for innovation, the development of new products and the formation of markets in which these products and services are traded. A significant service and consultancy sector has also developed. The most advanced markets with the largest providers of bioremediation goods and services appear to be those in countries where regulation is most stringent, leading to a stratification of bioremediation market development in Europe.

Strict regulation in Germany, the Netherlands, Sweden, Norway and Switzerland has led to a relatively large number of privately initiated bioremediation projects in these countries. Detailed site inventories have been prepared in these countries, which also provide prospective entrants with the basis for assessing a country's market size. France, Finland, Italy and the UK, on the other hand, fall into a separate market group. Less-stringent regulations and relatively fewer companies specializing in bioremediation have resulted in a less well-developed market for bioremediation. With still weaker legislation and enforcement, markets for hazardous waste remediation in Greece, Spain and Portugal have developed only to a limited extent, and there are very few entrants. Countries in the Eastern bloc have poorly developed environmental regulations and market evolution is at a very early stage (although they provide a potentially large export market for western European and US firms). Figure 15.1 shows approximate numbers of bioremediation firms in selected countries.

15.3.2 Structure of, and strategies in, the bioremediation industry

The structure of bioremediation industries in the US and Western Europe has, to some extent, mirrored, on a smaller scale, that of biotechnology industries in more fully developed sectors such as health or agriculture. However, the environmental segment of biotechnology industries in these countries is small, between 3 and 8% of companies. Health-care related biotechnology firms represent the majority of companies (30%–50%) (see Bullock & Dibner, 1995; Lucas, Muller & Pike, 1996). However, as with the health-care sector, the bioremediation sector can be divided into two: companies are either dedicated, having entered the industry to exploit specific biotechnologies, or they are established companies which have long been present in the market and in recent years have incorporated new biotechnological developments into their traditional activities (see also Caplan, 1993). In the health-care sectors of North America and Western Europe the dedicated companies are represented by the new bioscience-based start-ups, many of which have emerged from university campuses and as spin-offs from larger companies. Examples include Genentech, Amgen and Chiron in the US, Celltech and British Biotechnology in the UK. The established firms in the health-care context include the multinational pharmaceutical firms such as Merck Inc (USA), Hoffman la Roche (Switzerland), Rhone Poulenc (France), and GlaxoWellcome (UK) which have made major

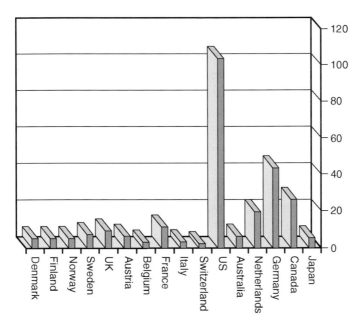

Fig. 15.1. Estimated world-wide distribution of bioremediation companies (data derived from Glass *et al.* (1995*a*,*b*)).

investments to integrate biotechnology into their traditional chemistry-based drug discovery programmes.

Some examples of dedicated and established bioremediation companies are listed in Table 15.3.

According to recent analyses (OECD, 1994), while about half of the environment industry is composed of small companies employing less than 50 people, product markets in North America, Europe and Japan are dominated by a few large companies. Japan has a particularly concentrated environment industry, as most of the major suppliers are subsidiaries of larger diversified companies active in several product areas.

A stylized representation of the structure of the environmental biotechnology industry (based on a classification of the industry by the technology focus of companies and their stage of development, rather than product sector) is shown in Table 15.4.

The formation of alliances and strategic linkages between these two types of company enables the smaller innovative companies to reach large markets and benefit from the distribution and marketing expertise of the larger companies, and to spread their technological and business risks. Conversely, while the larger companies benefit from scale and scope economies, they may rely on the innovative capabilities of the smaller companies in specialized technological areas such as production of bioremediation inoculants and design of bioreactors. Typically,

Table 15.3. *Some selected examples of established and dedicated companies in the bioremediation sector world-wide*

USA	Europe	Other countries
Established diversified companies	*Established diversified companies*	*Established diversified companies*
Batelle	Shell Research (UK, Netherlands)	Grace Dearbourn (Canada)
Du Pont Environmental	AMEC (UK)	Broken Hill (Australia)
Fluor Daniel	Solvay (Belgium)	Mitsubishi Petrochem
Groundwater Technology Inc.	Elf Aquitaine (France)	(Japan)
		Obayashi Corp (Japan)
Dedicated companies	*Dedicated companies*	*Dedicated companies*
Bio-recovery Systems Inc.	Viridian Bioprocessing	CRA (Australia)
Detox Industries	(UK)	Griffin Remediation
	Ebiox (Switzerland)	(Canada)
Oil Spill Eater	Biodetox (Germany)	Biocentras (Lithuania)
International		

Table 15.4. *Stylized structure of bioremediation industry*

Dedicated bioremediation company	Established diversified company in construction, petrochemical, engineering or utilities sectors
Typically:	Typically:
• Spin-out from university or large company	• Vertically integrated
• Niche products and services, e.g. microbial inoculants, nutrient supplies, bioreactor design, diagnostics, specialist consulting	• Engineering driven rather than bioscience
• Constrained by finance	• Contracts out licenses in innovative technologies
• Needs large company for distribution	• Strong distribution, marketing and regulatory functions
• Licenses out technologies	

these larger companies are engineering driven and may only have limited bioscience expertise (although they are beginning to develop in-house expertise and to spin-out bioremediation subsidiaries). An example of such a strategic alliance is Viridian Bioprocessing Ltd, a joint venture between the large UK construction firm AMEC Group, the French chemicals multinational Rhone Poulenc, British Nuclear Fuels, and the University of Kent at Canterbury (UK). The company specializes in effluent treatment systems, liquid and air emission abatement and remediation of contaminated land. This consortium arrangement is a strategy that enables academic groups, dedicated small companies and larger diversified companies to pool skills and benefit from shared expertise. Other European examples include collaborations between the French companies BRGM, Elf Aquitaine, and ESYS using *in situ* bioremediation to treat hydrocarbon-contaminated soils using nutrients and microbes.

So far, in this chapter, a description of the industry and the importance of regulation in shaping its development have been developed: however, a number of important conditions or factors are widely believed to be important in determining the spread and successful uptake of technologies, which will now be briefly examined in the context of environmental biotechnology.

15.3.3 Cost-effectiveness of bioremediation

Regulated companies or those that face financial charges for emitting pollution have an incentive to incorporate technologies which reduce their costs. Tietenberg (1995) has argued that charging systems create a greater incentive for companies to reduce their costs and adopt new technologies than command and control standards. This is because companies that abate their pollution outputs beyond minimum levels, can in some cases trade this excess with subsidiaries or other companies that fail to meet the levels. A market is created in which emissions are traded and, provided regulators set the fees correctly, market forces will lead to the desired technological outcome. In the case of standards, there is little incentive for a company to go beyond the regulatory minimum and indeed, because production managers within companies are more likely to be well informed about technical developments than the regulators, there is even a disincentive to innovate. This is because, by disclosing improvements to pollution-abatement technologies, companies will be forced merely to comply to stricter rules under the 'best available technology' principle. Whether in practice these hypothetical issues arise has not been widely tested, and there is a distinct lack of empirical studies comparing standards with fees and in particular, their impact on the incentive to innovate.

Putting this discussion aside, it is reasonable to assume that companies will aim to reduce emissions until it is no longer cheaper for them to do so, i.e. to the point where the marginal costs of abatement (the cost of an extra unit of pollution removed) will equal the costs of the penalty for excess emissions (in the case of standards) or the costs of the emission charge (in the case of tax or fee-based systems). The simplest theoretical cost advantages of bioremediation are illustrated graphically in Fig. 15.2. In this scenario, the marginal cost curve is lowered by an amount C_1-C_2 at the target remediation or emission level using bioremediation as opposed to traditional physical or chemical techniques.

The areas below the cost curves represent the total variable costs of using either technology. In Fig. 15.2, the marginal cost curve from using bioremediation (MC_2) is lower throughout the level of pollution remediated compared with using

S. Shohet

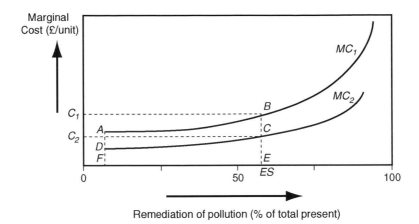

Fig. 15.2. Simplest theoretical cost advantage of bioremediation.

the traditional technology (MC_1) up to the environmental standard *ES*. On the
x-axis the area *DCEF* < area *ABEF*, hence the use of bioremediation in this case
would be preferred. The curves indicate that it becomes proportionally more costly
to remove contamination as the process tends towards 100% removal, i.e. diminishing
returns set in, though using bioremediation methods this effect is reduced (this
could be because microbes or enzymes can potentially degrade products to lower
end points than conventional methods could achieve). In practice, a standard is set
at what is believed to be the maximum desirable level of hazardous waste on health
and environmental grounds, which at the same time is achievable technologically
without excessive costs. More complex scenarios can be envisaged, for example,
where marginal cost curves intersect as shown in Fig. 15.3.

In Fig. 15.3, the marginal cost curves for a traditional technology (MC_1) and
bioremediation (MC_2) are again shown. Here, at an environmental standard where
only low remediation of a site's pollution is required (ES_1), the traditional method
has the lower total variable costs shown by the area *DCFE*, compared with area
ABFE for bioremediation. However, where a high standard of remediation is set,
(ES_2), bioremediation costs are lower (area *AEHK* < *DEHG*). For environmental
standards set in the shaded area, a company would be uncertain of the benefits of
bioremediation compared to a traditional method, at least in relation to variable
costs. In practice, a company may have only a limited ability to predict the level at
which a regulator will set the standard at a site, and this may lead companies to
minimize risks, and delay adoption of bioremediation. The investment decision
would also be influenced by the nature of the companies' fixed costs. If fixed assets
such as plant and machinery were sunk, i.e. only suitable for use with the
traditional approach, and where the second-hand (resale) or scrap value of these
fixed assets was negligible, the fixed costs of switching to bioremediation might be
high. Even if costs were not sunk, but installed machinery was depreciated over a

276

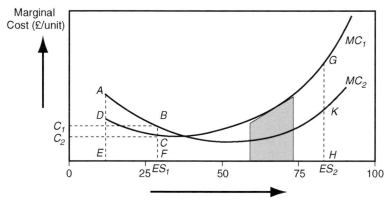

Fig. 15.3. Intersection of marginal cost curves of bioremediation.

long period, there would be limited incentive to switch to bioremediation in the short term. It is more reasonable to assume that bioremediation would be phased in, and that gradual replacement, or partial replacement would occur. In the marginal cost curves shown in Fig. 15.3, both technologies show some effect from scale economies, although in the case of bioremediation the effect is more pronounced. Such an effect could arise from economies gained by bulk production of inoculum, nutrients and efficient use of bioreactors as scales increase, although as Fig. 15.3 shows these benefits decline, and diminishing returns set in as the remediation levels increase beyond around 60% of total. In the case of the traditional technology, diminishing returns set in earlier.

A key difficulty in assessing the cost advantages of bioremediation is practical demonstration of this potential. To do this, companies have to carry out costly R&D that they may not be willing to undertake alone, particularly if companies cannot prevent competitors freely benefiting from the research. Here, public policy can play a role by encouraging collaboration between companies and universities or through government subsidies for feasibility and demonstration programmes.

A study of costs of biological and non-biological treatment of environmental pollution in the Netherlands revealed that biotechnology methods were less costly than traditional methods in relation to soil remediation, and air and water treatment, although the study pointed out that the feasibility is highly dependent on energy costs (OECD, 1994; see Table 15.5).

15.3.4 Other diffusion factors

It discussing costs it has been suggested that, although there are limited data available, there are situations where bioremediation can be cost-effective in comparison with more traditional technologies. This is a crucial factor in influencing the attractiveness of the technology and in terms of affecting its ability to replace

Table 15.5. *Summary of perceived cost benefits and disadvantages in the treatment of air, water, soil, and solid waste of using bioremediation approaches*

Air	Water	Soil	Solid waste
Biofiltration (+) cheap (−) not suitable for all pollutants or concentrations	Biosorption (+) could replace physical and chemical methods and be used at low concentrations	(+) low capital intensity (+) low energy usage (+) minimal site disruption	(+) selective concentration and removal is possible (+) operating and investment costs are moderate
Bioscrubbers (+) can clean highly contaminated off gases (−) high capital and operational costs	(+) recycling of heavy metals (−) water treatment plants are open systems (−) use of GEMs limited (−) stability and performance (−) not all organics yet removable (−) sludge production (+) low costs per m³ of treated water	(+) complete degradation of some products into harmless products is possible (+) treatment of soils containing low concentrations of contaminants is feasible	(+) overall waste volume is significantly reduced (+) recycling and reuse offer potential to add value
General (+) low energy and few secondary wastes; potentially lower operating costs of >20%		(−) complex mixtures are difficult to treat (−) variable performance	(−) low reaction rates (−) some wastes are resistant to microbial degradation
(−) empirical processes reliant on undefined microbial populations (−) limited biological competencies in an engineering-dominated sector		(−) rate of clean-up dependent on external factors such as pH and ground temperature	

Source: adapted from OECD, 1994. (+) = an advantage; (−) a disadvantage.

existing methods. There are, however, other important factors which may influence the commercial attractiveness of a technology and the creation of incentives to innovate. These can be grouped under the following four headings of appropriability, public acceptability, risk and scientific advancement. Each of these will be dealt with briefly in turn.

Appropriability

Appropriability refers to the extent to which inventions can be protected by innovators so that the economic benefits are captured by the innovator rather than imitators and competitors (Teece, 1986). Bioremediation is highly dependent on novel processes and it is widely recognized that it is more difficult to protect intellectual property relating to processes than to products, because process patents can be more easily circumvented without infringing the patent holder's rights. A US patent is required to meet the criterion that the invention is 'non-obvious' which may be difficult to demonstrate in the case of biotechnology processes where a number of widely used methods form the core of new inventions (Sorrell & Seide, 1996). Published patents may have the effect of revealing technical details to competitors and may not provide the expected intellectual property protection that a patent is intended to afford. Furthermore, bioremediation relies on essentially natural processes and the use of naturally occurring micro-organisms which are not in themselves patentable. While recent rulings allow the patenting of novel genetically modified organisms and gene constructs, their use in bioremediation has been limited by regulatory constraints. We can judge from this that the appropriability regime in the environmental biotechnology field is relatively weaker than in areas such as pharmaceuticals and seeds where there are probably greater opportunities for companies to establish strong proprietary positions. This weakness may lead to a diminishing of the commercial attractiveness of bioremediation, in general. Companies may, however, develop a number of strategies to ensure that imitators and competitors cannot easily obtain proprietary knowledge; most obviously by ensuring secrecy or through the use of trademarked and copyrighted products.

Public acceptability

Public acceptability is a crucial factor for technical success. Surveys of public attitudes towards biotechnology indicate that northern Europeans, US and Japanese consumers have concerns regarding the use of genetic modification in food and in animal genetics, but regard its use in environmental remediation more favourably (Zechendorf, 1994; OECD, 1994). Caplan (1993) argues that the successful use of bioremediation to clean up the shoreline of Prince William Sound, Alaska, following the Exxon Valdez oil spill (see Chapter 8) greatly contributed to the public acceptance of bioremediation in the US. However, use of genetically engineered micro-organisms (GEMs), rather than indigenous microbes, has been severely limited to date in both the US and western Europe owing to strict regulatory constraints on their use: this may be relaxed as more research and validation work using GEMs emerges. In theory at least, the potential to 'tailor' microbes to degrade complex (and previously resistant) molecules such as complex aromatic hydrocarbons using recombinant DNA technology offers major commercial opportunities.

Financial and technological risk

Environmental and product legislation in the US and in western Europe increasingly places the liability for environmental damage on the manufacturer and contractor. The US Comprehensive Emergency Response, Compensation and Liability Act 1980 (frequently referred to as the Superfund Law), for example, contains provisions which impose strict liability on companies. The law has a retroactive effect: a company that has operated under best available practices at some time in the past may still be liable to pay environmental damages for present clean-up costs. This type of legislation seems likely to make bioremediation companies act cautiously when considering the use of novel but potentially riskier environmental biotechnology approaches, such as the use of GEMs, which may have long-term, unforeseen effects on the environment.

More generally, technical uncertainty such as the variable performance of particular bioremediation methods generates financial uncertainty, especially in projects with a 'no cure no pay' clause. From the point of view of the venture capitalist planning to invest at an early stage in a bioremediation start-up, an investment would be perceived as riskier than perhaps in other areas of biotechnology, since projected cash flows, which form an important part of the basis for assessing the investment potential of a firm, may be more difficult to predict. This may explain the relatively small number of new environmental biotechnology start-ups in both the US and western Europe in comparison to other sectors such as health or agriculture. As we have already noted, there are a number of strategies which firms can adopt to spread this risk such as forming alliances with larger companies.

A further uncertainty, as we showed in Fig. 15.3, is that the decision to adopt bioremediation technologies can be highly cost-sensitive and is dependent upon the levels at which the regulatory authorities decide to set their threshold standards. An added complication is that while a government may signal its intention to set strict limits (which may favour bioremediation), actual enforcement may come much later, hence companies have to get the timing of their investments right. It is not unknown for governments to reverse decisions on environmental thresholds or for new administrations to 'move the goal posts'. Companies therefore need to develop a clear understanding of the decision process, and often this can involve intensive lobbying to influence regulatory agencies. In this case, alliances formed for strategic reasons can prove useful in terms of giving companies a more powerful say in the government decision process.

Role of the science base

Little has been said so far about the scientific and technological drivers which have led to the development of bioremediation. For agricultural or health-related biotechnology, the core techniques of recombinant DNA and monoclonal antibody technologies were initially developed not by scientists in the R&D divisions of large multinational companies but by groups of academics mainly in the US and Europe. Similarly, knowledge about microbial ecology and biochemistry, which underpins the science of bioremediation, has largely been developed from university research rather than from the private sector. In this sense, commercialization of biotechnology seems to have followed the 'science-push' model of technological development in that knowledge has flowed out from the public sector research base and has subsequently been taken up by the private sector. Since the development of an industrial biotechnology sector, a 'demand pull' from existing and newly emerging companies has been created. The commercial interest has, to some extent, shaped which areas of research receive public funding, because science policy in many countries (notably the US and the UK) has shifted to direct the research to exploitable areas. The UK Foresight Exercise, for example, highlighted the importance of remediation technologies as part of a set of tools for sustainable development (OST, 1995). There is also, as we have noted, extensive collaboration between biotechnology research groups and industry which is blurring the old boundaries between public and private research.

Technology transfer from the science base requires an efficient coupling and flow of knowledge especially because much of bioremediation at a practical level relies greatly on empirical 'trial and error' approaches, and requires a combination of bioscience and engineering skills. This requires a multi-disciplinary approach that is being achieved through the formation of consortia, and strategic alliances, both between private companies and between private companies and public organizations such as universities and research institutes: but in some cases new organizations and structures may be needed to ensure that this process works effectively. Continued provision of resources to the science base in areas that underpin bioremediation would seem to be important to ensure continued uptake and development by industry.

15.4 Overview and assessment

The available data, such as it is, suggests major opportunities for entrants into bioremediation markets which are forming in developed economies. These markets have been created largely through regulatory intervention by governments since there is good evidence to suggest that market failure occurs in the absence of regulation. This market failure arises because much of the environment is common property and there is little economic incentive for producers of pollution to bear the costs of pollution abatement.

S. Shohet

The regulations reflect public concern about environmental 'degradation', but in recent years companies have become increasingly convinced of the benefits of limiting the environmental impact of their activities, not least because customers and shareholders have exerted pressure more directly on them to do so.

Nevertheless, most governments recognize the need to establish and enforce regulations to control industrial pollution. The use of market-based approaches, such as fees and taxes, which act as indirect incentives to influence company behaviour, have not been adopted widely in the environment field, as yet, although there are some notable examples such as the US Clean Air Act. In this Act, provision was made to allow companies to trade their emission permits, effectively enabling efficient units to offset the costs of pollution abatement of inefficient units. At least in principle this could act as an important stimulus for innovation because a 'reward' is created for companies that limit their pollution outputs. While this approach can be applied to current emissions, the residues of past emissions that have accumulated as a stock in the environment, require the application of remediative processes, not just control or avoidance approaches. Historically, regulators have set minimum standards on the acceptable threshold levels at which these stock pollutants should be depleted. They have also 'forced' polluters to adopt particular types of preferred technologies (including bioremediation but not exclusively so) often with the *caveat* that there are not 'excessive costs' to be borne by the company. The ultimate aim of the regulators is to balance societal and environmental costs and benefits; although accurately assessing these costs is problematic.

As we have noted, bioremediation is a collection of biologically based techniques that can be used to remove these stock pollutants and enable contaminated land to be restored to levels of environmental quality as specified in regulatory standards. Bioremediation offers a practical adjunct to more traditional engineering-based extraction, cleansing and incineration processes with applications to a range of environmental compartments notably soil, solid waste and water (and to a lesser extent to air and gases). Cost is a critical factor influencing the adoption of bioremediation and, while new data on cost-effectiveness are continually emerging, there remains some scepticism amongst users who have, in the past, employed traditional methods. However, the relatively low capital intensity, and low variable costs in terms of inputs such as energy and inoculants are major advantages of the technology.

There are situations in which bioremediation is not often applicable, typically where the substrate is inorganic or highly recalcitrant to biological degradation (although in some of these cases organisms such as particular plant and bacterial species can bioaccumulate and mobilize chemicals such as heavy metals). The performance of techniques has so far proved to be variable and dependent on the specific environmental conditions pertaining; a problem that creates some uncertainty for those commissioning clean-up projects, and may lead them to choose less effective but more reliable options (such as 'clean' technology).

For the development of bioremediation a set of framework conditions is also essential, which includes a sound public sector research base, a favourable perception by consumers and the public more generally, and a sufficiently strong patenting regime to provide companies with an incentive to innovate.

In conclusion, common sense suggests that the problems of dealing with contaminated sites, and with the legacy of hazardous waste, cannot be resolved by scientific or technological 'fixes' alone. The issues discussed in this chapter underline the point that solutions require the complex coordination and effective functioning of social, political and economic institutions. Where these have been put in place, in, for example, the Netherlands, Germany and the US, markets have formed and evolved, providing convincing evidence that there is major potential for further diffusion and integration of bioremediation technologies. Novel economic instruments, such as fees and taxes that have yet to be widely applied in the hazardous waste sector, may also have a more prominent role to play in the future.

Acknowledgement

The author is grateful for support from the Gatsby Charitable Trust to the Centre for Business Strategy, London Business School.

References

Bullock, W. O. & Dibner, M. (1995). The state of the US biotechnology industry. *Trends in Biotechnology*, 13, 463–7.

Burtraw, D. & Portney, P. R.(1991). Environmental policy in the United States. In *Economic Policy Towards the Environment*, ed. D. Helm, pp. 289–319. Oxford, UK: Blackwell.

Caplan, J. A. (1993). The world wide bioremediation industry: prospects for profit. *Trends in Biotechnology*, 11, 320–3.

Glass, D. J., Raphael, T., Risto, V. & Van Eyk, J. (1995*a*). Growing international markets and opportunities in bioremediation: Part 1. *Genetic Engineering News*, 15(18), 6–7.

Glass, D. J., Raphael, T., Risto, V. & Van Eyk, J. (1995*b*). International markets, trends and technologies in bioremediation: Part 2. *Genetic Engineering News*, 15(19), 38–9.

Hardin, G. (1968). The tragedy of the Commons. *Science*, 163, 1243–8.

Lucas, P., Muller A. & Pike, W. (1996). *European Biotech '96 – Volatility and Value*. London: Ernst and Young.

Luken, R. A. & Fraas, A. G. (1993). The US regulatory analysis framework: a review. *Oxford Review of Economic Policy*, 9(4), 96–111.

Markland-Day, S. (1993). US environmental regulations and policies – their impact on the commercial development of bioremediation. *Trends in Biotechnology*, 11, 324–8.

OECD (1994). *Biotechnology for a Clean Environment*. Paris: OECD.

OST (1995). *Progress Through Partnership*. Report of the UK Technology Foresight Steering Group. London: HMSO.

Pearce, D. & Brisson, I. (1994). BATNEEC: the economics of technology based environmental standards with a UK case illustration. *Oxford Review of Economic Policy*, 9(4), 24–40.

Prieels, A.-M. (1993). Development of an environmental bio-industry: European perceptions and prospects. European Foundation for the Improvement of Living and Working Conditions. Dublin, Ireland.

Russell, C. S. (1993). Economic incentives in the management of hazardous wastes. In *Economics of the Environment – Selected Readings*. 3rd edn. ed. R. Dorfman & N. S. Dorfman, pp. 271–87. New York: Norton.

Smith, S. (1995). *Green Taxes and Charges: Policy and Practice in Britain and Germany*. London: Institute for Fiscal Studies.

Sorrell, L. S. & Seide, R. K. (1996). Patenting biotechnology process inventions. *Bio/Technology*, 14(2), 158–9.

Teece, D. J. (1986). Profiting from technological innovation: implications for integration, collaboration, licensing and public policy. *Research Policy*, 15, 285–305.

Tietenberg, T. (1985). *Environmental and Natural Resources Economics*. 4th edn. New York: Harper Collins.

Waxman, H. A. (1991). An overview of the Clean Air Act Amendments of 1990. *Environmental Law*, 21, 1721–816.

Zechendorf, B. (1994). What the public thinks about biotechnology. *Bio/Technology*, 12 (9), 870–5.

Part IV
Directional pointers to future environmental problems

16

Development of 'fail-safe strategies' (FSS) to combat biomonitored biohazards from environmental xenobiotics

Alan Wiseman and James M. Lynch

16.1 Perspectives in environmental toxicology

Toxic pollutants can disrupt the sustainability of ecosystems by relatively undocumented effects on species, populations, communities and related processes of interaction and survival. It is the molecular flexibility and elasticity of particular ecosystems that determine the long-term 'ecotoxicant resistance' (ER) that each may display under optimal or sub-optimal conditions relating to dynamic steady-state systems, e.g. with polynuclear aromatic hydrocarbons (Madsen *et al.*, 1996; see Chapter 4): other pre-steady-state or post-steady-state systems may not be so favoured (for ER) in their ability to shock-absorb the effects of ecotoxicants. This is especially evident at high-exposure concentrations associated with bioaccumulation where recovery is, at best, very slow due to lack of elasticity (deformation index: DI).

Real-time biomonitoring of ecosystems, therefore, may not be definitive in predicting collapse due to high DI into chaos, of the community relationships in the existing flora and fauna. It may then urgently require 'first-aid soil technology' (FAST). Some readjustments of the balance of contribution of particular species may not, however, be classifiable as ecological damage or disruption unless retention of the status quo is the only, or main, criterion of success, i.e. in preserving the balance of the immediate *'ante bellum'* period only.

The label of 'polluted' for a particular natural environment may have, in favourable circumstances, to be amended therefore, to 'exposed to known pollutants' as for a particular purpose such as pesticide or herbicide treatment or controlled treatment with necessary nitrogen fertilizer: or with appropriately genetically monitored micro-organisms and other organisms as desired for its economic or other outcomes. Here the risk : hazard index (RHI) referred to by the editors in Chapter 1 may need to be quantified clearly. Comparison between risk : benefit ratio (RBR) and clinical definitions of 'therapeutic index' may usefully be developed further. This is the dose required to achieve useful therapeutic results, divided into the dose required to exhibit morbidity or mortality. These must be predefined for individuals in each population, who may vary up to say 40-fold in therapeutic or toxic response: side effects may be 'unpredictable' however. For the environment, it would be useful to express these ratios or indices as a reciprocal exponent p^1R (0–15) to signify an increasing risk on a logarithmic scale (0–15). It is the effective dose actually encountered by each member of the ecological community that will lead to the displays of ecotoxicity that can be detected by whatever biomonitoring is arranged (or are observable naturally). Supposed dose, directly or by bioaccumulation, can be misleading if the real exposure has been ameliorated by, for example, soil-binding of pollutant. Soil-bound pollutants are examples of immobilized toxicants whose accessibility is controlled by an aqueous unstirred slow-diffusion layer that controls the permeability rate of relatively small molecules; but especially that of large biomolecules (and of micro-organisms, bacteria and yeasts). These soil-bound pollutants, at levels below the saturation limit of the binding material present, may constitute little immediate threat to the ecosystem present, provided that there is no sudden disturbance (or release) such as a period of freak weather as with unusual torrential rainstorm (or alternatively drought) or high-temperature prolonged exposure.

16.2 FSS in environmental toxicology

One prime example of a biohazard is the deposition from air or water (or dumping) of radionuclides. Their effects on ecosystems are, however, quite as unpredictable as less obviously hazardous chemicals such as polynuclear aromatic hydrocarbons (see Chapter 4) or heavy metal ions. Radioresistant bacteria are often generated (by mutation, or selected by growth ability) in radionuclide-contaminated environments such as soil or aquatic systems. Bioremediation opportunities (and some biomonitoring techniques) may involve the 'leaching' of the radionuclides; where micro-organisms affect this process due to modification of pH or redox potential (antioxidant–proxidant balance); and consideration must also be given to the organic binding molecules they contain or secrete (for review see Binks, 1996). Furthermore, nuclear wastes have been subjected to bioremediation by absorption on to particular biological products, such as melanins, humus, tannins, chitosan (Cuero, 1996), polysaccharides, metal chelating agents (Hockett & Mount, 1996), and whole cells (or cell walls) of yeasts and fungi (Roane, Pepper & Miller, 1996).

Fail-safe strategies (FSS) are particularly important for nuclear waste disposal, where thousands of years may need to be accounted for if natural decay of radioisotopes is awaited to lower the risk of water or soil contamination. The FSS concept might be better expressed as 'fail on safe strategy if left' (FOSSIL) to remind disposal agencies of the enormous timescales involved in prevention of risk from the unusually potent hazard of radionuclides (perhaps with half-lives of up to thousands of years). If failure does occur, as leakage from, e.g. buried or sunken aggregates that were thought to provide 100% containment, the prospect of bioremediation in some future era may look poor at the moment; but no doubt much better forms of bioremediation can be developed by research, compatible with the highly sensitive (also precise and accurate) detection systems already in use for many forms of radioactive substance. Although correct prediction is dangerously difficult, mathematical approaches might usefully be developed to describe the likelihood of recovery of ecosystems through bioremediation strategies. Such 'remission analysis' (RA) (not to be confused with regression analysis of actual data!) must involve the concept of elasticity (reversibility) of ecosystems: this should be considered over an appropriate timescale in every case, even throughout the aeons involved in recovery from radionuclide pollution. This is a daunting prospect. No doubt, highly efficient specific-binding agents (probably inorganic) will be developed for bioremediation of radionuclide-contaminated soil or water. Developments in clean technology (including clean-up technology) may include an engineered increase in efficiency (due to fragment production or surface area increase) of binding media when bombarded by the high-energy particles emitted: this is therefore another example of an FSS (with FOSSIL).

16.3 Perspectives in biomonitoring

The fundamental concept of biomonitoring, as distinct from physical or chemical monitoring, reflects the development or subsequent refinement of quantitative biology during the past century. It is paradoxical, therefore, that convergence of physical–chemical approaches with molecular biological and biotechnical methodology has occurred with startling rapidity. Now the responsiveness of enzymes, antibodies and of gene DNA is to be explored.

Early biomonitoring for explosive methane gas in coalmines involved the continued visible wellbeing (and audible bird song) of a caged canary; now an immobilized enzyme biosensor using methane monooxygenase could be employed. It is not immediately obvious, however, which of these two very different forms of biosensor is always the more useful: each can display visible and audible alerting feedback in response to a particular risk: hazard presetting that could even distinguish between explosive and asphyxiation risk to the coal miner (at a particular height from the tunnel floor). Newer techniques of biomonitoring offer a precision (accuracy?) that often stems from a remarkable molecular recognition ability both in binding specificity and binding sensitivity. For example, immobilized enzyme electrodes (biosensors) rely upon enzyme-substrate binding specificity in the range of, for example, 10^{-4} to 10^{-7} M binding sensitivity. These devices can be superseded by antibody-affinity electrodes in the range of, for example, 10^{-7} to 10^{-12} M binding sensitivity to antigen. The development of successful electrodes has often involved considerable research in biomolecular electronics to facilitate the rapid flow of electrons from aqueous solution to the metallic compounds of the electrode (using appropriate chemicals as electron-transfer aids: transducers).

It is clear that many future developments will depend upon biomonitoring for either the presence of particular sequences in DNA (see Chapter 5) arising from genes released into the environment; or the expression (into messenger RNA) of appropriate genes induced in particular organisms by pollutants (see Chapter 6). These similar-sounding gene-centred studies are, however, for very different purposes, which could cause 'public confusion' if not clearly distinguished from each other. Detection of, for example, undesirable levels of hazardous pollutants such as the polynuclear aromatic hydrocarbon, benzo(a)pyrene, see Chapters 3 and 4, in marine and beach environments was discussed in Chapter 6. These studies are mainly to alert regulatory authorities to risk of ecotoxicity in the biomonitored locations.

Establishment of fundamental 'ground rules' for released genes, by the biomonitoring of their spread (both horizontally and vertically), in particular, soils (Chapter 5), is a *sine qua non* for the confident release of particular genes under carefully defined and controlled conditions. Some remarkably sophisticated methods of biomonitoring for the presence, and activity, of such genes are being developed now in leading laboratories.

16.4 Perspectives in bioremediation (see Rhone, Pepper & Miller, 1966)

In bioremediation of soils, the soil can be mechanically removed, restored to acceptable composition (at an affordable price?) and returned to the site. Bioremediation *in situ* may provide greater challenges at present, with hopes of developing specific remedies for particular problems, such as the removal of nickel using complexation with histidine derivatives. Truly bioremedies may involve detoxification by deliberate 'doctoring' of soils with particular fungi (or of an agricultural crop) tolerant to growth in (and removal of) particular heavy metals such as arsenic (III); the latter can also be removed by oxidation to arsenic (V) in the presence of sunlight coupled with good aeration.

It is evident that bioremediation often involves aerobic metabolism of, e.g. soil micro-organisms including fungi and bacteria. The well-known concept, therefore, of quantitative 'biological oxygen demand' (BOD) could be extended to the more particular concept of 'bioremedial oxygen demand in soil' (BODIS) or 'bioremedial oxygen demand in environment' (BODIE). Some of the BODIS could be ensured as a fail-safe strategy (FSS), by routine co-burying of oxidizable wastes with organic peroxides or inorganic peroxides if available to provide a relatively long-term *in situ* reservoir of oxygen, which would greatly outlast co-buried hydrogen peroxide. Care would be necessary to avoid heavy-metal-catalysed rapid decomposition of co-buried (and relatively unstable) peroxides. Biomonitoring of, for example, iron (III) salts may be needed to avoid explosive admixture with peroxides especially where underground temperatures might build up rapidly due to climatic conditions, or even the much more threatening scenario of accidental admixture with radionuclides (see above). FSS strategies might involve the additional admixture with 'chain-reaction quenchers' either by specific chemicals or by cooling when water of crystallization is automatically released upon induction of rapid heating scenarios. Another approach would be to admix with appropriate gels that harden rapidly upon heating. Some of these desirable admix properties may be identified in sawdust (wood dust) lignocelluloses especially as the lignin (polyphenolic) content of these becomes subject to manipulation (usually to increase biodegradability) by recombinant DNA technology (see Chapter 9).

Biodegradability of mineral oil spills cannot be withdrawn from public attention for longer periods of time than those elapsing between tanker disasters world-wide (the publication of reminder lists jogs the memory at frequent intervals; see recent history in Chapter 8). Bioremediation at sea by strongly interventionist techniques may no longer be recommended despite the development of oil-hungry bacteria using recombinant DNA technology. Much of the spilled oil 'disappears without trace', and this is now thought to be due, in part, to speedy evaporation of lighter fractions (with evident wind-borne odour it seems).

16.5 Prediction and avoidance of future disasters in the environment

Much like the weather (climate?) in the UK, always a guaranteed subject of communicable interest, understanding assembled, even through precise modelling, can give only some degree of confidence in prediction. For example, future oil spill disasters involving large tankers whilst in transit near coastlines seem certain to occur from time to time (however irregularly in time and geographical location). Here, FSS might involve the admixture with the mineral oil of locating chemicals (e.g. fluorescent dyes) and sunlight-assisting or oxygen-assisting additives to promote rapid bioremediation upon spillage at sea (or upon beaches). There is scope here for chemical (or biochemical) remedies perhaps as a part of 'clean technology' (in combination with clean-up strategies for large-scale disposal of otherwise useless chemicals with BODIE problems).

It would be unduly pessimistic to assume that all predictable disasters will occur at some time, sooner rather than later. Most disasters will be avoided, or at least mitigated by FSS, once they have been predicted (recognized) because of admirable avoidance tactics associated with strict legislative control. A belief that 'it may never happen', although reassuring, must be followed up by continuous situation monitoring whenever possible, despite some financial outlay for research and monitoring development.

Nevertheless, progress of great benefit to mankind can be achieved, provided that knowledge is painstakingly acquired in ecology and ecotoxicology, in the general context of environmental toxicology world-wide. Recent progress, documented in this book, illuminates the increasing opportunities and benefits that appropriate research endeavours will provide in some of the most crucial interdisciplinary scientific fields in the remaining years of the twentieth century.

A. Wiseman and J. M. Lynch

Acknowledgements

The editors acknowledge helpful discussion at the University of Surrey with Mr M. A. Winkler, Department of Chemical and Process Engineering, on 'wastewater environment engineering problems', and with Dr R. H. Hinton, School of Biological Sciences, on toxicology.

References

Binks, P. R. (1996). Radioresistant bacteria: have they got industrial uses? *Journal of Chemical Technology and Biotechnology*, **67**, 319–22.

Cuero, R. G. (1996). Enhanced heavy metal immobilization by a bacterial–chitosan complex in soil. *Biotechnology Letters*, **18** (5), 511–14.

Hockett, J. R. & Mount, D. R. (1996). Use of metal chelating agents to differentiate among sources of acute aquatic toxicity. *Environmental Toxicology and Chemistry*, **15** (10), 1687–93.

Madsen, E. L., Thomas, C. T., Wilson, M. S., Sandoli, R. L. & Bilotta, S. E. (1996). *In situ* dynamics of aromatic hydrocarbons and bacteria capable of AH-metabolism in a coal tar waste-contaminated field site. *Environmental Science and Technology*, **30**, 2412–16.

Roane, T. M., Pepper, I. L. & Miller, R. M. (1996). Microbial remediation of metals. In *Bioremediation: Principles and Applications*, ed. R. L. Crawford & D. L. Crawford, pp. 312–40. Cambridge: Cambridge University Press.

Index

Index

Index